DOES THE SUN SHINE
IN HEAVEN

Does the Sun Shine in Heaven

One Man's Battle with Leukemia

John Amatuzio

iUniverse, Inc.
New York Lincoln Shanghai

Does the Sun Shine in Heaven
One Man's Battle with Leukemia

iUniverse books may be ordered through booksellers or by contacting:

iUniverse
2021 Pine Lake Road, Suite 100
Lincoln, NE 68512
www.iuniverse.com
1-800-Authors (1-800-288-4677)

ISBN-13: 978-0-595-31219-1 (pbk)
ISBN-13: 978-0-595-76041-1 (ebk)
ISBN-10: 0-595-31219-5 (pbk)
ISBN-10: 0-595-76041-4 (ebk)

Printed in the United States of America

Preface

I was once asked to write a one page summary about myself and my transplant history at a hospital function later to be passed on to other patients and families. Feeling lousy to say the least at that time, I stated that depending on how you look at it that could be accomplished in one sentence or several volumes of books. I am certain that many bone marrow transplant patients with complications would feel the same way. Any transplant survivor for that matter. The short route would go something like this: My name is John Amatuzio and I was once a handsome, healthy, athletic and energetic person. I was diagnosed with CML in 1984, had a bone marrow transplant in 1986, acquired graft vs. host disease and basically stopped living and began existing.

A doctor once told me that I would be trading one terminal disease for another terminal disease even if I survived that far back in 1986. The predicament was that I could only go from accelerated phase to blast crisis before passing away if I didn't go ahead with the transplant. This was my only hope to buy back time back then with the slim chance to not acquire the graft vs. host disease, or "GVHD" "post transplant. Well I never missed much of anything along the way in the world of "transplant allogenics". Liver failure, kidney failure, mucositis, "shake and bake", 106 degree fevers, ecoli's, edema, spinal tap blunders, marrow aspiration mess-ups, Hickmans, pneumonias, low poly counts, spleenectomy's, laminar rooms, "moon suits", missing life, getting burned to a crisp from the massive doses of radiation-TBI, powders and ointments, and GVHD. Cataracts, web strictures, choking, joints freezing up, feeling wrapped in Saran Wrap, wheelchairs, and being told that I would never walk again. Peg tubes, fist fights, "roid rage", moon faces, humpbacks and all of the other things that can go with the territory and some things that weren't supposed to. Bad reactions to med's, experimental protocols, FK506, Puva, Psoralen, photopheresis, column exchanges, thalidomide, cyclosporine, ATG, Imuran, blah blah blah blah blah…

I could have attempted to write that summary a hundred times on different days and in different moods and mindsets which would have produced a hundred different versions. From bouts of loneliness, a broken engagement, a torn family, soul searching, spiritual peaks and valleys and the search for hope. I've always found a way to muster up some hopes or fantasies of "someday", just hang in there" Often times after a hemorrhage or a bleeding fingernail episode, a hair falling out incident or a walking at cars irrationally on interstate 95 in tears fiasco, hope would always creep back into my heart somehow. Honestly though it came to the point where it all "got so old", the cycle of it all.

I continued on with this paper talking about those survivors who came away unscathed and in pristine physical condition, having movies and stories done about their situations. By enlarge back then and even today those wonderful stories aren't the norm. Most every patient has some particular predicament to contend with and shouldn't be skated over by the ratings powers to be. I am not one of these prime time candidates but I'm also very thankful to be alive.

I concluded this letter elaborating on how GVHD had perversely ravaged my body, mind and soul. On how I was treading water as a parameter on where I was in life. I stated that the young man inside of this prison shell of a body was working to get out once again. I talked about the man who had a tremendous personality, was great company, a hard worker and a funny guy with great faith and was still reachable. The same format applied at prominent hospitals across the country in attempting to release him from that overwhelming bondage of health related issues.

My closing sentence noted that he was a good hearted man that has been forced to be the kind of person that he doesn't want to be. And as this page illuminates some of the ramifications a patient has to struggle with on a daily basis, you can see where I was physically and mentally back then. I hope that the story, which I have written can enlighten you even more in an informative as well as interesting perspective.

CHAPTER 1

▼

It's February 23, 1997, 20 minutes to five and I'm going to Church. I've just had five cancer spots burned off of my face. I'm going to have my nose re-broken to fix three previous medical blunders. My legs are killing me. I'm so frail and mentally exhausted…going on and on…one fear I have is what will God do to me if I take my life. I'm so tired and sucked dry.

Well, here I am one hour later. I managed to go to confession by grabbing the priest on the way in. "Perhaps a bit of divine intervention here because normally, no confessions are heard before Sunday Mass at this particular parish". I had a good Mass, Communion and all, and I feel a bit better, just a bit; serene I'll call it.

Sunday nights the family comes to my mother's house for pasta (that's where I've been living, with my mom.) The visits are okay, I love everyone and I enjoy seeing them all, but I cannot help but feel distant; out on an island. The Flyers will be on in a couple of hours—playing the Rangers, a huge rival and always a great game for me. So I'll enjoy a few hours of ice time, I suppose. I've come to try and schedule things that take away the pain for me. I think to myself a lot. How long and what can hold my interest long enough to act as my morphine. Music works; the music I listen to is a great parameter of the mood I'm in. If I decide to become a doctor, I'll use some of my methods as therapy tools. With all of this time on my hands, I've noticed the knack I have for listening to the type of music that reflects the particular mood I'm in.

At home I drink "Metrx" shakes camouflaged with Breyer's ice cream to my liking. This, of course, is a decent way for me to try and get some nutrition in me. It can get expensive, of course, but when I talk to myself mentally to keep going on, I picture myself as I used to be—35 to 45 lbs. of muscle and more flexible joints ago, that is.

I say, "Keep pushing and you can make it back". Realistically, I doubt even coming close will come to pass, not withstanding a miracle from God or a medical breakthrough. So, I ask myself, why or what is keeping me alive or "afloat"? Copperfield's illusions, invisible strings, fake hair, I know it's not the shoes.

I'll be very surprised if this attempt to write gets finished. Several efforts have failed one of which I spent dictating forty-five minutes of blood and guts emotion into a defective tape in what I thought was a perfect session. Of course, much to my dismay, Murphy's Law comes into play. No offense, Jim, who is my donor (Jim Murphy)—without whom, obviously, I would not be here trying to express whatever it is I'm attempting to express. Needless to say, another attempt ended in the tape recorder breaking and I wanted to just scrap the whole idea. Who'd read it anyway? Well, I'd just like to see if I can get it out, what's "inside" of my insides and break loose or take a sigh. I want to get some kind of feeling from this endeavor.

Pearl Harbor Day, December 7, 1941, a day which will live in infamy. Probably every American of age knows this scenario. Of course, I'm versed in the whole historical happening. My father, Ralph, was a United States Marine in World War II. Entering just hours after he'd heard the traumatic news. My father was my idol. Needless to say, I grilled him often for every one of his war accounts. Just like that little cartoon mouse Seymour with the questions.

Pearl Harbor Day, December 7, 1984, another day that will live in infamy for me and my father, my family and some friends. This was the day the doctors informed me that I was diagnosed with leukemia. That's when it all started for me, in what is now some 18 years as of this writing.

My life and its surroundings have since been just incomprehensible at times. Trying to recant every aspect is probably just not possible. I would like to try and bring some of my prominent memories and episodes to paper. So, perhaps as well as some type of mending therapy and closure I can relate some feelings to ones that haven't had to deal with a life-threatening crisis. Obviously, one message here is that your health is everything.

When I was growing up in the City of Chester, Pennsylvania, it was a rough and tough city in most areas; "A small version of Philly's badlands or the Bronx perhaps". A city that became one of the most crime riddled cities around at one point. Gangs, drugs, vandalism, racism, somewhat I suppose, but in my childhood, it was home. I knew no better, my perspectives were that of knowing the one hundred block to the four hundred block. I played in a fenced in pen behind my house near the alley when I was a baby. "It seemed like a jail cell". We had neighbors in "the Mob" with locked doors, buzzers and passwords, and purple Cadillac's, as well.

As I grew up some to be the paperboy of the neighborhood, my range grew bigger, obviously. The cemetery I lived behind became a hangout paradise playground of sorts. Bike tag, army games, baseball and football—you name it. The kids could all be found in the alleyways, the church lawn or the "cem" as we called it.

I played sports as a young boy. I was an all-star in baseball and basketball. I also, played football for six years in organized club ball, junior high and high school. Nothing was better than suiting up and playing football. Maybe playing basketball in leagues or in the alley comes close, because it was the thing to do; everybody played hoops; uncountable hours with the guys or just by myself, shooting hoops.

I often meditated in basketball: dribble, shoot, ponder, and listen to a distant gunshot. Life was good—"ha-ha". It seems to me now that I reflect on my reflections, so to speak. I enjoyed my health and worked at keeping it, as well as improving my skills.

Of course I wanted to be Joe Namath, Turner Gill, Dr J, Steve Carlton, Sugar Ray Leonard and on and on…it didn't hurt as far as getting the ladies' attention either. Man, I loved women and still do today. I tell God it's His fault, I can't compete with his most beautiful creation. He's the one who made them so incredible.

In junior high, I was too cool to be an altar boy or too afraid, because on the days of the altar boy meetings only the so-called "wussy kids" went. So I sat as my peers watched and harassed those going—doomed to persecution. I formed an incognito alliance with God. I'd sit in the back choir loft steps for Mass, out of sight, and hit Masses I thought no other kids would see me going to. Actually, I may have made too much out of the cool thing, because I noticed more kids attending church after football season started; they were all around the choir loft as well. "Go figure"

As I got into high school (all boys), it was a prison for a guy like me. I think it even made me more girl crazy. Everything just seemed to center around them. Roller-skating was a big thing. Every Friday and Saturday night we'd go to the rink. This is where the ladies were in major numbers. I started dating and to my regret was a bit shy in those areas. Mostly the girls would initiate the first moves and all. I was really overwhelmed with all of these girls to see.

Well, my high school was a good school for religion in Catholic theology, so it kept me in the "classy gents mold;" That, and of course, nine years of Catholic education. I wasn't a prude but by then I had developed a good sense of "religious background." So much so that I remember putting rocks in my shoes as a kid in around the 2nd or 3rd grade as penance—after we learned about some great saint that day. Perhaps I took the study a bit too literally. In any event, I feel that the religious foundation I have is the glue that keeps any of this in any sense of understanding. Hopefully, you can see this later on.

Once I got that all sorted out, I found not enough time for school work, my job, football and girlfriends. So as difficult as it was I eliminated football as the only viable option instead of the ladies. Skipping all of those spicy details, I managed to get in sync with myself as a high school guy and for the most part, there were a lot of good times to remember. Of course, as we all would, if we could change some things, we would.

As things would have it, I finished high school and entered college as a prospective artist. I had received a modest scholarship and academically got off to a good start. The adjustment of commuting everyday into Philadelphia was a bit harder. For some reason I didn't get all gung-ho about the school thing. Our class schedules were set-up like a regular workweek, obviously to prepare you for the forthcoming career move.

I'd come home to work on my deadline projects and, as time passed, I found myself spending more and more time with the girl I was seeing and working on my truck. I was really into four-wheeling and fishing, outdoors and all of that good stuff. The grades slipped a bit, there were still some A's but mostly B's.

I worked for my brother in the morning, went to school all day, and came home to do homework, and fit my social life in between. Like many, I was confused as to what my future held career-wise. My friends and I even discussed the possibility of starting our own advertising agency together. It would have been a great thing but unfortunately it never materialized.

My artistic creativity spilled over into my truck hobby. It became my second love at the time. I did all kinds of modifications to it with the help of my Dad, my girlfriend, and a few of my friends and, of course, even my Mom. It had big tires, captains seats, cutout flares, overhead consoles, trick artwork, you name it "pure gluttony". I was obsessed even to the point of missing school and renting a garage to strip it down and start all over. Now I see it for what it was—dysfunctional insanity, but at the time I was materialistically consumed.

Days would consist of cheesesteaks, loud music, dirt, grime and lots of fumes—"my poor lungs". I say all of this now but when you are 18 or 19 you're "invincible". My enthusiasm drew me in like a drug. Slopping on paint stripper down to bare metal, I slaved away building my "ultimate" truck. I was so irrational with no concept of time about building a future or anything—hindsight is 20–20.

This project got so out of hand that I needed to get professional automotive help to finish what I couldn't do myself. How I wish now that all of the energy and gluttony spent was better served on a worthy cause. Nevertheless, I seemed to level off somewhat for a few months as I toiled with my career moves.

I developed a serious relationship with someone and got into a routine of spending much time with her. We became inseparable to the point of smothering each other I suppose, but I guess looking back on it now, we were just kids—just kids. I bought her the coolest dog from the SPCA; the runt of the litter complete with dog mess all over him. He was the only pup to emerge out of the pile to come see me.

Unfortunately, after being hit by a car despite our best efforts of buying a special cart for his paralyzed legs, my girlfriend put him to sleep. In that scooter of his, he flew around another year and a half giving us much happiness and joy. I knew for sure that he was a very happy dog as well. Some people criticized us for being cruel, keeping him alive & paralyzed, but his affection and panting smile assured me that he was happy to be alive.

With the need to let out some steam, I lifted weights more intensely than n I had in high school. I did the liquid protein diet and vitamins to conquer the world so I guess I thought. I'd gone through some depression spells in my childhood and in retrospect this probably was an episode. I was definitely restless.

Some petty problems with my girlfriend and me over one of her old boyfriends added some heartbreak to the fire. I can often feel the metamorphosis of physical change in depressed states to the point of getting ill. I managed to get through that episode although my sense of being and life were changing. I guess it was just part of life's "growing up".

That summer ended, and Fall was in the air. It was then, and probably still is my favorite time of the year: lower humidity, cooler breezes, and change of colors in the trees, holidays and football. As a kid I loved playing football and even after high school, I loved coaching it, watching it, every aspect of it. My father and I loved going up to Penn State for those fall classics. Games against Notre Dame, Alabama, Nebraska, and Texas…were some of our great trips. They were just wonderful memories.

In the season of 1984, I made two early trips to Happy Valley, and although I enjoyed them thoroughly, my stamina and overall zest of energy was fading out.

It was one of those feelings where you just shrugged it off, or just dismissed it due to a lack of sleep or bad eating, etc. I started noticing a pattern of this weakness. I even wondered that maybe I was just getting older, that this is what everybody goes through when you get older—that kind of thing. Well, pretty much I just kept this to myself. I was concerned; my basketball game wasn't as good; and I couldn't jog as long or as easy. I even remember back in college my getting really weak and very nauseous, so weak in fact that my friend, Kevin, had to take my work into class while I laid on the floor of he lobby next to a candy machine. Those occurrences I attributed to the Philadelphia air, subway and carsickness. I never thought I was in denial; I really just kept putting things off doctor-wise.

The late fall in October had a big game with Notre Dame, I believe, and some of my friends had a dorm in downtown State College. I was invited for the weekend trip and didn't hesitate to grab some clothes and "jet" up there. I'll tell you, it just felt great! The fall air, downtown campus, what an atmosphere! My adrenaline was giving me plenty of life; It ended up that I weaseled a couch to sleep on; "that's a big deal when 20 kids are in a box".

The time up there was fun, but draining. I kept feeling like I had kryptonite in my body. As the time grew closer, I learned that none of the guys that I went up with were going to the game. No rocket scientists needed here to figure out why, they were up there to party. So I found myself having to walk a mile or two to the stadium and I finally did get one other buddy to go with me. I think I had to buy his ticket or something and scalped fifty-yard line seats for like one hundred dollars each or something. At least they were great seats, directly behind the Notre Dame bench. It sounded like Heaven, but a monsoon of rain storms ensued which didn't help matters. I figured that I could block out the rain. I mean Penn State vs. Notre Dame, me on the fifty yard line, are you kidding? The only problem was that the once easy walk had found me drenched in a cold sweat underneath all of the rain's wetness. I just felt so numb and again pushing it on adrenaline.

I thought I got through it but it was the walk that did me in. Getting back to the dorm, I had a shower and just collapsed on the couch. I didn't move for the rest of the trip. Everyone else partied: went to a girlie movie, dinner and visited other dorms, although probably not in that order. I remember a war movie was on and I just lay there kind of distant. I knew I was definitely sick, but nothing registered as to what it could be.

The significant irony of my memorable trip was in meeting one of my friend's roommates who then, I believe, was a reforming party animal—spiked hair and all. He kept telling me about how he was going to change his lifestyle and get back to church and so on. He gave me an article from *The Catholic Standard*, I recall about his brother who had just had an incredible miracle. I took a bit of an interest because we all had attended the same high school back home. It was a moving story that I never thought would have had any impact on me.

Thanksgiving had arrived and at the dinner table over my sister's house, I was confronted about my night sweats and fevers that had persisted only at night. Evidently, my mom talked to my sister about it and they had enough evidence to convince themselves that something needed to be done. I reluctantly agreed to let my sister Carol arrange a doctor's appointment for me. I hadn't really seen a doctor since before high school, so all that I had was a pediatrician to go to as my MD. He and Carol corresponded and I was referred to a local doctor for a complete physical. This appointment was scheduled for December 7, 1984 for about 11am as I had mentioned.

That morning is still crystal clear in my mind even today. The modest and cluttered but cozy row home that my family lived in had me lounging on the couch watching TV as one eye kept peeking at the wall clock. Eventually I made my way to the hospital. I lived only several blocks or a stone's throw away if I cut through the cemetery. My dad was off or something although I now figure he probably took off work because he knew something was wrong.

After all of the clipboard questionnaires were filled out, I was ready to get this physical rolling. I often speak of photographic memories I have of certain experiences and this is one of them. A nice older nurse came in and gave me that fashionable gown with no back to it and asked me to get undressed after some blood work was taken.

As fast as she was in and out, I observed my skin go cold and ivory colored due to the chilled steel table I was on and from the vials of blood taken as well. This triggered a slight, rapid heartbeat of unknown nerves with the lousy atmosphere of old file cabinets and UFO lights hovering over my head on the table.

The doctor came in and introduced himself, did the reflex, stethoscope, eye coordination thing and then used his hands to push on my abdomen. As doctors often do, his demeanor changed and his body language gave him away. I then knew something was wrong but, of course, he said nothing much other than, "go back home and wait for us to call you this afternoon". The exact time turned out to be 2:55 pm.

The whole time I was home standing by there was a certain whistling in my ears, kind of like when I had been hit head-on in football drills. I kept figuring that I was anemic or had mono or something else real easy to take care of. So, when I reentered the office, I had convinced myself pretty well that I was all right. That was just until I heard the deafening silence of the whole staff.

I got a quick eye contact of a glance by one nurse and another nurse with a mother-like gentleness escorted me to the examination room. With my father by my side, I made some dry jokes to break the tension although it failed to ease him much. No sooner than I had sat down, the door opened and another doctor came in. This was the initial doctor's associate, and supposedly the first one had other appointments, so this gentleman was elected to give me the news. I still get sick every time I recount this moment in my life. We all sat in a triangle facing each other when the doctor said, "John, we think that you have leukemia." I didn't see my dad's reaction at that moment. I do remember smiling in a plastic, fake way though.

The doctor went on to compassionately state how some patients have lived a few years or sometimes a bit longer. Looking back, he was grabbing at anything I suppose to ease the shock. I'm sure it was a difficult position for him to be in. No sooner had he told me that I had leukemia, I abruptly inquired if there was a cure. He mentioned some rare cases of a permanent remission and invincibly I grabbed that for my initial comfort. I was told that I would have to be hospitalized immediately, because my white cell count was estimated at over one million and that the normal machine could not be used to count them. They had lab technicians counting by hand through slides and microscopes. My platelets were also ridiculously high at over eight hundred thousand, so basically my blood had become extremely thick and mud like for an analogy.

The surreal moment then was my father and I sitting in that quiet, long echo-filled hallway, waiting to be admitted to a room. My father just looked so down. His eyes were distant and broken. He knew more than I did about leukemia. Maybe he was thinking of how we could fix it some way.

The only thing that I knew about leukemia was as a boy, maybe 5 or 6 years old, I had a friend who used to come and play once in a blue moon. I can still see him in my mind running down the street to meet all of us kids and then not knowing how to fit in. He was pale and sickly, but determined to live life with a huge smile, just so anxious to have some fun. Now, of course, I can see why he was that way.

He was probably doing well enough at the time to get out for a special play session, and as us kids were, just totally awful. His reward from me was to trap him between our row home steps and torture him with my fake gun. Of course, he was convinced that it was real and I totally traumatized him. So much so that my mom came outside and grabbed me as he screamed fearfully. "Boy, what I didn't know then". We had some great fun times as well but my gift to you today, Eddie, is that I pray for you often in sincere apology. God bless you, Ed; now I know all of the pure hell that you went through.

Eddy passed away shortly after our war games. Other than that, in about the 6th grade, I was helping my dad panel my bedroom and listening to a Philadelphia Eagles game on the radio. They sponsored a drive called the "Frito Lay Eagles Fly for Leukemia". Then I remember asking my father what leukemia was. It's really something how those two memories have stayed in my mind throughout my whole life. It's almost like a premonition of sorts that I had initially.

I finally got settled in a hospital room by about 5 pm that same December day in the left corner of a twin room next to the bathroom. The doctors started administrating drugs called Hydrea and Myleran, I believe to try and start the thinning of my blood cells. Another of the assortment of meds was called Allopurinol. This was to assist my kidneys in dealing with the very thick blood and possible organ damage that existed.

The magnitude of this did not hit home for me all at once. It came in waves, from a brief calm into a full blown mess. Up until this time, I did not shed a tear and really believed that I would be real good about it. The next thing that I knew my girlfriend came in all smiles; I believe not knowing what was going on. I totally lost it and cried like a baby. What a "wuss" I remember thinking to myself a short time later but as I do now know, it did give me a much needed release. I regained my composure and tried to explain the situation to her. The great comfort back then was that she was "a rock to lean on" at the time for me.

The evening rolled in and my family made their way in like a mini-mob as little ants roaming around my bedside tending to my every need. My sister and I discussed my game plan to beat this and, ironically, the "card of hope' came in the form of my new oncologist, Dr. Mike Soojian. He would prove instrumental in my battle.

No sooner than he introduced himself it seemed that I hit him with the "is there a cure?" He glanced my way, pessimistic in expression, speaking of the permanent remission thing and some new drugs to prolong life a bit but just left it at that. Then, as in the movie "The Exorcist", where they refer to the exorcism itself as being kept back in the closet by Catholics sort of thing, he quietly muttered a possible bone marrow transplant. Those words barely got out of his mouth before the verbal pummeling began. Again, just like the little mouse cartoon Seymour I think who never stops with the questioning, we hit him from all sides on the issue.

The fact that I heard of a remote procedure may have been all that I needed to hear at that time for inspiration although I knew nothing about it. I still had major work to do ahead of me in the here and now just to get out of this local hospital. As I remember it to be complete with the usual hospital ritual of no sleep, vacuuming your room at 5 in the morning, people peeking in and out at all hours of the night, hospital food and so forth. And, of course, lastly the ever-present blood sticks at all hours of the night, in total darkness to boot.

I'd be the first to admit that I am a moody person, but I do try fairly well to go out of my way to be polite even when it requires extra effort. Not in a given situation such as 3 am in a hospital room, especially with it being a training facility. Very many students reeked havoc on my arms for sure. Well one particular stick led to the discovery of an isolated infection in my heart. One described to me as extremely rare and had baffled the doctors to the point of bringing in the infectious disease team.

By taking a shot at them now, I can say at the very least, that they lacked bedside manners for sure and that is putting it politely. I distinctly remember the group huddled together, busting into my room like a scene from a Clint Eastwood movie where the villains come crashing through the saloon doors. Without any introduction to my family or myself for that matter, they promptly started to clear the room so that I could be "interrogated" or, as they saw it, a routine examination. This was the first bad experience with doctors I had encountered and in a bad situation, as if it already wasn't bad. By that I mean that callous, robotic nature and disregard of any type of compassion or rapport. All that seemed missing was a swaying spotlight as they grilled me on how I could have contracted this germ. At the time I was very scared and intimidated just as they had intended I'm sure.

Underneath the seedy sheet of a half-gown that I had on, you know the standard no back issue; I had a rosary around my neck that I put on the day before for some sort of spiritual comfort. At that point, I do not remember if I could even recite it correctly to tell you the truth. Anyhow, the head infectious disease doctor with his grayish beard, chocolate brown suit, brown mustard shirt, and matching brown tie spewed of arrogance as he curiously attempted to probe my mind. Firing off insinuating questions like: How much crack have you done? Tell me how much heroin have you done lately," come on, you can level with me". We know you're a party kind of guy, right? All of these asinine inquiries while his cronies are probing and policing my body for evidence to support their conceited theories. I guess like lawyers and undefeated track records go, this staff had never been previously stumped.

Needless to say, those doctors never found any track marks or any other shred of evidence to support their theory. As of this writing, I've not received an apology for those accusations. Perhaps I'm not deserving of one either. They were doing their job; it was just the manner in which they conducted their business. I'd state that it was poor at best. As far as the staff could determine, the germ on my heart was one commonly found in burn patients and this hospital housed the biggest burn unit on the East Coast. So I'll never know for sure how I picked up that infection so fast, or how ever long it took to get there. It's also funny to me how this particular incident stayed in my mind all of these years with such a bigger picture to focus on—that being the leukemia, of course.

With that incident out of the way, I still remained hospitalized in lousy condition. After four or five days of big doses of oral chemo, my sludgy blood was now at a consistency where conventional lab techniques could be used to monitor my blood levels. I still clocked in around one-half million white cells and just about as many platelets. I was pale and withdrawn; the fluorescent lighting didn't help to flatter me either. I felt like a ghost with my white face staring back at me in the mirror, "Boo"…I was extremely lethargic, but not in much pain per se. I just "rested" in that standard hospital bed, if I could use the term rested at all.

Word was getting out that I now had leukemia and some people wanted to come in and see me. At that time, I really wasn't in the mood for company but couldn't ignore my friends who cared. The first two friends who weaseled their way in were a couple of my close friends from school, Kevin and Pete. Armed with the dry, David Letterman sense of humor that we were noted for and true spirit, they arrived on a mission to cheer me up. Kev brought me a truck magazine and Pete gave me a girlie magazine to boost my morale, the latter of which was absconded by a janitor from the wastebasket. But more seriously though, Pete had a little nephew who was already battling the same disease. He was at Children's Hospital in Philadelphia. So Pete had first-hand experience on what I had ahead of me. Chucky was Pete's nephew. He battled hard just as kids do and lived a while longer before passing. "God bless you, Chucky; a little bog hero!"

With Kev and Pete breaking the ice for me, I felt a little better about other friends visiting me. The next evening, I was totally blown away with over fifty of my friends and acquaintances coming to see me. I don't think the hospital enjoyed it as much as I did because they had to wheel me into the lounge and close it off to accommodate my visitors. All tolled, it ended up that about a hundred people came to see me with cards and support. That was such an overwhelming moment for me to see so many concerned people showing that they cared. "whew"…

I believe that I was improving just as the doctors had hoped in the initial phase of treatment. The plan was to try and get me out of the immediate life threatening danger up to a point where I could go home and be treated on an out patient basis. I continued to get encouraging cards and visits and even some of the neighborhood girls came to visit me, who brought flowers and candy. I thought that was great but I'm not so sure how my girlfriend felt about it at the time. I guess she knew that I always kind of liked them, who knows?

It took a total of about ten days to two weeks staying in the hospital, until the doctors were satisfied that my counts were sufficiently stable enough to be discharged. So I came home feeling rubbery and sluggish but glad to be back where I belonged, only four blocks away but home is home!

When I initially got in my front door, it was a funny feeling for me. For some reason and I still couldn't tell you why, I just remember sitting on the living room couch looking at the television and then over at the clock with the afghan draped over me. Maybe I just couldn't believe that this was happening to me. I definitely felt alone. That whistling in my ears and the clammy perspiration along with a misfire in my heartbeat kept me company.

One thing that also stuck out in my mind was a visit that my brother and his wife made to see me. They had brought with them my sister-in-law's nephew who was slightly younger than I was. He wasn't known for his emotional tendencies, yet I could clearly notice compassion by the look in his eyes and the tone of his voice. As sincere as the gestures may have been, it only triggered me to analyze the situation further. Internally I could see, or thought I saw people looking at me with pity, like…"the poor guy is doomed to die." There was no doubt that the way people treated me then was gentle but morbid. They were scared for me and now I was getting really scared for me. I mean I felt that I was feeling better, but what about later on? "Man, I'm gonna die." I just ate myself up with fear inside for sure.

I was eventually scheduled weekly for blood counts and maintenance sometimes three days per week. The office was tucked away in the basement of the hospital back behind the incinerator, trash bins and storage depots. It was small and typical but attempted to be cordial. "Blue light special" paintings hung, twenty seats, a coat rack and the sliding glass window partition between the nurse and the waiting room. This place became my second home it seemed with week after week after week checking in for blood counts. My medicines would be adjusted almost weekly as well. "Counts rising" was traumatic and my mood would revolve on the climatic results, whether it was okay, up or down. The "counts rising" in my mind was like getting closer to dying—I'd convince myself. I just brutalized myself emotionally.

As I mentioned earlier, my doctor gave me a window of hope in his mentioning the bone marrow transplant. So, obviously I had to address the issue with him again. I think I waited perhaps one visit. This doctor is a great guy and I believe that we have a very good rapport. I'm sure that I have been put out with him about some things over the duration that he has or hasn't done but all in all I feel very fortunate to have been teamed up with him.

Our initial discussions were brief at best. He seemed to almost dodge the transplant issue, most likely because he knew the crunch numbers on the odds of survival and I didn't. With the type of leukemia that I had (CML), the only successful attempts were those involving a sibling matched donor, i.e. a brother or sister. Even if that was the case, other than a perfect twin being used, the odds in 1985 were lousy.

Chronic myelogeneous leukemia was unique in the quest to cure and this is a good time to state that there are various kinds of leukemia, some curable and some not. Most people hear the name leukemia and lump all of the forms together, which in turn leads to problems with misinformation. At any rate in the 80s the odds of a family member being compatible as a suitable donor was one in four. We talked some about making arrangements to have my family members tested, but in reality it seemed as if months were passing by with no definitive plan. I was now learning the very nasty side of politics, perseverance and management. Whether it's right or wrong, whether the doctors are at fault, I could not say. I just have my personal opinions to go by.

The system just does not hold you by the hand and escort you to a finish line or direct you otherwise in any direction for that matter. "Most of the time you simply are on your own". If you do not ask, you will not find out the answers. You either have to get mean, be obnoxious or, at the least, come off as pushy or aggressive at times; it really is a kill or be killed kind of mentality. A lousy thing to have to find out when you're terminally ill, I suppose. I'm just very fortunate that I was able to put together some help and support units. I feel as if I was in a war in many respects. That is what it became and still is now. It becomes just a matter of how far you wish to take it and I still cannot believe it has to be this way.

The whole issue of finding a donor is for the vast majority of people, complicated, tedious, vicious and terribly exhausting. Television has often depicted wondrous stories of success and ease between twins or family matches, parents having children for donors and so forth. Those types of stories are incredibly great, and I am very happy for them; it is truly a miracle. Those stories are great blessings from God. But in reality, I would say that 99% of all of the cases just don't end that way. I cannot help but get watery-eyed thinking of every person in families involved or enduring any type of transplant especially when it involves searching for a donor outside of your family.

In my experience with all of this, I've even seen patients underestimate the seriousness of the matter. Things such as dragging their feet until it is too late to pursue a transplant or realizing what type of commitment it really takes on the part of the patient as well as the family. The whole ordeal in searching for a donor that I have mentioned is sometimes for the very blessed, not such a big deal. In cases where you have twins involved or relatives that match up real well, obviously, that is the best place to start.

When we first learned that the statistics on suitable matches was approximately one in four, I immediately psyched myself up mentally with positive ways to match, including my mother and father, sister and brother, as well as two nephews and three nieces. I actually had nine possible chances, so I thought. It was encouraging for me to think that way, but at no time did that nauseating butterfly feeling ever pass, even when I became optimistic and teased with hope.

I must say, that while I make an attempt to recant many of the memories through this mess, I do not believe any words could justify or express the gamut of emotions that I have lived. That may sound like a cliché, but there are many times, even today when I still feel like I'm in a fog or living a nightmare that I cannot comprehend or escape from.

At any rate, the family dinner discussions became heated as to who thought that they would match me and why. Everybody had reasons why they would be a better match. Either it was because of the way they looked, acted, or just wanted to will it that way among many other crazy reasons, so they thought. Of course I was glad that they all were so eager to help. Now we had to go and set all of this testing up.

Initially, my mother, father, sister and brother were scheduled to go into the hospital for some blood workups. From what I remember, the first phase of typing would take several weeks to determine whether those tests could be further developed. If so, the steps could go to tests such as MLC and DR typing etc. I really did for a good while anticipate a match and envisioned each and every member of the family being close enough to use as a donor at one time or another.

The waiting turned out to be brutal and as we all know, the time felt longer than it actually turned out to be. The rapport that I had with the doctors was just okay at the time. I was under the care of a group of oncologists, hematologists.

For a long time of follow up visits, I would not know which of the doctors that I would be seeing in the rotation. So basically each guy had a unique personality and style that I would grow accustomed to eventually.

In the beginning, it was very awkward and upsetting for me to say the least. As it turned out, I drew Dr. Vivaqua on this particular day. No sooner had I sat on the examining table than I could notice his body language and demeanor suggesting bad news. And so it came, the quote was "There are no matches…" His eyes looked down on the chart and he made very brief eye contact with me, then just silence. As dead as the sound is empty, I could hear that whooshing in my ears again. Then a recollection of a heart skip kicked in.

Nothing much else to remember from that visit except the start of many more no match visits. In what became the norm, I would come home beat-up and try to retreat and regroup in the confines of my home, most often in my bedroom. I knew that I still had my nieces and nephews to type, so that was a good defensive mechanism to use as a tool for my sanity at the time. As testing eventually started on them, pretty much the same situation of waiting and hoping arose. There was a funny rumor of my nephew Tommy passing out during the stick, but I couldn't confirm it. Looking back on things, I notice some patterns in attempts at making some humor out of this mess. I do not believe that I was as aware of that then as I am upon reflection now.

The results of the kids came back and I believe that it was my sister who informed me over the phone one day, that there were no suitable donors within the family. As bad as it was hearing that from Carol, it was way better than having a doctor inform me. That possibly was a psychosomatic attempt to find optimism in my sister's voice, who knows. I do know that I was crushed. I laid out back of my house on the old car seat that we had in the alley near the basketball court. I just stared out in to the cemetery that was behind the house, not seeing the irony in that back then. I couldn't come up with a game plan and it was an empty sick feeling. I don't believe that I coped with the situation well at all during that stretch looking back. It simply passed by tick by tick by tick, and my counts were not doing all that peachy either.

One thing that I had to do was find some serenity somewhere. I thought that I might step up with my faith and perhaps start going to Mass daily. I was never a morning person and Catholics know, most all of the daily Masses are 6 am or 8 am, something like that and that's it—maybe some 10:30 am Mass or Noon Mass somewhere. Well, I had to find a way to grow spiritually from where I was, if for no other reason than to just stay calm and somewhat sane. I can't count the number of times that I felt like exploding. I was just a time bomb with my emotions.

I have always been and still am an emotional person; but these episodes were unbearable. I'd often thought of it as a person wanting desperately to express himself but not being able to do so. Anyhow, I started looking in the area for Masses and low and behold, I found a 5 pm evening Mass within driving distance. It turned out to be the old parish of my Godmother and became a great spiritual "private Idaho" for me. The particular church was St. Rose of Lima in Eddystone, Pa. This was something that I desperately needed to cope with things for sure.

As it turned out, my first visit was very close to being my last. The girl that I was dating was a Catholic, but not brought up in a parochial school setting. In her innocent way, when she received the Blessed Sacrament of Holy Communion, she cracked a smile most likely in shear embarrassment due to her ritual form. The priest serving Mass was very "old world" pre Vatican II and ultra-reverent in his own way. Well, he stopped the Mass and scolded her crudely as I saw it, that it was all that I needed to go off. "I didn't need this crap I thought," and was prepared to storm out with my girlfriend, in arm and vowing never to return, "I'd show them all", I thought. As it turned out though, I guess that the Holy Spirit kept me cool enough to finish the Mass.

Now, just as I was leaving the church, right in front of me appears this cool "Clint Eastwood" kind of a cowboy, in form only. A great presence and aura, but all compacted in a slim, neat, regular kind of guy. He seemed as if to seek us out to chat with. Perhaps he had witnessed the incident and felt that he would like to shed his priestly side to us, and I am very thankful for that. As it turned out, he was the new pastor and it was his first day there. Just the "coincidence" I needed, because he calmed me down and became my close friend and spiritual director, his name, Father William Fahey.

Father Fahey was in his sixties and in control. A man of God that could help me grow and I believe that I did. I have to believe that God put us together. It sure seemed like it. Thus, I had my hook up to daily 5 pm Masses and obviously, that was instrumental to my life.

For the time being, I was better in terms of my frame of mind. The counts bounced all over and I had my medicines adjusted accordingly. I was able to pace myself and adjust my lifestyle to my energy level. All in all, I did a fair job of faking it while I attempted to still fit in with everything. I needed to still do as much as I used to do and it was pretty easy on the outside. I even had some brief times where I would forget that I was sick, albeit, very brief.

One of my rituals had been to hang out near my friend Kevin's house. Kev's father was and still is very active in church functions. One day he mentioned to us about a talk that was to be given at a local church one night. It had to do with this young man who went to our high school and had a religious healing happen to him.

This extraordinary story involved a miracle, and a priest that is up for sainthood who will be canonized by the time I ever finish this book. It had all of the good stuff that you like to hear about. In fact, this man, Paul Walsh, has been on television's "Unsolved Mysteries" and now is a good friend of mine. I cannot forget to mention that this gentleman was the same person whose brother told me the story back up at Penn State before I had been diagnosed with leukemia! All of this I now know but didn't at the time.

So my friends, Kevin, Pete and I decided to go hear that talk at this nearby parish. I believe that we were the only young guys in the hall. Mostly there were older parishioners and parent-type individuals. We got there in time to hear the dramatic events that led to Paul's miracle. In a short synopsis, Paul Walsh was involved in an automobile accident; his brain and skull were crushed. He lapsed into a coma and had approximately 72 spinal taps. He battled meningitis, numerous infections, and diabetes insipid us, among many other setbacks. No doctor gave him a surviving prognosis, so his mother investigated into the people in the church that were up for sainthood.

In the Catholic Church it is believed that miracles of God can be obtained through the intercession of Saintly people. In this case, a Franciscan priest named Padre Pio was chosen for the job. I say this humorously because Padre Pio passed away in 1968. He bore the "stigmata" or wounds of Jesus Christ, and has had many miracles attributed to him. As a matter of fact people all over the world pray to this holy man today for his intercession to God. Padre Pio has recently been canonized a Saint by the Catholic Church and Paul's case was one of many used in the research process.

As I still skim the surface of this incredible story, witnesses say that Padre Pio was seen in the hospital room of Paul's just before he regained consciousness. A bedside roommate attested to this as well as a nurse. A CAT scan revealed a healed brain and normal functions. This was not the case before the healing took place. Paul's brain tissue had been smashed in certain regions and thought to be permanently damaged. Paul is a regular guy. We fish together have an occasional beer, and do the things friends do. More can be learned about Paul and Padre Pio by contacting the National Centre for Padre Pio in Barto, PA (610.845.3000).

By giving a briefing on Paul's story, you can see why I was so fired up by it with a new sense of confidence and hope. If Paul is a guy like me and God helped him, may be I could get that help as well.

The talk that evening gave me fuel for awhile, like a high, I suppose, euphoria and all of that. I didn't need to worry I thought, I'll just bug God. I took with me that evening a prayer card of Padre Pio and it had a third class relic on it, a piece of cloth touched to his tomb. At that particular time I was not very knowledgeable on relics and the like, but I had great reverence though I didn't believe that it was a case of idolatry or anything like that.

The lecture concluded and a mention of a healing mass was stated for a church in Norristown, Pa. So I guessed that it was close enough to drive to and I needed to get to it. I hope people reading this can notice a pattern of coincidences or connections. I can't really put it in a chronological order, but the ongoing series of events seemed meaningful to me. This was such a strange time in my life, I'll never forget, but things were being put together without my being aware.

I received directions and my sister, Carol agreed to take me to this healing mass. So when the date arrived, off we went. The church was Holy Savior in Norristown, Pa. a nice church that, of course, was new to me so we settled in around the middle rows. It was a nice mass with talks about Padre Pio and various miraculous stories on him were included. At the end of the mass, everyone lined up to be blessed with a glove worn by Padre Pio. They were used to conceal the visible bleeding wounds of Christ that he bore; I was pretty geared up to be blessed, admittedly, thinking of an instant cure once I was touched by it. I know that is not how God usually worked but, at the time, I was convinced that my next blood counts would be normal.

The oddest thing that happened to us that day was indirectly linked to the Mass, but more bizarre than I could imagine. A nice lady approached me after church and asked me if I was John Amatuzio. I answered yes, of course, and she promptly asked my sister and me to have dinner with her and her husband at their home nearby. Her name was Peggy Parker and she was so nice, although it sounded crazy to have this happen, we reluctantly agreed. I still do not know how she knew who I was. Perhaps I will find out someday, but the story gets even more eerie. Mrs. Parker told me that her son had one of the very first bone marrow transplants, in 1969 I believe. He had a relative as a donor and lived another 10 years after that post-transplant. His name was Jacob

When my sister and I entered the home you could see immediately a drawing of Jacob and Padre Pio together on the wall. The Parkers mentioned that Padre Pio had been a part of their experience. Who was I to argue with this going on. "I was thinking that Rod Serling from the Twilight Zone was in the kitchen." Mr. Parker was a rosary maker and after dinner he showed me techniques used down in his basement. We looked at pictures of Jacob in a photo album they brought out and talked a lot about him. The issues of my case were brought up and I relapsed into the panic sensation that I did not have a donor and that things weren't looking good at all.

I had explored all of my options family-wise and thought that was that. The next thing you know Mrs. Parker said "Let me call my daughter-in-law's mother." As she was dialing, I was thinking, "What the heck is going on here?" As it turned out, while her son was in Seattle, WA. having a bone marrow transplant, an older brother or sister fell in love with this woman's son or daughter, respectively and they ended up marrying. The big deal is that the in-law's mother was a big boss at Seattle's Fred Hutchinson's Cancer Research Center in Seattle, WA! Basically that is the best place to go in the world for bone marrow transplants for "CML", especially at that time.

Actually, the procedure was developed by a doctor on staff there, Dr. Donnell Thomas, the Nobel Prize winner who later would become my doctor. Go figure the odds on that. This woman, Marion McCarty, talked with me and after a few minutes, she told me to get my files and fly out as soon as possible to see what they could do. This was the miracle or the start of many little miracles I thought I was looking for at the time. Of course, as you will see, I wish it were that easy. So here I am in a surreal mindset driving home from a healing Mass, having eaten with strangers in their home, and now getting ready to red eye from Philadelphia to Seattle and back again. Talk about witch hunts or craziness; it was plain and simple desperation. That's how it appeared at the time.

I had never flown before and that was kind of exciting for me. I figured that the whole trip would be easy for me because it was a Monday marathon. We would take off, fly, visit the doctors, eat, take the last flight home the same day and be back home. I'd take a 6am flight out and a 10:30pm flight back, something like that. Little did I know about jet lag or cramped seats, stale air, those peanuts, and all that good stuff. It seemed to me that the flight was okay, but long of course. The trip went by fast across the country on the way out. I didn't know about Seattle's rain either. But I'm told there are good rain days and bad rain days. I guess that I came to see it that way too, eventually.

My first experience at Fred Hutch, or "Hutch" as they call it, was scary and intimidating. That had to do with the particular area I was in. I believe that they were building new facilities at the time. The floor that I first entered in, now the old building was just that, an old building. The old elevator crept up to the third floor I believe, and upon stepping out you could see graphic poster size pictures of mucositis. This is a very severe condition that many bone marrow transplant patients know by heart that occurs in the mouth and throat. Often blister-like open sores and gaping holes as horrible as your mind could imagine. There were also photographs on the wall of graft vs. host disease patients. The often occurring reaction from donor bone marrow that is the most hideous of all at the very least, that can involve virtually any bodily organ or function. You can think of it as a spin of the wheel as to what you may or may not develop: organ failure, internal bleeding, infections, severe skin burns, throat problems, joint pains, stiffness, and even death. This is a very much crippling and debilitating disease, as I mentioned, and often fatal. If you are fortunate enough to survive at length dealing with this disease, you can develop all of the symptoms that I mentioned and even many, many more. It is definitely perverted; there is no other way to put it. These pictures pulled no punches and this is the truth, they don't tell lies.

All of the staff members I encountered were courteous, polite and compassionate. It was the atmosphere that spooked me. Today they have a Taj Mahal compared to this visit that I am talking about now. As rough as this was, I couldn't imagine the environment that Jacob had in 1969, uh! My sister and I were escorted to a room. I guess that it was normal in size to anyone who has been in hospitals. I sat upon a gurney and a curtain was used to separate one side of the room from the other. Whereas often was the case, more than one patient shared one room. Obviously, this was a screening room and by no means a patient area. Next to me was a family from Asia. The curtain blocked the view, but we could both clearly hear the goings on between us. There was so much tension, fear and anxiety; you could just cut it with a knife, such a horrible feeling.

I was asked oodles of questions and I succumbed to what to what Carol and I called the "roto-rooter", a mammoth sized needle hooked to a hose. Now that I know needle sizes, I now request number 22gauge, that being very small, whenever I can possibly get it; (The higher the number being the smaller the size needle). That big needle must have been in the negative numbers I'll tell ya. It's all that we talked about on the way home and we did mention it to everyone, who knows if they ever believed us.

As if that was not enough, during my consult, the Asian couple evidently received bad news that they weren't candidates for a bone marrow transplant. The woman or girl just screamed and went crazy. It was so traumatic; everyone's nerves were just on edge. At that moment, I couldn't tell you how I felt. I had to give a good bit of blood for tests and things, so that didn't help my energy level at all for the trip home.

We had a bit to eat and were told that at that point in time, no one with chronic myelogenous leukemia had survived at all, using a non-related donor, in the whole world, he stated. He advised me that I could go check the University of Iowa, UCLA, Sloan Kettering, Johns Hopkins etc., but no luck. He stated that the survival count was 0 for 20, but if I wanted to see about finding a donor, they would consider me for a transplant. The big decision for me was that they felt confident that they could cure the leukemia, it was the infections and graft vs.host disease that they lacked abilities to control. They presented the toughest problems in my case. The doctors stated that the procedures of radical chemotherapy, extreme total body irradiation, toxic treatments, and all of the other things were more aggressive therapies than at other centers doing transplants.

Well, really there is no decision when you are terminally ill, at least for me there wasn't. I thought, you're going to die if you don't try it, and by trying you could just make it! I agreed to enroll and try to find a suitable non-related donor. Through their donor bank system back in 1985, it was very slim pickings, but it was all that we had. I would just get psyched up to think that someone has to be out there that's all. I had to leave this marathon journey on somewhat of an optimistic outlook. The door was open again for a chance to get this leukemia out of me. I was exhausted from my first flight experience, but I seemed to have something to work with.

By this time, I would say that three months or so had passed; that put us around April or May of '85 I believe. The things going on in Seattle concerning a donor match for me were slow and tedious. Evidently my genetic makeup in the blood work didn't match any initial computer numbers. Otherwise, I'd probably be contacted and quick arrangements for a transplant would have been made. It was clearly now a matter of beat the clock, because CML advances into stages of progression, namely an accelerated phase, and ultimately blast crisis. These are terms used to describe complicated matters of the disease. When you advance into these areas, the chances of being cured are jeopardized greatly.

I didn't have any of the signs in my blood work or marrow aspirations to indicate either one of these advances had taken place, so that was a good blessing. Every patient differs in the time frame that it takes to deteriorate, to put it bluntly. It can occur in a matter of weeks to months, and in some cases, several years. Nothing is a given with chronic myeloygeous leukemia, so that was just one more mental anguish angle that I added to my psyche mind set, as if I needed it. Maybe another week or so after this, my sister received a call from Hutch that nothing was coming up as a suitable match. Lousy news for me, but since I was feeling good physically, it took some pressure off for the time being.

By now Carol had officially become my public relations person; she was my agent, my secretary, you name it. She took it upon herself to start aggressively pushing my whole case. Carol had the privilege of working for my brother at the time as a bookkeeper. That gave her access to use the phone in her office as a "war room". I feel this too came to be a blessing from God. There isn't any way that this undertaking could have been done without the flexibility that she had. My brother came into his own business two years before I got sick and, ironically, shortly after the majority of my treatments were done, he sold the business. The coincidences keep mounting. Individually, it may not appear as anything big, but in adding them up you can see why I feel the way that I do.

In processing my blood for potential donors, all of the work-ups showed that I had a rare chromosome named a 244X. I'm still today not a blood typing guru, but it is a potential problem to have these rare features in your makeup. It was fouling up all of the tests so far, but as some luck would have it, my 244X would later come back and be instrumental in helping me. The donor bank ultimately exhausted its attempts to match me with someone, but nothing showed up. In the inter-workings of all of this, Carol established a great rapport with the Fred Hutch staff. They all in turn linked up with the Puget Sound Blood Bank. Among the many awesome people helping me, there were Doctors Fred Applebaum and Pat Beaty. Their interest in my case was instrumental, as were all of the staff members, of course. Again I cannot express this in words.

Some discussions ensued as to me perhaps having any other family members to try and test. As far as I knew, it was case closed. My dad's mother was alive and my mother had a sister that was alive, but that was that. I would say that by this point I had stepped out of the donor search and let Carol single-handedly take over. Like I said, she was my agent and I had great confidence in her ability to help me. The next thing I remember was that they were convinced into giving some blood for testing. Carol also hired a private investigator to help to see if there were any other distant relatives.

This turn of events took a new direction because, although nobody matched as a donor, my grandmother possessed the same 244X chromosome that I had. That led them to pursue my father's side of the family. I don't completely understand how, but this also enabled doctors to search for other indicating match factors that they didn't previously have. I also didn't know about the 60 or 70 other distant relatives that they came up with somehow, either. Everything that you could dream up in a soap opera was occurring. Attempting to track these people down was unbelievable; from some, flat out rejections of consent to help, to my brother and sister driving for hours to locations, only to be blocked by vicious dogs, to others trekking in monsoon rains. I believe people were even contacted and tested outside of the country. Even up to today I have not met any of my distant relatives. I can never thank them enough for trying to help me. I did receive some best wishes through the grapevine. God bless them all, even the ones that didn't want to help me, I suppose. What can you do...

I'll also say that this is another huge hurdle, to just overcome the testing. People do not realize that it costs money for each and every person that you set up to be tested. Insurance does not cover this in most cases, and in 1985 not at all. I don't believe that it does today either, but I remember the cost being about $75.00 per person back then, just to draw one or two tubes of blood.

Another coincidence "if you could call it that" is that our family, namely my sister had a friend who was an attorney, Mr.Archibald. I never knew it for a long time, but this man arranged for Carol to have the testing set up and he would pay the costs, plus airmail to Seattle. I have no idea how much he contributed silently, only God knows. Once again you can see why "Thank You" can sound so insufficient sometimes. If only people could see inside of your heart and feel the sincere appreciation, and I'll probably never know of every individual who contributed to my recovery. Perhaps in the next life I can show them how much it meant to me.

Well, my immediate family was ruled out as donors. My brother was doing well at the time business-wise, and along with my sister, decided to take the family to Disney World. I think everyone helped out somewhat, and it was a great way to step back out of this mess for a week, I thought. I recall wondering if the whole idea was to get the family out for a big memorable trip before I passed away. I can tell you that I had many goofy thoughts like that through all of this. In any event, the trip was planned for the upcoming summer and it couldn't come soon enough. I still had people being tested, those being some new distant relatives that turned up. So I wouldn't be losing any time by going, and the positive side of it was that maybe a match would show up while I was there. My plan was to use that mindset and try to have a great time.

I would try to forget that I had leukemia for a week. The fact is that it didn't work. I dwelled on it a lot but in spite of that, I still managed to have a very good time. Amongst the fun was an episode where my girlfriend and I got in a fight for several days down there. She came along with us so that was neat. It turned out that when we took a horse riding tour, the guide and I flirted a bit. Just chitchat and the guide put me next to her and my girlfriend in the back of the group. What is even funnier is that the guide was also the part time "Alice in Wonderland". I had to decline seeing her later, but I always joke that I could have dated Alice in Wonderland.

During that week I lifted weights a little at the Contemporary. I had started a program to get in better shape for what was hopefully to come. I laid around the Polynesian a lot and I remember meditating and drinking it all in. All of those happy people: the kids, the air, and the sun, all of the ambiance. I got a kick out of this big bass that startled me in the lake. I was just wading and floating around when I decided to take a peek under water. I opened my eyes and—boom—there he was with his face right in mine—eye-to-eye, cheek-to-gill—very startling. Of course, we did all of the Disney attractions and it was great.

The trip definitely helped me regain an edge of sorts on living, for a bit. Although I was terminally ill technically, I was feeling pretty normal at that time. When that trip came and went, we of course found ourselves back home in the routine of life. As Carol had the donor search going with everyone included, I started a ritual of calling her every day at work for updates while trying to stay positive about things. Some of the latest early results were trickling in, but as of yet there wasn't anything good to report.

I often played basketball behind my house and subconsciously waited for the phone to ring. I would race in and grab any call hoping that it was Carol or Seattle. Most often though, just false alarm regular calls. The daily 5pm Masses were still going well. Usually there would be ten or twelve older people attending, and most of them being woman. I was the only "kid" around but that was okay. It got to be where everyone recognized the daily visitors. Every now and then a different face would show up, but most of the woman belonged to the blue army. That is a group devoted to the Blessed mother. They wear baby blue berets and follow strict obedience and reverence to God.

Well, one of those ladies turned out to be a real character. Her name was Jean; at least that is what she went by. She was in her sixties I suppose but could have been much older. Jean always wore a long skirt down to her ankles, and probably knee high stockings, a baby blue sweater and matching beret. She walked hunched over and carried a rosary everywhere. Jean drove a huge boat of a station wagon and she would often just make it to Mass or be late upon entry. The side church doors would open and in she would mosey. Even the Priests would get a kick out of her antics.

So one day she started some small talk with me other than the usual "hello". Jean mentioned that she noticed me making the sign of the cross at a particular part of the Mass that some people didn't. It was the Glory be to the Father, and to the Son, and to the Holy Spirit part. Not that it's right or wrong; it's just the way that I was brought up in the Ukrainian Catholic and then Roman Catholic schools. In any event, Jean showed an interest, like I mentioned she was a real character.

Days would add up with weekly doctor visits and blood counts. I was fairly stable but by no means was I in any type of a remission. Adjusting the medicine doses seemed to be keeping the numbers in check for the time being. My routine was very repetitive, kind of like a "wait and see" state of mind. After Mass one day, Jean, who I privately started calling "Jeannie the Beanie", asked me if I would like to take a ride to the Padre Pio centre, then in Norristown. She had been there before. I'd bet that she had been all over the place, just like a gypsy this lady was. The real irony was that she mentioned Padre Pio and I had never mentioned to her any of the previous coincidences I had happen to me. As I said, this lady could have passed for a gypsy because she was a character in more ways than one.

Well, I agreed, and we made arrangements to go. We took her Bat mobile one day and we were off. Upon entering the office, Jeannie took off strolling down a skinny aisle. The counter girls, who I would later become very close with, were very helpful that day. On this particular visit, Christina, Vera and Maria Calandra I believe helped us. Another coincidence mounted there because as a boy, I used to be intrigued by St. Therese of the Child Jesus. Better known as the Little Flower—a great Saint of the Catholic Church.

Christina had shown me a first class relic of St. Therese,(an actual bone fragment from her) and I ended up obtaining it for my own. I also took some literature on Padre Pio along with a few medals I believe after a nice visit and an overall good experience there. As for Jean, she managed to get me to pay for all of her things: gas, food, goodies and all. I'm not complaining, I just think that it is pretty humorous, all of those shenanigans of hers and everything.

Jean and I stayed friends for a long period of time. I'd still see her at St. Rose's almost every day. She even convinced me to buy a statue of the Blessed Mother from her. Often she would have something to sell out of the back of that station wagon of hers. I think I paid her thirty or forty dollars for a ten-dollar statue. She mixed capitalism with religion but still, if it wasn't for her taking me to the Padre Pio centre and adding a piece to this puzzle, in which way I was directed, who knows what would have unfolded. I may not have become good friends with the Calandras or any one else in this story for that matter.

I ended up taking a couple more pilgrimages with her here and there and found out one day that she owned a tiny little candy shop tucked away in a distant town. That's what she did, she sold penny candy and lived behind the shop in an apartment or something. Who would have thought that? One of those ventures led me to what was known as Padre Pio Day in Doylestown, PA. It used to be held at Our Lady of Czestochowa Shrine. Somehow I was volunteered on the spot for the rosary procession around the church!. Obviously, someone nominated me and I guess I couldn't turn it down.

I was both honored and nervous to carry a flag around this huge church when, low and behold, my new friend, Paul Walsh, stepped in next to me. Evidently he was recruited as well to carry another flag. Anyhow, there we were strangers becoming friends in front of a couple of thousand people at least. We were both in good enough shape to make the mile or so trek around the church. The grounds were lengthy but we arranged to make the journey with relatively no problems. That didn't prepare me for the super gust of wind that came swooping down on me, targeting my flagpole especially. I'd say that it didn't prepare the Bishop either because I ended up taking him out along with his cap. After he picked himself up and dusted himself off, the look I received was about as far removed from Christianity as you could get. I can't say that I blame him but at least it wasn't a couple of nuns that I had in grade school that I wiped out. I would have been taken out with more than just a dirty look. More like that clicker or those dreaded pointers. Well, sorry Bishop. That is one of the humorous moments of this trip, I must say.

Through all of this, I found myself getting more involved in Church and the whole faith thing. I think that the people who know me wouldn't say that I am a fanatic or anything, just deep in faith. I did a lot of things that Catholics or any Christian would do for that matter in their own way. I learned about many saints; read all kinds of literature covering A to Z, especially on miracles. At times, I found that it was so easy to just relax consciously and hope that God would make it go away. There was even a time when I probably believed that I could get healthy without a transplant. I would just will it or pray it away—just in denial, I know now. But there were some sincere thoughts to these notions for sure.

Somewhere I learned of very rare instances when a spontaneous remission would occur. There were so rare in fact, that notions of a misdiagnosis take precedence over the so-called cure. I may have even pestered Dr. Soojian and his colleagues over this phenomenon. They may have even thought that I was crazy, but patients want to hear things that they want to hear, especially terminally ill patients.

You can say that I was looking for thrown crumbs of hope alright for anything positive. I'd even gone so far as to read books on macrobiotics. That has to do with your diet, curing or making you well by what you consume. I now can see the lengths that you will go to for any type of positive feedback. There isn't any harm in a good diet and all, but I realized that there were limitations to what can be accomplished with respect to holistic medicine in conjunction with modern medicine, but in my case, not exclusively.

My religion definitely carried some weight and with all of the coincidences occurring and still mounting up, I had to take a look at what I saw going on. The summer was starting in 1985, I believe, and I had a chance to go to Wildwood, NJ with my friends for senior week. It was kind of a tradition that previous graduating classes such as mine could come back and join in on the fun with the younger classes, at least in my old school St. James. I was feeling okay for the most part and my life was in limbo so to speak. Carol was working like a mad woman to try and track down anyone that could be tested. I could set up my doctor appointments at the end of the week, so I decided to go. I was able to get a cheap room in the "home base" hotel where the guys were going. It was the central hangout amongst three or four nearby hotels being used. Just simple rooms with beds, bathrooms and showers down the hall—no amenities, but it was great.

Nothing was better for me than to be in Wildwood back then. A Penn State football game would be close but this was June. Across the street, an all girl high school was staying. They were girls from Archbishop Prendergast High. Nothing but beautiful girls all around me, and my girlfriend was back at home. It was major pressure for me to behave, but I survived with only two or three close temptations. Now I'm looking back with regret acting as if I was married

The coolest thing was that the Catholic Church was just 50 yards up the street from my room. I had the whole island of Wildwood to stay on and we landed right next to the church, go figure. I could try to relax, have fun and still get to Mass everyday, another coincidence.

The church was air conditioned and so therapeutic. I felt like I had some control with things such as church, so it was like work in a sense. I would get up early, go to church in shorts and a sweatshirt, eat breakfast, and go with the flow with the guys—from lying on the beach, to playing waffle ball, to sitting on the porch rating woman passers by. Someone made numbers from 0 to 10 and one guy would have the job of holding up the majority vote that we all decided on. It really was pretty entertaining. We would whistle and invite them up for a beer, or try to invoke a reaction. Not only was it easy to meet the girls, we could judge them if they blew us off. I ha with me a sort of secret weapon, it was just a simple plus or minus sign that I could add to the group total without the guys knowing .

So I had final say of a good score or bad. I didn't give many negative ratings though I mainly just flattered the gals.

This was helping me cope with my sickness a bit by just keeping my mind on other things. The whole weekend was wild—non-stop partying. I lost track of all of the cases of beer building up on the curb for trash collection but it was a small mountain. Not to mention all of the kegs on porches and keep in mind that there were hundreds of graduates around this area. I didn't drink because of the medicines that I was taking, but I sure enjoyed watching other people make fools of themselves. In fact, I couldn't resist being a little kid once in a while.

Like for instance when one guy had gotten so intoxicated that he dropped his room key. My friend, Brian, and I hooked up some fishing line to it; when he would reach down to try and pick it up; we would pull on it just a bit. It ended up with us pulling key all the way down the hallway without him having a clue as to what was going on. I finally came out and faked like I threw the key over the balcony of the porch. While my friend kept him occupied, I sketched a quick map. We went on to tell him that the key had been buried out on the beach. Another friend ran ahead to draw an 'X' in the sand.

We all watched in tears as our buddy was counting paces in the sand. He then proceeded to dig like a dog in the middle of nowhere. I think I wet my pants and hyperventilated a little in hysterics. When this was all over, we took him back and made sure he was safe and sound sleeping off his over indulgence. A girl onlooker almost did slap me though; she didn't see any humor in our little prank.

Many other shenanigans took place that week. The girl's high school banner was taken and stashed under my bed without me knowing it. Luckily it disappeared before the police were called and I never found out the scoop on that. And my room key turned out to be a master key that enabled us to spy in on friends and keep a good supply of fresh towels from the closet. I did turn it in though. I could go on and on with good stories but I wanted to touch on my attempts to step away from this leukemia even if it was brief.

I noticed a pattern of me waking up and within 15 to 30 seconds I'd get this lump in my stomach, a sensation reminding me not to have too much fun because I was sick. I tortured myself with that bad voice inside. I wonder what fun I could have had if I had gotten a handle on that voice and queasy sensations, but those kinds of trips were better than not having anything at all I suppose.

Among the things that I was doing at church were Novenas. I was given a blue pieta prayer book that I thought was a super prayer source. It contains prayers to various saints, meditations and so forth, prayers to Padre Pio and St. Therese as well. I said rosaries and made special requests to God, so I kind of engulfed myself in this for a period of time that I look back on now as something special. Like I had mentioned, I do not believe that I was ever, or am now, a fanatic. I just used things that were available to me in the church and found myself sticking to them.

My faith was growing and I was at a point in my life where everything enabled it to do so. I really didn't have a steady job any longer; I was terminally ill and young—maturity wise, in some areas. I also had enough help to enable me to get to church and about regularly. My faith is childlike in many ways. I want to keep that, if I can, but human nature and questioning doesn't always help. In one of my art classes I was named the class realist. So for any reason good or bad, I guess I see some things in concrete perspectives.

As I started really taking a look at what it was that I believed in religion wise. Once I had examined these beliefs, I needed to apply them to the here and now. If I believed in anything, I would have to accept the fact that some things I just cannot humanly comprehend. Like the universe for example, the big bang theory, evolution, whatever it might be, I can see all of these things in human nature and so forth. No matter how you look at it, one cannot explain where everything originates. Infancy and infinity to us must have some beginning and end, yet we keep learning more and no one can exclusively define it all or reproduce it for that matter.

Well this I had to apply to the Lord and His workings, all of the mystery of Jesus and His miracles, his death and resurrection. The Apostles handed down power to perform miracles. Through the history of the church up to modern day saints and their miracles obtained from God through that same church. It is so overwhelming, but in reading scripture, participating in Masses and everyday life, there are parallels to them, then and now. It isn't very different if you believe and apply it to today.

By looking, you can find what you need, I thought. I would read about miracles and religious occurrences and say, "Why can't this happen to me? I can get that too if I believe and ask God." if it was to be, it still wasn't answered, but God's will. Just like in the Bible, searching and finding quotes that can apply to your situation. I can only speak for myself because God knows I know about unfortunate situations that don't end up the way that we want them to. It can easily get to you as not making any sense or being hypocritical. Why some die and some don't, etc. even though they may do the same things. I even crudely justified it to myself once that this thing of faith was something that I would just have to surrender to. If I'm wrong, it won't matter but if I am right, I have all of my efforts into the glory of God.

My surrender of faith was for a time looking at various stories of miracles and scripture. I believe that the ones fortunate enough to get out of the ordinary happenings of life are God's tools and "presents" for us to cling to in times of trouble. It's easy to say all of this and, of course, life itself is a miracle because we cannot explain it fully, yet we are a part of it. Still if you look you can come up with every day ordinary people who have had unexplainable events happen to them. Regardless of what others say or feel you cannot convince them otherwise. Many even have medical testimonies to show that science couldn't account for their particular recovery and so forth. People just accept it and most often attribute it to God. While Christians have the Holy Spirit to guide them, and I often prayed myself to be guided by the Holy Spirit and still do today. I'll say again, I don't expect everyone to agree with what I have to say, it is just the way that it happened and unfolded for me—religious wise.

One day Carol called telling me that there was possible good news from Seattle. One of the distant relatives showed some initial testing similarities, but it was just the first stage. I believe that the DR typing and MLC were ordered. I was really psyched up. It felt so good to hear some good news for once. All that I did was tell everybody that somebody may have been found as a donor, but I wouldn't know for several weeks. I made the mistake of getting too fired up about this, because it turned out to be a false alarm.

There are cases where people can match up with some numbers that indicate a possible match. As the tests progress, the ultimate screening is performed when both the patient's blood and the possible donor's blood are mixed together. The process can indicate whether they interact or not with each other. That is simplifying the procedure, but it gives you an idea in "layman terms". Unfortunately, even before you advance that far, most people are easily screened out as was the case with this relative that they called about. He was eliminated "on the front lines" so to speak, but that was even further along than we had been thus far. A pattern of ups and downs was forming. The "roller coaster" effect, I call it. You get teased with some possible good news and then you get slammed with the bad news.

Eventually Carol started screening me from those situations by just sitting on any "possibles", and waiting for some concrete information to come in before telling me. That probably helped me due to the number of distant relatives mounting up into the forties and fifties. There were a lot of early potentials but as with the others just false alarms.

The ups and downs were outside of the leukemia realm as well. I have always been an animal lover and in the span of a week, my great dog, Sam, was put in the vet and ended up passing away. Also the dog, Kong, that I had bought for my girlfriend was hit by a car and paralyzed, as I mentioned earlier. There was a stretch where I laid in the back of the animal hospital with both dogs trying to comfort them in those 5'x 5' cement cages. And I wasn't in the greatest of health for sure. Not to dwell on this, but soon after Sam died we made arrangements to have Kong fitted with a K-9 cart. The two back wheels enabled him to fly around for another year or two. We gave him so much love; despite the fact that people thought we were selfish or cruel to him. I am positive that he was very happy and not in any pain. Both of those dogs were a great source and energy and love for me.

I eventually began saying some thirty-day novenas in church and I did the same barrage of prayers that I mentioned from the Pieta book. I concentrated on God and church, actually talking to God almost incessantly. I got to a level where my conscious rapport was with God. I still played basketball a lot, I jogged and worked out attempting to do all of the "normal" things that I did prior to having leukemia. I even made the mistake of playing football without the equipment. I tackled a guy, who was twice my size, which would have been no problem attempting in full gear. My friend, Bruce, collided with me and I came up dizzy with a bloody lip. That memory was like a defeat in my mind, I was no longer dominating but instead took a shot and didn't rebound as quickly. I attributed it to my being sick, instead of just realizing that the guy was a moose. Perhaps the medicines had made me over sensitive, I don't know, it may have just been something to center on and use as an excuse.

I became dejected about everything. I moped around a bit and even though I acted out, I was starting to repress my real feelings. The counts were elevating and I was terrified that I would loose a grip on them. Some new medicines and dosages were introduced along with the Hydrea and, I believe Myleran was the big one. It was administered in heavy doses for a certain amount of time to try and induce a remission. If it worked, I would stop taking everything and wait to see how long I could remain in that state.

Once again I had to clear my head and get a grip on things. I tried to focus on the positive things that I had going for me: family, friends, church, my personality, and so forth. I had gotten good at retreating and regrouping, figuring out a new game plan strategy. Either that or I was good at bullshitting myself. In any event, it brought me some sanity time.

Some of the things that happened to me over the fall of 1985 were just as unbelievable for me. I cannot help but think that God was giving me some encouragement to persevere. Because some of these events are physical, I can say that I was sane and I did not make any of it up. I was not irrational whatsoever, so I used them to back up other occurrences mixed in that wouldn't hold up in a court of law; God's perhaps, but not in our skeptical world.

My mom had a knick-knack—antique—kind of store in the area. She would get all kinds of different articles in, from refrigerators to new beer signs. A good old flea market under a roof, I guess you could say. One day when I stopped in she told me to take a look at a statue of who she thought was Jesus and the Blessed Mother. The statue was very old and my mom, being the angel that she is, was brought up a Baptist and another denomination before converting to Catholicism, when she married my dad. Back then she wouldn't know the difference between any saint, let alone the Blessed Mother. She is better now after what we have been through. The statue was of Jesus and St. Therese from the early 1900s, and another coincidence because she was the saint that I had been praying to.

Well, I scooped up the statue from my mom and still have it today as a reminder of faith for me, and God's love for us. Not an idol just a reminder. I was really feeling good about this incident, and even my counts became relatively stable once again. They weren't terrific but not in the real danger zone any longer. This was a pretty good assurance that the new medicines, in conjunction with the old ones were keeping things in check for the time being, and with that the fall was setting in.

One of the traditions my dad and I had was going up to Penn State when we could. Usually one or two trips a year, we would make weekend trips out of them and stay up in the mountains in a cabin at Stone Valley. Those trips were so memorable to me. I always wondered if that trip in 1985 was the last trip that my father and I would take up there together. I have pictures that I reminisce with from that frozen time in my life. I looked pretty good; probably no one could tell that I had leukemia or what was going on inside of me for that matter.

With the good things going on lately, I enjoyed the game and trip. I can still see myself sitting inside of Beaver Stadium and looking out over Mount Nittany amongst 90,000 fans or so back then, and thinking if anybody else in the stadium had leukemia. I also calculated the odds of one person in the stadium matching me. With the initial odds that they gave me, it was 1 in 180,000. That would have meant two Beaver Stadiums filled back then. A mass of humanity and only one potential match technically.

If that wasn't daunting enough, after my rare 244 X chromosome was introduced, it became more like 1 in 1 million. "Damn", this is just how I thought, back and forth from optimism to pessimism. I had to really fight to stay on top of things mentally with the roller coaster ride of emotions unfolding in front of me.

As Halloween and Thanksgiving were approaching, I was still holding my own. There wasn't anything new with any possible donor findings. Carol could never disguise her facial expressions very well to me so, I would always know if something was cooking or not. I had to go in for a bone marrow aspiration one day. That is a procedure where a needle is placed through your hip or your sternum and bone marrow is extracted out of the bone cavity. For me, this was about the worst procedure that I had to undergo at the time.

I know of people who breeze through it but, as I mentioned, I am not that lucky, for whatever the reason. I would get all worked up because the pain would rush up and down my back and legs, like the feeling that you get when you eat ice cream too fast, or have the most massive of tooth aches—but to the 10th power, throughout your whole body and it doesn't go away for days. Well for me it didn't anyhow. Perhaps I was hypersensitive to those procedures, I don't know.

Last but not least, I forgot to mention that sucking sensation, it was such a killer of a feeling for me but enough of that. Periodically the test was needed to check for blast crisis or tell tale indications of an accelerated phase. My results came back okay, so I was still on a good ride so it seemed. Now if I could only get a donor match to show up.

I believe it was around October of 1985 or so by now and I had gotten another dog and named him Yukon Cornelius, after that guy on "Rudolph the Red-Nosed Reindeer". My girlfriend got one too and they were both AKC. white haired, blue eyed Siberian Huskies. They ended up having a big litter of puppies, one of which we gave to Father Fahey. Yuke lived with my parents and I, and one evening my mom brought home a huge statue of St. Therese. Some man brought it in to her after hearing about my condition and devotion to her in prayer. When my mom first brought it in, Yukon started looking at it wondrously, howling, as he stood motionless like a white wolf. His obsession with this statue may have been the normal response from any dog, but I was taking anything that I could get for a spiritual boost. It was bizarre the way that he reacted.

Back then, I believe that God was subtly giving me something to work with and pushing me ahead for a week, a month or whatever it would take. In this short period of time, I had received two statues of a saint, whom I knew a bit about, not to mention the relic I obtained, and I would get to know a lot more about her as time went along. I bought a few books on Therese Martin and her life. I even found a videotape sort of documentary on her. The "little ways" she had, as you may be aware of, were something that I could totally relate to. I noticed some similarities between our mindsets and that just naturally attracted me to learn more about her. Keep in mind that this was happening spontaneously, and as I said, since these were all physical occurrences, I'm sure that I was of a sound mind.

I also believe that this may have been a period in my life that I will not equal. Perhaps it was a spiritual peak, although I don't think that I could stop growing in my faith. It's just that these things I describe do not occur any longer by enlarge. They seemed to have appeared at a particular time—in clusters—at a moment that I needed something most. Father Fahey once told me to hold on to these memories, which I'm about to share, when times are especially bad and nothing seems to be right with anything. He also said that nothing spiritual like that had ever happened to him, so I should be very thankful and count my blessings.

In the readings of saints and in particular, the readings of St. Therese, it said that in the intercession of her prayers to God, often people would report manifestations and occurrences. Things such as roses being given to them by people for seemingly no occasion, or the visiting aroma of floral perfume and so forth. Those beautiful fragrances to the person praying have also been associated with answered prayer requests as well. These are what I believe to be another one of God's "spiritual boost tools" so to speak of spiritual support.

Of course this is simply hog wash to those that do not believe, but that old adage of "for those who have faith no explanation is necessary, and for those that do not believe no explanation will suffice." In any event, as I became aware of this, I attributed the statues as little signs to trust in God. I mean I never sought the statues out, and my mother didn't know how to distinguish St. Therese from Adam. They just conveniently made their way into my possession.

I had even yet another unusual addition to my collection. It came one day when my girlfriend's sister-in-law had a celebration party of some sort up at her house up state. I believe it was a Christening. Anyway, when we arrived at her parents' home, down in the recreation room where everyone was gathered, there hung a beautiful watercolor print of St. Therese. It had been in their family for years and belonged to her mother who had recently passed away.

During the party I mentioned something briefly to Colleen about her picture and just kind of forgot about it. It was hanging off to the side, so it could have just sounded like I was making small talk. When we were getting ready to leave, Colleen took the picture off of the wall and gave it to me. I really tried to say no, but Colleen insisted and said that her family wanted me to have it. I would say that it is one of my favorite sacramentals and a very gracious thing to have done for me.

CHAPTER 2

▼

Now unwittingly, I was building my own little shrine. My friend, Kevin, joked that I could build my own saint with all of my accumulating articles. I still wonder about all of these things that were going on. I have to believe that they meant something. It was uncanny the way that things would happen. To the best of my knowledge, Colleen had no prior information as to my other statues and relics, nor did most of the other "contributors" involving these incidents.

Meanwhile, it was getting cold and snow had fallen some. I really enjoyed the holidays: football and more football, chocolate chips and cold milk. Kids' holiday shows like the *Grinch Who Stole Christmas* and *The Year without a Santa Claus* with those Heatmiser and Wintermiser characters.

My girlfriend and I took a bus trip with a group of church devotees. I would say that we might have had a few fanatics here. But with what was going on with my life, how could I dare to judge what they may have thought or known. God does work in mysterious ways; so, this trip was to Flushing, New York, next to Shea Stadium, in a park where the World's Fair was once held. I'm a big Jets fan so I always wanted to see Shea Stadium anyway. Allegedly, the Blessed Mother was appearing to a certain woman up in that area with spiritual messages and, at the time, it was big news amongst church laity. Although the Catholic Church's official position on it was that they didn't recognize it as a true sign of apparition, it had been or was still under investigation. Very often these sights take years to investigate one way or the other. This helps protect against fraudulent cases.

Lots of people had claimed to be cured of illnesses and to have even seen the Blessed Mother for themselves. People would take Polaroid cameras to reveal what they said were miraculous photos. Superimposed rosaries or messages on the pictures were often circulated through the crowds. I even witnessed a few that actually resembled the Blessed Mother's image. I saw one publicized as writing from one of the Fatima children, Jacinta. It sure was very interesting stuff I'll tell you. A funny and ironic thing was that the very same "old world" priest that scolded my girlfriend early in the story ended up blessing her little Polaroid camera. This is so funny to me. Evidently, it was urged to have the cameras blessed for the miraculous photos to appear so I was told.

Well, it turned out to be so cold, I mean, I had been deer hunting before in places like Potter County, PA where wind chills were in excess of around 32° below for hours at a time in freakish storms. This may have rivaled or surpassed that insane temperature on this night. I wore my blaze orange hunting suit and remember kneeling in the snow and ice, looking up at the starry night saying my rosaries. I may have been crazy, but there were about one thousand other pilgrims outside besides me.

I took a bit of solace in that as I saw people in wheelchairs, on crutches, gurneys, you name it. All walks of life came to pray the rosary and possibly get a miracle from God. It turned out to be a nice visit with mixed feelings. At the very least, I made a sacrifice and did recite some rosaries, probably 15 decades. I wasted nothing spiritually I suppose, but wondered about things. After all, who am I to determine if people were seeing the Mother of God or not?

It was now Christmas time, a time of greatness and wonderment. We had a modest but quiet stretch. Clearly, for me, it was not as hectic as I had become all too accustomed to. By that I mean the rat race of shopping, visiting all over kingdom come and everything. I stayed in for the majority of the time and tried to enjoy football. I did much soul searching of what was happening to me. It wasn't a bad dream, I was really, really sick and, on top of that, I noticed what a toll this was all taking on my family and even some of my close friends as well.

My family was working hard to make everything normal. Unfortunately, not one of our faces can keep a secret if something is up. I could definitely feel all of the love, but in turn I began to kill myself with guilt. How can I do this to them? I convinced myself that I was personally responsible for my illness, that I induced it or something.

A year had come and gone and I wasn't any closer to getting well. By some estimates, I had overextended my given time to live. I definitely believe in the correlation between depression and illness because I could feel my immune system fading. I was sick to my stomach with the nerves and worry. There was so much stress and anxiety that it became unbearable. As if I needed this to occupy my energy, up and down, I was so exhausted.

One night shortly after the holidays had passed; I hit the sack and started saying my prayers. I had established a real ritual that I stuck to. I made some musical tapes of relaxing wordless music off of a late night college radio station, WXPN in Philly, I believe. One of my favorite shows, stars end or echoes. I would put it on and pray and pray for at least an hour or two at night. This was on top of the daily Masses and prayer as conversation with God without ceasing throughout the day. It was kind of thinking and mentally talking to yourself, but directly addressing those thoughts to God instead. I wonder how many people at traffic lights looked over and saw me talking to "myself"?

Anyway, this particular evening I was just ending my list of prayers when for a good ten seconds or so, I had the strongest sensation of roses or extremely sweet smelling perfume right below my nose. My heart just raced and I thought that I was really losing it this time. Nobody was around late at night, and this? I couldn't decide if this was good or bad. Was I manifesting what I had learned about subconsciously? No, I wasn't, because I didn't sit there and think about anything like that ever, actually. I know who I am and what I am, so eventually I fell asleep and filed the experience not mentioning this to anyone at that point.

I couldn't decide whether to confide in somebody about it or not. I mentioned it to a few friends, my priest friend Father Fahey and my parents. All in all, I was given supportive feedback, but couldn't help feeling angry that I thought they thought I was loony. The funny thing about it is that it was just the start of more things to come, in which this would pale to in comparison. If I thought that they thought I was crazy with this story, wait until I hit them with the others.

Approximately seven days after the smell of roses, I began a 24-day novena to St. Therese, using a popular prayer card version I had. I think it went like this, "St. Therese please pick me a flower from the heavenly garden and send it to me with a message of love, oh Little Flower of Jesus, ask God today to grant me the favors I now place with confidence in your hands. St. Therese help me to always believe as you did in God's great love for me, so that I may imitate your little way each day. Amen." This is one of the prayers that I used back then and I have to believe it if I had any kind of faith, that I was lucky enough to be blessed with a true sign.

As I was still doing the daily Masses at St. Roses', one day in particular changed my view on spirituality. As I mentioned earlier, these Masses drew all of about ten to fifteen people a day. Mostly older folks spread out inside a nice sized church. In 1986, the church still had the old marble altar rails where you would kneel to receive the Blessed Sacrament. Since I sat in front most of the time, I had my own little territory so to speak. For whatever reason, the majority of the parishioners sat on the left side of the church; "Perhaps because the statue of the Blessed Mother was on that side, along with a first class relic of St. Rose herself". Maybe it was just convenient, I don't know. Whatever the case may have been, people often prayed silently before and after Mass over on that side keeping to themselves. This would always leave me virtually alone on my side to receive Communion. Many times Father would start with me and move on down the line methodically with his slight limping walk. The church was beautiful yet quaint in a setting that made it special to receive Communion from Father. I considered him a true man of God.

Well, as I was saying, the Mass began and soon the time came for me to kneel and prepare to receive Holy Communion. I made it a practice to look around and take in the church ambiance in just a solemn time. As I prepared for Father as he stepped over to give me the Blessed Sacrament, I can never forget what happened next as this was one more dramatic sign along the way.

I distinctly remember having my hands folded in front of me, elbows to the rail and looking down meditating. When I raised my head up to receive the Host, I routinely made the Sign of the Cross, paused and again looked down, bowing my head in reverence as I prepared to get up and return to my pew. Just then, there it was right in front of me, a very, very tiny and delicate purple flower! I nearly hyperventilated in seeing it! I instinctively picked it up and as I trekked back to my seat, there was not a soul within thirty feet of me! I am absolutely sure that this flower was not in front of me two minutes prior! Father Fahey surely did not slip it there, as he had enough of a challenge just maneuvering his body with the Chalice.

Furthermore, he was a holy man of integrity and wouldn't do such a thing, even if he could have maneuvered that daring feat off with his health. The icing on the cake to this bizarre happening was that I didn't initially realize that this was the 24th day of the Novena that I had started to St. Therese.

The Mass ended and I still couldn't breathe right. As everyone filtered out of the church, I raced in to tell Father about this. He was definitely astonished and again I can assure you that this man was not the type to lie of course or do something like this. Even if he could hold a Chalice, say Mass and remember to hide a flower and then predict where I would be along the rail, I don't believe that he would do that to me. He was as astonished and intrigued as I was.

We sat for a good while and scoured the area for other flowers or signs of something to indicate a coincidence. We finally concluded that there wasn't anything around the area. Ironically, this all took place just under the St. Therese statue that discretely sat on a small shelf above the candles. The only flowers there were plaster. My father made me a case to seal it in and I can say to this day that I have the flower, still as tiny as the sliver of a fingernail and it is still bright purple. It still blows me away when I look at this flower; "A little flower."

The very next week we received a call from Seattle that one of my distant relatives was a two-antigen mismatch. That meant that in a last ditch effort, if no better matches were to come up, he could be a suitable donor. He was a second cousin and in a life saving attempt, I had at least one option. It was not a good match by any means back then, but useable if need be.

Another series of coincidences during this time began and I really, really started to think. Could you blame me! If nothing else, these were some weird happenings taking place. Not only did it effect me and leave me in wonderment, how do you put things like this in perspective? I sure don't know but it was the continuation of extraordinary happenings, for me and some of my family members. I was praying for signs and evidently I was getting them.

While this stuff was taking off, I do believe my friends supported me in what I was telling them. I am sure that I was the same old me in all other respects that I used to be on the outside, except for being sick. A breath of fresh air in life for me was when a bunch of my friends invited me to go in on a beach house for the summer in Wildwood. I think that I paid $150.00 for the whole season with my own house key, albeit that was with 14 other guys. I think they asked me if I was a lunatic for saying yes. It felt nice to feel human or "normal" for a spell. It was still only February or March of 1986 and the house rental didn't start until June, but I couldn't wait.

With all of this going on, it didn't slow things down any with the donor search especially since the match I now had was not a good one to begin with, as I mentioned earlier. Carol and the hospitals were still pounding away at any possible prospect or direction to look in. My counts remained still just "okay" in terms of a danger zone. I even managed to take a break one-week from the needle sticks and thought that was the greatest thing at the time, a great big deal and a moral victory.

My going to church and "storming heaven" as Father called it didn't cease. In fact, just a month or so later, after the flower episode and donor deal, I had a moment surpass that amazing time for me personally. As deep as my convictions were for St. Therese, they were equally increasing with Padre Pio. In dwelling on the initial happenings I mentioned earlier about the healing mass and the Paul Walsh story, etc. it was so intriguing that I wanted to learn more about this holy priest.

There is so much literature on Padre Pio out in circulation you wouldn't believe it. Videos, books, articles, testimonials, you name it. I had no problem getting a feel of personal knowledge of this man. I recommend getting a video or book for I feel that you would see the many sides of God reflected in this man's undying love for Jesus. Without getting carried away here, I'll just add among the many attributed healings from God through the intercession of Padre Pio here, a cure of an Italian girl that is still alive today who can see without pupils! That's right, without pupils.

Doctors documented her as a medical phenomenon not explained by modern science. You should inquire about this story. Also, Padre Pio bore the stigmata of Christ as I mentioned earlier. They are the bleeding wounds of the hands, feet, back, the crown of thorns and so forth. Padre Pio succumbed to very, many skeptical doctors at hospitals who even attempted to sew his wounds shut at one point without success. They would always reopen and it is documented that he lost the equivalent of cups of blood daily. On top of this, upon his death, no marks whatsoever could be found on his body. No scars, not even from all of the stitches initially placed in by the doctors! As I mentioned, he was featured on televisions' Unsolved Mysteries show along with Vera's and Paul's stories. The only thing you can say about this is that he was truly a man of God. I do not believe that God would trick humanity by letting evil come in a manifestation through this man, a profound follower of Christ.

Well, I hit the sack one night with the same routine again that I had been adhering to for months now. I finished up my prayer session and shut off my wordless music for the night. At the time I was sleeping on a skinny love seat kind of couch bed. God only knows why my bedroom was a disaster area. I dozed off for the evening hoping for a good night's sleep. As God is my witness, I turned over on my side having the most beautiful fragrance in my nose that I have ever encountered. It was the kind of thing where I remember coming out of a sound sleep and being directly woken up by this aroma. It wasn't going away either.

I sat up swiftly amongst the darkness of my room. I could see what I thought appeared to be a silhouette of Padre Pio himself! It was defined, but just a silhouette, as I mentioned in a lighter shade of darkness overlapping the pitch black bedroom area. Perhaps like a tree in front of the dark sky at night. I do not believe that it was life size, maybe three to five feet in front of me, or something like that. Then my eyes seemed to dilate into the darkness of the whole room. Just like that the silhouette disappeared, but not the fragrance!

It was so, so very strong, until the day that I die it is an impression that I will never, ever forget and no one could convince me otherwise. It was just so incredible! I got out of bed and burst out of my room into the bathroom just outside of my door, then to the hallway, then to my parents' room—all in about 20 seconds or so. My mom and dad were lying down downstairs watching television with Yuke my dog. I yelled down for my mom to get up here, "You've got to see if you can smell what I smell, come on!"

As soon as my mom got to where I was, she said, "That smell—it's beautiful", something like that. We both scoured the upstairs for the source, but it was everywhere and not in a particular spot that you could pinpoint the traces of its origin. All of a sudden it seemed to move to the steps and, down it went, with my mom and I following right behind. Then this fragrance traveled from the steps and into the dining room, to the kitchen and then back to the living room where my dad was.

Well, by this time he was just about bouncing around like a punished little kid because he had a severe head cold and couldn't smell a thing. He watched helplessly as my mom and I went berserk, flying through the house. One moment I even breathed in and out, in and out, in and out, almost hyperventilating really fast to suck in this awesome fragrance. This manifestation lasted for over one-half hour and, ultimately, ended up with about ten minutes in the front room directly underneath the crucifix hanging on the wall. On top of that, Yukon, my dog, was staring at this empty space with his ears straight up, a straight eyed, no blink, eyebrows slanted, concentrated look. I'm telling you this was probably the most unbelievable spiritual night of my life! Probably my mom's and Yukon's as well.

At this point I had just about lost it. All of these things had been mounting towards good circumstantial evidence that I was crazy or that God was telling me something. I could only surmise that it was to hang in there and to keep the faith and hope. I would think obviously, that if you had something like this happening to you, you'd feel great, and I did. But I was also confused and scared at times, wondering if you could even trust your own feeling or not. Once again, looking at the circumstances, I did have my mom as a witness along with my dog acting funny, with his two episodes of staring into space. Three new relevant statues from out of the blue, a picture, a mysterious tiny flower and a possible donor to use, all in this time span, not to mention that fragrance episode. And the nice lady who helped me at the healing Mass. Staying with Paul Walsh's brother before I even knew who he was at the time—on and on and on, whew!

I certainly didn't make any of that up, so it positively reinforced me to happily accept these occurrences as best I could and move on with confidence and faith. It was really a time of ecstasy and unparalleled duration in my life and we still talk about that eerie and incredible night as though it was yesterday.

With all of this, I should have felt almost on top of the world, you might think. It sure helped but my human nature kept me on that roller coaster ride of emotions; up and down, up and down, all the way through into the summer. I have been my own worst enemy; despite the fact that I believe these signs came from God. Nevertheless it isn't that easy talking to someone about these happenings and still expecting them to respect your integrity. Well I have shared them with a few people and now here for all to scrutinize. I just know what happened to me and that is how it was.

As the summer was approaching, I attempted to figure out my strategies on coordinating the weekly blood sticks back home and commute back and forth to Wildwood. One night I overheard my family talking about how my transplant would be paid for if, in fact, it took place. By this time into things, I was not included in those types of conversations. I guess they figured that it would save me some stress, and actually that angle I had not even considered. I just assumed that my dad's insurance would cover it. I was covered on a separate policy of my own, but unbeknownst to me, this transplant was going to be much more costly than I could ever imagine.

A bone marrow transplant in 1986 was still experimental and not always covered by insurance. The costs could range easily from $250,000 to excesses of $1 million dollars or more. Upon hearing this I just freaked out! "How the heck am I going to be able to pay for this", I thought. I mean we were fortunate enough to grow up in a home, with food, an education and everything but by no means could we afford this kind of expense. I believe that my sister calmed me down by schmoozing me with some story to get me relaxed a bit, just like a car salesperson she was.

What was worked out to buy time by my family and keep things moving along was a plan to put my parents' sisters' and brothers' houses up for collateral if need be. They were second mortgages I believe and I didn't become aware of this scenario until years later. By the grace of God, shortly before I left for the Jersey shore, my insurance company agreed to cover a portion of the bone marrow transplant. This procedure was eventually to become the preferred treatment for CML. Thus, my family's backup plan could probably be nixed. Primarily, I consented to be involved in a government study to pay for a significant portion of the expenses if accepted. This transplant study entailed additional tests and A to Z procedures for research purposes. Almost as soon as I had heard about the expense issue being mostly taken care of, it lessened the taxing burden of things for awhile. "Now I only had nine million other things to worry about."

Another area that is most likely trivial to many here despite my health issue was my love for women and my libido. Trying to uphold the "standards" of a Christian gentlemen or whatever you would like to call them was a test of faith to say the least. I would almost bet that my drive was overboard and probably still is with the land mines of, lust, fornication, celibacy and so forth in the way. Many people could care less about the commandments and sin today, but as a Catholic Christian, I did when struggling with those powerful temptations of the flesh. I was supposedly a strong Christian yet, at times, I was so weak.

My falls would end up with immediate calls to the rectory to get to confession as soon as possible. I would hop in the car to be cleansed of my sins. It got ridiculous; over and over I would fall. Three confessions in a week was at one point a routine spell. I was addicted to the sex it seemed but for every ten urges and holdouts, the eleventh was trouble. I even had a traumatic experience of a priest telling me not to bother coming back and practically tossing me out. He said that I was making a mockery of the Sacrament. I was crushed and about drawn to tears.

I had all of these pressures to contend with and now I was canned from God. I recall some panic attacks and it wasn't until I caught up with my priest friend Father Fahey, who erupted in anger, when I told him what, had happened. "How dare he say that to you?" Give me his name he said. I didn't, but he assured me to go back whenever I felt the need and to keep doing my best. Father told me that God knew what I was dealing with and knew my weakness', He created me. Of course he didn't condone my faults, but only God and I knew how hard I was trying. I believe that it was a pretty good effort myself.

I tell God today and joke that it was His fault for making women so beautiful. He also made me the way he did. Nevertheless I did abstain almost totally before leaving for the beach. The place for female land mines and ironically enough, I just about shriveled up like a prune there with the abstinence. I ate my heart out, boy, and man the fun I could have had. God had to be proud of my victories over temptation in Wildwood back then. Speaking of which, it had finally arrived. I was on my way to the beach for a summer of fun and rest, just normal life so I hoped.

For the people who have never been to Wildwood, NJ, in 1986 it was just the greatest activity beach you could ever want. An island nicely sized and equipped for fun. I think it's around a two-mile boardwalk along the ocean, lots of rides on piers, loud music and games galore to play. There are frequent benches to sit and relax on watching the passers by. Water slides everywhere, tramcars, pizza stands, stores, nightclubs, etc. If you can think of it, it's probably there. And last but not least, the ladies—lots of beautiful ladies.

The house that our crew rented was right on Rio Grande Avenue. This is the main entrance and exit to the island. We had the top floor with a big porch and a deck over top of a back yard. Everything sat on top of an empty store. Just outside was a phone booth, a 7-eleven and a McDonalds. For a group of guys, what more could you ask for. Fourteen young men, each with a secretly made key to come and go as we pleased, consisting of three bedrooms, a living room, and a kitchen. I had my own tiny bed in the back room and that was just fine for me.

It wasn't long before the refrigerator was converted into a beer miser, all the racks out and in with the keg. I traveled light, with a trash bag of clothes and a bit of money. We had a television and a stereo, so it was all set to lounge around in. I think about a day went by before the usual attendance would hover around 30 to 40 at one moment or another. Friends of friends of friends and strangers, "who knew"? Mostly on the weekends it would be crazy and non-stop goings on until Monday mornings, then for a few days it would thin out. To recant those stories by themselves would take a book to cover, I'm sure of that.

On my first trip home to see my doctors, I arranged to have one of my tee shirts sent to the Padre Pio Center so they could get in touched to his tomb in Italy. Christina Calandra suggested it and I felt that it sure couldn't hurt wearing it around for spiritual juice. For the early part of the summer, I only drove home if I had to get a blood stick. I was able to connive out of a week here and there to stretch my beach time.

Wildwood was a surreal period for me. I now see it as a time that I lived some, but mostly watched people living. Just as if I was a spectator, not intentionally but it ultimately turned out that way. I came to enjoy watching the people moving around like little ants, scurrying here and there. I would spot a guy walking by and imagine what he may have been thinking. I wondered if he was aware of the beautiful day that I myself was noticing. Or the "Guido" from South Philly in his sleek Iroc Z28 driving by with his boom box stereo blaring; him with his gold chain and jet dried hair, arm out the window, just cruising by chewing his gum or whatever. He never noticed me looking down from the porch at him and analyzing his life. He's not terminally ill, I'd stare, nice car. Just out of high school and his whole future ahead of him. He was on top of the world.

Anybody that I saw I had a thought for, you would have figured that I was invisible some days, hanging out on the boardwalk or particularly at the water slides. I so much enjoyed the feeling and sensations that I would get by sitting around that atmosphere. That's where I was, invisible, sitting in the bleachers watching people. The awesome breeze and the smell of the ocean air along with the chlorine mixed mist stirring in about, as the wind would kick up—loud music and girls everywhere. I don't know if you would call that enjoying life, or feeling sorry for myself, or what. My guess would be that I pondered a lot because I was scared. Nevertheless, the waterslides gave me a warm feeling inside from looking out at the distant ocean and ambience many times.

I also enjoyed lying down on the beach and shooting the bull with the guys. "Drilling for oil" was the term we used if a pretty girl nearby prevented one of us from "getting up" with our bathing suits on. It was funny at the time, if we all decided to take a dip in the water and somebody couldn't leave his spot until he was "his old self again". I didn't feel that unusual for a change, I wasn't the only guy who loved women!

I took a lot of walks on the beach and thought about that famous "footprints" picture and prayer a few times, and rode my bike here and there. That is until my friend borrowed it only to have it stolen one night. That's what friends are for, right Tim…

A good amount of time was spent by myself wandering around town. Sometimes down by the bay, at the fishing docks to see the party boats roll in and get a glimpse of the day's catch, pretty much this and that. For the most part, the week was quiet until Thursday or Friday, when the troops would return from working back home. It was interesting to see this one or that one pull up at all hours of the night, never on a schedule but always with goodies of some kind. Every one would bring their share of food, beer, and boogie boards with of course, the required wiffle ball equipment amongst the other necessities.

It got to a point where just my friends Tim, Kev, and Larry would be there along with myself and, out of all of us; Larry and I were the late night owls. Three or four in the morning was commonplace. Being the insomniacs that we were, our wee hour creativity set in one night. Only to have us invent some crazy game called "lamp ball". A rolled up pair of socks and using only one hand we each had to bat the sock into the other guy's lamp shade; this, with a working bulb in it, to highlight or illuminate our respective rims. Needless to say, it got brutal.

Not only did we eventually break the lamps, but lots of bulbs. I must say it was foolish but hilarious. Larry was always "feeling good", and when you add in a 4 AM starting time, this was cheap entertainment that was tough to beat. That's what I guess we thought anyhow, I don't know. We had the goofiest stuffed koala bear mascot hanging from the ceiling. Somebody named him Wizzo. He had cheap sunglasses, a scarf, hat and a beer can glued to his paw. I think he was rubbed out in August, feathers and bean bag balls all over the floor. He was a trooper though enduring that menagerie.

Some of the awkward things were the ways that the guys started treating me. I mean they were always good and all, but I started getting the "king treatment" with the way that everyone was so polite. "Can I get you anything?" "Are you all right?" Larry even cooked me a huge steak with mushrooms one-day. Another one of my friends, Steve, was soft spoken and out of character, treating me like I was a piece of china. It really made me feel good because these guys were animals, "regular tough guys". They did a lousy job of hiding their concerns, but it really helped here and there. I never mentioned it, kind of like a pact guys have about not showing the emotions and all I guess.

By this time I wasn't getting to church every day. I was on the other side of the island, so it became pretty much a weekly thing now. I still prayed intensely, perhaps even harder in meditation with God. Up early or late at night, I'd burn the candle as one of my new quirks, having been spoiled so to speak with what I thought were signs. I began looking for or expecting them after what I had gone through previously. Possibly I expected it to become an ongoing thing. One enjoyment for me was gazing at the stars while I prayed at night on the porch. I would say, "Give me a sign God, a falling star, perhaps tongue in cheek", but to no avail. I would see falling stars, of course, but random ones, not specifically when or where I wanted them to be. I enjoyed it even though nothing was happening; another one that I had fun with asking for a specific song on the radio. Here and there I would tune in to a part of one here of there, but actually I never placed much stock into it. I did stay focused on prayer though, I know that and it was childish in some ways, but then again I suppose a lot of my faith was child-like.

By this time I guess that it was late July or early August and I still was having a pretty good time at the beach. I would call Carol daily from the pay phone or occasionally the landlord would come track me down for a call through the office. I have to say that any sound of a phone now freaks me out due to the many bad phone calls I received over the course of my transplant procedures. In any case, Carol continued to tell me the same thing; that being nothing new to get my hopes up with. So as usual I would keep trying to keep my mind occupied with other things.

Wiffleball games were one way to do that. You would have thought that these guys were getting paid, the competition was so fierce. I remember a nice girl named "Marina" caught my eye during a game and I made a big error. By the heckling I received for it you figured I'd just lost the World Series. It did feel great though because, for a time, the guys forgot or didn't care about the leukemia. I screwed up and they hated it.

One of the nights had me coming in from dinner only to find my friend, Larry, all cut up from a fight that I had just missed. I had to rush him to the hospital for a broken jaw and neck injury or something. All of that didn't stop Larry the next night. He didn't miss a beat showing up for our nightly lamp ball game—neck collar, bandages and all. A true dedicated lamp ball player for sure.

The volume of lady traffic was taking a toll on me. The girl Marina, who I believe pitched for Rutgers softball, was staying next door—a very attractive girl who tempted me seriously. I did escape that danger zone and all in all would say that I got out of five or six risque' opportunities. I remained unscathed and loyal to my girlfriend back home. Confession after I went home loomed eminent.

The last thing that I needed was my libido's secret weapon to make me fail. In 1982 I had seen a beautiful girl from Michigan named Kristen and fell for her. The travel, distance and my getting sick nixed any long term ideas between us back then. But this girl got a notion to drive from Michigan to Wildwood and track me down for perhaps another shot some 4 or 5 years later. When she showed up at my door in Wildwood, I practically melted.

I always did around her and this surprise blew me away. I was even more attracted to her than before. I just broke down inside because she didn't have any idea as to the extent of my illness, and I couldn't bring myself to really tell her either. We spent some time together; all of which I toiled inside until I finally had to come up with something to tell her that could redirect any new thoughts of love. I just couldn't do it knowing what was in front of me.

I ultimately gave her some line of a story and now, regretfully, stayed on the straight and narrow with God and my commitment with my girlfriend back home. I would probably do it all differently now, knowing what I now know. I was terribly depressed with all of this. I was just losing my perspective of everything. What life I now had was dictated and held captive by this horrid disease. I even was so ignorant as to leave a wonderful girl who truly cared for me, a stinking note and sneak out of town later that night. I hope that someday she will read this and understand why I acted the way that I did.

I think I cried half way home driving through the Jersey Pine Barrens at 3AM. in the pitch black darkness, with bugs flying into my beaming headlights. I'd taken the long way home without even realizing it, just wondering what the hell was happening to my life. I was convinced that nobody could possibly understand. People treated me well, but for what? For what reasons, I wondered. I drove and drove into the night with a "Box of Frogs" cassette in the tape player. So whenever I listen to it now, that moment is frozen in time for me.

Back then there wasn't a clue about my future to look at. In going home, I didn't accomplish much. My state of mind was lousy and most likely I wasn't good company for anyone. In fact I remember getting into an argument with my girlfriend and walking 3or4 miles home one night from her grandparents' home. Maybe I attended Mass; otherwise, I lived in bed up in my room for the most part. By the end of that next weekend, my restlessness took me back to the beach in desperation to relieve my mental anguish and exhaustion.

After a few days early in the week of quietness, I strolled in from the sand only to find our apartment filled with people. I believe ten or fifteen girls along with most of the gang; more friends and friends of friends having a big blow out party. From the porch in front to the balcony in back there were wall to wall people. I mingled a bit pretending to fit in and wound up sleeping out front in a rocking chair. I couldn't have slept in my room, even if I made my way to bed, as everyone was strewn about. And when I became tired and ready to hit the sack, the fact that I couldn't sleep fired me up even more. It turned out that all of these girls took over my room to sleep.

I had one of my friends, Brian, out front with me on the porch and he came up with a great equalizer. It was now around four or five in the morning, so he decided to go to extreme lengths. The summer was almost over and there were holes in the walls from horsing around so our security deposit was shot for sure. Secondly the building was slated for renovation. So, without my knowing it, he climbed up on the back porch and stuck a hose in the window and turned it on full blast. The next thing that we heard was yelling and banging around; a bunch of curses, some laughs and some wet people. By this time the sun was coming up so I slept the whole day in peace and quiet after the room dried out and everyone vacated.

With a few days left until Labor Day weekend, the official last day of my vacation, I felt like getting in some last minute activities that I had planned over the summer. One was to jog the length of the boardwalk each way either 2or 4 miles. The other was to play some serious basketball with a few of the guys. A couple of my roommates played college ball and were in a summer pick up league down at the courts. I had no problem weaseling in to some of the games and, for the most part, I enjoyed myself. The big problem was that I started really slipping in my game again—energy-wise being the primary problem. On top of that, I could feel something happening, but wasn't sure as to what. Be it my appetite or fluctuations in my perspiration, my overall strength and my moods or a combination of things, I just felt something. Even now I still couldn't give a complete definitive pinpoint as to what it was.

After more phone booth powwows with Carol, I had convinced her as well as myself that I needed to see the doctor. I spoke with him from the same phone booth to the hospital at home and eventually persuaded him to accommodate me with a bone marrow aspiration. Despite my dislike for them and acute reactions to them, I emphasized the fact that I could feel something different about my physical condition going on. According to the weekly counts and charts, he indicated that I was okay but he arranged for further testing probably to accommodate me and ease my mind. So just like that I instinctively packed up my things and left for home.

I mentioned earlier how much I disliked the aspiration, so I had to prepare myself mentally for this procedure. This marrow extraction for whatever reason was the least of most of the other treatments in terms of pain, but it was still lousy for me, the best of the bad so to speak. It seemed as if no sooner had I gone home and been tested that the pathology reports were back. In reality it was a few weeks I believe, but the worrying just accelerated all the time as much as it dragged it out.

I didn't mention that my family was in the process of moving and that the new home was just where my doctor tracked me down. The kitchen of the new house was ground zero for my news. Dr. Soojian, informed me that the pathology reports showed changes in my bone marrow with more blasts and that I was starting to progress into an accelerated phase. This was the worst news that I could have possibly wanted to hear at that time. My "spider senses" were right and boom, just like that, I had to make plans for the transplant within a few weeks or else. If a blast crisis set in, I would have virtually no chance to survive or be cured and jeopardize even having a chance to attempt the procedure.

I still wonder about what it was that made me push the issue with a marrow aspiration because most likely, if that didn't occur; all of our work would have been thrown out the window. As I said, we jokingly refer to it as my "spider senses" a.k.a. Spiderman's extra sense. A funny sort of irony was that I experienced both relief and fear equally. The relief was the explanation of my erratic behavior I'd been going through and at the same time, I was totally fearful of not having a good match to use. If no body had yet survived a non-related transplant with a so-called "good match up" what did that say for my chances? A second cousin was my only alternative, so I needed to turn this into something positive. "I'd think, God gave me this person, he will take care of it." That sounded great but the reality of it was my human nature ate me alive. On the outside I may have looked excited and strong; but on the inside my thoughts and feelings were being magnified and realized.

By that evening, my whole family had been notified. Carol had tons to do and again I don't know how any of this could have been managed without her help. One of the first issues was to go back to my local hospital the next day for another CBC count. The test was concise and to the point and could tell me where I was in conjunction with the marrow studies.

All of these visits by now felt like a Chester fist fight. As usual, I chose to drive into the hospital by myself and face the wrath of pessimism ala solo pilot. My photographic memory lives on especially with this visit. As per usual, the ritual proceeded with my registering way down the hall, pit stopping in another room for blood work, and moving to another office to sit and wait. From there I was escorted to the second hold where my weight and blood pressure would be charted. The door would close and I'd wait to be seen by the doctor in the same chamber.

My pulse always pounded with anxiety in those days with so much uncertainty to toil over. This day was rough because even though I was certain in my transplant decision, any normal person would have had second thoughts after this particular session. The real stress of it all magnified while I laid on the gurney looking up mostly at the drop ceiling. The examining room door was behind my head and the hallway just outside of that. You could often hear bits and pieces of conversations going on amongst other patients, nurses and doctors. Well, this day was no different except that what I was hearing was pertaining to me!

Dr. Keough, one of the associates, offered some of his thoughts to another colleague, Dr. Lebetta, right outside of the door. He touched upon the possibility of my having an autologous bone marrow transplant. For many readers not familiar with this procedure, in 1986 this type of transplant offered no chance of a cure for the type of leukemia that I had (CML). You see the autologous version is a process that attempts to cleanse your own body's bone marrow outside of the body and then it is reintroduced into you system. Essentially, you are your own donor. This sounds ideal and perhaps one day will be, but as of 1986, no fool proof method of irradicating the leukemia existed. So ultimately the patient would undergo the extensive procedure only to buy one's self some extended living time. This could equate to roughly months to another year or two at most.

When I heard these whispers outside the door, I totally freaked out! It's probably the closest I ever came to passing out up until that point in my life. "If I hadn't of already been lying down who knows if I would have dropped or not." I immediately reverted to my prayerful instincts that subconsciously emerged. Just mouthing, probably heard as a simple light whisper, was my own self speeding "Hail Mary full of Grace, the Lord is with you. Blessed are you among women, and blessed is the Fruit of thy womb, Jesus. Holy Mary, Mother of God, pray for us sinners, now and at the hour of our death. Amen." In the span of about eight seconds I had it done. Now another and another, then another thinking, "Make it go away, please God."—Don't let them force me to have this kind of procedure. Obviously, the idea of prayer isn't the quantity but the quality in this context. Nerves and fear equaled the gamut of emotions for me at that moment.

I heard some other muffled conjecture and then you could hear the preliminary clicks and jiggling of the wooden door about to spring open. Still, at this time in my visits, I didn't yet have one doctor exclusively seeing me. I never knew which of the four associates would see my on any given day. So as the white coated silhouette appeared, it narrowed it down to Dr. Keough or Dr. Lebetta. The other two doctors wore suits generally as a rule. Immediately I distinguished Dr. Lebetta's face, so maybe, just maybe, I may have misunderstood everything that I thought I had deciphered through the door. This was total denial at its best and in it's finest moment.

Dr. Lebetta is very professional and forthright in these serious natured matters. It may be difficult to hear things hard and straight forward, but that is his nature and his job. After briefly skimming the autologous option by me, I informed him that I planned to go ahead with the transplant using my distant cousin. I believe that he was aware of the work we had put into this, but I don't know if he knew to just what great length everyone had gone so far.

You could see the look of concern on his face as he proceeded to suggest that I would ultimately be exchanging one terminal disease with another terminal disease. That being graft versus host disease. With no living transplant survivors thus far anywhere other than that of a donor being an identical twin, a statistic that in and of itself tore me up, I convinced myself that I would be the first and that was that. I doubt that I convinced him and in some gesture of compassion he attempted to humor me somewhat I believe, but I understood his duty to explain to me exactly just what I was getting myself into.

The disease that I would be trading leukemia for, according to Dr. Lebetta, was called graft vs. host disease; a totally hideous nightmare that I will go into a little further along. But just in itself, Dr. Lebatta's synopsis was intimidating. GVHD is just what it stands for. The graft is the donor's bone marrow trying to "graft" its way into your body and function, versus the host, that being the patient. Instead of a rejection (which can happen initially, or at other intervals, aside from losing your graft) the body and bone marrow engage in warfare.

From my experience, depending on the severity of GVHD ranging from Phase 1, 2,3 or higher, Chronic or acute, it can vary to a great and complex degree. The marrow sees the body as foreign and an enemy; therefore, tissue damage and organ failure can occur, along with countless other terrible manifestations. This is just a scratching of the surface in describing it. Again, despite hearing this, I theorized that my leukemia was a given to be fatal and that I'd have no chance to survive unless I give this transplant a try. Even though they both projected out as being fatal, the feather tipping the scale in favor of the transplant was, obviously, the hope of a chance.

We exchanged some views and ultimately I'd like to believe that all of my doctors respected my decision. I don't believe for a minute that any of them thought that I would return home let alone survive for any length of time though. That's what my "spider senses" thought anyhow. Over 16 years have come and gone and I still feel residuals from the ware and tear of that time frame and dealing with my doctors. This visit wore me down so much that I went home and slept for hours and hours only to wake up not feeling much better. I think I spent some more time alone or with friends, just like always trying to adjust to this hell still.

Yet another strange moment unfolded for me several nights later that may be trivial to some, but nevertheless it happened. It was about 12:30 AM on a still, hot, clear night that found me lying on top of my big truck. I had a 1976 Chevy Blazer, at the time, with big tires and a lift kit. It was a big four wheel drive truck that we had fixed and probably was over 8' high at the roof, so I enjoyed climbing in and catching the view from up there. On this particular night I was parked outside of the house but not ready to go inside. I hopped up on the roof and started gazing at the stars, thinking and praying. I envisioned what Jesus must have gone through in the Garden of Gethsemane. Not that I was making any parallels, I just couldn't imagine how his ordeal must have felt when I knew how lousy and scared I was feeling.

I laid up there for a good half-hour and had some tears brewing in my eyes by now. I could feel this inferno of anger erupting and trying to blame someone or something including myself. I felt so helpless and out of control, yet I had at least a chance of surviving through the operation despite it not yet working for anyone else as of then. I struggled so much to believe myself, it could work, it could work, it could work—think positively—breathe in, breathe out, relax. I took a deep breath, sat up, and just for the hell of it said to myself to God, "Please God, let me know if you're up there and if you really are with me. Let the Blessed Mother show me a sign or you give me a sign with a falling star shooting across the sky in Jesus' name!" Exactly at that moment, the most awesome bright star appeared and shot across the sky like a meteor! Not only did I slip off of the truck and bruise my back, I ran into the house probably waking up a few neighbors in he process of telling my parents.

Perhaps they thought, here he is with another nice little story, but after they had witnessed some of the same things that I was experiencing, I'd like to believe they believed as I and took this as a positive sign of hope. Obviously, this is a case of faith only because any scientist could rip my story apart with logic and probabilities. Nevertheless, I know I asked and it appeared exactly when and where I was looking immediately after asking. Luck or no luck, it was good enough for me at that time and just like that I was back on an upswing with a new tank of optimistic gas. Believe me, I am still leaving out many details to move this story along, up to the final countdown flight trip out to Seattle.

I became hyper and running on adrenaline. Even though I was desperately sick, you may not have noticed it right about then. We packed what we had to pack, All I was taking was at the front door and you could have cut the family's tension with a knife. My husky, Yuke, was practically a wolf in his nature. He was very high strung and emotional, he seemed to know that I was leaving. With his acting funny, I began to play and rough house with him. The other dog, Kong, that I mentioned earlier who was in a cart, I had trained to show his teeth if I made a fist. It was a funny smile of a gesture and I was trying to teach Yukon, but it wasn't nearly as easy or successful.

Instead of me showing Yukon, he showed me by biting me severely in the chest. Here I am getting ready to leave and now had a bleeding wound to contend with. It turned out that because of time, I had to fly across country to Seattle with the wound patched by my Mom until I could receive medical attention. Man did it hurt!

Not twenty minutes after the dog bite, this episode was eclipsed by another of my story's oddities. It came in the form of a phone call and I mentioned earlier how that sound effect's me; well, this was no different in its sound but it was in the content of the call. Believe it or not, I was notified from Seattle that a closer matched donor, in science terms, had been found. "Leave your cousin home", they said. I still can't believe all of the accumulating scenarios. This phone call came on the very evening that I was leaving.

Needless to say, I got lost in emotions. At that point I was not as knowledgeable about matches as I am today; so, any good news from the top was good enough for me. I immediately assumed that my chances of survival would be greatly enhanced and it still may have been the case. Although I didn't know about all of the specifics back then, I just rode the wave.

This new and intriguing update gave my brother, sister and I fuel for conversation during the flight across country. For the moment, though, we had to notify my distant cousin whom I didn't even know that we would not be needing his assistance any longer. He was very disappointed and, although I still haven't met him to this day, I consider him a donor in every sense except for the marrow. Bill, wherever you are today, God bless you always. The very irony of this all still gets me now: a distant cousin was packed, and ready to go to Seattle with us. On the very evening that we were leaving for the airport, we received a phone call from the state of Washington that I now had a donor from the state of Minnesota. It's really uncanny.

Well, off to the airport we went. Upon saying, "I love you" and all of the other airport sendoff stuff to my parents and girlfriend, before I knew it we were in the air. I still felt the pain of the dog bite for sure. The flight was long and tiring. We landed with some idea of where to go and so far the people were very nice. The first order of business after catching a cab was to check in with our local designated hospital apartment facility. Carol had arranged it all over the phone and, since this whole situation arose so abruptly, we did not have the luxury of shopping around for another place to stay. The place we were given was called the Monticello. This was a three or four story complex similar to a motel setting with each unit having its own exterior door and balcony.

We were just a few blocks away from the Fred Hutchinson Cancer Center and Swedish Hospital. On a clear day you could see Mt. Rainer, a great spectacle. When one enters or leaves the Monticello, you experience an eclectic blend of scenic tile, throw rugs and color. This doesn't sound out of the ordinary except the particular combination did catch us off guard. We came to adopt our home away from home as a humorous and eventually comfortable abode.

A bit loud and damp at times, our Monticello unit consisted of a 12' x 12' living area, with a couch/bed that connected to about a 6' x 6' kitchen area, and then right to 2 double beds into the bathroom just like the letter 'L'. Our bathroom had a pink tub, a blue toilet and a yellow sink. As unsightly as it was initially, I quickly realized that it had just caught me off guard in terms of what I had envisioned. We proceeded to "soop up" the place with Halloween decorations in our window, some knick-knacks from home, etc. We had to rent a television from a store across town and viola; it was our home sweet home, i.e. "Home Sweet Seattle".

I had to check in at the hospital briefly and was scheduled to start some work up procedures for the next few days. I filled out some forms and was given an itinerary list of appointments and times along with the locations and so forth.

The rest of the day was open, so we decided to walk the rustic hilly town and just goof around a bit. We may have stuck out to the locals with our "Philadelphia" accent and for sure after I decided to go in and have my head shaved into a Mohawk. On the sides it said, "Marrow man", and so the legend began. Well more like whispers of "look at that nut", but it did turn heads. I knew that it was going to fall out anyway, why not take the opportunity and psyche myself up creatively some more for this ordeal.

One of the first orders of business was to meet with some of the doctors in a conference room with ten or twelve other incoming patients like me. I remember briefly introducing myself to everyone, and my exterior facade of contentment stuck out from the crowd. You could hear a pin drop as the doctors explained again the severity of the transplant and to a certain degree what it entailed. I learned much later that their policy was not to speak about every detail because of the individualized problems that may or may not arise. Also because they felt that it could possibly be demoralizing and counter-productive to the patients, so it was just acquaintance formalities for the most part.

This briefing rattled me and again I felt like a yo-yo man with the emotions of fear, confidence, reassurance, being scared, getting weak, growing strong; whew, I was a mess. But it was too late to back out and what else could I do? I often would think of songs that fit my need of expression. Right then it could have been Queen's, "The Show Must Go On". The doctor-patient session lasted about 1.5 hours then I could go lick my wounds, so to speak. My sister, brother and I met in the lobby; so, home to the Monticello we trekked.

This was the eve; I guess you could say, before all of the wheels were to be set into motion. The next day was the start of transplant work-up procedures. The list of things to get done concerning work-ups was divided into days instead of cramming them in all at once. Perhaps two or three procedures in a given day would be performed, but the rest of the day would be free to us. Some of those work-ups included seeing the dentist to ensure that all of the hygiene needs were taken care of. I was aware of this back home, so I took care of that beforehand.

Dental hygiene is a high priority for bone marrow transplant patients due to chances of infection. Also, some of these tests included pulmonary function tests such as lung capacity, oxygen intake, dioxide ventilation and so forth. Also included were eye exams, body fat measurements, range of motions, food intake and, of course, lots of blood work. These were just some of the pre-admission tests that I needed to finish.

On those afternoons off, we would mosey around town and try to see some of the areas' attractions. Although my brother and sister took in some good sights,

I'm sorry to say that I still don't know much about the area outside of "Pill Hill," i.e. the hospitals. The first initiation of "real" operations under the knife in store for me was scheduled within the week. This was the insertion of my Hickman catheter. Every patient gets one "installed" as required gear. What it is literally is a pipeline tube from just around your collarbone down into your heart. This becomes a lifeline and vital tool for the medical staff. Anything from blood being withdrawn or infused, to medicines, to nutrients can all be administered through this Hickmanline.

Most patients are pincushions by this point from all of the previous blood procedures that they have endured. Not only does this spare the patient tons of pain and potential mishaps, but it would be virtually impossible to perform everything on the patient using just arms, I would think The Hickman is also the tunnel that the new bone marrow will be infused into me with.

When the day arrived to have my line put in, I was shocked to find that the performing doctor would be Dr. Hickman himself. This was a worldwide famous device, so you would never think that the inventor would be anywhere around. I would have guessed that this guy would by lying out on some tropical island collecting revenue checks from his creation. Well with Dr. Hickman that wasn't the case. He put many catheters in at Fred Hutch and I was one of them.

I had no idea that I would be awake for the procedure but, once they wheeled me into the O.R. and things got started, I realized I would be awake. I managed to get Dr. Hickman to fire up the radio so; at least I could get tucked and prodded in ambience. What I remember most about this was the intense pressure that I felt as the catheter made its way down through my artery. Not pain per se, more like a burn or the smashing of your hand, with a hard pressured movement from the head down into the heart. It took about an hour or so to get it all over with and I was free to take my new catheter out for a test drive. Dr. Hickman and I got along so well that he later came back to have lunch with me one day down the line—"Pardon the pun".

The catheter needed constant care and maintenance with cleaning and keeping clean. Initially my sister cleaned it for me using Beta dine, with special pads and ointment in a kit form, after removing a crust that would try to form at its base near my skin where it went it. This was occasionally bothersome with the scab forming and being so sensitive to the touch once it was cleaned off. All in all, anyone who ever cleaned that thing did a great job, and I'm very appreciative.

When this was all taken care of, I had several bad days of pain and discomfort but eventually my body became accustomed to it as best it could I suppose. The next order of business was another bone biopsy and marrow aspiration. What I refer to as the "cork screw". By what I could always feel I envisioned the type of apparatus used to remove a cork out of a bottle of wine. I mentioned earlier for some reason that this was and always is a difficult procedure for me. The bottom line is that feeling and sensation-wise it tears me up. Again, I know other people that don't experience these types of problems whatsoever, so here is more evidence to myself that I am a freak.

This procedure usually only takes 15 or 20 minutes to get over with but, as is the case with most things in my life for whatever reason, it wasn't uncommon for the staff to have to try 2 or 3 attempts. For me that meant separate corkscrew attempts. Evidently, the bone marrow can sometimes have air pockets present or something, which can occur to make the extractions difficult. We even tried a Lamaze technique with ice packs tapping all over my back and everything. Nevertheless, they got the bone sample and a marrow sample needed so I could go home to the apartment and retreat for one day.

A bright spot and break for me amongst all of this poking and prodding came from a very nice social worker at Hutch. I believe her name was Mary Shroeder She had managed to grab me a pair of Sea Hawks vs. Jets tickets down at the King Dome. The Jets being my favorite team coming into town to play worked out great and I could get to see them. The season started off that year 10–1 and for Jet fans, we grew accustomed to know how rare that was. The Jets won and it was a real relaxer to fit in at that slot and recharge for everything that was to come next.

With all of my pre-admission testing now finished for the most part, it was time to rumble. This was it! I was going to take the shuttle bus over to the Hutch and not be coming back out for awhile, if ever. Even today I hate that inner voice that revisits those bad flashbacks, which I've acquired and have to beat them back to stay in control.

I really didn't know what to expect. I had seen the laminar airflow rooms (LAF) on *60 Minutes* with a segment they had on a gentleman by the name of Zumwalt, but it wasn't the same as being face to face right there when I arrived on the floor. From the cozy lobby we passed housing all of the baseball hats and trophies displayed therein the big cases, I went to the left, up the elevator and into another world. I'm not sure but I think I remember 25–30 rooms or so wrapped around the outside of the floor. The center housed the kitchen, nurses' station, showers, tubs, closets, medical paraphernalia and so forth.

Upon reaching the nurses' area, you could not help noticing the adjacent LAF room with a patient and family doing battle. It was dimly lit, and very quiet with just the sound of pumps beating and EKG machines beeping. In the distance, sounds of many other beepers and pumps came to fill in the background.

The laminar airflow room unit, as I mentioned, is essentially a self-contained free room. This was supposed to be a 99% germ-free environment, isolation area that the patient stayed in. It was approximately 8' x 8' and "closing in fast" as I remember it to be with a partial open door frame, protected by a wall of circulated air via fans. The other partition was a vinyl curtain-like material, but sealed with a plastic oval window, and surgical-type gloves reaching into the patient from the outside area. Some may remember the show *"Lost in Space"*; it had a robot with long slinky-type arms and I couldn't help but always think of that robot saying, "Danger, danger, Will Robinson". You really know where you stand when you see rubber arms coming at you from the other side.

Well, as I first stopped at the nurses' station, I checked in and awaited instructions. What I needed to do first was get "decontaminated". I had to take a shower with anti-bacterial soap and play twister getting into a germ-free moon suit, as we called them. From stepping out of the shower and into blue booties and pants, matching top and cap, with gloves and a mask, I got pretty good at it actually after several of my few bubble breakout episodes. I then would be wheel-chaired or escorted across the hall to my room. The first half of the room was a regular environment like the rest of the hospital and outside. From the entrance of the airway, I had to coordinate the jump over into the "safe zone" by removing the suit as I entered the "bubble".

Once I crossed over, I was on the inside looking out like a gold fish in a bowl, that's how it felt Just like those little ones you toss ping pong balls at to win at the carnival. All that I needed were gills. You never get used to it, you just try to tolerate it. Actually, from about day one I started climbing walls. All that you really could do was pace a few steps, lie down on the "cozy" cot-sized bed, or watch TV. One of the many strings Carol and Tom pulled for me was to get me a room that had MTV and Atari. Atari! That's how far back it was to date it all. As a matter of fact, that is a perfect analogy for the progress transplants have made in this time frame. Atari to Sega is the progress in transplants from then to now. I wish I had Sega progress and today's methods in 1986 for sure. I could have saved much living. Well, I didn't; so, in any event, I also was given an exercise bike to cruise to nowhere.

I could keep busy somewhat with these activities for a little while. I'd learn that time on my hands was the least of my worries. Everything was beginning to hit full swing at this point. I was to start 10 days of chemotherapy, and then about 14 days of total body irradiation (TBI), something along those lines—but, first, the chemo for a beach head.

I didn't want to look too far ahead but I'd already envisioned my road map of how things would go. I'd just breeze through all of this early stuff, pray a lot, get the marrow and, just like that, poof—before you know it, I would be home. "Boy, do I wish it really was like that Lord".

A lot of pre-testing had been done to determine exactly how much chemotherapy and how much total body irradiation, or (TBI) I was to receive. The doctor told us that "they wanted to go as far as they could and come as close as they could to killing me without killing me." (And that was a quote!) My weight and my intake, etc. were crucial to monitor. Unfortunately, patients had, in fact, died just from the chemo and or TBI so it was a very serious business of precise calculations for sure.

I remembered during one of the previous pre-testing days, in the afternoon we stopped into the Saint James Cathedral, located up the street from the hospital, for prayer and Mass. A big statue of St. Therese was on the side in back, so for whatever reason; I plucked a strand of my hair out and stuck it under the statue. Only God knows why we do things like that, but I guess it gave me a link from the church to this stinking bubble. One last piece of the old me here, maybe; who knows?

One of the now funny but then painful, regrettable and unusual things happened, all in one storm right out of the gate. Since the chemotherapy I would be getting was so toxic, the inner bladder lining was expected to shred and break down along with sporadic internal bleeding. The protocol called for a catheter to be inserted in my penis by one of the nurses who was assigned to me. I can never say enough about how compassionate all of them at Hutch are.

In 1986, the nurse's work there was so intense and stressful that they worked for 7 days straight and then they would be off for 7 days. I'm sure that all nurses are special to their patients, but I just think bone marrow transplant nurses go a step beyond reality.

Back to the catheter story; well as I mentioned that it had to be "installed" before the heavy-duty procedure started. Not that this was not heavy duty to me! I was petrified. Calm and cool on the outside—I was initially, but frantic inside. I'm thinking, "How is she going to jam that big hose up inside of me?" Uh, I had so much anxiety. On top of that with a pretty nurse, I was worried about getting excited down below, if you know what I mean. Well, that didn't happen but what did was about as bad. Evidently, I was given a sedative to relax those organs and make this an easy affair. Whatever drug I was given quickly turned me into a lunatic. The nurse managed to insert this catheter thing in me and up there (which is still brutal just thinking about it). It was so very unnatural and uncomfortable of a feeling, something I didn't even consider as a part of the transplant.

No sooner did she get the catheter in me than I went on a loony binge of hysteria. Laughing uncontrollably, standing up on the bed, having diarrhea all over the place and I pulled the catheter right out of me. All of the work she did to get it in and I just whipped it right out! Flinging it around and around like a lasso, whooping it up until, like a drunk, I became dizzy, collapsed, and puckered out. I fell right on the floor. That was some kind of sedative for sure, just not right for me.

After all that poking and prodding and cringing to get that damn thing in, I'd gone and yanked it right the heck out while my brother and sister watched as their jaws dropped in disbelief. Now I had to be subjected to that same stinking procedure all over again, this time I'd be cleaned-up and with a different pre-med for sure; "A rough lesson in mixing catheters and pre-meds in private parts".

Okay, I thought it's not the worst thing that could have happened. My first in-hospital procedure went awry, but I could just shake it off and easily move ahead. Having no control of my bladder and that queasy pressure sensation down there did rattle me but it was just the beginning. Oh, God hear my prayers and help me, I said many times. If for nothing else, I hoped they helped the nurses who participated in these fiascoes.

Once this was taken care of, I was pretty much ready to start the chemotherapy sessions that were on deck. I think a couple of days may have gone by before I actually started. On the outside it looked like an innocent enough procedure. A couple of clear fluid I.V. bags and it was just to be infused through my Hickman line and that's all, a simple hook-up start. Just prior I was given another pre-med popularly known as Benadryl. This was supposed to help my stomach with the nausea that the chemo would induce, but I encountered my second big problem consecutive procedure attempts.

As my luck would have it, I was very allergic to the Benadryl with severe reactions. Nobody would have thought that I would be allergic to this frequently used medicine. My heart raced, I got hives all over, and became irritable and fidgety, as well as having a difficult time breathing. This ruined everything and for a reason that I never knew, it was decided that I would try to be given the chemotherapy with out any kind of anti-sickness medicine whatsoever. Evidently, I had a big problem with pre-meds. Now that I think about it, if I'd had two successive violent reactions with just pre-medications that, were supposed to help me; how the heck did they think I'd react to the chemo? My only guess is that the doctors feared perhaps a combination of the two as being even a worse reaction. I couldn't imagine it being any worse than it was for me though at the time.

My convulsions and spasms from those days of chemo were intense. I spit up blood, tons of mucus and black bile from my stomach and intestines. It was so bad that the staff prepared to operate if my esophagus ruptured. Thoughts of stopping the sessions were serious enough to call several big pow-wows among the doctors. Ultimately, the doctors and I decided to get through each remaining day however we could, if we could. There weren't any other options. The retching and spasms lasted only a copy of hours a day until I became exhausted and slept the remainder of the day. I never knew humans could throw up black "tarry goo".

My parents were scheduled to fly in about this time and I'm glad my mother missed this horrible mess. I don't know if at any point I ever really had a perspective of what was going on. I did acquire serious damage to my throat, as a result of that which I still have today. On top of this, I had several injections in my spine of a drug called methotrexate. It was to aid in the killing of cells in my spinal cord; this was painful and pushed me to start climbing the walls. I couldn't deal with all of this at once, I guess, maybe I cracked some under the pressure.

I was planning my escape from the bubble unbeknownst to anyone else. I hinted to Carol by complaining as to what it was like inside there. Like an FBI crime negotiator, she pleaded with me to stay in. "Stay in—stay in", she said. I think what tipped me over the edge was the fact that, now with the chemotherapy over; I was to be carted out for 14 days in and out of this laminar airflow room. Each time I'd have to shower down, moon suit up again, and then strip down upon re-entry, over and over. I'd get a taste of the "outside" and then back into the bubble.

After two more days or so, I think, I blew a fuse. Pacing back and forth like a lion at the circus, I edged closer to the doorway. Finally, I remember yelling to Carol in a threatening tone, "I'm coming out. I can't take it any more." She stood in a slouched stance with her hands stretched out in defense, "No, no, no, don't!" Boom, I crossed the forbidden zone. I was now "contaminated". The entire ruckus rounded up several nurses and staff members as they peeked in to find me lounging in a nearby chair. They were speechless. I was plenty drugged up, flustered and demanded to speak with a doctor to negotiate.

I needed to cut a deal. You see, across the hall were several patient rooms that did not use the L.A.F. or "bubble system". Depending on what protocol you were slotted into determined whether or not you would be placed in isolation or not.

It just so happened that I drew the isolation set-up that was chosen as best suited for me due to my illness.

Now it seemed as though I had gone and flushed the research right down the drain. Nevertheless, I had to get into one of those open-air rooms and it just so happened that one became available that day, unfortunately, due to another patient's passing. I clearly upset everyone on the staff but I felt that I had to get some control of my situation and buy some time, at the very least some mental recovery time. I really got out of the gates pretty lousy, what next? I still had 10 or 12 rounds of TBI left before the technical term of day zero of the transplant even began.

With some compassion and luck, the staff agreed to move me across the hall and I got a much-needed boost of morale. I just was not prepared for the claustrophobic environment initially. Only God knows if I could have stayed sane if I'd have gone back in there at that particular time. Well, the transfer was made and I felt somewhat like a human again. This room was somewhat similar to a typical hospital room. It also had cable TV—ESPN and MTV—so that was great. Now I needed to get some rest so that I could resume the total body irradiation the next day.

I fought to convince myself—"Stay calm and positive, you've barely skipped a beat." Obviously that was stretching it a bit but I had to use whatever would work. I must have shaken the staff's confidence in me or just out of concern, maybe even my family was in cahoots with them. But whatever the case may have been, I was scheduled to see a social worker/psychologist for some quick counseling. This turned out to be the same woman who got me the Jets tickets, so I knew that she was nice and sincere.

I was always a bit skeptical about therapists but I really didn't have much of a say in this matter. Basically it was just an informal conversation with the therapist, my sister and me. One of the things that she suggested was relaxation techniques and visualization techniques. It very well may have worked but, at the time, I thought that it was a crock. I was told to envision a pleasurable place that I'd been to before and try reenacting, creating an experience. I was somewhat put off by this as I perceived it as insulting my intelligence, or it as being some sort of hypnotism attempt. I thought, "Okay lady, you want a fishing trip? I'll give you one."

The therapist would question me with things like, "Are you in a boat?" "Yes, I'm in a boat." "Have you caught anything yet?" Yeah, a line of bullshit, I joked to myself. "No," I said, "nothing is biting." On and on I took her around the lake until I figured that it was time to catch the big one. I think Carol detected my smart aleck sarcasm and I winked to her a few times, but I don't believe that the therapist was aware of it. I didn't mean any disrespect to her at all; I just had a little bit of an attitude. I believe that it was fear that made me a bit defensive to all of this. Yes, I do believe fear dictated a lot of my thoughts and behaviors right then. Perhaps the therapist was using reverse psychology on me by letting me think this session was ludicrous. I wonder, in any event, it may have helped me with the channeled anxiety.

Well, with all of this going on, you'd think that I had thrown everything out of sync. Actually, since all of this happened in a few days, the total body irradiation didn't conflict with the turmoil, because my first scheduled "nuking", I believe, was in the late afternoon or evening. Now that we were all back on board from the derailment, the TBI was my next hurdle.

I was now out of the LAF room, as I mentioned, so I did feel "unattached" if you will, except for the catheter in my privates and the Hickman catheter in my neck, and 2 or 3 new blue pumps that every patient becomes all too familiar with. This baggage reminded me of when I was four or five, playing army out in back of my house. I probably was all of about 2 ½ 'tall, but was loaded with tons of pretend equipment. You know my dad's work hat for a helmet, a toy gun, the canteen, a rake for a bazooka and so forth, dragging it up the alley to nowhere to save the country. Now I was lugging this growing acquirement of paraphernalia but, at least, in a bigger area to roam.

Of the many surreal moments I had through all of this, the total body irradiation ranks right up there! Now dressed in regular hospital scrubs that I weaseled from one of the hot nurses, I was ready to be gurneed down in the speedy wheeled stretcher. For the first time a pre-med didn't affect me like somebody tripping at Woodstock, or someone swallowing Drano. It felt "good" not having any "complications before any complications so to speak".

My throat was still raw and sore from the retching but I felt that I had some decent strength left over after the sickness had subsided. For a fashion statement, they stuck a cap over my Mohawk. Actually, I believe it helped with the sterilization and so I was ready to be escorted to the basement. My pre-med was to kick in shortly after the radiation had started and then the hope was that I would sleep right through the night.

The nurses' team escorted me out the door, down the hall, up the floor through a tunnel and into the "dungeon". For me, there was one room that I passed, the animal research area which was upsetting. I have no idea what, if any, harm is done to them but I can't imagine anything being pleasurable. I don't think that I'm an advocate of animal research and I chalked up another emotional scar; "As if I needed to see them at this moment."

The "drive" seemed lengthy, like I was journeying to a distant, remote and secluded area. I t seemed that way all right because that is just exactly what was going on! "Man, this stuff is so dangerous, it must make you glow", I thought. I knew about us cancer patients going through various forms of chemo and radiation but this was ridiculous! I then remembered that statement made to me by the doctors that they would try to go as far as they could to try and kill me without killing me. Now the magnitude of that statement hit home even more so than before. I'm thinking, what the heck are they going to do to me? I felt like a freaking Martian in that environment!

Even though I was getting groggy, I remember entering the cave, or bomb shelter like structure "if you will", that I was to be nuked in. After a drive up and down tunnels and hills (it seemed like it took at least 15 minutes to get there), we approached big doors with the classic Danger Restricted Area signs and all of the labels. Even the well-known radiation symbol of the black and yellow triangled logo stared back at me. This is the moment in which every body scattered and left me to be had by the monster. Kind of like, in King Kong where the natives leave the offering just outside the huge wall for Kong to come down and feast on. Man my imagination was flying inside although I was cool and humorous on the outside.

When the button was pushed and the doors opened, I was parked in the center of the vault. That's just what it was, very similar to the kind of operating room you may have seen on television, where there is an elevated window just above eye level. Behind the glass of the room were all of the controls and work fronts. I could notice the operators looking down at me communicating via an intercom system. As if this wasn't freaky enough for me, the whole room was a pale shade of pink. Yeah, stale pale Pepto Bismal like pink!

A very old black and white television on a stand was in front of me to watch if I chose to do so. This TV had a tin foil antenna stuck to the back of it. I was probably so far underground that nothing else would work except a pre-historic dinosaur TV and that foil wrap for reception. I still can't believe I didn't make this stuff up even with a waterfall of emotions running through my head. I'd love to know my pulse at that particular time.

For the most part, the first round of TBI seemed uneventful. I'd swear though that I could feel the waves and vibrations of radiation skimming and zapping through me. I don't know if that's possible. Maybe I just experienced a psychosomatic reaction but, I believe that I felt something during those sessions for sure.

I never lasted long staying awake for the whole duration. Always about half way through I would doze off only to wake up in my hospital room back on the transplant floor or in the hallway somewhere on the gurney going back. When I managed to get a few days of this radiation under my belt, I got a quick but false sense of security and confidence because initially I didn't feel much different. "If this was the brunt of the stormy hell, this was a piece of cake." "I'm cruising", I thought.

Looking back, I see a fine line between a fat head of confidence and being humble. I never could have persevered without the confidence level being high or continually looking for a positive aspect to psyche myself up with. One of my tough lessons though was that I wasn't invincible in simply doing this all by myself. Of course, I was the central player but the layers of support and help needed go far beyond the self. From as far up as the Lord above, and as lateral as every hospital staff member, friend and, of course, my family.

Not only did my music have great power to it, they actually had relevant and meaningful lyrics. One of which was my choice by Rainbow titled "The Power". Perhaps hard rock to some but roots tied to heavy metal for sure. Anyone familiar with this hidden tune knows that the lyrics speak totally of what it takes to survive a transplant. This was my transplant anthem. From Madonna to Motorhead, Jimmy Hendrix to Led Zeppelin, of course the Rolling Stones, Yes, Iron Maiden, Metallica, The Beatles, Pink Floyd, you name it and I had it all. Those plus my special wordless tapes to relax and sleep to meant that I had some very good crutches to rest and escape with.

When I wasn't listening to music, often times I had devised a brilliant plan to escape and relax with even more by taking as many baths as I could. At the end of the hall were two or three rooms with bathtubs in them. You might call them the "tub rooms". All of the patients could take baths if they chose, so in between each use a nurse would have to sterilize it for the next patient. Often the nurses assigned to the particular patient would take care of his/her turn to prepare it. It got so bad for a while I remember nurses bickering with each other because a patient had jumped in and used a tub that was already prepared for another patient. I can't blame them. It took fifteen or twenty minutes of hard cleaning each time to sterilize the unit. Finally, a reservation sheet was made up. That's funny to me now, fighting to get clean!

Well, my motives for a bath were strictly for relaxation and escapism purposes exclusively. I'd run water as hot as I could tolerate, bringing along my tape player, and melt away for as long as I could, often pruning up. "The Prune Man", if the water would start to get cold, I'd drain some and fire up the hot water again. I definitely hogged the bath although it eventually ended up that I was one of only a couple of patients to use the tub facilities. It even came to a point where nurses and family members would frequently check on me to see if I was okay. I'd hear a tap, tap, tap, tap, tap, hey, are you okay in there? I guess they weren't used to the way that I enjoyed escaping from my hospital bed the way I did.

A funny thing I remember was that, for safety reasons, none of the bathroom doors had locks on them. So it did come to pass that a nurse or someone else peeked in to see for them self if anyone was in there. One of the first signs of radiation was my pubic hair falling out. Initially I was self-conscious of this, so I started taking an extra wash cloth to cover my private area. The catheter hose would just serve as a tent pole out to the pump outside of the tub. It worked out pretty well actually. It's so funny, I'm terminally ill with leukemia and worrying about people seeing me without hair. What was I thinking?

This all continued for the duration of the TBI. I was now wearing the dress code familiar to all bone marrow transplant patients: sweat pants, sweat shirt, mask, and white socks with slippers or sandals (whatever could fit without being painful); "Easy maintenance and access to all of those pumps and hoses". Another pass through the basement tunnel one night and I couldn't help noticing an area where several of the patients who had passed away were being tended. I was so chilled by this, it left yet another emotional scar on me that I just vaulted.

By now my radiation was all but finished. In those early days, I didn't really feel any different other than being extremely tired and weak. This and the fact that my probable imaginative body vibrations were buzzing so I thought. Thus fair I had been administered the methotrexate directly into my spine, received all of the chemotherapy and the fourteen days of total body irradiation. As if this wasn't enough to kill me besides the leukemia, the doctors had one more trick up their sleeves to spring on me. This was called a column exchange.

One day I was wheeled down into a room much like you would see in a blood lab or a forensic medicine unit. It was real quiet in there and I was put up on a stationary bed that reclined somewhat. What they now were going to do is change my blood type believe it or not. Two incisions were made in my femoral artery, a major bloodline to the legs and heart located right below the groin. I was split like some kind of wishbone and, after I was locally anesthetized, tubes were inserted up into the artery itself.

Connected to the tubes was a big box about the size of a console television set I guess, that looked like it in turn linked up to a larger unit resembling a computer. I think I remember circular glass donut shaped windows that you could see the blood visibly through. One tube would be used for in-flowing new blood and the other tube was for the "old blood" so to speak to exit. I guess as the ratio of blood went in, in turn the same amount left me. I believe this process was to further insure that any doubtful sign of possible remaining leukemia cells would be eliminated from the blood stream, as well as the bone marrow. I think this procedure lasted several hours and, with those tubes all in me at once, at that time I resembled something out of a Frankenstein movie for sure.

A day or so after this final big step to kill off my leukemia, I finally started feeling it all catch up to me. The column exchange had literally changed the blood type of mine to another. I believe that I may have had the rare AB negative type and now what became O positive or something like that. I didn't know that it was possible to do, but evidently it is. In what seemed like a matter of the blinking of my eyes, I went from just feeling tired to feeling tired and miserable. So much fatigue was setting in, I felt like I weighed a hundred pounds more than I did.

At about this time, my girlfriend flew in to stay with us. Now this meant I had my mom, my dad, my sister, my brother, and her for support. This was my my immediate family, except my in-laws, nieces and nephews, so it felt good to have them there. I was real curious as to why my girlfriend waited so long to get here and I later found out. Back at home all of my friends had been involved in a big fund raiser party in my honor. When I found this out I was so speechless and overwhelmed. It's one of those bright spots in my heart, in my life, obviously. Everything was taped on a video and it was going to be sent to me so that I could watch all of my friends helping us out. I just don't have the right words to express how I felt and say thank you to each one of them. You all know who you are and I'll never forget what you did for me.

With my girlfriend arriving and the news of the fund-raiser, it curtailed my downward spiral to some degree. My spirits were boosted for a good long while with her being there but, ultimately I started sliding again. Now I had to start to wait until my blood counts hit zero. Actually a literal count of about 5 or 10 cells was pretty much the same difference to the doctors, I believe. I think it took several more days to achieve these kinds of numbers that the doctors needed to see.

My moment of anticipation was inching closer. Those few days of waiting found me lying down almost constantly. I think I was close to using a bedpan, if I wasn't already. I prayed a lot and kept my St. Therese relic next to my bed on the night table. Along with that my stereo and the Padre Pio shirt I started to drape over my eyes to try and sleep more with in the form of catnaps. Meanwhile, my family kept rounds of clockwork watching over me. It was very comforting to know that they were there to support me through this ordeal.

I started to receive some get-well cards and had a collection growing on the wall. Even they helped more than I would have guessed. Next to them was a big wall chart that Carol made to count the days down to the transplant day designated as day zero by the medical staff. So the days mounting before day zero were negative days on the chart. I could clearly see the big Xs blotting out each day, wondering which upcoming day would be the one.

I thought about who my donor could be. Was he or she a famous athlete or not? Were they black or white? Were they a fireman or an artist? Perhaps even a forklift mechanic? Okay, maybe I didn't come up with that one but you have the idea. The possibilities were endless and intriguing. It was entertaining, joking about who it could be; would I inherit their qualities such as craving for foods or personality traits? Who knew? The suspense was a healthy thing to use to keep my mind occupied and positive.

I could tell that my body was starting to show big damage symptoms, but I denied them off subconsciously as long as I could. The day and hour had finally arrived when the okay was given to get the ball rolling with the new bone marrow. My counts were in the 0s to 10s range in numbers so they said that it was good to go. I had so many anticipatory ideas of what to expect, if you named it, I'd probably envisioned how it would go. After all of the work that my sister, doctors and friends had done to get me to this point, the big moment of truth turned out to be an anti-climatic event in and of itself. By that I mean my nurse entered the room holding up four big bags that for the most part resembled bags of blood. This was my new bone marrow. It had been diluted in saline solution and flown in earlier that afternoon.

The much-anticipated operation of infusing the bone marrow into me consisted of simply hooking up the bags to my Hickman catheter. Once my nurse Ann made the connection, we all watched it trickle down out of the bag as it made it's way into my body. At that point I was wondering if I would actually feel it enter in me or see any signs of something noticeable to react upon.

I pretty much just laid there for an hour or so as it finally emptied all into me. I had a lot of emotional thoughts, some of which paralleled the feeling you get when you purchase something expensive and then have second thoughts. Anyway this feeling was the same for me when I became briefly saddened to have the new marrow go in. Not so much because of the new bone marrow itself, but rather the fact that my own marrow had been destroyed. Kind of like a part of me had died. I also had sensations of relief and fear mixed in at the same time. I'll say that it was a rainbow of emotions that I went through from sadness to elation.

All in all I was still feeling positive for the most part. Looking up at Carol's wall chart, we had arrived at day 0 and marked it in. Now I had to fasten the seat belts for those critical 14 days or so to come. Two weeks or so is the significant time frame for everything to start unfolding. This is when the bone marrow begins to "engraft" itself into the body by producing new white cells and so forth. A literal engraftment into the "hollowed out" bones themselves, i.e. bone marrow.

Besides the impending infections to come, the major concerns were now to having the marrow graft, or take to the patient, to losing the graft, which has even been known to occur as far as one year post-transplant or further; Although that is not the "norm" with graft vs. host disease, if and when you acquire it. This was the disease the doctor back home had told me that if I survived the transplant, this disease would ultimately kill me. Remember that quote I mentioned earlier? "You'll be trading one disease for another and both will ultimately kill you." As if I needed to remind myself of this everlasting embellished statement and kiss of death, but my personality being what it is, I did just that!

CHAPTER 3

▼

Now that I realized I was still moving my toes and blinking my eyes so to speak, my frame of mind was adjusting to the fact that I was still living and with some one else's bone marrow and blood inside my veins. This is something that I toil with occasionally. Just like when not to long ago, a Jehovah's Witness explained their view to me that I shouldn't have exchanged blood from one person to another. In a sense, I should have died because it was against God's law according to them. After this briefly shook me up, I came to my senses and researched my Bible and so forth. I concluded that they may have had good intentions but I feel they were speaking out of context.

The God I hope and believe in is all loving and compassionate. That and the fact that I had all of those incredible "coincidences"; I'll nicely call them, and truly believe they were for a reason. I even found humor in the fact that if I should already be dead or have sinned using someone else's blood product, why they were so interested in converting me. They insisted on return visits, maybe God wanted them to see it my way. Never the less, reflection on the new bone marrow is a part of my life, even today.

I recall the first two or three days as not being too bad, with only basic symptoms of nausea and extreme fatigue. This most likely was due to the fact that the doctors administered major steroids to me at that point. This is a process of suppressing the new bone marrow or controlling the speed, if you will, of the rate at which it grafts and grows in me. The reason being that in theory this can slow down or lessen the chance or severity of graft vs. host disease. A procedure that I still wonder about today because, the method of thinking in 1986, was that it was better to get a little bit of GVHD rather than none at all. They speculated that GVHD. could aid in preventing a relapse of leukemia itself.

The problem with this is where do you draw the line in the use of suppression drugs? In retrospect I wonder how well I would have fared if my initial suppression had been more aggressive so as not to contract any GVHD whatsoever. No one knows if this could have even been possible, but any surviving patient with serious GVHD would agree with me I'm sure. I won't go into explaining how the immuno-suppressive drugs govern the new and hopefully, growing bone marrow. It would sound like mumbo jumbo in layman's terms, as would much of the hematology oncology field to "common Joes".

I remember hearing some updates of other patients on the floor and to many of the families I believe that it may have been like a sort of contest type of thing. Not so much as a competition of who was better but, I feel with all of the emotions flying around, everybody was eager to report in on anything that they thought was any type of good news. As humans go, the bad news also leaked out like water everywhere, at least out of the majority of the rooms anyhow.

Some of the other patients got off to early starts with new graft counts coming in. With some patients the doctors permitted them to leave the hospital in as little as 20 days or even sooner. When I heard that, I set my goal to be the earliest patient ever to leave. This could be an extra incentive to use and hope to get out and back to the "confines of the multicolored Monticello". Surely, I thought at the time, if I could do this it would be a good parameter of how I was doing. "If you can leave this place, you must be doing okay", I thought. A girl down the hall was reported to be in the tens by the hallway gossipers. A real nice man named Howard next door to me had some good early numbers. This one, that one, it felt like a primary election with the counts coming in.

As wiped out as I felt, I was just as antsy to have my snails pace of progress pick up. For me there was absolutely nothing count-wise for the first few days. I don't even know if the other patients had the same protocols being used as mine, so I shouldn't have compared what I was hearing to my particular situation. Things were going very slow however, and I silently panicked that my graft wasn't going to ever materialize. "What then?" I tortured my inner sanctum.

Thinking so far ahead is a curse to anyone's sanity in transplant hospitals. Adopted mottoes of 'day by day' became the norm. One day at a time could easily fill your quota of anxiety and gamut of emotions. When I earlier referred to my back home doctor visits feeling like fistfights, they paled in comparison to Seattle's battles. My father served in the Marine Corps during WW II, so I was very versed on all of his battle experience: Pellilu, Siapan, Tinnean, Pavuvu, Okinawa, Guadalcanal, Henderson Field, etc., all places where my father fought. This was becoming a similar line of thought for me, each ordeal taking shape like one battle at a time in a big-pictured war.

A couple of days more had passed and patients began separating themselves from the crowd so to speak. What looked like the cream of the crop to a bystander or family member turned out to be for many patients simply a mirage? You just could not tell anything this early. Yes, one or two people were cruising and on their way to their homes away from home, to then begin daily commutes back and forth to the hospital as outpatients. Yes, this still was the goal of all the green novice transplant patients. But only in living through this was I able to realize that going to the local apartment didn't mean very much in the big scheme of things.

At this point I had spiked a fever of about 101° which I was assured was very common at this stage. The gentleman next door to me was suddenly and rapidly struck with graft vs. host disease and severe radiation burns to the point of being extremely life threatening. I had seen him pass by my room with his newly wed wife. I believe they actually had a ceremony in his room. He would trudge on by with all of his pumps and eyes peeking behind his masked face look in and give a little wave to me. He, a patient with the burnt red baldhead glowing from the overhanging hallway lamps, if any one deserved to make it this man technically spending his honeymoon here certainly did.

One of the girls that jumped out count-wise had taken a slide with an infection and reports of several others getting pummeled whispered in past my ears despite Carol, and the gang's, effort to shield me from this news. My priorities dealt with what was going on with me and I had to try to block out other patients' outcomes either good or bad. I never mastered that tactic but there soon came a point where I wouldn't have to worry about concerning myself with others. Slowly but surely a typhoon of crap was going to hit the fan for me.

I really wouldn't have any time to think about anything else but pain, God and rationale. My numbers squeaked in around day 14 or 15, I guess, and they were not anything to write home about except for the fact that they were finally being recognized as an amount that could be monitored. Even though, as I mentioned, measures were taken to control the rate of engraftment. To me, it seemed as if no sooner than I started getting in numbers to be happy about, I was hit with an impending wave.

The radiation and chemotherapy had finally caught up with me. As If I had gone to bed and woke up, in that same time frame, I began to look like a mulatto. An overall "tannish hue" that rapidly had a metamorphous into major skin burns.

My whole body had been torched, and to what degree I'm not certain. I wouldn't be surprised if they were combinations of first, second and third degree in severity. Just like when you place your hand under running water to get it hot, from very cold to very hot is what my body felt like. I was coated with ointment and salve from head to toe. Aquaphor, and some others thickly applied, with many compresses to try and draw the burn out, as well as try to prevent extreme skin cracking and scarring. Today my skin has healed a lot but many burn scars remain. I still can envision Carol smearing that thick jelly like goop all over my body.

The next week or so, I spent lying as still as possible and barely sleeping at all. You just can't really doze off or get quality sleep with sap over you especially stinging incessantly from top to bottom. Obviously, my record setting goal of leaving early was now a pipe dream. Some of the other patients had checked out of the hospital and into their apartments as out patients. I was a bit demoralized with all of this going on and I'm sure a good deal disoriented. At this point, some time and relationship to what was going on are a bit vague as to date the hours and months by incident.

My second room in as many months was now like by cocoon. The only contact to the outside world was the television and people coming and going in and out of my room. My family had tried to keep it from me as long as they could but the gentleman, Howard, next door passed away. He had been very badly ravaged by graft vs. host disease after a valiant struggle. It's unfair to have such a perverted disease existing. Not that any disease is pleasant. I just feel that GVHD violates you in every way. It is a rape of mind and body and soul, bottom line.

If GVHD was a traveling disease, you could say that it left Howard and it came knocking at my door. Obviously, that isn't how it works. It happened to be about a day later that my problems increased. The burning and stinging persisted and a bitterly frustrating itching began to creep in. The catch 22 here was that if you scratched the itch, it stopped briefly but you in turn immediately induced the pain of the burn. There was also skin cracking on my lips and elbows; so pads were tried on my arms to try and protect them, and salve was applied on my lips as well. I can't say how well they worked though.

Any one now in my room was required to wear masks or instead have me put one on. At times I preferred everyone to use them but I became obsessed with germs prone to infiltrate me, so I donned the mask myself if for no other reason than to empower myself. I still had the Mohawk but some clumps were falling out here and there. That, with all the other symptoms, showed that it was clear that I had graft vs. host disease of some degree.

To try and go through GVHD would get into volumes of books. Unfortunately, I have come to learn that it is not just the public that lacks a common knowledge of this disease but, more alarming for me, was the realization that even doctors in the mainstream are misinformed of its many traits. Even more sadly, some cannot accurately define it. Thank God for me this has only involved secondary physicians and not my main doctors who regularly monitor me. With the detailed specifics linked to how GVHD works, I can more easily explain how many symptoms can manifest themselves. Then you can have some understanding of what can take place involving a patient's trials. I will most likely miss some symptoms but this is a general overview of onset GVHD

First, the disease is broken down into two main classes. Acute and chronic, much like leukemia itself in this respect. Depending on the severity and duration of symptoms, a patient is classified into phases, those being 1, 2, or 3, i.e., chronic phase 2 or acute phase1. This boils down to complications and affected areas of the body with respect to severity.

GVHD can attack any vital organ such as the heart, liver, kidneys, lungs, etc. It can attack all or none at once or combinations of organs. This is a result due to the genetic matches and mismatches, which occur in the new bone marrow and the patient's body. As of this writing, science can identify 6 antigens I believe, in the complexities of blood and tissue typing. There are a vast amount of other presently unidentified antigens and the like that in theory can dictate GVHD and its severity or lack there of. For the most part, the line of thinking is that other unidentified antigens could also conceivably match without being presently identified.

In what ever the case may be, GVHD can also involve the skin, eyes, muscles, stomach, hair, joints, ligaments, fingernails, gums, teeth, intestines, bones and, I suspect, even the brain. Picture a big game wheel where you spin it and whatever the arrow lands on you get. Just like the *Price is Right* showcase showdown, but as this being no game, you can get many or all of these combinations to deal with.

Many times GVHD attacks a vital organ and it becomes fatal; usually within the first few months to a year post transplant. Acute GVHD can be associated with the more rapid death rate, and chronic GVHD a slower deterioration and death. I feel that they are both equally hideous, in their own respects. With chronic GVHD you may live longer, but ultimately, die of infection or a progressive, tormenting and debilitating perversion of symptoms.

Although it has been theorized that when dealing with GVHD overall, it may go away and "burn itself out" or simmer down to the point of existing with the body over time, i.e.., the longer you live the better your chances are of it subsiding. I am now skeptical of this school of thought but remain equally hopeful. I will continue to elaborate on the GVHD a little further along.

At this point, I guess the total body irradiation burns were taking a bit of a back seat to the GVHD for now. I still needed to have the new marrow engraft and produce blood cells but, at the same time, we had to try and control the GVHD with the immuno-suppresive drugs. This technique has to have something to do with luck or fate, because how they can pull this off is beyond me. If you suppress the immune system (the counts), the new marrow engraftments may be jeopardized while attempting to combat the GVHD and, also, this makes the patient extremely more susceptible to infections. This is the precise and fine line to draw between possible improvement and catastrophe.

Some of the routine tests that they do to detect, diagnose and monitor GVHD are skin and lip biopsies. This primitive looking tool used to dig and scoop out flesh reminded me of one those used to clip nose hair. You know, the aluminum or cold steel shaft that spins with the inside blades turning around like mini propellers. You are generally localized at the targeted area, and soon afterwards pressure, scoop, blood. Just like that! I usually didn't feel much pain until the local wore off. Then a major pulsing beat of you body's heart rhythm would kick in at the spot where the piece of skin was just confiscated.

When the pathology tests came back, all signs indicated acute graft vs. host disease. No one in my family wanted me to be aware of this and it spawned a new trend of what I'd call, "keep it from Johnny". They wanted to shelter me from any news that might upset me or dampen the positive spirits I may have built up. It has now gone on for years and irks me to no end. Despite their best efforts, they all stink as actors; just as a neon sign that flashes, "Eat at Joe's". All you'd have to do is examine each one's demeanor and facial expression to detect trouble. That plus the fact more activity was now buzzing in and around my room.

For the first few days I was internally terrified, and becoming increasingly paranoid of what to expect. When I did confront everybody and get them to 'fess up, I was quickly conned by Carol not to panic; to remember "a little GVHD is good theoretically". We still had to find out where the GVHD was attacking me. At that time, I do not believe I had the knowledge of the specifics of GVHD symptoms I touched upon earlier. When I heard the word GVHD and acute mentioned together, I thought about an immediate death sentence. But I didn't even know what that actually meant exactly.

I had never been in a situation that felt like I was in a closing box. The earlier diagnosis of leukemia was tempered some by the fact that I was soon out of the hospital, and had transplant prospects to get me out of that tailspin; (Aside from the medicines and doctor visits). Also, for the most part, other than stress and mental anguish, I could live a relatively normal life at that time.

From the traumatic pictures that I had seen in the hallway, during my first visit to Seattle, and being given some brief explanations of GVHD, I knew it was bad. With nowhere to go "because this is where I planned to get well", I told myself anything to stay calm and that everything would still be OK. The problem now was that the symptoms were getting even more painful. After another week or so of the same mess, my counts remained very sluggish to respond, but I think this was a time when the doctors were beginning to narrow down the areas where the GVHD was attacking.

My dark tannish skin was turning into an orange-yellow mess and, while my heart, lungs and brain were temporarily eliminated from the suspected areas harboring GVHD, my kidneys, liver and skin were hot spots. This can be detective work for physicians because everything is or can be out of whack at the same time, related or not. Electrolytes, blood counts of all sorts, platelets and literally every bodily function is at the mercy of a bone marrow transplant, especially using a non, related donor. Virtually everything has to restart in the body, so to speak, so determining what may or may not be a result of GVHD is tedious and un-nerving at best.

I believe the final conclusion was that I had GVHD in acute phase of the skin, stomach and possibly my liver. I was eating less and less but, even worse than that, my stomach was not absorbing the nutrition from my food intake. The nurses started a hyper alimentation line consisting of primarily sugar water, electrolytes and vitamins such as zinc and magnesium among other ingredients.

A major break that I had fed on was the fact that a leading killer among the procedure was an infection called cytomegalovirus (CMV). Through the breakdown and mechanics of its nature, if the patient and donor were both screened as CMV negative prior to the bone marrow transplant, this danger was automatically eliminated. This was the case for me, and one huge weight was lifted off of my psyche. I'll have to say, though, with everything going on, who knows if I could have been able to distinguish what symptoms and problems went with what disease or virus.

We watched some numbers rise as I feasted on daily helpings of mega dose prednisone and cyclosporine "A.K.A. Quaker State motor oil". Swallowing that crap should have been enough to kill me with the first gulp! I remained in pain, gooped with salve and fidgety, but the drugs started the increasing presence of mood swings. I mimicked the Incredible Hulk's metamorphosis from human to green animal. Except in my case, I was going from orange to a pale-colored yellow. The yellow wasn't a funny pun but rather indicated big trouble. Now, even the whites of my eyes were gone, they now eased into a sickly tan yellow—the telltale sign of jaundice. So, now amongst all of this to stay on top of and sort out, my liver was now taking the limelight.

When the obvious yellow sick glow of my body overshadowed the counts and cracking of my burning skin, I think that the doctors may have assumed this was simply a manifestation of the GVHD itself. A common deduction but the thorough nature of Fred Hutch's staff quickly concluded that something else was the problem. I felt like the unlucky patient of the month club winner again and recipient of the prize. What seemed like the end to this story and kiss of death, was a problem called veno-occlusive disease (V.O.D). This is a fatal liver disease that ultimately ends in death due to extensive organ damage and failure. When this surfaced, I would say, the wind came out of the staff's sails. I could be wrong, but it seemed as if that spark of confidence had fled and I was mentally, in their minds, demoted from a star patient to a probable statistic. As I said, I may be totally mistaken, it's just the vibes I felt at that time.

Obviously, things were horrible. All that I had to do was take a look at myself in the mirror. It looked so bad to me beforehand and now this. I had given a poor showing for all of these true Christian-like people. I quickly learned that my Billy Ruben was escalating at very dangerous levels. Levels that, if you were to calculate the rate of increase and estimate a death numbers-wise, it would equate to a matter of hours before I would expire.

The bilirubin is a key number of the liver's health and function. I believe that the normal range for this number is something like point 00 something. Abnormal ranges are single digits and high single digits become very dangerous to health. My particular numbers were taking off at rate of 2, 3, 4, 5, and so on every other hour.

My only recourse then was to revert back to my habitual instincts of prayer. I donned on my Padre Pio shirt along with my relics, prayers and fired away. The liver numbers were ridiculously increasing into double digits before long and still with no signs of subsiding. I had Carol going to Mass for me along with some other family members and assigned her the task of getting a priest to come to visit me. As usual she produced and not long afterward a man of God came to the rescue. His name was Father Carmody. A laid back young to middle-aged priest who connected with me spiritually from the instant we met.

Our visit lasted 30–45 minutes or so. We prayed intensely as well as conversed getting acquainted with one another. Our visit finished up with Communion and a bit more prayer. "I guess inside I had hopes of hearing the Ave Maria and poof—a miracle." This is where my childlike faith could lead me at times. I would just will it in the Name of the Father, the Son and the Holy Spirit, while the veins about bulged out of my forehead with intensity. That and, perhaps, hemorrhoids from the muscle contractions; "All of this intense praying but to no avail so it seemed." Father left and I remained with a bilirubin at lethal levels with still no signs of them subsiding.

So I was now in that technically life ending zone. Just like that, this fast, I thought, "Mother F——er! I mumbled. All of this f————g s—t. All of this work, for what?" I think my anger was magnified by the steroids, antibiotics, cyclosporine, and everything else being infused into me. Knowing what I now know, I can say that I was fortunate enough to turn my anger into an ally. Whenever I got angry, for the most part, I turned it against the problems. Maybe now that I think about it, I envisioned this mess as a good vs. evil scenario. I believed that the devil was trying to break my will and beat me or try to get me to quit. So, in turn, I would channel all energies to wage war now including positive thoughts and beat back those voices of pessimism.

Maybe another day went by in what was a horrendous time frame that was more than enough stress and suffering to equal a whole transplant duration quota. My family still green but becoming savvy in BMT warfare was on the brink of collapse. My sister, brother, girlfriend and father were taking shifts to stay with me in 'round the clock vigil form again". This spoiled me but perhaps I would not have gotten through those times if not for their support to lean on.

The climax to this battle occurred not soon after this memory when my bilirubin was posted by grim staff members at 27. Not point 27 but plus 27! Bets were probably being laid down as to when I would kick the bucket somewhere in that sanctum.

My family continued the prayers, going to daily Mass and even had a prayer bombing raid on Heaven from friends back home. Having said that, with my not having an elaborate drawn out and climactic story to tell here other than the incredible mentioning of this. My bilirubin simply began to reverse as quickly and dramatically as it rose!

Absolutely no one could believe what was going on! In fact, testing was repeated after the initial declines for fear of error. This was obviously not the case and I was going from complete liver failure to normal ranges about as quickly as they elevated. Forgive me if I include this as one more mounting coincidence that we could lump in as a miracle. Who knows, maybe little ways of God through faith and intercession? That, and soon after the massive prayer barrage, you tell me.

Everyone was elated when this happened. It was like a football team getting back a starting player. There was restored hope in my recovery, and to top it all off, certain residual liver damage that should have been imminent was not to be. Not one trace of damage to my liver existed besides a slightly elevated number that had been there since before I went to Seattle. Now with this bizarre skirmish in and out with no rational explanation to speak of as to how it resolved medically, it was awesome. But reality showed that I still had a graft to obtain with counts to speak of, and the acute graft vs. host disease remained present to contend with.

As the liver episode had unfolded, it was clear that this battle was on. I now had my feet wet with the unimaginable goings on and as if I had a coach calling for a time out, you could say that I received one. Shortly thereafter we were informed that my GVHD had changed from the acute phase to the chronic phase. I don't know if this was actually a break or if it is at all ever common to have occurred.

In reality, the only break was the fact that my chances of dying soon due to organ failure may have been lessened a bit. It isn't like I physically felt much different because all of my symptoms persisted. It just sounded better to me then and, as I mentioned, I was not as educated on GVHD at the time either. Relatively speaking I may have stabilized a bit but the next big concern on the list was my lungs and my overall conditioning. A number of reasons existed, including infections of course, fluid in the lungs due to being bed-ridden, and de-conditioning in just normal breathing itself.

My father being the Marine that he was decided to enroll me in his boot camp. He took it upon himself to get me out of bed and escort me out to the floor hallway for laps. This was a routine attempted practice for the patients who were up for the task. From my transplant bed you could easily see the hallway passersby and among the traffickers were bald, sick struggling bodies, often dressed in the mask, knitted hat, robe and slippers. Oh, yes, leashed to the patients were the poles, pumps and buzzers that took on their own identities as your twin. Sometimes you could get a wave but more times than not patients were oblivious of anything except hanging on to surviving which included those laps.

To try and describe the struggles around the "track", I can only speak for myself here. It was one of those things where I overestimated my stamina in envisioning my old self before the radiation, tubes, chemo and all. "Just a cruise around a simple floor pathed in a rectangular shape road wise" I scoffed at the initial cadence of my dad to get moving. My cocky pride that I was being slowly stripped of did not take into account any of the debilitating emotions that my body was now facing.

I made my way out of bed okay and probably even to the hall but, after that, it was crash and burn. Either my legs or lungs gave out first, I just don't remember. I lasted for about 30ft, or maybe 1/10th of the course only to have my dad carry me back with the help of my brother. One thing that I could compare these sensations to is, the one you may have had coming out of the water after holding your breath too long or being held under. That back pounding whoosh in your head and neck, accompanied by your own heartbeat pounding furiously in your ears.

When I recovered somewhat physically afterward, my psyche was still in need of repair. If I was this weak now after being in such good shape, how could I endure another setback? Again, I needed to go back and recondition myself especially mentally. I would clear my head and start to peck away at the distances around the hallway. Then I would be able to use the increase of distances as a parameter of progress, it just took some discipline to do that. We had to pace the intervals and take breaks in the hallways so that's just what we did.

Little by little I advanced until about a week later I was able to go the distance. I had to squish the fathead that was swelling in achievement and keep it in perspective. This constant battle with the little voice upstairs in me was draining to say the least; a seemingly non-stop regulation of too up or too down. On one hand I needed to be very positive and, on the other hand there was so far to go that I didn't have any time to bask in the moment of a trivial victory. "Get a grip!", I'd say to myself along with many superlatives.

Well, I got back to a certain degree of stamina and had the routine laps down to a daily event. I now see first hand how massive toxins induced into the body can strip you raw of the equipment with which to fight, i.e., strength, appetite, dignity, patience, will and so forth. Nobody can prepare you for this experience. I don't know if other types of cancer procedures are less severe or if it's all simply relative to the patient.

My dad and brother helped out a great deal with the laps. They may have enjoyed the work, somehow feeling as though they had contributed to the recovery cause, which was definitely the case; even if for no other reason than the family interaction between us which was generated. I can still recall one particular corner of the floor in the "back". It had a big bay window overlooking a high school across the street. I'd use that windowsill as the last pit stop toward home— "my room". Most of the time, I would arrive to the corner window revealing a cloudy, rainy and spooky day. It was still a Halloweenish to Thanksgivingish back drop of a scenery around town.

For the most part my lungs remained clear and in the big scheme of things, this was a calm recovery time frame. It may have lasted four or five solid days that I would term as good until the next barrage ensued. With some sporadic physical therapy sessions using color bands in bed or being carted down to the exercise area a few times, they were pretty uneventful. Why I tried the bench press knowing that my strength was down, I'll never know. I literally had gone from bench-pressing 210 lbs. to barely struggling with 20 or 30 lbs. You talk about a major downer, this was inconceivable to me, yet another barometer of the traumatic undertaking that my body endured back then.

I had my brother and sister finagle to get me the exercise bike like I mentioned, so that I could try and maintain some sense of flexibility and conditioning. The bike became the stage for another one of my vivid memories and flashbacks. With all of the possibilities of problems discussed prior to the transplant, one virtually inevitable issue to contend with was a trauma called mucousitis.

Again, without delving deep into the doctor jargon, this is basically a devastating and vicious attack on the mouth, throat, esophagus and related areas. All brought on as a result of the massive doses of radiation and chemotherapy administered to kill the bone marrow and, hopefully, the leukemia cells. This is a very significant hurdle to overcome due to the serious nature of damage it presents. If you could envision poison ivy blisters that ooze, or a severe burn blister, or yet a deep open wound, then place it inside of your mouth cavity on the top roof and bottom, the gums, throat, and down to the solar plexus, this is truly mucousitis. The severity also varies from patient to patient.

First and foremost, it presents a major source for infection and often times manifesting into much larger complications. It also stands to reason that a bloody, scabbed and brutally painful mouth presents major eating problems. The gums are often ravaged, as is the inner pouch on each cheek. Since my aspirations of setting world records to get out of the hospital the earliest were up in flames, I was now laying the groundwork to vie for the longest tenure ever of a patient's stay at Fred Hutch.

My mucousitis torched me big time, starting out as a rapidly progressive and burning sore throat. Then my gums started throbbing until they burst with gulps of blood cascading down the back of my throat. Next, and probably the most painful of all of these symptoms, was the splitting of both cheeks in my mouth. I had two gaping gashes that resembled a cut into a medium rare sirloin steak. You could visibly see the raw pink skin flapping about. I can say that the pain was so intense it felt as if a can of salt was being poured into those open slits every time anything entered my mouth including water or air.

To try and combat this somewhat, heavy doses of antibiotics were administered on top of the growing list of pill cocktails. In addition, a long suction hose similar to one you would use at the dentist's office was brought in. As gruesome as it sounds, the suction would pull fragments of dead tissue and blood out of my mouth to aid in healing, as well as remove the germ fertile mess away from my body. The bike comes to mind because I often recall trotting along at a snail's pace looking out of my window with this Loch ness Monster of a hose coming out of my mouth. Even today, the sounds of the slurping serpent can still be heard in Fred Hutch hallways, I'll bet.

The final mucousitis-fighting weapon was a "lollipop-sticked, foam headed, snowflake-shaped swisher resembling a toilet bowl brush, conveniently sized to swab the mouth". Patients would go through dozens of "these 'so-called' mint flavored taffies and dispose of regularly. I suppose they helped a great deal to scour and loosen but man, could they sting." I was more fortunate than some with this, and less fortunate than other patients. It ranges from one dying of mucousitis to barely getting nicked up or falling somewhere in between.

I would say that it took several weeks to get under some control and simmered down to a manageable state. This enabled us to keep pushing ahead although I must say that I still have two line scars on the inside of my mouth. During a flare up, the pain can still wipe me out this long after the fact. I have always wondered if any patients had the gashes go all the way through their cheeks. Mine did not but came about as close as it could without doing so. I wouldn't wish this one battle on anyone—let alone the entire transplant. The mucousitis once extinguished down to a residual state, had me irritable, tired and left with a raw sore throat whenever I swallowed, awash with a reverb effect bouncing off of my cheeks.

Needless to say that I was wiped out and needed to recharge for any other unforeseeable problems, that could arise. Not at the time, but now a humorous episode occurred shortly thereafter. I spent as much time in bed as I could, milking any way to avoid the laps, bikes, physical therapy and so on. I was trying to escape in my musical land of meditation, so as not to occupy my mind with the real thoughts of fear that I felt had been increasing. Perhaps I may have been placing myself in danger with this mindset; who knows, but someone on the medical staff saw it that way.

Of all of the many wonderful staff members at Fred Hutch, I developed some super-friendships while I was there. Of those, one was with a feisty physician's attendant, or known in the business as a P.A. Essentially they are doctors in every aspect except they answer to a residing MD. . This "gentleman" I guess I could call him was named Rick—I'll call him Dr. Rick. He would razz and wage mental head games with me from the beginning. Upon him seeing me in a 'lazy' mode according to his standards, he launched strategic tactics on me. One incident had Dr. Rick burst abruptly into my room and with a mellow dramatic throwing down of his clipboard; he went on a tirade of how I was a quitter. "You let me down", he griped in a disgusted, low but stern voice.

It wasn't bad acting now that I can look back on it, but even then his reverse psychology methods paid off. Just as if he knew exactly how to push my buttons—he did. Boy was I ticked off! In so many words that he launched at me, just as fast was he out the door, down the hall and gone. This completed his charade with his grumbling akin to Ma and Pa Kettle. The cartoon bears that can interpret each other, but no one else has a clue as to what the heck they're saying! Off went the mumbling about me as it faded down the corridor into the distance.

I'm sure that was a risky task to spring on a patient, given their personality. I guess he calculated that I would respond just the way that I did and not sink deeper into a shell. Perhaps I am giving him too much credit for the shrink impersonation, but I do believe he had it planned out just the way it unfolded. Rather that than him being really down on me. Right, Dr. Rick…

The "win one for the Gipper" type lecture of sorts fired me up and in taking it personally, I vowed to myself to return to the 'strip' (the hallway). Soon after this I ventured out into the hallway to cruise a lap. Obviously the whole floor took notice of any patient out of his or her room, so I wanted to send a message and prove Dr. Rick wrong. Probably playing right into his hands, my brother and dad took over the reins again to guide me around town. I surely did not cruise though; once again it was more like walking on hot coals and donning a 50-lb. boot camp backpack. I sucked a lot of wind and did the academy award winning performance as I passed the nurses' station. After what seemed like an endless journey, I passed all of the rooms, each corner and back into my lair.

I again had seemed to bounce back from an attack and felt a false sense of calmness, security and relief. The days were mounting and I think the next number after day 14 to shoot for was 45 or 90. That was a prescheduled optimistic return home date for successful patients. I don't think that I equated all of the setbacks that I was having into the big picture though.

You would think by this time that I would have learned to be wary of trouble, but a relaxing break of another week or so only set me up for another horrible downfall. This came in the form of a very nasty infection known as a gram negative. I believe there are also many specifics to this infection that I won't go into detail with but it totally rocked me big time. This was about the longest period of time up to this point that I felt a constant state of suffering without it letting up. For whatever combinations of reasons I suppose it was just a relentless torment. When I reflect on situations and give thanks, this infection incident often comes to mind. I don't know medically if this more life threatening than any of my other encounters, perhaps not, but life threatening is really the same across the board I suppose.

I'd say that I was very helpless here and didn't do anything that I can remember consciously to fight back other than will or grunt cadence for the relics here and there. Some whimpers for relief and comfort accompanied them as my infection in the bloodstream spiked fevers that would make you believe that I was making it up. Insane temperatures of 104°, 105°, 106° and, quite possibly, higher ravaged me. The risks of brain damage were imminent if not already occurring. I was packed in ice and transferred to an air-conditioned bed. I would swear that I could feel the ice melting on me as they packed it on. The throbbing throughout my body made it seem as though I had a vibrating mattress underneath me. Now I was dehydrated and slipping into what's known as septic shock.

With the green tee shirt I had the Calandra's touch to the tomb of Padre Pio, I shrouded my face in a shell-like fashion. The raging fever had me shivering with sweats and chills, both hot and cold to the point of major hallucinations. I was administered a "superpower drug" called vancomycin, I believe and, if that was in fact the correct moment, whatever it was induced a reaction that the hospital staff called "shake and bake". You would still keep the ridiculously high fevers but fluctuate with symptoms in between burning up to utterly freezing.

One of the things the staff used was microwave ovens to heat blankets constantly and wrap me up in a mummy-like fashion. Family's would dispute over who got the hottest ones as well as the quantities. I was fortunate in a bit of a dog-eat-dog scenario because I had enough family members to insure that I would have my fair share of blankets. There were plenty for all; I just think that some of the families panicked in emotional states watching as their loved ones were getting torched.

Imagine that in the span of a minute, having all of the covers completely off to fully burying yourself under them, to practically getting naked again. A nurse even placed a pencil between my teeth at one point to try and lessen the intense chattering going on. I did chip a tooth minutely and am reminded of that incident whenever I get that distinct cool sensation there. Despite that chipped tooth, my mom, sister and girlfriend hand held and fed me many a freeze pop to my mouth while I lie there shaking and trembling in bed. They were of some comfort to me, if for only the brief time it took to gnaw them up.

The staff worked non-stop like ants on a trail to keep me hanging on. The dehydration caused severe muscle cramping that was barely noticeable from the other shake and bake convulsions. I managed to blurt out some directions for Carol and my dad to massage a leg each. My hands clamped in like claws due to the contractions also adding to the helpless frustration. It just seemed like a hideous nightmare that wouldn't go away. I must have looked like someone possessed. Finally, I received a blessing when the doctors and nurses with the medicines and prayers got the insane fevers to break. I was down to a balmy 103° and feeling much better, relatively, of course.

I was hydrated heavily at regular intervals and began a new custom for me by peeing in the hand urinal off of the starboard side of the bed. It was such a great relief not to have to walk three feet to the bathroom and I actually got a bit of a high in not having to leave the bed. The infection seemed to be responding to treatment and, officially, I believe no brain damage was detected; although my friends and I sometimes wonder about that. Another crisis had seemed to be overcome and the 'one day at a time' motto, which echoed through the halls surely showed why with this battle.

Naturally, the similarities between the families in what they were going through brought some of them closer together. Several families bonded with mine and among them were good old patient Paige's parents. Her mother and my sister enjoyed each other's company when it could be shared as a pattern of crisis, humor, collapse, crisis, and more humor was unfolding. I'm sure that had something to do with the seriousness of everything and human nature with the defense mechanisms coming into play.

The "Mata Hari's" that they were, Paige's mom, my girlfriend and my sister Carol, decided to go out and treat themselves to a new hairdo. All of them looked fine as they were, so I thought, but women will be women and off they went. As a team they ventured out into the downtown Seattle area or outskirts, not knowing much of anything about the surroundings. Evidently the ladies agreed on a salon and the makeovers began. They sought out new looks and that's just what they got all right. Three perms in all and three hideous outcomes!

As deathly ill as I was I had to use precious reserves of energy to hold in my laughter in front of them as they emerged into my room. Standing in front of me was absolutely fried hair to the roots. What a laugher for me! None of them were happy. They each had received cuts, perms and whatever color jobs they selected that totally backfired big time. I think my girlfriend stole the show with scorched orangish hair badly resembling "Annie". Paige's mom came in a close second with the retro Shirley Temple doo. Carol managed to salvage some dignity with mousse, curlers, and a smoke and mirrors coverup. Even though I would look better in a clown wig that was to be bought for me the upcoming New Year for sure! It was just what I needed to persevere at this point.

The holidays were approaching so I could focus positive energy on the time of the seasons. I can say for sure that with my personality, the timing for this transplant was perfect even if I had no say in the matter. If I could have scripted it to unfold at the time of year that it did, I would have . The late summer into football season with the summer to prepare for it; football throughout the fall and winter plus the holiday season to help keep my morale up. That is how it looked anyhow to me, the bad hair days was just a sideshow.

As my condition briefly continued to plateau in terms of the problems I was encountering, I had a few bright spots and special moments to also touch upon here. What may not sound like any type of big deal whatsoever, to me this was yet another example of the hospital staff's true compassion and concern. My throat and mouth seemed to respond and take comfort in those cold ice pops, ice cream and plain crushed ice in small bits. Outside of grape and cherry, I think, my taste buds were quickly fading away due to the radiation, chemo side effects and or the mucousitis itself. My mind was conjuring up those "good old Wildwood boardwalk chocolate dips on a sugar cone days", and the tastes of a big chocolate Dairy Queen shake. My all time favorite was a Mr. Softee shake from the big blue and white truck that drove through the old neighborhood streets in Chester, PA, but Seattle was quite a ways off!

One of the nurses, Laney, got wind of my craving along with some input from my other nurse, Linda. One afternoon Laney mentioned that she might be able to stop on her way into work one day at the Dairy Queen to grab me a shake. That was so cool to hear! This intense craving was ravaging my remaining taste buds. If I could beat the clock and drink one before they fizzled out all the way, I figured I'd have a bit of good old enjoyment restored somewhat. Well, lo and behold, the next day, sure enough, Laney moseyed in with the stash in hands. Good old Dennis the Menace on the cup with the big red straw that could be slurped with no worries of a "cave in"! This was great. Holding the cup and gulping that perfect creamy rich consistency mix down took me away like the Calgon bath commercial. For those few minutes anyway I'd come as close as I could to forgetting what was happening to me in the real world!

The biggest part of this little tidbit of information was that there were no Dairy Queens in the city area! Laney, I later found out, had to drive out of her way, about a half hour each way, to reach the closest DQ. Can you imagine a regular nurse doing this? I was so appreciative that she did this for me, but then again this was no ordinary staff of nurses. They were the Fred Hutch "into a nearby phone booth, super nurses". Why should I have been surprised? All in a day's work for them, Linda, Laney, Anne, Doyla, and every BMT nurse I ever had, thank you so much, you will be reward ten-fold for sure.

With these few humorous stories that I mentioned, the fact was that outside of my room other patients were being pounded as hard, if not harder. Sadly, a couple of others had passed away due to complications from the transplant, namely, loss of graft, infection or GVHD. Just a glimpse or mention of any bad news would unnerve virtually the whole floor. I wish the subtleties of good news circulated had boosted morale as much as the sad news brought us all down.

Even though I had made acquaintances with a few of the patients, I never got to know all of them. But even so everyone felt everybody else's roller coaster of emotions to some extent. As I would hear the bits and pieces of other goings on, I did try to again refocus after each hit I would take emotionally. I really did have more than enough concerns to handle myself but I wish that it were that easy to block out the other patients' news.

One of the things that did make me focus was, of course, those daily counts, blood draws, medications and so forth. Lord knows the cyclosporin and the various other liquid elixirs were enough to make you throw in the towel as it was. Another was the daily platelets brought in to infuse in me. This was ions easier than woofing down those sloppy cocktails while holding my breath so as not to toss my cookies all over the place. The platelets in the early going were spun off and delivered from the local blood banks from nameless and generous donors; "Yet another hidden group of heroes, contributing to this huge undertaking to save lives." I'll try to talk about attempting to thank all of the people later on as that will pose a monumental task for sure.

These platelets were required due to the fact that my new bone marrow had not as yet begun to produce sufficient amounts needed to survive. Many days my platelets would be "chewed up" or used as fast as they went into me. They came in tiny little bags and varied in color, which always puzzled me. It even spooked me initially as did the sensations I received as they were infused. I would get a tingle or shiver while clearly feeling a cooler temperature I surmised from the liquid going into my body. Due to the fact of my graft coming in so slowly and the GVHD itself, my receiving platelets lasted the whole duration of my stay and even at home for nearly a year afterward.

As I mentioned, the football season was in full gear and I kept abreast of the action almost as well as I would have from back home. Even though I remained in critical condition and was having complications, in relation to where I had recently been and now was, the staff had another surprise in store for me. This one was huge at the time and I didn't have a clue it was coming.

My social worker and volunteer, Ron, felt the time was as good as any to spring it on me. First, I heard the buzzing of commotion in the halls and by the way that people flew around and briskly walked by my door, you might have thought that there was a code blue somewhere. Thank goodness that wasn't the case. The next thing I knew a couple of photographers knocked on my already open door with big smiles on their faces. As they introduced themselves, I watched them dip their hands into the hanging box of disposable masks on the door. When they grabbed a handful more than just for them, I became even more curious.

All of a sudden I was seeing faces of men that I knew from television only. These guys were Seattle Sea Hawks. My string pulling social worker had swindled five or six players to come cheer me up. It was so great! I think my dad may have enjoyed it more than me! Due to the masks covering the player's faces, it was difficult to distinguish everyone but clearly I remember a few of them.

They were very down to earth and personable, so it wasn't very long before we exchanged football stories and razzed each other a bit. I received a team photo with autographs along with bedside pictures taken. The one player that I had hoped to see was former Penn State running back, Curt Warner. He was an all-pro with the Sea Hawks and I followed his career. In fact, I have a poster size photograph that I took myself of him crossing the goal line to beat Nebraska on their way to winning the National Championship in 1982. Curt was not there but I gave the players a run down to relay back to him and to give best wishes.

We concluded the visit of about forty-five minutes or so and, no sooner did I lie back to ponder what just went on, in walked Curt Warner himself. Penn State's all time leading rusher, him and I, person to person, it was great! Of course, I had a picture taken with him and tried to enjoy the moment as best as I could. I've heard that he has a car dealership in Seattle and hope to stop in and say hi again someday. Once I got the pictures back, it was hard to tell who looked better, Curt or me with my orange skin, slits for eyes and mask covered mouth, "it's pretty close, ha ha". Thanks very much for taking the time Curt, and all of the visiting members of the team. God bless you all!

Well, with this nice boost to my morale, and anticipating all of the holiday bowl games to watch, it would have made a nice segue to the next story if I had a continuation of good fortune. As you can see, the true roller coaster pattern that I mentioned is unfolding. As truth is stranger than fiction, I didn't make this stuff up. The streaks of ups and downs were uncanny! Of course this is much better than to have all downs, or I wouldn't be writing my story.

My appetite was becoming non-existent. I just had no appetite as fast as that, and even what I did eat was nothing to brag about. As with the many symptoms unfolded to a patient having a bone marrow transplant, my lack of hunger was consistent with being "bombed, basted and fried". The real tip that this could be more serious was the duration and accompanying lethargy. The final giveaway that I was in trouble again was dark urine and the lack of it, which was discolored and pungent barely filling the urinal. In about the time it took resting through a nap and eagerly peeing in a cup for the doctors to analyze; the results were back; "The true meaning of the term stat". The next attack was on and this time it was my failing kidneys.

With the lousy track record that I had compiled thus far, the first line of order for me was to be placed back in the bubble, a.k.a. the L.A.F. room. The same coop that had me climbing walls in just a few days the first time. The same pen I went AWOL from and that was before I had the transplant, the infections, liver failure and the other problems to boot! This is the last thing that I wanted to hear. If hell has different levels, I was being demoted to the basement in my mind; right back to being the hamster in the Habitrail. The boy in the plastic bubble had a mansion compared to these units. Again I had to find a quick way and get a grip from the looming panic attack in my mind. "Just relax", I'd think and, "It will all be okay." One day at a time was becoming one hour at a time.

Well, they convinced me that I had better get my butt along with my new growing marrow over to the other side into a laminar air flow room. Everybody packed up shop along with my things and all of the cards that I was receiving and had growing on a wall. The Santa picture, my Penn State boxer shorts, the relics, everything; I had to decide what things would go into the bubble with me so they could be autoclaved, or "sterilized" before I received them. Once I did that it was off to the scrub down decontamination shower, into another "moon suit" and over to the dark side. For my family it was just a short walk across the hall, for me it was like preparing for a shuttle launch.

How could I have missed explaining about powders, lotions and ointments? Instead of depriving you of this ritual, I'll institute it right here because in 1986 at Hutch, powders and ointments went hand-in-hand with laminar airflow rooms. Once the patient maneuvers out of the 'moon suit' and over the threshold of air, into the controlled environment, these powders and ointments were to serve as your "friend and ally" of further protection so to speak. Also, of course, was their trusty companion, the extra long Q-tip swab.

The christening of the L.A.F., which gets more intimate than you or I or most people, would care to know. The purpose of these applications is to try and build a further barrier wall from the body and infections. A third line of defense, I suppose, in a manner of speaking, every orifice of your body has to be coated. The sprays aren't so bad as I recollect because they were only used in your nostrils just like a decongestant. The powders were obviously used all over your skin areas. This was a head to toe application not to be skimped on—between the toes, the groin, underarms, etc. It got a little annoying because the process had to be repeated three to four times a day. I was really getting sick and the weakness I incurred made it more of a struggle to get up and do the procedures. I imagine that I could have had a nurse gown up and assist me, but I either didn't think of it or felt uncomfortable asking.

I didn't forget the Q-tip and ointments, which were the least desirable of all. Besides feeling a little degraded of some dignity being stripped, I had to bend over the slide bed rail and get this goop up and around my backside. Also crossing the front of my private area and fully cover the insides of my ears to round it off. It felt like peanut butter had been caked on me in these areas but I know it was a small price to pay for added protection from the germs.

Of course I never did become comfortable with those procedures and honestly, I probably cheated some with respect to the number of applications and thoroughness. Now that I had a sealed-up butt and all, I was once again on the inside looking out from behind the plastic wall with the robot arms. With just a simple partition, separating me from my sister outside playing with the gloves, Carol grabbing me was all that it took to make me feel the way that I did. I don't know if I mentioned that I get a bit claustrophobic in certain situations.

Well, the transition was made and I was in my new pad, now the main reason why I was back in there took center stage. Right away I didn't equate failing kidneys with kidney failure. That sounds odd, I suppose, but it blew right by me in those terms. It didn't sound as final. The counts were rolling in and steadily dropping or elevating—whichever the case may have been. I believe it was the creatinine levels that revealed the toxicity in my system.

The inability of my kidneys to purify my body of certain poisons was just what was happening. I think that I was given extra fluids and the drug allopurinol again for assistance to the kidneys, but nothing short of trying dialysis seemed to work. That is, until we powwowed around and decided to storm Heaven again. With the past track record of all those 'coincidences' that were mounting, why not keep trying some more.

I think I slept through the night and woke up to a big ugly dialysis machine, double-parked right in front of my plastic window. It terrified me to the point of having those heart misfires of adrenaline. I had no idea how it worked, I just remembered a few of the people that I knew who had to endure that horrible process. To them it was a Godsend in prolonging, or saving their lives. I can't say how much empathy I have for anyone undergoing dialysis treatments.

My already growing array of tubes, holes and lines going in me would have made it difficult to cut into me even more. Perhaps they were going to use my Hickman catheter or install another femoral catheter in me, or just drill through my back into the kidneys. I had no clue of what to envision. As if things weren't bad enough, my other blood counts were erratic. That may have been related but the anxiety just rushed through me to the point of a collapse. I was witnessing first hand how much our body's can withstand pressure-wise.

Before long my dad, mom, sister, brother and girlfriend were all in for a visit and we made plans for a Father Carmody visit. I had the bat signal out for him and he would be over that evening. Meanwhile my total fear of that dialysis machine gave me a brainstorm to buy some time. Isn't it funny how some things strike fear into some people and not other's. Anyway, I came up with a diversionary tactic to buy some time to mentally prepare for this threatening undertaking. I plea-bargained with the doctors after a host of opposition to hold off my dialysis treatment for one more day. I was becoming a reputable car salesman at this point with the wheeling and dealings of transplant floor life. To my credit, or against it, I was pampered with an extension.

I made this out to be such a thorn in my side mentally, my stinking artist mentality of imagination. Like another cartoon I remember as a kid. There was a boy, Ralph, who was always in trouble at school for daydreaming with his overblown perspective scenarios. This was the case with me—and my race against the clock, hostage situation in my irrational and sometimes scared mind.

Trying desperately not to panic, I comforted myself in thought that at the very least I'd have one more night's sleep and a day of not being "dialysised". We all prayed with and among ourselves with my intentions to have God spare me from the procedure or, at least, help me to endure it. I knew that I could do it physically, I estimated, but it was my being 'my own worst enemy' that I feared the most.

That morning turned to afternoon and rolled into evening and the latest count checks still revealed a declining kidney function. I then began pounding myself that I had now wasted a whole day's treatment and would regret it. I waited a little while longer when finally Fr. Carmody paced in. We all conversed socially and informally as a group for a bit, to lighten up the mood of us all. After a while just Father and I quietly spoke between the plastic divider wall, "kind of like a see through confessional". I tried to remain upbeat and positive, again on the outside but inside, honestly, I was crumbling.

My urine was horrible with the smell and color just on the golden side of brown. Weakness was taking over my personality but amidst all of our talking, I conveyed to Father that I really did have great faith so I thought, and I needed to dig it out into the forefront. We prayed for about 20 minutes or so and he finished up with some positive and sincere small talk. For whatever reason, that night I went to bed and slept very soundly, just the opposite of every other LA.F. night.

One of the tricks I picked up on was the control button to the speed of the doorway barrier fan. I noticed that the button was within my reach with a pencil. Nurses would turn it way down low at night and all of the sounds of the hallway would pester the heck out of me. By tapping the switch to high, it gave me enough of a continuous whoosh to drown out virtually all the exterior ambience. This tactic began the same night of "dialysis eve" I believe. More importantly, before retiring for the evening I had come to some sense of acceptance with respect to the dialysis treatments. "It couldn't be any worse than what I have already endured and could possibly help to get better", I concluded. That didn't sway my preference not to have the dialysis, of course, and I emphatically made that clear to God before "turning in".

I have lost track of the "coincidences" so far that have been occurring to me throughout the story. Thank the Lord that there are many, many witnesses to attest to my dictations. The next day came swiftly and upon my waking eyes, I peeked a glimpse of the 'machine'. It was still parked right there but little did anyone know my body would not need to be subjected to hooking up to it. With the push of an eraser I clicked the fan motor down to reveal the bustling of what sounded like people coming my way. The click, click of high heels and dress shoes echoing so slightly along with inflections of growing cadence. Not long after that, in burst a group of three or four nurses and doctors grunting "good news, good news, great news". "This morning your kidney functions are perfectly normal! This just has never happened around here that dramatically, ever! Possibly with some dialysis treatments but not without it that's for sure." You are one lucky fellow, fellow!"

The guy blasting out those statements was Dr. Buckner. He reminded me of that Trapper John, M.D. TV guy. Needless to say my family and I were elated. The first order of business I told them was to get that darn machine the heck out of my room! I still felt absolutely terrible but with the mountain being lifted that I had created mentally over this mess, I felt a load of weight drop away from my conscience. So chalk up another one for the God who works in mysterious ways, or place it in the growing coincidence column. Your choice, either way it happened!

With my kidney failure back to normal in the span of one evening, my blood counts were still tipsy at best. I remained lethargic and still wondered if the kidney problem set my counts plummeting or if it was something unrelated. Even though they were dropping, it was hard not to gloat over my near miss situation with my kidneys. Besides, those numbers were always off of the danger zone. They were a definite concern, of course, but nevertheless not a crisis situation and I didn't want to look for reasons to worry, I had enough. My next task was to try and finagle a deal to get out of the bubble and back into a 'normal' room. My grounds for this appeal tactic were a.) I evaded the kidney crisis, and b.), my sanity.

With the help of my family and my social worker, we pulled a coup. In just a few days I had gone full circle back into my old room, technically my third. Naturally, with Christmas on the way, I directed Carol to decorate my room again. This time she even brought in the heavy artillery, twinkle lights! Thanksgiving was a day or so away but I wanted to get a jump on everything before Black Friday. You might have thought that I was going shopping somewhere the way that I hastened those elves to decorate.

My Thanksgiving was quiet and uneventful for the most part. As with most holidays, I go through emotional highs and lows, so this was no exception. I couldn't help reflecting on my very good fortunes and blessings while, at the same time, feeling lonely even though I was among family; perhaps missing something or some place to go. In reality my Thanksgivings consisted of football and family dinner. I had that here but still my mind stumped me again.

The remaining taste buds I had receiving signals could barely distinguish turkey from cardboard. I think all of my food was autoclaved anyway so it wouldn't have mattered even if I could have tasted it. Carol and I joked as I mocked like a person feasting on gourmet delicacies when, in reality, I couldn't taste much of what the heck I was eating! We all had a sense of humor about it and were in very good spirits then because my remaining immediate family members were scheduled to fly in.

I believe that my nieces, Danielle and Nicole, arrived earlier than this and surprised my sister. They are her children and Carol eventually made arrangements for them to stay in Seattle as well as go to school there also. They were somewhere between second and fourth grades, I'd guess. My brother's wife, Denise, and their children, Tommy, Tony and Lauren all came in to surprise me by sneaking into my room while I was undergoing a procedure. It really made things a lot better getting to see everyone.

I remember the floor seeming more quiet than usual; a sense of peace among all of the critically ill patients. The biggest memory of that holiday was simply reflecting on life and trying to grasp what was going on. I can still say that I really find myself thinking this nightmare was a dream and not really happening, only to realize that it definitely was happening. I find even now that it is still hard to take it all in and comprehend this huge undertaking.

My mother recalls the rest of my family eating Thanksgiving dinner at a nearby soup kitchen for the needy. I was oblivious to the fact that money was so tight for reasons other than my mounting bills. Simple everyday costs of living on top of it all took its toll on their savings. So, needless to say, everyone was further humbled with that experience. I've since gone back myself to help out at a few of these centers and I feel that everybody would appreciate their blessing much more if they were to do the same. I assure you that you will have a changed perspective of things.

Another patient passed away shortly after Thanksgiving, which again eroded at my rusting armor of mental toughness. A piece of you goes when someone else goes. My counts were hovering somewhat, not increasing or decreasing. On one hand that was good, but on the other hand, much still needed to take place engraftment-wise. My mouth, my hips, spine, joints, you name it, were increasingly becoming bothersome to me. You could almost feel somebody or something turning up the volume on the pain. I would go from having heat flashes to ungodly cold surges in my fingertips and toes. I have never had frostbite but judging by what patients who have had it say, I would believe it came close to paralleling their descriptions sensation wise.

My gums would throb, an occasional nosebleed and sporadic attacks of those killer cramps would dive bomb my legs, hands or jaw at any given moment. It all became so debilitating to me that the doctors prescribed morphine. Initially, I think it was given to me in pill form possibly combined with Versed or something similar. Whatever the mixture, my pain tolerance was dramatically improved. As a matter of fact, the shot of Demerol or Versed was so successful; I'd look forward to the rush of the needle injection into my Hickman line for relief. I figured that I could rest assured that no pain would rule my demeanor while being taken care of in this manner.

I would often conk out soon after my shot and it became routine for me to sleep through the pain, I believe for me this was a magnificent tool and I came to combine it with my wordless music tape that I made. By doing that I could totally try and submit to letting go and relaxing to alleviate all of the stress. It was a pretty successful ritual for that stretch and I don't know if I could have maintained my composure or endured that pain spell without it. Of course, everyone who has been through serious hospitalizations or medicine use knows that the downside to drugs of this nature, are the side effects themselves. I could never stand to place myself in those predicaments unless it was a very serious situation such as this, because of the mood swings and overall changes you incur which come close to surpassing the initial problems.

Luckily for me, my lousy mood outbursts occurred at times which I didn't offend too many people, I hope. I know I was snippy to my family at times and my nurse, Linda, got hammered somewhat. I have since apologized to all of the recipients of my tirades but they all understood. Except that is for a clown and a local Santa who came to visit all of the patients. I don't remember if I dreamed it or, if I threw both of them out of my room with a verbal bon voyage to put it politely. No one else remembers either but I do have pictures of a clown and a Santa in my room and my look is cruddy; "If I booted you out Bozo and Santa, sorry about that". Perhaps that's why I only got a couple of gifts that year?

One of the next things I felt I had to attempt was an escape from the hospital for a visit to the apartment at some point during the holidays. This was a pretty much out of the question feat with my track record being what it was. Some of the nurses planted a seed n my head that if I could get a break with everything and stabilized at bit, I may be able to finagle a three-hour pass to leave briefly. Alas music to my ears! Nearly three months had now gone by since I had last breathed real fresh air or stepped outside. The doctors tired to be low key with this idea since I had so many complications and everything. My main concern was to get lucky and not have anything else pop up out of the blue.

Just in case, though, I had my family prepare a strategy to make the trip if it came to pass that I could go. The only major factors to work out were the van ride and making sure that everything I needed, such as platelets, medicines, etc. would be administered before hand. As a stroke of luck would have it, I felt lousy, but nothing new had developed. If that alone could hold up and I could get out of the coup, this Christmas simply feeling lousy was great with me.

Some time passed with all of the, "regular goings on" happening. Such "regular things", as high fevers, pain, skin burns and the itching for example and basically, everything that I had discussed earlier. They were all pretty much commonplace with ninety-nine percent of all of the bone marrow transplant patients in the hospital in 1986. So when the time came and nothing else symptom wise had been added to that list, the doctors felt comfortable enough to grant me a three-hour pass after all. The family apartment was only a couple of blocks away so if anything popped up I could be whisked quickly back to the lovely confines of Fred Hutch.

Christmas Eve arrived and for me, even thought this mess that I was in had dampened my spirits, just like in "The Grinch Who Stole Christmas" when his heart grew ten sizes or whatever, I still had plenty of reserves to bask in the holiday moment. I think that I really enjoyed my Christmas Eve day even though I was in a hospital room bed. The fuel of anticipating my Christmas Day excursion to "Monticello Lodge" was invigorating to say the least. After all of these months, I couldn't wait to breathe some fresh air once again.

It finally arrived, Christmas morning. The Christmas of 1986 was, I believe, probably the most memorable day in my life to that point. Nothing has compared to what I experienced in a personal sense. I mean I didn't smell or receive any flowers, or have visions or anything like that. I say that it was so very memorable because of my real sense of awareness of what was going on in my life. Absolutely everything was in focus for me that day. I felt it from the moment I officially declared myself up from a "fantastically lousy night of sleep".

I guess around 10 AM or so my dad and sister came in to see me. I believe that my girlfriend-then, may have spent the night on the cot, I'm not sure. The nice, serene feeling that you can get on Christmas from the still ambiance in the air was affecting me in a very positive way. One look in the mirror should have "bah humbugged" the whole deal holiday-wise by the way that I looked. You could sum it all up in a quote that I heard a year later and will mention that in a bit. In the meantime I slowly but eagerly prepared for my trek "home away from home away from home".

Of course I had to uphold the honor of the official, unofficial dress code of a BMT patient. This called for extra measures. Not just sweatpants, sweatshirt, white socks and slippers, but brand new sweatpants, sweatshirt and white socks! Same only slippers but who knew! I'd further dress up the attire with the vaunted knitted cap and, finally, the outfit maker and sign of the times, the lemon yellow mask! You could play the theme from "Shaft" as I prepared because that's the type of swagger I felt. The pre-game festivities of medicines, platelets and everything were finished, so around one o'clock or so I slipped into my corduroy 'Fonzie" jacket and away we slugged.

I set no time records I'll tell you because I walked at a snails pace for sure. Just the change of scenery from passing the elevator upon doing my laps had my mental awareness senses picking up the "new environment". Stepping into an elevator once again was even, and the swoosh of my belly lifting ever so slightly from the decent had my heart pumping. I got a little bit of an adrenaline rush just from the trip and van ride down the street alone.

My radar was in high gear. I remember sitting up in the front seat of the van without even asking if I could. I just hopped, well actually was plopped in and started jabbering with the shuttle driver. I believe his name was Leonard, he could have passed for Shaft himself; he was so cool. "Who's the man who can drive that van? Shaft", actually, Leonard. Driving the length of three blocks or so, I resembled the family dog going for a car ride with my eyes bulging to drink in all of the scenery. My head shot in every direction, scanning for fire hydrants practically, I was so excited.

When we did arrive into the valet-type curve at the lobby, I thanked the driver and calmly stepped down barely assisted. I inhaled the most refreshing breath of fresh air since I had been in the Pennsylvania Mountains. The day was briskly cool and cloudy and a lot milder that the East Coast winters I'd grown accustomed to while growing up. Often back East, snow would have fallen already but the only Seattle snow here was on top of Mt. Rainier. From what I'd heard that was about as close as I would get to seeing any around Seattle itself.

Obviously I was pretty excited about being out although my energy level was way down. The fact that I was unhooked and free from all of the I.V. pumps and machines lessened the load by about forty pounds I'd say. My newly found freedom was just enough to let me make the difficult trek up the staircase. The apartment was on the second floor and had a balcony overlooking a small side street. From this vantage point I could see a good bit of Christmas decorations around and about the area; A Santa here, a Nativity scene there and, of course, the sprinkling of many eclectic lights.

Not to be outdone our family always had a tradition of turning our homes into the North Pole. Since this was the next best thing, Carol and all of the elves performed magic on our cave, I mean "Taj Mahal". That's a bit harsh because home truly is where you hang your hat. These guys hung a lot more than that with all of the decorations! First, the front door was wrapped like a big present in bright red foil with green ribbons and a bow. Next wrapped around that were colored twinkle lights strung all along the weathered door jam. From the moment we paced into the apartment, the determination to celebrate Christmas as normal as possible was clearly evident, despite or should I say, in spite, of the conditions we were all facing.

The first thing that I noticed inside was that a white Christmas had fallen here anyhow. I guess it does snow in Seattle because our window was avalanched in with wind drifts of blown accumulation. Well, really in actuality the crew had made paper windowpanes and sprayed the fake snow on from a can. Complete with Santa and the reindeer streaking across the skies of Seattle. It was so cool.

Next were stockings dangling about from the walls. Mom's, Dad's, Danielle's, Nicole's, my girlfriend's, Carol's and mine. Garland was strewn from the ceiling and a sprinkling of lit candles accompanied by a few twinkle lights made it even more inviting. The finishing touches were some Christmas carols playing lightly in the background for ambience and, of course, the tree itself. Our tree was closer to the Charlie Brown variety than the White House skyscraper.

Our tree symbolized to me everything we were there for. Carol had borrowed a very old artificial tree from the apartment manager and I must say that by the time she got finished with it, anyone would have been proud to display it in their home. It had lights, balls, garland and tinsel too. Underneath the tree were our gifts. Most years found our tree barely visible due to the many packages camouflaging its presence. Even though my parents were not wealthy by any stretch of the imagination, they still managed to bombard me with gifts as a child. Perhaps they did know Santa better than I did.

This year was different. Seven of us in one little room and maybe there was a total of ten gifts to divvy up. Actually it turned out to be one for everybody except that Danielle and Nicole each received a teddy bear. When Charlie Brown's friend, Linus I believe, made the statement that "Christmas isn't about giving presents, it's about giving yourself", that statement in the story, fictional or not, is very difficult to top. Nothing at all could be closer to the truth in my mind. Maybe it had to come down to all of this for me to thoroughly realize it though. That phrase was lived out by my family and most likely every other family going through the transplant ordeal. For some more than others perhaps, but I'd estimate that the numbers of personal reflection that Christmas was pretty high.

The Christmas story of the Birth of Our Lord, Jesus Christ, as depicted in the Silent Night song had me envisioning what that moment must have been like; very cold, quiet, difficult, intense yet wonderfully beautiful for all mankind. I combined this thought with my previous reflections of looking to the stars at night and visualized myself as being there with the few onlookers. Coming back to earth I drank up the encirclement of my family being there with me so far from home. It was such a calm, serene and comforting moment even though we really were two thousand miles from home. All of these people loved me and took time out of their lives to save mine along with the whole medical staff. And somewhere out there was the person who made it all possible besides God, that person being my donor.

For legal reasons it was against the law for me to know who he or she was. I thought of that person on Christmas and knew that somewhere else somebody had given to me of his or her self. "No greater love hath he who would lay down their life for a fellowman." That love was conveyed to me and yet a life did not have to be given. Many transplant organs are from deceased donors who fulfilled God's words, but my story had two bonuses. One being the donor, and two, he or she was still alive and well. I definitely intended to find this person someday, some way!

We all enjoyed Christmas Day, masks or no masks. It was and still is a beautiful memory for me. It may have appeared humble and plain to the naked eye, but to the heart and soul it couldn't have been much better, except for my having to be in the predicament that I was in to realize it perhaps. I was so taken by the moment of Christmas outside of a bubble after the time spent in it, that I cannot express to you completely, what a great gift I received. I just know that the feelings I have drawing from my Christmas of 1986 are ones that every person should be able to experience and keep for a lifetime of reflection.

After basking in the comfort and cozy confines of the modest apartment improvised by my family, I'd say that we all had an uplifting visit, and I then returned to the hospital. Even though it was for only three measly hours, I got a good boost from it all. I now had even more incentive to try and get to the point of staying at the apartment full time as an outpatient and only be in the hospital for three hours a day; "A good old role reversal of sorts". No one could say if or whenever, that time would come, due to my erratic counts and varied complications I was producing; Also, because they weren't God. This inner motto that I adopted within myself must have evolved with all of the religious connotations and conversely the pummeling I was experiencing. I affirmed mentally that no bad news could stay permanent if God didn't want it to. If I could convince myself that no matter what would happen, if anything and what bad news I may receive from the doctors, it was just that—simply news from the doctors, humans just like me. No disrespect to them but on the contrary, I also thought that they could be perceived as the hands of God.

St. Padre Pio encouraged people to exhaust the ways and means of medical science in conjunction with prayer. "Pray, hope and don't worry", he preached. "Trust in the infinite wisdom, goodness, and mercy of almighty God." I don't know if I can take any credit for the state of mind that I acquired other than the fact that I developed a habit of bugging the hell out of heaven; more politely stated by Fr. Fahey, "storm Heaven".

All of that which I have mentioned about my renewed found attitude internally does not mean that I became Superman. By no means! As you will see I conveyed all of the same emotions as most patients. I just think to myself how much of a degree worse my mental frame of mind would have been if I didn't improve on it in this manner. I'll confidently wager that I may very well have died just from a mental breakdown alone because I was on the verge of one with the stress of all this before my emotional reprieve. At that time you could feel a sick, engulfing presence, which "felt of death itself".

With the rest of the week of holiday time to be spent in my hospital bed, my next crutch to pass the time with was football, and lots of it. Between NFL games and the college bowls, I would use up a lot of TV hours feasting on pigskin participation. Being the football freak that I am, you would sometimes think I'm still playing. Like all of the pretty woman who have exercise videos today, I should have made one on how to do aerobics as a volcano erupting, vocal, jump around TV spectator fan. I know I work as hard as those lady instructors, but who would go for a bald, masked dude with yellow and red eyes, tubes all over the place, and expensive blue beeping pumps as weights; No one, but Howard Stern perhaps.

One of the fun things as I mentioned earlier was that the Jets were 10–1 after defeating the hometown team, the Sea Hawks, with a late field goal, I believe. They managed to advance into the playoffs for the first time in a few years so I could watch the big game or games if they could continue to win. Even more exhilarating was that Penn State was playing Miami in the Fiesta Bowl for the national championship. Ironically, my two favorite teams, having great seasons at the same time and, just when I was being nuked and bombed to boot! Every fan knows that Penn State has perennially been a championship or bowl contender but, ask any Jet fan how rough times have been and you'll know how sweet this moment was for me.

Anyway, this all turned out to be a great diversion to occupy my mind and overall time while my body attempted to respond and heal. Of course I still felt horrible but mainly in spurts and intervals. For me, football alleviated some of the aches, pains and twitches I had in the mix. I conjured up another brainstorm of sorts to escape again. No rocket science here, but I first simply planted a seed to maybe get another pass for the Fiesta Bowl. I then discretely pestered the heck out of them.

The days were going by and the Jets lost to Cleveland while my dad and I cringed and grunted. Like the old beer commercial where the guy takes his dog in to the game through the television screen, I would have taken my dog Yuke and gone in through my screen if I could have. Well a couple more bowl games were played and New Year's Day was up next, a virtual smorgasbord of football! I could accept watching these in the hospital room but the Penn State game was so big that I just had to be pump free! I actually think they moved the game back to the January second so every one could see it.

The game was slated to start around 8 or 9 p.m., so it presented a bit of a challenge to the staff if I was to be able to leave. My family assured the doctors that they would rush me right back if anything what so ever happened. That plus the fact that I was so pumped up for it gave them no alternative to refuse, just the incentive to oblige. It was positive waves. One of my favorite movies *"Kelly's Heroes"* had a character named "Odd Ball" who talked about those positive and negative waves all of the time. I think, to the doctors, I was an oddball all right but this wasn't a movie.

As it turned out, my overall condition was acceptable for the doctors to let me out for the game. My excitement level and adrenaline was so high. If it hadn't been for my body being beat up the way that it was my mind was almost the same as if I was well and back home getting ready to watch. I hid a nosebleed and was off to the apartment to see (and participate, if I had any say in the matter) the game. Now that I look back on it I wonder if God let me enjoy this game so much because of what was waiting in the wings for me. I'll file it as another modest "coincidence". I was even able to taste food that night which was a bit odd due to the fact that my taste buds had stopped working shortly after Christmas.

Carol made shrimp and the cocktail sauce was awesome, the little bit that I had. The reason that I remember tasting so well was the hot sauce. I sure wouldn't have wasted their money woofing down shrimp that I couldn't taste. It started out of curiosity by me dipping into that hot spicy dip, and upon biting down the most outer regions of my taste buds were lit up! Maybe I'm making a big deal out of nothing because many patients can taste food as well. But by the same token, many patients swiftly lost their taste pallet for any sensation other than pain. All that I know is that I couldn't taste anything. Then I could and then I couldn't again for months and months! Needless to say, I scoffed down enough shrimp to turn into one.

Anyone who saw the 1987 Fiesta Bowl knows what an exciting game it was. A classic for the books, which on the first play from scrimmage, it looked as if all of my finagling to see this game was for naught. Miami dominated early and then it evened out to a stalemate. Finally, the Penn State defense rose to the occasion and slammed the door on Miami with 5 or 6 seconds left on the clock. A final play to see who would win and a Penn State interception by Linebacker U sealed the Nittany Lions victory 14–10 adding another national championship, how sweet it was! I wanted to touch on these bright spots along the way because they certainly differed from the norm.

From the moment that the holidays had passed it seemed like the whole roof began to fall in. Or with my roller coaster analogy, I was on the very top ready to plunge down the steep rails and toss my cookies, as my old girlfriend Kristen used to say to me on those Wildwood rides. Well, no more than two or three days later I spiked a fever that was higher than the norm for a patient at that point of the procedure. The tests were run to try and trace the origin of infection but nothing as of yet was showing up.

With the three-hour passes I was getting, it kind of spoiled me into expecting to get one here or there routinely. Since I really didn't feel much worse and my fever hovered around 101° or so, I somehow schmoozed another escape. Besides 101° was nothing to me now as I can say that I survived a 106°+ death threat! This was to be my last pit stop to the Monticello because my sister and dad pulled some strings to upgrade the apartment and move over to the First Hill complex. That complex was considered a step up in creature comforts and amenities.

About an hour into my "three hour tour", I indiscreetly started having massive pains in my groin and lower abdomen. I may have been foolish to play it down since it was at a persistent level and duration. I just had my mom or Carol fill up a hot water bottle to place between my legs and over my groin. The hotter the better I demanded. The heat was so soothing that I was taken by a false sense of relief for the moment. I sat and "roasted my nuts". Pardon the pun, but it's funny to me now. Back then I'm sure that I wasn't making any jokes. Anyway, I had received a letter from one of the guys back home and it was great to hear from the home front.

Although I stated that I didn't want any visitors, if in fact they could afford to fly out, but I never said anything about not writing. I imagine that the fund raiser video sent out was their best form of communication; that and the giant get-well card that everyone signed. Some wrote and some didn't. Well with that the pass came and went so back to the hospital I trekked. We even got so bold as to try and walk the few blocks occasionally instead of using the van, but since I was in discomfort, the van it was. Those walks by the way were nothing of beauty either if you watched me wander and sway on my frail and deteriorating legs.

I don't know if I mentioned the lower pain I was having to the doctors or not but nevertheless, it remained, as did the fever. The thing was though that no abnormalities were showing up on any test results. The only speculation was that it was marrow and or GVHD related and possibly graft versus host disease of the gut but still no proof.

My need for platelets increased so more donors from the blood bank were recruited to moonlight and spin them off just for me. Those different bag sizes and colors filled with various shaded platelets still amazes me. I don't recall ever needing blood although it's possible that I received that as well at some point. To make matters even cloudier, as the luck of the draw would have it, my feet were now starting to throb and tingle incessantly.

The doctors continued investigating the source of infection or cause of the fever I was sustaining. Now this skirmish included feet and circulation problems, a lower stomach and genitals constantly throbbing, a 101° fever on top of low platelets, nosebleed trickles and graft vs. host disease with lousy engraftment counts to boot! This was all mixed up and served to the staff to try and sort out. Just an everyday occurrence with most bone marrow transplants—that aren't wrapped up for television syndication. Like I mentioned earlier, in the late sixties, seventies, eighties and even the late nineties, the majority of transplants do not go anywhere nearly as smooth as the success stories you hear about most of the time. I can see the public relations ramifications to that though. A lot of people do not want to hear the truth if it isn't nicely packaged to their liking.

Indeed this was a "sticky wicket" as the British chaps say. The doctors and nurses along with my family did a good job of containing my pain and comfort level with all of this, another tribute to this first class hospital. As enigmas go, so to do bone marrow transplant occurrences often go. Mysterious symptoms and problems arise as fast as some dissipate. They can crop up and vanish without a clue as to what may have caused them. Needless to say this is something to get used to. Those same aforementioned scenarios of the pain and origins showed up on the radar and then vanished like a UFO bleep so to speak, especially my heart misfires.

Some more days passed by with still the same ups and downs lingering until after a cycle of about four or five episodes of "peek a boo" subsided. The counts plateaued, the platelets stayed with me a bit longer to the point of needing fewer bags per day, say from five to three or so. The pain medicines controlled my unexplained groin pain and the GVHD was, well GVHD, perverted in its nature but temporarily now hogging the limelight. My appetite for tasteless cardboard was okay so, if nothing else erupted, I could go to see the new apartment in a few days. Unfortunately, I was slammed once again.

The infection took off just like that and I was on my back again in a matter of hours. My schizophrenic-like emotions were thoroughly yanked as once again I was feeling like a prisoner. One step forward and two steps back. I wasn't lobbied for to get back into another L.A.F. room as of yet but it seemed like I was right back where I started. Even with all of my self-proclaimed faith to fall back on, as the case was with me, the dents from feeling all of the physical pain were taking a toll on my God theory that I touched on and embraced. It was a lot harder to deny what the doctors were telling me now, when I was feeling so drained. As they gave blow by blow explanations as to why I was deteriorating, I'd second-guess myself somewhat. This shaken confidence was a definite concern.

Daily rounds were the norm and you could estimate the herds of doctor arrivals by the increasing volume levels of their discussions. Being the suddenly moody creep that I was, I would make it a point to initiate my old eavesdropping tactics that I had used to employ at my hospital back home. This was a major blunder because I totally undermined the positive energy that I had hoarded and jeopardized my mindset strategy. Any little innuendo that I would pick up through the doors gave me palpitations and it's a wonder that I never hyperventilated.

Before I would even be evaluated, the thoughts of my various problems being kicked around in the halls out there in discussions were taken by me verbatim. Like Dracula sucking the life out of his victims, those words were my vampires. The old adage of 'defeated before you've tried' certainly applied. Since I couldn't distinguish a routine problem from one serious in nature comparatively, everything freaked me out. Old houses creak and groan and I equated all of the pain, gurgles and sensations in my body as trouble. I was in this new body of a house so to speak and the tiniest inklings of something I'd not been accustomed to were related to danger looming; a feeling that you cannot turn off right away, or escape from. It wasn't a question of just taking off a pair of shoes, it was a mental stockade.

CHAPTER 4

▼

The infection that I incurred turned out to be serious but not an extreme, major concern. Evidently whatever it was they had encountered could confidently be knocked out with another course of particular antibiotics. That's just what they did and it took about seven to ten days or so. My paranoia wasn't totally a self-induced affliction because it turned out to be that the various changes I was feeling were real and weren't just with this bug. The antibiotics took care of that infection and the fever, so it appeared as if they were attributed to the core of my complaints. I perked up physically a bit after this incident and I was put on a possible three-hour excursion alert again by the staff.

Nothing with bone marrow transplants is as predictable as its unpredictability. I think if it wasn't for the concrete evidence of symptoms and manifestations, a patient could easily be accused of crying wolf. They are so bizarre some of these occurrences that they can mysteriously arise and then vanish just the same.

Next came a setback with simultaneous explosions of pain and blisters. This was herpes zoster or shingles. All down the right side of my back were excruciating nerve shots which ensued .It is now known as post-herpetic neuralgia. This entire ordeal unfolded over the initial week of the infection with some blister like weeping. It finally was controlled to the point of a poison ivy type of condition. The post-herpetic neuralgia, which is a residual condition that damages the nerve endings has lasted years and still visits me regularly with knife stabbing accuracy down right my side even today. These complications, when they hit, are perverted, plain and simply put. In any event, I skimmed through this episode to keep moving along. But that's certainly not to say that I'm making light of this ailment because anyone dealing with this chicken pox relative knows how painful it is.

Since things aren't always as they seem, a lot of my observations as well as the doctors' were pretty much up in the air. My zoster was not doing any more physical harm to me at this point other than the pain itself, so the staff mapped out another game plan to allow me out on a three-hour pass. Possibly now even a swing over to the new apartment to stay there and begin commuting to the hospital every day, and I was certainly up for it! I'll bet we all needed a break from each other, myself and the doctors and staff members included. That's just my hindsight personal opinion because professionally they were there until the very end for you. I just speculate now of what a jerk I must have seemed like at times with everything going on. This does seem like a good time in my recollection for them to have wanted to boot my butt out of there for a time out.

The First Hill apartment, where we were now attempting to reside in was another dejavous for me because several years back I had watched a "60 Minutes" special on Mr. Zumwalt who I mentioned earlier. He was a previous patient who happened to stay here so I had a television tour of this place so to speak. The First Hill Apartment was a very nice facility. Our unit was on the second or third floor with a view of the airplane traffic patterns among the many other colorful and interesting sights. Ironically, the planes taking off and circling to land became big time festivities for my tiring and wary parents. You might have thought that those two had a front row seat or were in a car at a drive-in to a feature first run movie the way that they watched.

The window that I speak about hovered directly over the bed in the front room where my parents slept. This was off across to the right upon entry into our apartment. Aside from the bed and entrance was a cubby-hole vanity leading into the bathroom. Making a left there was a couch bed that Carol slept on facing a swivel television that turned to the kitchenette side. Above that was a loft with two single beds tucked away only accessible via a spiral wrought iron staircase. The lofts half-wall looked down on Carol's sofa bed from a cathedral like ceiling. This was a perfect "hide away escape, the world secure kind of lair" for me. I took the bed farthest to the wall and my girlfriend, took the bed closer to the stairs. I felt some sense of protection up there and for the most part reinforced myself with this thought to sleep "relatively well". As for my nieces and nephews, they must have returned home by this point I presume.

When this transition took place for me, keep in mind that everyone else was already settled in by this time. It didn't take long for me to disrupt the flow of things. The evolving stigma gaining momentum was now the ring of a phone or the sound of a beeper. This was partially stemmed from my stay at the First Hill. The beeper was hospital oriented, and the phone ringing was 'home' related.

What caused this traumatic complex were phone calls from the hospital also. It seemed like every time that I established a routine of "life at First Hill" and having to go to the hospital for only several hours a day, a new complication would arise. The middle of the night's quiet emptiness would be disrupted by the shrieks of ringing tones. The conditioning of bad news to follow equated with phone calls was simple. That phone was not used for anything much other than patient to hospital communication and vice versa. I never had anybody call me with good news, just nervous news.

More than a few times I had to leave the First Hill at wee hours of the morning only to be re-hospitalized. The corner bed of the loft may have served some quirk purpose of hideaway escapism but no one could be spared from the wrath of a ring. Luckily, and I say luckily facetiously, my problems were only staph infections and the like. Definitely serious in they're own right but only a jigsaw puzzles piece in the transplant scheme of things.

Between the mini-hospital stays and longer tenures were the walks. I don't remember whether or not I was encouraged to walk to and from the hospital to the apartment or not. Perhaps I was trying to prove something to myself, I don't altogether recollect. I do, however, remember one distinguishing stamp mark on those treks, the burning chest pains. For some strange reason, the crisp, cool Seattle air in January of 1987 was very different for me.

All the inhaling that I worked for torched my airways. It wasn't like a de-conditioned stitch in the side of your belly after a taxing run, or that of even being short of breath per say. Though I was really weak it wasn't a question of my gasping for air. The radiation, mucousitis, damaged esophagus, and or GVHD I suspect, was at the center of the cause. It was slightly invigorating on occasion to feel this sensation as my lungs felt as if they were bursting past capacity, enflaming with feelings which borderlined the pleasure-pain threshold. My mask provided that backlash of hot oxygen as I exhaled through the material. Although this moisture felt very comfortable, the condensation resulted in the chapping of my lips, spawning yet another source of discomfort magnified by their extreme sensitivity.

For the few days that I did manage to salvage staying in the First Hill apartments as a 'tenant', the walks and chest pains went hand in hand. The steep and windy hills that taxed my aching feet and deteriorating legs, would make any reader wonder why I would go to such lengths of an inconvenience, or even be permitted to do so for that matter. I can only speculate on behalf of both parties that it was a way in which to keep the body working and give the patient some sense of control in hopes of a recovery.

Those walks did take me by a unique building that worked on hot rods and even old wooden horses for carousels. Often times in that stretch the highlight of my day was to pass by and peek in the open garage door. This fueled my imagination of envisioning my future wild creations, if and when I could ever return home and be well. That stroke of luck noticing the shop helped prolong what sense of sanity I had for the impending bubble sabbatical.

Just before that nightmare erupted, my appetizer for personal traumatic Richter scale manifestations came knocking. Those evenings at First Hill were becoming eerie instead of rejuvenating. This was mainly due to the previously enjoyable silence. After everyone else conked out, The Catholic Christian and musician in me could quietly hum verses of Jesus Christ Superstar. When Jesus asks the Apostles, "Won't anyone stay awake with me? Peter, James, John."

Again I would reflect on the Garden of Gethsemane; lonely and fearful with plenty of confusion around. Just as hypocritical as my anxiety was, my girlfriend and Carol would send me into orbit with a quiet rage playing freakin' scrabble all night. Whispering as they may, triple word score letters and dictionary lookup laughter often elevated the volume meter. From a buzz to a roar, buzz, roar, on and on, I could have killed them! I was up in the loft and they were in the living room/kitchen/plane watching tower. I'd like to take credit for never screaming below to them but more than that, I'd attribute it to nerves and preoccupied other thoughts rushing through my mind. Now, when the girls finally called it a night "or morning", my girlfriend would "quietly but noisily" creep up the squeaky spiral stairway and boom, just like that, all were asleep but me, of course. Just me and the sounds of silence…

A couple of times during the night I'd have to use the bathroom and made efforts to tiptoe down and about. Sitting on the alien toilet and scanning the foreign tiles with complimentary towels, I pondered life, what better place than the bathroom, right? So here I am one late night-early morning with everyone catching Zs and me posing as the statue of David. Finishing my business, I debated whether to flush and wake up the entire building (because every flush echoed throughout with a loud roaring whoosh), or drop the lid and plead the fifth. This night I didn't have any say in the matter because I stood up to make the move on the handle when I saw that the yellow toilet was now filled with a crimson red color. Not just a food coloring cherry thin watered tone but dark, catsup like in thickness and brilliance.

I quickly checked my backside and, when I concluded that it wasn't coming from there, as a man my most breath-stealing fear was confronted. A last denial check to my groin area at my catheter sights for blood but to no avail. This blood and what now appeared as tissue or wet red paper came from my front organ. "Oh dear God, no ', I gasped to myself. Not knowing anything about this kind of occurrence, I thought I was dying. Discombobulated jargon now leaked out from my mouth and made its way to my sister's ears as she woke up from the ruckus.

One look into the basin and she inhaled aloud. Not one to hide emotions very well, fear was written all over her face. With her hands scratching her hair and arms flapping to get her bearings on the matter, a quick call on the bat phone and; needless to say I was whisked away one more time back to the hospital. After examination it was determined that the inner lining of my bladder was deteriorating and it was most probably due to the total body irradiation. The paper thin substance that looked like wet Kleenex was just that, clots and tear remnants of the bladder wall passed through urination.

The overused phrase of words cannot explain this or that is the only thing that comes to mind here with this, yet another, setback. The all too familiar discussions of whether or not I should re-enter the laminar room were now underway. As foolish as I may have been, I sold more cars with B.S. talk and held off that idea, because I didn't want to die in a bubble. There really wasn't anything that they could do, short of radical and invasive surgery, to try and repair or save the bladder except administer some medicine to slow the bleeding and give more platelets. With my condition being so bad health wise, the only option was to wait and hope my body could repair itself. I simply wouldn't have survived any more invasive procedures then.

Those platelets that I was receiving were being used up as fast as they were being infused so many more than the normal amounts were administered into me to combat the life-threatening situation. There was hope that the lining would stop shredding and eventually taper off if I could start the process of healing on my own. Since I wasn't up for the bubble unless the staff felt it was mandatory, I still stayed in the confines of my family's apartment and, obviously, taking note of every discharge.

For several days nothing changed, no increase or decrease in the clots. Silver dollar sized slices would eek out of that comparatively mine hole in my penis. I squirmishly had to assist in pulling some out, as they were so stubborn. I became mortified that there would be a blockage or something, so with that I tormented myself, of course. I was so concerned about this that my sister took me to a separate urologist in the city to be reexamined. I guess for reassurance that everything was being done for me that could be, so in that respect it did calm me down a bit. I brought a jar of clots with me to show him and after a brief but expensive consult we left with no other news or answers. The pain of the waiting game had seconds turning into what seemed like years of anxiety. I don't believe that I didn't flip-out with this ordeal.

Days rolled by at a turtle's pace it seemed until I finally got a break. The clots slowed to a minimal pace and the doctors were confident that the damage done would repair itself in time as long as no perforation broke through. I don't know what I would have done then and I didn't want to find out. I took their hypothesis and ran with it. A funny thing here is that with all of the "coincidental" occurrences throughout my story, I don't remember really attacking this problem spiritually with prayer. But then again I had people back home and my family to keep me on auto pilot.

One last episode that I'd like to touch upon before the reality of a Warren Zevon song kicked in appropriately stated. "Send lawyers, guns and money, the shit has hit the fan", and "Dad get me out of this". That "normal" activity I saw was a trip in a car for the first time in four to five months. I took the shuttle, of course, but no journeys outside of a two-block loop. This might not sound like a long time to many but for some reason I was affected in a strange way. A Speed Racer cartoon had a story when I was a kid about a car so fast that you had to drink a special potion to drive it or else the surroundings would freak you out. You may or may not have seen that famous "GRX" episode but like a savvy Trekky who could blueprint any show for you, the Speed Racer fans will relate. For those of you that have no clue who Speed is, my reflection will explain what I meant.

My brother and Carol decided to take me to the mall after my heckling forced them to crack. We took a cab from the notorious fleet of Seattle cab farers and upon taking off I immediately became engulfed by fear and disorientation. The stops, starts and traffic lane changes had me a total wreck. The motion seemed to be magnified like a time warp. I don't think I became acclimated whatsoever and simply closed my eyes and listened to the radio. That took care of the visual aspects of things but my equilibrium knew better. We barely managed to arrive at the mall, which was a good half-hour from town, when I bailed out and held off the vomit with just a few dry heaves. Man, I thought I blew it again in listening to my stubborn hard head that I developed with the help, of course, of my Irish, Italian, American Indian heritage.

We were far enough away from the hospital that any serious complications would have been difficult to tackle. Within a few minutes after arriving and leveling off, I had settled down to the point where we could walk a bit in the mall. I tried a slice of pizza and something to drink but couldn't eat much because of my mouth and stomach problems. We then ended up browsing in a nearby hobby shop where my brother bought a model and just like that we were on our way back to the apartment. I did get sick on the return trip but it wasn't that bad as I recall. Tom finished building the model car and so went my climactic mall trip story. With this excursion I still wonder if I helped my condition in anyway or hindered it. Only God knows for sure but this point started where the meltdown began.

Within another 48 hours or so I'd say, I found myself back in the very same spot where the last dilemma took off; that being the bathroom in the late hours of most peoples sleep time. Once again with my being fatigued and exhaustingly contemplating all of the bad dream/reality experiences I was having, on top of everything else. The routine pass by the adjacent vanity mirror exposed my burned and battered body staring back at me with contempt. Upon my usual gaze over to see what else was shrinking away, I noticed just the opposite. Though it was slight, the left side of my abdominal cavity was protruding out. I gently pushed into the bulge apparent to me but evidently no one else. I couldn't get anybody to acknowledge my findings since I had no discomfort in this area. With all of the other active hot spots for pain throughout this human aperture, I filed it and convinced myself that I was simply looking for problems here. At this point it was easy to believe that because my feet decided to take the center stage for awhile.

As quick as an inflating raft, right before my eyes, my feet ballooned into a horribly painful swell. This was so dramatic that suddenly I could not even slip a pair of shoes on over them. The pain was so unbearable that I had no choice but to re-enter the hospital. All of this gave me about a week or so of total time as an out patient between the last clot fiasco and now exploding feet, "that sounds like a band name" let alone the truth of the matter. This escalating problem became very serious when my skin started to literally split open and weep. From clear fluid to blood, my pain tolerance threshold was pushed to the max! The stinging and cracking along with the bleeding left the doctors no alternative but to place me yet again in the bubble. All of my thoughts were entrenched in pain management so I didn't have any qualms about that whatsoever. I think for the first time I surrendered to the pain.

Severe edema was the culprit most likely induced by all of the massive changes and chemical imbalances that I'd incurred thus far. I was immediately placed in a traction-like elevation. Due to the severity of all of the body pain, a morphine drip was initiated with my being in control of the strength in dosage. I had a little ball governor on the I.V. line to increase or decrease the flow of the morphine. I don't know if I could have remained conscious without it. Thank the Lord for the hands-on control!

Another instantaneous directive was given to administer a drug or substance rather called albumin. This came in an I.V. bag as most of my goodies did. It closely resembled tree sap and or heavy maple syrup. I recall many air bubble type circular formations in it as I watched the gooey glop slither into my catheter. It's a wonder the lines weren't clogged up by this stuff as thick as it seemed to be. With the morphine quickly taking charge, the albumin became a festivity to watch. My feet are split open, bleeding and hoisted at half-mast but I soon could care less. Relief had set in, pain-wise anyway.

A lot slower than the inflation process, my two blimps eventually decompressed into a resemblance of human feet. You could witness the metamorphosis of the spectacle right before your very eyes. In a few hours the taut, pruned skin was fairly normal in size but scorned with road bumps of lesions. The blood subsided, leaving several open, brush-burn-type caverns and in what appeared to be a break in the action, turned out to be a Catch 22. If I were to lower my feet at the normal lying down position, the swelling process would immediately begin again.

I was left with no other choice but to hang my feet for a week or ten days—night and day, except for bathroom usage, i.e., my potty seat next to my bed but that's a whole other story. That was a case of beat the clock unto itself to try to go and get back into bed and get elevated in the harness before the rush of inflating fluid began again. All in all that totally rotted. Five or six blue pumps with beepers hooked to me, drugged up and increasingly becoming more miserable. It was bad enough to remove the bag used in the toilet seat and maneuver it over to the fan airline barrier to the nurses to be weighed. But with giant swollen feet, I felt like a homicidal Donald Duck out of frustration.

I know that I had to be unbearably irritable. Being tied up to a block and tackle didn't help but, finally, after what seemed like forever, the stability in control of the edema was manageable. It got to the point where I could maneuver again for several hours without the swelling acting up. Then I could elevate my feet for say twenty minutes or so to bring them back down to a tolerable size again.

The activity wasn't like I was going door to door. My Habitrail of a house had no connecting tubes, but I could at least sit in the chair for awhile now. Back outside the confines of club laminar, there were again whispers circulating of my being released soon for yet another attempt at out patient acclamations. Of course that was music to my ears, not like my hard rock and heavy metal music that was reported to have annoyed the neighboring patients just a bit. I still don't believe that it was loud but I did turn it down for them anyway. Some more days and nights tug boated by and as was speculated, I was granted a release from the dungeon. The way that these peaks and valleys occurred is just how they unfolded, almost as if they were pre-scripted and systematic in retrospect.

With winter in full bloom the reports from back home came in about huge snowfalls that had recently fallen. I sure could have used some snow in downtown Seattle. But that was just about like snow falling in Tuscaloosa, Alabama from what I was told. Before we found a donor when I was sick at home for those two years, I used to play a game of sorts with Carol. On the day that St Therese became a nun she asked God to let it snow that day if he was pleased with her decision. Well it snowed and she filed it as a sign from God. Anyway I would call Carol at work and let her know the day before that I would pray for snow as a sign. The percentages for snow where I lived were better there so the few times that it did come down, I'd joke to her that I ordered it. Honestly, I batted almost one thousand if you include flurries on some of those days.

I'd bet my family humored me with all of the ribbing I took from those incidents, but when I decided to fire up the prayer line to Heaven for a dose of snow in downtown Seattle, they panicked. Those percentages were very different here so "coincidences" couldn't really make me look good, or God first and foremost for that matter. You could sense that they were afraid that when it didn't snow my faith would be crushed and I would end up in a tailspin of more depression. Well, no disrespect to my family but they weren't God. So I rolled up my sleeves so to speak and shot those prayer vibes out!

It was great to be back in the First Hill and just to sit on a couch and have a rug on the floor gave me more reflection on the many blessings of life that we simply take for granted. Naturally, this is me we are talking about so the apartment may as well have been a drive-thru McDonald's excursion. Well, of course it wasn't, but my brief stays there sure could remind someone of me being the passing cars going in and out of the pickup window. We actually did get to go to the local McDonald's during this quick visit to my home away from home away from home. The oddest thing was seeing other bald, yellow masked patients in there taking over the joint. Most of them were ready to go back home soon and well ahead of me with the recovery process.

My meal in itself didn't taste any different than anything else I could eat due to my fried taste buds, but it was just the thought of doing what regular people did that spurred me on to try. After a one block cab ride back to the apartment, I was bushed. I went to bed early evening, around six or seven o'clock to try and "Calgon" my way out of this situation and recharge some.

My passing of a clot was rare at this point and my feet, although cut up and scarring, were not blimping up any longer. My counts were rising ever so slowly but, at least, they weren't dropping. All in all things looked encouraging once again.

The old familiar nightly family roar of the ladies Scrabble game faded out as I drifted off and caught some Zs. A good night's rest comparatively and in fact we even made it back to a St. James Cathedral daily mass the next afternoon; That in itself being another surreal moment. I was the only masked man in a huge cavern of holiness. I convinced myself in a conversation with God that I could be excused for wearing my Jets hat in church to cover my bald dome. Nobody said anything about it and I attributed all of the stares to my glowing yellow skin. Maybe it was because I was just so handsome, yeah, that was it.

Whoever was in charge of the job of blasting people must have pulled my name from the Rolodex because the very next evening, the phone reaper came calling. It seemed as if no sooner than I had undressed and hit the sack, the now ominous sound of those rings did just that. Well with some lucky guessing I figured it was for me. This time it was concerning my counts and how they were dropping according to the latest blood work results. "Whoopee, once again back in the shoe box." Dress up, cab ride, scrub down, powders and ointments on, sap up my butt and voila, life in "laminarville". Man, just like that in the blink of an eye I had gone from flying high escapism to a one hundred and eighty degree turn.

I didn't feel the affects of the declining count numbers for about another day or two but, luckily, I was in the 'germ free' environment to help protect me. I guess I was protected, more so in fact then if I was in a regular room. I'm sure of that but it was too late now to prevent a picked up infection called E. coli. I do not know how else to recount these events without flirting with monotony but it just kept coming. Who knows if I would have died had I remained as and out patient but in any event, I spiked another fever while my side seemed to be getting larger to me as well. No one else felt this was a concern at the time. With this going on, I also had one of my lungs partially collapse all at the same time. I was of the mind set now like "something would get fixed and better and something else would rise and get worse".

When I couldn't breathe as well, I went through a few seizures and cramping episodes that were fended off by the super nurses I had. They and of course the massive doses of Prednisone to boot. The seizures, cramps and collapsed lung all dissipated and I was now left treading water fighting just the E.coli and failing counts, 'that's all'. The E.coli reluctantly agreed to die off after good fortune and lots of help from massive I.V. antibiotics. This was a huge blessing and how my body withstood the infection pounding with falling counts and a beaten silly shell of a frame of mind—God only knows.

As for the main reason why I was reeled back in, that being those dropping counts, more battle plans were in the works. Platelets were being scoffed up and used by my body so fast that the doctors concluded I was building a tolerance to them per se. They suggested that we try using my sister exclusively for my platelets instead. The platelets harvested at the blood bank were just not working. It seemed as if Carols' earlier bags had lasted longer in me. If she was up for the task, they were going to accommodate her night and day and spin off her platelets. This did work for me pretty well but now I wonder what kind of toll this took on Carol. Every action has a reaction, and she devoted her whole being to saving me. We were so close but still, how can you express the level of gratitude I wished that I could have conveyed.

Days were also being scoffed up and I was becoming a caged animal. The heavy doses of Prednisone on top of all of the other stinking medicines that I had to take in didn't help matters much at all. I had the side effects of steroid mood swings or "roid rage" and now as my feet had done, my whole body was blowing up and inflating rapidly with fluid. My face was deforming, my side that I was concerned about was being hidden by the weight gain.

Any of the muscle definition that I had left in my stomach was done away with due to the fluid as well. Not being a super hairy guy I, was now turning into the Wolf man under a full moon. This hair was so coarse and wiry I couldn't stand it. A mustache that I often used to grow was now a giant floor mop stuck under my nose, thick and gangly. Disposable razors were no longer a match for the beast, so Carol bought me an electric razor that didn't harvest much more of the mammoth growth. The only advantage it had was that the electric lasted longer than just one use, unlike the disposables. Carol, by now, had given me a nickname of tungsten steel, obviously not what these razor were made of, by their performance.

Claustrophobic symptoms and deeper depression were once again setting in. There was still no definitive reason as to why my counts were dropping the way that they were at this point. Even the doctors couldn't agree on their speculations and my rapport with all of them brought in different theories and feedback from each. This was the start of pure hell in not knowing anything. I knew my legs were shot and I was bloated from the kneecaps up and had two upside down Louisville slugger bats standing as my calves, shins and ankles. They connected to the scarred up soles, toes and overall skin on my feet. The only thing that could keep you from not going into despair was not to look at yourself as best you could. No easy task when you can't escape the reminders manifesting all over you.

There was no possible way for me to leave this bubble in this condition that I was in, so everyone was pulling out all the stops to try and keep my spirits up. Two of the biggest weapons of optimistic hope came from my friends and loved ones back home. More impressively I presume from God, what do you think? That promised forthcoming video from the fundraiser on my behalf showed up via airmail. A VCR was heisted with a monitor and parked right outside of my plastic window. The statement I like to get a lot of mileage out of is "what can you say to people who help to save your life?" What? Thank you? I just always hope that God conveys my overwhelming appreciation and gratitude to them some day for their generous tasks of kindness.

The fundraiser tape brought laughter, tears, happiness, sadness and longing for home into my hospital room. It went a long way to restoring my anger for self-preservation. I had to turn on the juice like my adopted song and transplant anthem "the power" by the band Rainbow. I had to get home. I had to see my buddy Yuke, even though he had bitten me; he was still "the man" in my eyes. "I had to this, I had to that". I pounded my mental regions until they all were in agreement with my soul. A lingo that would be on a par with the entire fund raiser participants could be "I love you man!" As awesome as that video tape was to my state of mind, the only person capable of stealing the show and topping that, short of my donor walking in, was God Himself. I believe even my donor would graciously take a second seat to this particular and "coincidental" story.

Call it irony, call it a stroke of luck, or at the least call it no big deal if you like. I really don't care what it's called but I know it floored me. Waking up from a lousy night's battle with the pumps, beepers, hoses and the damned bed itself, I sat up. Upon gazing out of my window to the city below, I absolutely thought that I was hallucinating or simply dreaming, but the whole town was covered in white! The sky was white, the air looked white, and the streets were covered in white. It was freaking snow! About an inch or two had slowly and silently fallen through the night but this was enough to paralyze the entire city's traffic. As funny as that may seem to regular snowfall recipients, Seattle has major hills and the drivers simply were not prepared nor were the highway crews. I believe that I mentioned that Seattle proper itself, rarely receives snowfall. Of course in the surrounding mountains and higher elevations circling the city, snow is more prevalent. But in the city of Seattle, rain is king.

Well, a beautiful warm serenity engulfed me from head to toe. I talked to God, wondered about life, my future, good and evil and pondered about people even worse off than me. Little Paige was struggling down the hall as well as a lady named Grace who had a daughter going through a transplant. Who's to say who was worse off but it was pretty much all relative, in many respects. I thought of the great sacrifice that my family was giving for me by staying with me here. I felt very sad and somewhat guilty that I put them through this, but I don't know if I could have made it without them being there. If I had let them down I would have to make it up to them someday, somehow. I missed they guys back home. The band that I played in which received a short record contract, until I got sick. I missed pounding those drums and bickering with our talented singer/musician, Darren. I missed playing sports and just hanging out. I missed it all. I missed everything that wasn't what this battle with leukemia was.

While I thought of all of the things that you could think of, I sat bedside just watching the snowfall, oblivious to the surroundings for a good while. I definitely drifted off. The little ants below that were people scurrying about looking so disoriented made me sure that this was real. The approaching voices of my cheery, upbeat family members coming down the hall reinforced it. Yep, snow in downtown Seattle. All things were possible with God I smirked.

A very cool souvenir for me was a picture of a snowman that Carol and my girlfriend had made in front of the First Hill apartments. It took the whole yard of snow scrapes to build it but they did it. A thin man in his own right and for sure by East Coast standards but for me, this guy was the symbol of perseverance. My niece, Lauren and nephews, Tommy and Tony who returned home also sent me a mug shot of a snowman that they made. He was holding a six-pack of Coke, my favorite beverage and a florescent spray painted message draped across his belly for me. Now we had our very own Seattle snowmen. I don't think that God was finished showing His hands in things, they just kept adding up and getting more impressive.

Well with yet "another rejuvenation of my outlook on things", my frame of mind was temporarily spirited. But the fact that my life in the laminar room was indefinite it challenged those spiritual recharges for sure. In trying to make light of the predicament that I was in, my warped sense of humor piloted the ride with dry banter for awhile. This started with the food as I have mentioned. Although I now couldn't taste much of anything, it was a natural area to target with witty banter. As I alluded to earlier, laminar food had to be autoclaved or "sterilized". The same type of machine basically that purifies tattoo equipment and surgical equipment. It was used to cook food as well. Any flavor of Kool Aid essentially was colored, tasteless water to my lips. Whatever menu dish that was brought in tasted like soggy papery goop. Those early jokes of fillet mignon and lobster resurfaced as well as the rips on cereal. When I speak about not being able to taste anything, I can state that I always did experience a residual backlash of something nasty erupting over my pallet. As finicky as I was, I would say that was a miracle of sorts in itself just to get what I could in. I reluctantly shoveled the "delicacies" in, and for the most part kept a good bit of it down.

My legs were now on strike so the exercise bike was just collecting dust. Well, zero point zero point one percent or so, was germ-free right, so it was clean dust, if any, huh. Another nickname that I was tagged with later on by my friend, Kev, was now appropriate. He called me Yoda. Perhaps not so much for all of this knowledge, insight and wisdom that I was being forced to acquire but instead for the humpback and moon face I now carried on board from the drugs. Yep, a bigger and yellowier instead of green version of Yoda was I. "John, may the steroids be with you".

Some more mail came in but rumor later had it that a letter or two from an old girlfriend Tracey had been thrown out by someone, and I never received them. My dad searched high and low all over town without my knowing for a *Vette* magazine and a Four-Wheeler mag to boot. A Modern Drummer mag, a pair of drum sticks, and some stuffed animal gifts sent from home were all cooked up to cross over into the Twilight Zone to help keep me company. They did help some.

My baldhead was now a sand paper heavy grit crop and I still destroyed razors with the swift stroke of a blade. As I mentioned the Werewolf-look was in Vogue, at least in my cubby hole of society. Atari football, tank, baseball and other games, grew old and surfing channels was common knowledge. The music was holding ground but after all of those crutch tactics were used up, I ran out of ideas and tools, to pass the time and stay afloat.

I developed yet another infection of the annoying and treatable kind, but unfortunately, my counts were still slipping. In the L.A.F. room I was even more alienated because I couldn't eavesdrop as well on anything going on outside and was being filtered from a lot of the bad news trickling down; The filter, of course being mostly my family.

When the doctors and nurses showed up in the moon suits, to invade my region, I knew something was up. With their crossing over the barrier, I also knew that my back kidney area needed to be drilled. This was the rich domain of fertile tapping grounds. A bone marrow aspiration needed to be extracted for analysis. Little did I know but suspicions of me loosing my graft were at the top of the problem list for the doctors.

In fact, the discussions were so hot and furious that personal arguments ensued between some of them. A legal technicality prevented me from being allowed to have a second bone marrow transplant from my donor, so as not to place him or her under undue risk of harm. Keep in mind that these battles were all going on in other parts of the hospital. So I had no clue of what was at stake at the time. It was so ugly at one point that my sister and an undisclosed angel of a person, and high ranking employee, actually broke into a file room one night to obtain confidential information as to who my donor was. They were prepared to secretly fly to him in and get his consent no less for more marrow to try to save me. As far as tests went thus far, they indicated that I was in fact loosing my graft and not responding to the new bone marrow. In other words, I was dying.

My back was numbed "somewhat" and cut into. Once again this was me we are talking about and not some super patient responding perfectly to the trans-plant procedure "Hollywood script". The first pressure filled, painful procedure drew absolutely nothing. Evidently bone marrow can have different air pockets, so in they went once again and still nothing. Like drilling for oil, they finally hit pay dirt on the third tap attempt. Bone marrow was extracted and like the alien autopsy, the hovering huddled clan disbanded to leave me lying on the bed, vir-tually motionless and wiped out. I mentioned about how I felt the bone marrow aspirations being so hard on me, and this episode had just been like three separate pulled teeth extracted without a local anesthesia.

More time passed by once again and I drifted off into a morphine drip coma like state partly due to exhaustion as well. Probably the best endorsement for family support during these battles was Carol keeping a watch over me late one evening. What happened could happen to any BMT patient and through no fault of the staffs; I was quietly sleeping through my possible death.

For a reason only attributed to the beating that I had taken thus far in trying to save me, my body didn't coagulate the clotting factors and stoppage of my blood. I began hemorrhaging at the three aspiration sights. Initially they did respond and were bandaged up right after the procedure. At some point in time afterwards, the bleeding started again with a slow trickle. Eventually, the light stream turned into a steady flow. Just by chance, Carol closely peeked in through the plastic instead of using her regular chair view that would have only shown me quietly resting fast asleep. Instead Carol stooped over only to discover me besieged in sheets of red. From my neck to my shins, the bed was saturated. Her loud gasp like scream startled me to awakening and of course, now I could feel as well as see the terrifying mess.

In the blink of any eye nurses swarmed to get the situation under control. I was slowly pulled out of the woods of danger so to speak. Perhaps a quart or so low of oil but still running. Carol was immediately whisked away and once again sucked for platelets, taking more of her to give to me—no greater love.

In addition to this, there were at the very least several instances where my I.V. lines would reverse and back up, filling the bags and bottles with my own blood. Unbeknownst to me, or to anyone else for that matter, this would happen fairly quickly once those bags and bottles emptied into me. Gravity I assume would simply reverse and like a siphon back went the flow. This was remedied immediately upon discovery of course by simply flushing the blood back into me with saline and heparin solutions. Any passersby would have thought that I was receiving a transfusion for sure in the way that it appeared. As we know, things aren't always what they seem.

Naturally, all of his didn't help my strength whatsoever. I was even frailer now than ever before up to this point in my life. This didn't escape me and the seriousness of the situation was magnified and comprehended. I guess this was actually the first time that I really had to think about dying. Although I had thoughts along those lines, due to the nature of the leukemia I had, it never gripped me so tightly as now. I had always talked and psyched myself out of the many other crises but, then again, I had a lot more strength and energy to give also. I guess the key factor distinguishing this stage of things was the level of fear. I couldn't deny what was going on around me any longer and kind of felt like I had run out of "tricks" to use.

To make matters worse, the hospital Chaplain made a point to come into the L.A.F. room on my side all gowned up in the moon suit. He also requested that my girlfriend also be in there with us as well. The Chaplain's name was Percy and he was a very pleasant man. He reminded me of Glenn Campbell the country singer that I had seen on Hee-Haw or something when I was a kid. Percy had polio as a child and then had a transplant with a related donor for the same CML that I had on top of that. Those hurdles themselves that he had to overcome, I respected him for. It was only fitting that this gentleman became a man of God in a transplant hospital.

Percy conversed with my girlfriend and I about a lot of things. How serious we were in our relationship, marriage, children, etc. I told him that she suggested that I use a sperm bank for future use if need be, and that I declined after looking briefly into the program and felt that God would take care of the children if he wanted to. Commitment issues and other topics arose but the core of his mission was to let us know that I very well may die soon and to offer support. Although Percy wasn't a Catholic he still was first and foremost a Christian for me. His words hit home and I went into a bit of a tailspin.

Without getting into all of the specifics of my 'tailspin', I'll just say that my emotions were spilling out from A to Z. As I mentioned earlier, those steroids magnified my perspective at times and I displayed some irrational thoughts for sure. One of those was a selfish line of thinking as well as one of the funniest time frames I had upon reflection. In a ridiculous gesture at that moment while thinking about it now, I asked my girlfriend to promise me that she would become a nun if I died. I thought that I didn't want anyone else to have her. Boy isn't it funny how you can look back and notice the most ridiculous things that you may have said or done or felt only to feel like, "What the heck was I possibly thinking?" Needless to say, I'll attribute that ludicrous statement to all of the medicines I was feasting on!

Shortly thereafter, Percy and my newly vowed nun of a girlfriend left the bubble as Father Carmody arrived to administer the Sacrament of the Sick and Last Rites, a very serious ritual in the church. Once again this was a red flag to the nails going in my coffin because I didn't ask for this visit; the doctors had informed my family how bleak the outlook now was. A bleak outlook perhaps yes, but not lacking any suspense for sure.

All in all I must have received Last Rites or "Extreme Unction" about nine times through my whole bone marrow transplant ordeal; "He's up, he's down, he's in the hospital, he's out of the hospital", etc. My dad's face said it all. The Marine look that we were all accustomed to showed signs of pain and helplessness. As did Carol's feelings show through her pale complexion and total exhaustion due to the platelets that she had been donating to me. That coupled with everything else added on to her shoulders, lended to her tiring appearance as well. My girlfriend had formed a habit of escaping to call a friend back home every evening for what started out as about an hour or so. At the time I was comforted for her sake that she had a refuge from this hell, but I would later wonder about the real reasons for those phone calls.

The counts were coming in as lousy as my stare out of the window was lonely. Slight ripples of my brother having to leave for home due to business, and doctors and nurses changing rounds with shifts of patients due to protocols, plunged me deeper into the hardened shock of what was happening. I was wrongfully furious at my brother for my wanting him to stay, even though he had a family and career to take care of at home. It was more hurt feelings of emotional scarred notions of being abandoned but, what can you do, life goes on. You grow to learn that we are all just a number or commodity of sorts. Not that that's a good thing.

I sputtered with my attempts to jump start the new physicians attendants and doctors on my case as they had to be updated on everything in a very short span of time. I never quite understood why there was a need to shuffle nurses, doctors and P.A.'s who were familiarized and intertwined with a patient and family. It seems to me to be somewhat counterproductive to all parties involved. I resented the round changes because just as in cramming for exams, you can sometimes miss and overlook some subtleties, where as with filling in a new group of medical members, certain bits of information are inevitably going to be bypassed.

My not so pleasant demeanor went even further south as I can remember furiously launching a cup of putrid yellow liquid medicine that smelled as nasty as it tasted. This tasted worse than anything I could attempt to describe, "And that's when I supposedly wasn't able to taste anything". The pea yellow chicken broth like elixir broke the sanitary side of my barrier like an exploding paint ball pellet. It wreaked minor havoc sliming and oozing all over the adjacent wall on the other side of my confines. As great a release of anger and frustration that this was, I paid for it dearly because of the pungent smell that was left in the room. No smoke bomb that had ever reeked of rotten eggs came close to this foul emanation. I lost some good brownie points with staff members and I believe a janitor friend, Joe, who wasn't to thrilled about having to excavate and decontaminate my dirty work, or the medicines' dirty work that is. Sorry, Joe, and thank you for being a friend.

One of the few good things about my case in reference to the staff's round changes was that inevitably, I had double the staff input in a sense. The previous crew became so involved and familiar with me and my family, that they moonlighted to stop in and participate on decision making. P.A. Rick was one of them and again offered his support for me not to give up, ever. My feisty and somewhat rocky rapport with a few of the new doctors persisted but the one still incredible coincidence then for me with the changes in staff was this. Dr. Donnell Thomas, who is the Nobel Prize winner in medicine for initiating bone marrow transplant procedures, was scheduled to arrive at this time. He pioneered the procedure years ago in 1969 or thereabouts and was now retired. Once a year he made it a point to come in and do rounds for a couple of weeks just to oversee things.

I don't know if it was true or not but I was told that Dr. Thomas was vacationing in Maine or Canada when he was informed of my case and condition. He then postponed his trip and made it a point to come and see what he could do for my situation, as well as the other patients, of course. I think this could have been another little miracle myself. In any event I welcomed the great news. This would be like the Dr. J or Michael Jordan of transplant doctors helping out you might say.

News of this didn't change my physical condition any right then. My spirits were lifted but I was in the worst condition so far and continuing to fade. Things were so bad that my family couldn't hold back the tears any more. They tried to take turns going to the lounge and crying themselves out, but upon their return trip revealed blood shot eyes, and remnant tears sparsely trickling with runny noses abound. All of this would occasionally accompany streaks out of my room to exit and cry some more. I felt so laden with guilt putting them through all of this.

Still moving along, with months passing and still nothing but the same, slow, deteriorating and miserable monotony, the time came when a major family conference was to be called in my room. About six o'clock in the evening it all unfolded one night which included me of course, my family, doctors and heading them was Dr. Thomas himself. This conference was another one of those negative memories photographically embellished in my mind. When it all finally unfolded after hours of hell and anticipation, the mini-herd of medical professionals milled in and quietly took their places behind Dr. Thomas. The pin-drop silence was broken by the echoed clicking of the closing room door. Those doors were rarely closed, if ever, as curtains worked for privacy, not the doors.

Dr. Thomas, a Santa Claus looking kind of chap in my mind, could have part-timed at the local department store as Chris Cringle himself. He cordially greeted my family and slid a chair as close as he could to the air bubble barrier between him and me. The various pumps and hoses escorted me to the foot of my bed next to where I attempted to sit. Actually, I leaned more or less propped up resting against the end of the mattress. Facing about a foot apart from each other, I could easily see the uncomfortable and compassionate expressions being conveyed by his face. What was to be discussed was essentially what my family had already been informed of. I concluded this due to all of the surrounding evidence. With empathetic watery eyes and a slow washing of the hands gesture, the tender and subtle voice expressed all of what we feared most.

The doctor said that I had put up a gallant battle and fought hard but that we had run out of any other options to try. I'm assuming now, that besides the legal ramifications preventing me from having another dose of bone marrow at the time. That coupled with other factors such as my very frail condition, not being able to withstand anymore damage, i.e., more extreme doses of chemo, total body radiation, etc. And also the evidence of me losing my graft, gave hints that the bone marrow was not compatible. On top of that, the graft vs. host disease brewing heartily and it simply was out of the question.

The one suggested option that I was given was that they could try to pump me up with more mega doses of nutrition and vitamins to perhaps get me strong enough to endure a plane trip home. They felt that if I could make it home that I may have a couple of weeks possibly to be with my family and friends along with Yukon my dog, and the comfort's of my own home to pass away in.

Everything hinged around a number called a poli count. The poli count evidently revealed much information to the doctors about my overall condition relevant to the marrow engraftment, cell growth and so forth. I believe that the "life line" or crucial number of a poli count for me was around fifty. Anything above that was tolerable to sufficient for stability or improvement. Anything below the number fifty was life threatening. That particular day I was like fifty two or something I believe. Dr. Thomas tried to give me a "you're going to die speech" as humanly compassionately as he was able. There isn't anything that I respect more in a doctor than compassion and understanding. I'm sure most patients would agree with me about that. "A lesson here for many physicians out there as well as other hospitals staff members to think about". Everything concluded with my at least knowing that I'd have some more time to try and "b.s". or think of a way to get better. It would take a week or so to try and pump me up for a possible plane ride home.

To break the ice amongst my somber family members, although I take no credit for the spontaneity of it all, I somehow made them laugh. I poked fun at my bean pole legs shooting out of what looked like diaper sized underwear. "Look, I'm Olive Oil; what do you think?" This gesture was a good, all around positive move. I also came up with a better idea in convincing the doctors to allow me to stay in the laminar room as long as my poli's were at fifty. Inevitably, whatever it was that I said was for the better. Perhaps they accommodated me by humoring me in anticipating my downfall at any moment. Or, they were still indecisive among themselves as to who made the eviction notice decision. At any rate, it worked out the way that it did, so chalk up another one for that coincidence column.

This stage of mental attrition was much more difficult than the physical debilitations I had racked up. I wish that I could go back and change the way that I sometimes behaved toward my father and others. In what would all come down to about a five second window in the early morning hours, determined that whole day's outlook and demeanor. A simple index card-sized paper would be posted in the lab indicating my actual poli count. My super father would rise first thing, early from the apartment and hurry over to sit and wait down at the lab room. He would then intercept the incoming data and bring it up to me. All that I had to do was take one glance at his face the second that he emerged through the doorway. I didn't sleep most nights by now, just pining, pondering and praying.

The big plastic divider wall that housed the robot-like gloves became a decided war room wall chart for my dad and I. Scotch tape and four by five pieces of paper started adding up. Early numbers of fifty five, fifty nine, fifty, fifty seven, forty five, forty one, forty six, fifty one and so on flowed in. Within seconds I was good for the whole day or snippy and isolated on my part for the day. That was terribly hard on my family and on top of that, it found me sleeping the day away from night insomnia and exhaustion. If I didn't already use the quote of "low point of my life", this was it. If I did use it, I was wrong.

Again, waiting like a dog for its owner, I toiled until my dad arrived. At least three or four weeks went by and probably more like six or eight because I recall something like fifty or sixty papers up before I asked my dad to pull them off. In a funny way I likened those strips to the World War II bomber planes and fighters who painted swastikas and rising suns on their fuselage to designate successful missions and kills. I could have looked at the poli counts as a victory of survival with all of those strips taped to my bubble wall. I should have thought of that then instead of in hindsight, all that I saw then were death cards amassing.

With no marked improvement in the numbers, it was obvious that they really weren't going to raise to encouraging poli counts. I guess that it was somewhat of a hopeful sign that although they didn't rise, they didn't fall far under fifty either. I was reaching I suppose, but this was a definite enigma in that it didn't add up medically. They either rise to normal recovery levels or they bottom out and you die This very much puzzled everyone involved.

The same old things were killing us all. My irritability, the family's emptied exhaustion and the doctors' frustration left us all cracking from the pressure. The most horrible scare came when my numbers arrived in the thirties meaning that I could technically die at any moment. I guess they ruled out my leaving, at least alive anyhow because I would never survive a plane trip across the country. The airlines had stipulated that my family had to sign legal papers waiving their responsibility if I died on the plane. I had given power of attorney over to Carol, my brother and/or my dad but as long as I was coherent and could convey clear thoughts I figured that I could still make decisions.

Literally having no strength left and the slurring of my speech suggested that I was expiring. I desperately tried reciting Hail Mary's and Our Father's of the rosary but couldn't remember the words. I do recall telling God to accept my prayers as they were and to come help me please. I'd get a bit of energy here and there, just enough to converse briefly and somehow I'd confidently think that God did intervene to urge my family, and me on. One of those touching things was in getting my prayer requests out to my family. I asked them to start getting to Mass as much as possible now, even if it meant not visiting me for awhile. I also asked them to summon Father Carmody again.

Something kept him from visiting the first night, and just as if it was scripted, I had another incredible evening of calm serenity that I would only compare to one or two other ever of its kind. I pleaded with my girlfriend to pray as hard as she knew how. The prayer cards of the Sacred Heart of Jesus, the Blessed Mother, St. Padre Pio and St. Therese taped facing in towards me on the bubble wall were once again recited with as much fervor as I could muster up. Of course, more so by her than I at this point due to my declining state.

My childlike faith implored my guardian angel to finish any prayers that I couldn't articulate, remembering this from teachings as a boy. Another one of the vivid memories I have is that of my girlfriend lying out on the chair bed that evening. In the middle of the night I found myself awakening from a short rest only to find her still up. She had a sheet pulled over her head and a flashlight scanning the prayer cards underneath. I found tears trickling down my cheek from being so touched as my nose ran amuck at the same time I burst into a quiet, reflecting and thankful laugh. I doubt if "Tweety" as I called her noticed me watching her due to her big feet propped up and sticking out of the sheets. Those big feet in those white tube sox wiggling away at twenty miles an hour.

As that night turned into day nothing changed with my poli counts. The whole day was centered around Father Carmody's expected arrival along with constant prayer; "Simply talking to God in conversation as prayer". Some of the nurses must have thought that I was delusional and talking to myself but I didn't say anything. A particular cleaning lady made a social event out of coming to my room and not leaving. God bless her but I was like, 'please get the heck out of here!'

It wasn't until the day eroded away with intense waiting that the good Father whisked in from the hallway. Disguised somewhat in a hat and trench coat covering a red flannel shirt, he explained how he occasionally ran through the neighborhood on calls incognito. This was due to the couple of bad areas that he had to sometimes travel through. I remember his generic collar being made from toilet paper or a paper towel that he took off while settling into the chair and laughing about it. I believe the reason had something to do with the quick visit and improvisation.

Father Carmody had visited me three or four times in this now growing span of seven months, not including the Masses that I attended at St. James Cathedral. All of the visits were good but this one differed in two ways: One of course, I was dying, and two, Father had brought with him a fiery spirit, perhaps the Holy Spirit, and a collection of relics of Saints. With our developed rapport over the past visits, Father knew of my St. Therese and St. Padre Pio relics as well. With the sharing some of my insight as to how I felt faith and spirituality wise, he came to express some of his as well. Of the relics that he brought, I believe a couple of them were of the very first Apostles of Christ. St. Peter and Paul I want to say as well as other historically highly recognized Saints in the Church. It bothers me that I can't recall exactly which ones he brought but I was in very bad condition for sure so I'm surprised, frankly, that I can retain any of this information for that matter.

Father Carmody had a vigor engulfing and fueling him that evening, as if he himself was in the zone and on a mission. I believe that he felt my faith was sincere and wanted to help as best he knew how. I received Holy Communion from him in the form of a tiny piece of the Host due to my weakness. I then was given Last Rites, also known as Extreme Unction once again and we got down to business. That evening visit was like we were two spiritual architects at a card game. I say that because the room was cleared except for the two of us and it seemed like the dim lights and ambiance were appropriate for the analogy in my mind. Father conveyed the personal meanings of his relics and how he felt they had helped in other times in his life during crisis situations. I'd guess that my expression of faith wasn't the norm for many Catholics, sorry to say. Perhaps he picked up on something that made him help the way that he did. Just as he would do for anyone I'm sure, if they would only ask for it just as I did!

Our visit this evening lasted about an hour consisting of intense prayer to God, using such scriptures as when two or more are gathered in my name anything asked of the Father in Jesus' name shall be done. I sincerely pleaded with God in conversations as if he were right in front of me. Together we torched the skies of Heaven with all of our vigor and tenacity that we knew how to fire up. I cheated and slid my hand through the air barrier to his hands and joined together in prayer. The relics were touched to my wrist and prayers for the intercession of those Saints were recited. This was the point in time where I really felt like I did everything that I knew how to do spiritually and left it in God's hands, with no fear or regrets of forgetting anything. I still had a fear of dying at that point of course, but serenity in weakness plus the morphine flowing through my veins gave me confidence that the pain or fear wouldn't get much worse. I don't think that I was afraid of death in the sense of what was in store for me but more of a not wanting to leave my family, friends and life in the "human sense".

When Father Carmody left, I think I conversed with my girlfriend a bit when she hit me with a quote playing a Cyndi Lauper song, *"True Colors"*. "I can't remember when I last saw you smile". Teary eyed, she moseyed out of the room for a moment to the lounge. I'll never forget that moment and think of her whenever I hear that song. I really thought that night could be the one that I didn't wake up from and pondered about the other side experience. Exhaustion took over and I must have blanked out.

With another morning to wake up to, I realized that I was still alive or Heaven or Hell didn't look any different. I really did think that briefly as funny as it sounds! I soon glanced out of the window to see a rare sunny morning (at least in the months that I had been there). To stay true to form with the character of the script, it was about time for another miracle, or coincidence if you prefer, to take the stage. Seriously though, this is just the way that it unfolded with the records to indicate it all, it just kept coming.

The morning ruckus in the hall was earlier than usual; so you could tell that something was up. The question was who all of the fuss was about. I was aware of another acquaintance patient passing away from hearing and noticing the family members in grieving in hysterics. "More traumatic scars to file" My heart died a little more from that and just as I was about to dismiss the bickering out there in the hall and attribute it to the same family crisis, the herd of white coats entered into my room.

The sudden lump in my chest, stymied by that jolt of a drum thud sensation and burst of adrenaline rattled my pool stick legs. "What now?" I gasped to myself. "What now?" With focused attention as if they finally were on the same page and in cahoots with each other, I was dealt with a proposition. Caught with complete abandoned surprise and now sorry to recall every physician's presence, the crafty proposal was just the crack in the door that I was praying for. I just knew it. I absolutely knew it!

Dr. Thomas, sitting on the chair with a lingering twinkle in his eye and my family banned right behind him. Above their heads Dr. Buckner hovered and Dr. Rick the p.a., lurked in the shadows wearing a candy-eating grin as if to say, "I told you so!" (He was the guy that told me not to give up or go home. He never believed that I was loosing my graft to begin with). Several other prominent doctors were present who had just as much to do with this coup as any of them. They were specialists so my recollection isn't as precise although I do remember agreeing to mail a case of Rolling Rock beer to one doctor when I returned to the East some day (I haven't as of yet.)

The whole scheme hinged around a hypothesis of a chance of success. Evidently the recollection of my comments about my side feeling enlarged was brought to the forefront at one of their meetings. A hunch, that a remote possibility of cells being harbored or accumulated in my spleen, could theoretically explain my predicament. Since the counts hadn't died out yet, but hadn't elevated either gave some validity to this notion. Obviously, there was no proof as of yet, but it was evident that I wouldn't continue to live without trying something.

Dr. Thomas suggested to me that a possibility of improvement might exist if their theory was right. He said that there had never been a case like this but "we can try to remove your spleen and see if the counts rise". The catch is that you will most likely die from bleeding to death. I'd probably die, "hum…where have I heard that so many times before…" Dr. Thomas also candidly noted that "frankly, if we don't try it you will most certainly die." Well, being the Rhodes Scholar, rocket scientist that I now was, my keen deduction abilities chose the former. Since this was an alternative to just sit and hope, I felt that God had given me a route to go by. My spirits did in fact rise as much as they were able and I cracked more jokes about my legs and underwear being a perfect fit "for a cartoon character".

The majority of the doctors agreed that this was an appropriate step to take at this stage, so that in its self gave me some confidence considering the circumstances. My family was fearful, of course, but you could see a change in them as well because they were workers of sorts. This was a direction to go in so they geared up for the ride. Buzzing like bees, they scattered every which way to the phones, to the apartment, to the church and probably to the bathroom. I just felt so positive now and never had a second doubt to go ahead with the procedure. Even though the doctors felt that my chances of dying from the spleenectomy itself were about as high as they were without having it. Like I said, it was a last chance and they wanted me to decide for myself whether I wanted to go home and die in peace or die "with my boots on" trying, as the group I like, Iron Maiden, sings. My being the son of a Marine, Semper Fi Dad, let's go! That's a bit melodramatic I know but I was ready.

Since time was of the essence, surgery was slated for that afternoon. Poor Carol was in charge of saving me again along with the doctors of course, as they planned to hook her up to a constant platelet line for me. This was to try and counter the massive blood loss anticipated with her counter infusions. Despite how it may have sounded, I was still relatively hopeful. Like Underdog and his power pill, you might say that I took a power pill filled with emotion and was flying high on it. Why not, I mean all of this time here, with the escalating costs, and nothing left to lose really, Carol deemed me the "five and half million dollar man and escalating, marrow man". My faith was taken to the wall and I was ready to prove it. So I hoped, it sounded good anyhow.

Once that I decided to go for it and everyone arranged their roles in their respective positions, the whole afternoon whip lashed by to welcome in show time. It would have been neat to cue up the ring announcer who rolls out the infamous one-liner "Let's get ready to rumble"...that's how pumped I was. Then along with that as fighters often do, they pick an entrance song to express their intent state of mind. I'd blare the timeless theme from the movie, "*The Good, the Bad and the Ugly*". It can stir up emotions for any cowboy or war movie buff, it's wordless so it reinforced the adage that talk is cheap and most of all the song smokes! I love to fire it up for a Penn State television game. Like their uniforms, all business, that's what I focused in on, all business. As a psychology major, I truly believe that the patient can contribute immensely to his or her outcome with the mental tools at their disposal.

Being positive can only be contagious to the O.R. staff and the doctors fighting to save your life. Your confidence in them can only inspire and convey that they like a teammate know that you'll give it everything you can just as they will for you. The verse in the Bible that states, "If God is for you who can be against you" is yet another example of how I deliberately attempted to surrender all of this mess into God's hands. I could hear the crowd in my mind or envision the fighter pilot saluting the fellow allies as he engaged into take off on a mission.

As corny as it sounds, I was capped and gowned up, stuck on the gurney and whisked away. Perhaps you can see the analogies that I made. The cap and gown was the required garb, my gurney was the F-16 of the hallways, and the trip to the O.R. was my flight plan, the O.R. was my destination and the spleen was my foe. Why I made all of those puns and connections, I assume, was a defense mechanism to cope and feel more involved instead of being just a patient on the table. "Clear for takeoff, Houston."

If my body was as close to ceasing in these hours, I don't recall, at that point, it having any bearing on my demeanor. I feel yet another example of mind over matter, you have to pick an inspiration song word for word, and then climb a mountain or two. Of course, the mother of all lies would be told if I said that I wasn't deep down inside a "bit" terrified.

I suppressed any feelings of 'this could be the last time you are conscious or alive' and instead rattled every other thought that I could call upon to bombard my family, doctors and anyone that would humor me and listen for that matter. Only God knows what I shot the B.S. about. I'm sure no one today would have a clue. Of course, the gamut of emotions attempted to surface constantly but I was fortunate to escape these fearful human inner voices. The countdown began backwards from ninety nine, ninety eight, ninety seven, etc. and fluttered away with a probable giggle as the knock out juice effectively sent me to la-la land.

Presumably several hours elapsed and only from being the big story in the hospital that day with the staff, my family was informed of how lengthy and difficult this operation was turning out to be. After the staff had worked their magic again, a dastardly but not regrettable nightmare of a scenario unfolded for me. When that moment finally arrives that the anesthetic wears off into post-op park job time on the gurney, it slowly brought me back to consciousness. I vividly remember talking to myself mentally, while the distorted tones of conversation other than mine came into focus. As the brilliant lights from the ceiling above rained down through my now radiated and thinned eyelids, my first comprehended sound was that of sobbing. Evidently my girlfriend and or sister had been trying to communicate with me. Due to my non-existent pulse to the simple touch, they presumed prematurely that I had died. Either Carol or my girlfriend b-lined down the hallway frantically as the crying sounds of a single person were recognized by my blurred orientation as one of those two people. "John…John…, he's not breathing (hiccup—hiccup) I heard murmured. I'm tuning into this saying to myself "You must not have died." "I heard that, wait a minute I'm still alive!" "What do you mean I'm not breathing?" acting as though my family had the presence of mind to pull out the always carried feather and stick it under my nose to see my breath blew against it.

My first attempt to speak ended up in a silent gulp-like whisper. My throat was as dry as the desert and evidently getting an endorphin rush from knowing that I was still alive. I used my regained motor controls to grab my girlfriend's arm and exclaimed as best I could, "Boo!" I probably could have killed her I guess, but the tension was broken with the family elation realized through the false alarm. Initially I didn't realize it but when I reached to startle them and celebrate, several staples popped out of my stomach that had been used as partial sutures. I wonder how far they flew. Little circles on my belly often remind me of this fiasco. Needless to say, we all had taken a ride on the world's latest roller coaster again.

When that trip ended I found myself right back where I'd started, in the bubble, in critical condition and still in Seattle, but I was alive. Only now burning with hope and curiosity as to whether or not this ingenious brainstorm of a hunch would pay off. Spleenectomies are sometimes performed on leukemia patients, for sure, but never in a condition such as mine. Now that I seemed to have pulled through this procedure, we all had to wait and see what came next.

Resting and hopefully now recharging real counts to speak of, the humorous buzz among the nurses was the record setting size of my spleen. It was so bizarre that it was carted down the hall dubbed the pot roast from John's side or something like that. My spleen went over to the University of Washington for research I believe, but the obvious size and proportions described concluded that it harbored major volumes of cells. Now we had to see if those cells were my old leukemic cells or new healthy ones from my donor. That and my body's response to being spleenless would go a long way in determining my hope for this recovery. Incidentally, everybody got to see that spleen of mine except me, I never got a chance to gaze at that glazed ham of cells. I guess by the size of my scar that you could say I had a vertical Cesarean section delivery.

Desperately needed good news came from my body several hours later. Counts that appeared to be on the rise! Relief was at the tips of our tongues and when pathology revealed a spleen of healthy donor cells! The champagne could be shaken! It took about three days or so to confirm for sure that the spleen theory indeed was the big link to my decline. Steady increments of rising counts in the days that followed established the fact that the engraftment was taking. Even though I still had many other complications to deal with such as GVHD and chronic infections, with any luck I could be envisioning going home soon. I mean home home.

The marked improvement after this superb tactical maneuver allowed me to step up from death's door to the first landing. Staff members were genuinely happy and excited with my upgrade. This had to boost the morale for all fellow "transplantinians" on the floor as well as their families. I absolutely feel that the opinion I earlier stated about "as long as the heart is beating there is always hope" still stands first and foremost to express and convey my story. Obviously, by that I mean that state of mind to dig down, not to ever give up, and to fight. God is the presider and my quote is the very link of confidence I and we all should have in Him.

Roughly two more weeks went by and I still was in the laminar room. Seemingly climbing walls in my mind. I elaborated on my improvement, but what seemed like miles of positive strides taking place was actually a snails pace in reality. In terms of possibly flying home soon, I could envision it coming but even then I would need to be hospitalized there most likely, in order to get plans rolling for flight arrangements and so forth. I had to establish a solid dietary intake aside from the hyper-al tubes feeding me. I would have to consume 500 calories a day, so this gives you a great perspective of where I was. I think there's 500 calories in a lousy candy bar but to try one was like swallowing a sword at this point.

Strict records of intake were taken so, obviously, quality and nutrition was critical. More L.A.F. tasteless goo was rousted up for me and once I had a fixed number to fly the coop with in my mind, I could motivate myself to achieve it faster, so I thought. As I mentioned all consumption as well as my bathroom output would be measured and charted. The second criterion for release from the cave was no fever. Coming down from one hundred and six plus you'd think that ninety nine to one hundred was a milestone! In itself it was of course but in my situation, ninety nine point five and above was potential cause for alarm. In trying to get in these 500 calories, I was required to have food other than sweets. My stomach had atrophied so much that it was compared to a tennis or baseball in its capacity size.

Fevers did in fact erupt and I became symptomatic of diabetic tendencies. Insulin injections were administered after every food intake. I tried to get it to stop the "falling down an elevator effect" in my stomach and with my equilibrium. This condition lasted a couple of weeks, I believe, and as a linked complication to my condition, it just added more crap to sort out as to its origin.

Leap frogging past the many days of blood count charting for sugar levels along with marrow related statistics, things finally simmered to where I could think about lobbying for departure times. This being a good time for more personal humor reflections, a real enjoyable memory for me was a day or two before I actually said, "Adieu". I was so frustrated in my accomplishments to eat food that my devious dark side prevailed. With more looming depression and anxiety squared right behind, I brainstormed my patented juvenile food trashing scam. I could be the first bone marrow transplant patient to toss out those scrumptious delectable, delicacies of laminar cuisine!

In a desperate attempt to go AWOL, I persuaded Carol to do the dirty work of my mastermind calorie fraud fiasco and trash the stuff. It was all going according to our synchronized watches. Actually the clock on the wall and I would meet hands with Carol at the air lock, dumping and camouflaging the mess as I directed her so as not to leave a clue. Carol "grabbed and chucked", poetry in motion in my mind and seemingly it was too good to be true.

Could it be that we had pulled it off? Like two excited thieves finding pay dirt, our basking in the moment was shot out of the sky like a clay pigeon. Caught stealing cookies from the cook jar; Carol was nabbed red-handed with plate in hand in the trash can. Carol was the perfect Catholic schoolgirl and, as advertised, she was destined to get busted. She couldn't do a dastardly deed and get away with it if her life depended on it. Well, a nurse entered the room and I failed to plan ahead and counter the infiltration of staff members. All I would have needed was a third party recruit to signal danger. Thinking back now, why didn't I just empty it all in a bag inside my bubble and then toss it over? Oh, what a tangled web we weave when to practice to deceive…The punch line to all of this was my biggest fear being realized of getting squealed on and held back longer from graduation.

I was sick worrying about the potential tattletale as it all unfolded. Either I was snitched on without retribution or the nurse was a double agent and didn't crack under the pressure. I don't even know if it ever came into play with respect to my release but what is hilarious to me today was no laughing matter in 1987. Eight months and counting as a prisoner and you can see why! Believe it or not, after I have spilled my soul recanting my story, this point is just the warm up in the big scope of things to come!

Finally, the end of the rainbow was in sight as far as the escape from Seattle 'weekend excursion' was concerned. No fever, sufficient calorie intake (with or without my trash can food plot) and another painful marrow tap gave an okay for the travel arrangements to be given clearance. The legal papers were signed for the airlines to relinquish them from any responsibilities. For my health status, flying home came down to one last night of sweating it out hoping not to spike a fever, etc. The very earliest check out time was five thirty in the morning during the shift change. I employed Carol to map out the quickest escape route possible. I'd even go disguised incognito if I had to, I bantered to myself. "like I could have blended in as a normal person". While my family made all of the arrangements and took care of remaining business the previous evening, Carol stayed in my room that night to ensure rapid get away at five thirty sharp.

With the evening ticking away into the next morning, the moment of truth arrived. In the most anticipated episode since watching the bone marrow trickle into me some eight months ago, I slithered down the back hallway one last time as a patient, I hoped. Regretfully, I did not get to say good-bye formally to everyone that I would have liked to and promptly made a clean jail break, leaving my bubble vacant for a new life-saving attempt. The recollection of my trip home is very vague. A slight memory of being whisked away like a tornado rings a bell but photos we have from the moment show me as being extremely frail, battered, masked, yellow and totally exhausted. My girlfriend who stood next to me for the most part showed signs of war time fatigue and a slight inkling of relief in the anticipation of going home.

One of the small conversations between my parents and I is paramount for me in my life. In my not formally thanking Father Carmody before leaving, I vowed to write or call him as soon as I could. My mom said that she thanked him for everything that he had done for us. His reply to her was "No, thank you." "My faith had questions that I had toiled with but after seeing what I have witnessed; my faith is even more reinforced in God. So, thank you and God bless you all for what you've done for me." That is so awesome for me to hear words like that from a man of God who you look to for your guidance. The Lord definitely does work in strange ways.

The final touch in departing Seattle had me insisting that Carol throw that darn green sweater of hers she often enjoyed wearing out of the plane window! Yes, it was expensive and yes, it was lovely but no, I couldn't stand to see it any longer! Actually I think she left it for a homeless person along with a bag of my no longer fitting clothes.

Upon arrival to the Philadelphia International Airport, my girlfriend's father picked us up in a van. We all fit fine and I believe that the rest of my family was waiting at our home. All of the past months in the hospital left me very disoriented on I95 and the surrounding area that only a year ago was all too familiar to me. I was drugged up but I really felt drugged up as depicted in television movies with the LSD hallucinations of spinning, falling, dizziness, etc. I closed my eyes and talked silently to my Id not to panic! I convinced the ego to ride it out, I'd be home in fifteen minutes, and so it was.

Vaguely remembering that first night back, I recall my waterbed and my room feeling a bit strange but I eventually became acclimated to the old comfort zone. Exhaustion helped me sleep through the night only to wake feeling like I had slept for years. The fifteen second clock that alarmed inside my mind telling me that I had leukemia instinctively went off. This was about the first time I began to try and recondition myself of this stigma. I was supposedly now leukemia free at this point but my psyche would have none of that. It merely plunged a new dagger of thoughts in while removing the old one. Every bone marrow transplant patient knows that the first year is the so-called year to hold your breath and hope against a relapse. Some occur even after that time frame, so it wasn't conducive to my outlook being informed of that tidbit of information.

With this going on inside my head, I was given the choice to try being treated as an outpatient at my local hospital or simply be admitted. It was a tremendously difficult decision that took me all of about the blink of any eye to decide on this tough one. Thanks but no thanks to the hospital! The hospital staff then led us to coordinate the maintenance arrangement between my family, the doctors and myself. The first line of business was to have me go in to see my original doctors and assess the directions to be given.

Dr. Mike Soojian had progressively taken over my case as the primary physician in the associate oncology group. I would and still do see the other three doctors on occasion and our overall rapport is good. Upon my father driving me to the hospital that afternoon, I again have a distinct memory of Dr. Mike outside the doorway waiting for me. I guess this was exciting for him as a doctor being very involved to see me at least make it back home. I joked to him as I also did previously with a fitness club manager, Doug that I knew, if they didn't see me in a few months that I would probably be dead. Obviously, I was five months longer in returning and still alive." I think I was anyway at the time...

Doctor Mike greeted us warmly and perhaps even more so than his usual office type of demeanor in his mannerism. As funny as it sounds, I cannot recollect any of the visits' goings on, just the greeting from Dr. Mike. The next memories I have swiveled over to my sister and I returning to the same hospital to arrange for her platelet donations to continue to be infused into me. This was a cubby hole of a room somewhere down in the basement of the hospital I believe. It was set up with the all to familiar standard chairs and vein drainers, etc. i.e., needles and bags, I.V.s, machines, and so on. Poor Carol had nothing left as I felt her "normal" platelet reserve lowered in top off count numbers by as much as fifty thousand to sixty thousand or so. In other words, her previous normal level was in about the one hundred and eighty thousand to two hundred and eighty thousand range, where as now it resided around one hundred and ten thousand to one hundred and fifty thousand.

Further reflection on this time frame was that of Dr. Mike and his staff success in training my girlfriend to withdraw blood from my Hickman catheter line. This enabled me to stay home a lot more initially and recuperate there while my drawn blood could be taken to the hospital daily for count analysis. I think it was a wonderful gesture to allow me this option. Luckily, I had tremendous support from my family.

I feel one of the obvious setbacks initially was my frame of mind in relation to having visitors or see friends. For infection reasons I wasn't able to leave for the first several weeks. I continued wearing a mask around family members and outside to the hospital. My self-conscious complex about my appearance was excruciating for me. As the days accumulated, the encouraging news was good in that it was that much further along which I had survived, but the downside of it was I felt that with each passing day my appearance was looking worse and worse. The apparent cease to my bloating, the total body irradiation that was still fermenting and ravaging my skin, the massive chemo damage to my insides and the heavy pay load of medicines that I now had to take daily were candidates for a Guinness Book or Ripley's Believe It or Not story.

My then, soon to be ex-, brother-in-law was an amputee veteran of the Vietnam War and one of his indelible contributions to this story was a one line statement that he pitched in one day right around this time. He said something to the effect that he would rather have to lose his leg again in the war he fought in than to have to go through the procedures he saw me go through. I guess this can give credence to the term "it's all relative". Although I have no doubt that I would have fought for my country, I can't help but wonder about that statement when I have read so much on war itself. Having said that, I would now myself have gladly traded a limb in exchange for what I have come to know and experience without a doubt. .

With time still gradually creaking by, the first attempt on a social excursion was to visit my girlfriend's grandparents' home. This was like a second family to me by now and there were so many of them. After a big greeting of reunited emotions, I enjoyed becoming a fixture in their living room. Several long visits ensued and it sparked a ray of hope to graduate to the next phase of seeing loved ones— my then friends. The grandparents' home was a great place also to see some of the guys who would stop by and attempt to re-bond on lost time and happenings. Initially, I had no idea how much could change in eight months of a hiatus. That was another shock to me perspective-wise as well.

With some of the reunification groundwork laid, the next order of business now would be to extrapolate on those pills and medicines I touched on. I guess that I would start with the high-grade motor oil substance called cyclosporine. Three to four times daily I had to try and consume a shot glass sized equivalent of the castor oil suspension based immuno suppressive. I often either bailed out or had bad gag reflex spasms every single time that I swallowed the thick goop. Camouflaging it again with chocolate syrup and milk went against some theories of absorption and function. Others posted the notion of whatever you can get in is better than nothing at all. Levels were of course, monitored. The only hint of a remedy for me was a cold coke chaser down the hatch immediately afterward to try and flush away the nasty residue of slime coating my throat. "No offense cyclosporine, we just weren't a match made in Heaven" as was the case with other patients. Some could handle it and some couldn't.

Cyclosporine caused hot flashes and occasional heart misfires inside of me as well as sporadic episodes of profuse perspiration spells. It has been tabbed 'AIDS in a bottle' by some physicians due to its potent ability to suppress the body's t-cell counts. That occurs in HIV as a major complication without drugs and, ultimately, contributes to death. Whereas, some evidence suggests that GVHD as living on the opposite side of the tracks with t-cells initiating damage to the body. The jury is still out as far as all of the active factors involved though.

Next, doing damage to me was the villain prednisone; a bigger bully to me in its own right. Namely, that "roid rage" of immense mood swings that would catch up to me later on. For now I was just amassing fluid on top of more fluid. I became a living Macy's Day Parade float. Milligrams as ridiculously high as around eight or nine hundred mg twice a day, I believe, which for those of you that are familiar with this medicine, is a purely insane level to fly on. It very well may have been higher than that. A protocol taper was attempted but due to all of the complications that I was having, it was put off and my own specific mainte-nance strategy was implemented. Bactrum and pills that were Herman Munster sized for those of you who have seen the show were also now a main staple, which I took several times a day. Incidentally, I choked on them dangerously more than a few times due to the esophagus problem I had incurred and a now due to a developing stricture that was forming. This so-called 'web' of scar tissue would eventually lead to a dilation operation in my throat down the line.

On top of these were magnesium, potassium, iron and handfuls of other beau-ties. All of these toxic medicines and supplements to destroy me in a sense and, at the same time, try to make me well. I was taking poisons to mediate the not-so-perfect "perfect match" of fireworks of new cells trying to move in and co-habituate with organs that were old to me, but definitely very new to the bone marrow. The prophecy of Dr. Jim's statement about trading one fatal disease with another fatal disease seemed primed to begin unfolding if this medicine cocktail didn't soon get a foot hold. I'll also throw in with the mix here additional daily side effects of nauseous vomiting spells that I countered somewhat with the breeze of a fan on high in my face while breathing in and out. "Panting, you might say." Diarrhea, fatigue, tingling fingertips, cyclosporine/prednisone hair now black and curly, and more perspiring along with insomnia and nightmares were the norm. Lots of fun I'll tell you. Again, in attempting to piece together events that occurred some fourteen or fifteen years ago, and counting, I probably can only recollect the prominent events that stick out the most to me. I am certain that I have blocked out or forgotten many more interesting pieces of this puzzle.

During this course of attempted recovery, a few rather enjoyable moments consisted of some past pleasures. For one thing I was able to again get to visit my good friend Father Fahey. We actually had a private Mass of thanksgiving in the church. Just him and I up at the altar, including St. Theresa and St. Padre Pio along with the Blessed Mother and everyone that had a hand in helping me in our offerings to God. It felt so nice to be home and actually making it back to church again. This was one of the only times though that I was able to do this, for another hiatus not of my own doing, was soon to follow.

The few months of summer away from hospitals as an inpatient were memorable. In fact, at one point, I seemed to be making some awesome progress. So much so that I was able to take the stage and play drums with an all-star menagerie of my friend musicians again. This stage and performance took place in my girlfriend's grandparents' huge back yard where frequent parties were held. The guys built the stage and set all of my drums up and we were ready to play. My usual fan was hooked up and aimed right on me just as I always preferred it to be. Getting to sit up on stage back behind the skins was awesome! Hardly missing a beat my adrenaline levels soared while that new marrow fueled my body through a few killer sets in the course of about an hour and a half or so. The normal set breaks of about fifteen to twenty minutes allowed me to fire up my squirt bottle to the face as well as throwing a cold cloth all over my perspired body.

The spark of rain showers into thunderstorms felt refreshing to me but seeing those corded guitars and the players diving for cover was no laughing matter to them, although it cracked me up. This storm was for the best I assume because I had unknowingly passed my fueled levels and was at the point of collapsing. The moment of fun just basked my mind into the days of old as almost to the very minute I entered the house, I had to be carried up to a bed where I wiped out. My girlfriend's brother's wife aided me by applying more compresses, blankets, and the like. The buzzing in my ears, I figured initially, was just the ambiance of everyone downstairs but it turned out to be my ears! I totally overdid it. What I'd lost in physical wear and tear I'd like to think was gained back with some signs of being human again even if just for a few hours.

Another favorable moment I believe came in the late months of that August in which I miraculously conned my sister and father into letting me drive a car again. By no means was it real road driving per se but I was taken to a state park and permitted to cruise practically at idle speed around the isolated areas including that always thrilling parking lot. As vanilla as it was I did acquire some sense back for the feel of the road that I had all but lost back in the war zones of Seattle.

With the good came the bad as I made a classic drugged-up irrational decision that still haunts me. After much finagling by my poor mother and father on my behalf; the awesome 1969 sunflower yellow Corvette, a convertible with a black soft top, yellow hard top, side pipes, 4-speed and centerline champ 500 wheels, was soon to be piddled away. How? By my stupidity and foolish way of irrational thinking, that's how. I'm not saying that I was never irrational before the transplant but definitely concluded here that the drug mixtures were the main culprits.

I somehow in some foolish way decided to sell the 'Vette. I must have misconstrued the thoughts of clutching and shifting along with no power steering as a major hurdle to overcome. I had lasted through all of the other things and then let a stinking clutch sabotage everything that my parents had done in labors of love for me. Remember when I stated that we didn't have much money; well, we didn't!

I guess it hurt my parents so much that their son was dying from leukemia that they would stop at nothing to find the funds. And my being a selfish, narrow-minded jerk like of a leech unknowingly knowingly sucked them dry. I wish to God that I could go back and change all of the materialistic gluttony, relatively speaking, to where we were financially, a hair above being poor, and where I was mentally. Comparatively we were poor in the big picture but not in spirit.

Well, what transpired was me having my parents take me on a distant journey to see a shyster of a car dealer who sold sports cars and hot rods. At the time I didn't know what a fraud and thief this car dealer was. To make a very painful and long story short, I was taken alone in a back office with this shyster. He explained how a guy like me was in no position to drive a big powerful, stick shift 'Vette and what I needed was a smaller automatic of some kind.

The car that brought me there in the first place turned out to be a show car that they often used as bait. It was a very awesome, pristine 1968 Firebird with a 455 engine and all "pro-streeted up" or customized with every conceivable accessory you could imagine. Candy apple wine-glass type paint and I wanted to trade for it. Ordinarily my right mind would have known that my 'Vette was worth a good deal more. Well, that was my initial plan until I was persuaded away with a story of how the Firebird only got 3 miles per gallon, wasn't ready for sale and so forth. He slickly eased me over and into a 1969 Camaro that was a clean driver but not in a league with my 'Vette for value, "the car he stole". It is hard to own up to this story but readers can get an idea of what the massive drugs, chemo and irradiation can do to the human mind as well as the body.

My mind was completely in an altered state, no doubt about it. So much so, in fact, that not only did the maggot get my '69 'Vette but, I believe, a thousand dollars on top of that! In return I got a very average Camaro worth about $3,000.00. It was a clean driver, automatic, power steering but no even up exchange, not even close. Now the hardest part of the story is I later found out the guy turned around and sold my 'old car' for around $13,000.00. More than double of what my parents had originally paid. Can you feel that painful lump in my stomach also? As for the thief who conned me, he has to meet up with God eventually. What goes around comes around...

CHAPTER 5

▼

With these few stories passed on here, the summer had ended and the change of seasons brought with it all of the things I enjoy the most: brisk air, colorful scenery, holidays and football. The time had elapsed by rather quickly and, before I knew it, the Thanksgiving dinner was being served. The then-family tradition had us at Carol's house most years. I was seated in the same familiar chair in which my sister coaxed me into going to the doctors some four years earlier. It was "deja vous" and I had a special feeling of the thinking that this was all just a bad dream, which had seeped into my mind. As I mentioned earlier, that very sensation really does occur now and then, and it's very eerie to say the least.

With my health improved comparatively over from where I'd been, aside from the fact that my paranoia of a relapse which I had mentioned, I had an improving sense of victory. The pessimistic side of me still waged battle against me daily but I would say this stretch was a true break from it all. Some of my strength came back, although not nearly to what it was prior to all of those toxins and transplant procedures done to me. I had enough though to slowly attempt a mall trip and go out for pizza, which incidentally did start breaking through my fried and previously tasteless taste buds. Chocolate chips still tasted like wet paper but, as for the pizza, it was extra sauce please!

I rested enough to blow all of my energy again for another performance, whether it was a wise decision I don't know but I feel that the positives of it outweighed the negative aspects. This show was a Christmas party among our friends and families at a rented out local firehouse. I actually had one of the band members/friend, Ted, carry me up two flights of stairs in a Philadelphia recording studio to rehearse and plop me down behind the drums. Other than the free lift "pardon the pun", once I was up there and seated, I didn't miss a beat. My other buddy and singer, Larry, moonlighted as Santa Claus during the music breaks for laughs. We were the only band on the planet that had St. Nick singing lead vocals for us. I guess you could have called us "Cringle and the Elves".

I was able to see and thank a good many people for all of their love and help. Again, my girlfriend and soon-to-be fiancé, and Colleen, her brother's wife, lent a helping hand with my drinks, fan set ups, food and so forth. A big help to me back there behind the drums I'll tell you. That's a nice memory of "the little things people did and not knowing how much it meant to me". The most pleasing and serene thing about that evening for me was that I drove myself to a nearby restaurant before the show and quietly ate some pasta. I can remember feeling so very emotional, thinking to myself "you did it man, you're cured of that. 'f-ing' leukemia" This is a special memory for me, among many, many memories, both good and bad.

I guess things were good enough for me to think about proposing marriage to my girlfriend. I had been dragging my feet due to my situation and honestly I had no idea how to pull it off. She had always made it a point to stop in at any store that sold wedding rings to coax me into the thought of it. After having her stay with me for most of my sickness up to this point, I figured that I owed her at least that much. Believe it or not, my "spidee senses" again should have prevailed in this matter because as strange as it may seem, I didn't feel that she was in love with me ever. I knew that she cared for me but to what extent I couldn't say. The turning point was when my sister ranted and raved to me about how much she knew my girlfriend loved me. Carol would say "just look at the way she looks at you"—"she loves you so much." On and on she bragged until finally I was convinced from her lobbying and bantering. So one day, my then brother-in-law, drove in to Philly to 'jewelers' row', a supposed hot bed of rings and value for your money. I knew what I wanted to pick out, so it only took a few hours to find the ring of my choice and seal the deal. All of this included of course my stealing one of her rings to match the size.

Initially I planned a big announcement at this last Christmas beef and beer I talked about but the way things turned out, it wasn't meant to be. I actually came up with many extravagant ideas but when all was said and done my health dictated a somewhat conservative presentation. Since she was drawing my blood and helping me with my Hickman line, many times she would stay in our spare bedroom that she sort of adopted. Christmas Eve was no exception, so most of my modest plan fell into place. A few years back I had bought her a giant six foot stocking to put her gifts in. As stockings go, we all know that they are all hung by the chimney with care.

The next best place for Santa to enter at my house was the front door since we had no fireplace or chimney from which to enter. Magic dust or not it's a big belly, right? So I hung the big red sock on the back of the door and almost pulled off the caper without a hitch. I dropped the wrapped nugget down to the big toe and left the rest empty just as if it was for decoration only. I forgot the darn door had big fake leather strips with bells strewn along it that exploded with jingles if you even gazed at them wrong. The sneak of a snooping elf that my girlfriend was, keyed in on the chimes so she knew from her room that I was up to something. This was unbeknownst to me at the time. I slithered back up to my room as best as a recovering transplant patient could, so it was more like thump, boom, crash—silence, pitter, patter, plop. The plop was me falling into bed.

I had a great night's sleep thinking that I had pulled off my mission, only to find out later that those noises did give me away. I even wrapped some cheesy gifts to put under the tree so it would look like the normal stash was with ours. When it came to rise and shine and go down to the rec room, the crud ball had already peeked down to scan the situation. Like a bigger kid than I would even profess to be, my first glance at her revealed that trademark smile of hers; the same smile that inspired me to give her the nickname of Tweety Bird. "She had soft big lips and curvy cheeks with squinty eyes smiling from ear to ear, which I couldn't resist". The grin had more to it this Christmas day though. Her grin had a touch of mischief to it that revealed clues as if she already knew.

I never found out for sure if she did, in fact, ransack the sock beforehand or not, but she did fess up to hearing those damn cowbells the night before. You know; when no one is supposed to be stirring, not even a mouse. No mice just Tweety. Anyhow she mauled through those bogus set-up gifts and with an apparent empty stocking. Her prior knowledge or womanly instincts grabbed the big toe part of the big sock and felt the lump. The eclipse of a grin somehow impossibly grew larger as she giggled and plunged an arm and hand almost disappearing into the cloth of red to clutch the goods. A brief flight off the ground while simultaneously opening the wrapping and then the box itself found her, I guess, as happy to receive it as I was to give it to her. I never had time to formally propose then as she rammed the ring on her finger while hugging me as tight as she ever had. I took that as a yes, of course.

Further remnants of the holidays bring back moments of her driving me over to her relatives to show off her new jewelry as well as those of me just paralyzed in thoughts of what I'd been through these past few years. Pondering and reflecting became even more a part of who I was. Throughout my life I had always contemplated things although now they were magnified from all of this. I also remember attempting to regain some of the intimacy that my girlfriend and I had prior to my illness. I think we managed some rendezvous that was pretty good for me, and hopefully for my then better half as well.

I probably got to embrace again being a bit more secure of my health really, for the first time that I wasn't sick. Perhaps with that interlude I forgot about everything if for only awhile. Any cause for continued celebrations would be out of character with my track record. It just wouldn't be right. I often jested that God or somebody spun the Rolodex and noticed that I had been left alone for too long. Alas true to form I was to be chosen and pummeled again.

One particular evening at home found me dizzy with fever on a horribly rainy night. This is when I murmured to Carol and my mother looking out at my television screen of a window. I saw monsoon rains and rolling hills into misty moors. Brews of fog escorted castle-like silhouettes off in the distance. A blow-by-blow account I recanted to my family from an impossible vantage point, my water bed. Soaked to the bone with fever, I clearly was hallucinating. These wild visions accompanied chills and slight twitches of convulsions, so the obvious deduction was to rush me to the hospital!

The Hyde of all Jeckles! Everything from starting to look normal and promising to having the roof once again instantaneously cave in. My rain and medieval fields traveled with me along to Crozer Chester Medical Center and my new home, Two South, the haven for cancer patients. After the ritual of blood sticks and plenty of I.V.s on top of I.V.s, the only consolation was that my castle drifted away. My being severely dehydrated led me to those moory mirages!

Over the period of an evening and morning, one of my typical encounters, that being a group of physicians or student interns entering my room and scoffing at our mask wearing rituals. To those uninformed personnel whoever you are, I hope that you have educated yourself on bone marrow transplant protocols as of late. I Pity you fools who may be so unfortunate someday in having to undergo a bone marrow transplant of the kind that I had. You know a CML accelerated phase blast crisis cusp non-related allogenic. Go have your blood type changed, do the procedures you must and then make fun of it. Perhaps then your lack of understanding and compassion will be acquired to replace the ignorance that seems blatant if that is possible on your part. If not, we will all have to meet our maker some day.

A complimentary blunder, as if I needed one, took place at my expense. Yet another intern or understudy, call them what you like, I have my own name for him, initiated a poking and prodding fiasco across my still healing and very tender scar on my abdomen. This prospect of a doctor I hope learned a lesson on communication abilities through this, as along with the jabbing and manipulation came also what he must have perceived as rhetorical questioning.

This man asked a million of them it seemed and my family and I competently obliged with relevant answers. You could have fooled him; and I guess we did because as bizarre as it sounds, one of the precise, crisp, clear and to the best of my knowledge of American tongue vernacular was used to explicitly state that I HAD NO SPLEEN! Over and over this jackass impersonated a Carol Burnett show skit of a vaudeville act on my body. By now I was not only very ill, but getting ready to clock and drop this guy via my erupting adrenaline surges! I finally sat up and bodily grabbed his hand as well as I could under the circumstances, and shoved his sorry looming presence away from me.

Disgustingly sitting further up now in utter disbelief and amazement of this treatment, I must have put up with this clown thinking that he knew what he was searching for. I was correct in my thinking that he knew what he was looking for all right; so, now I'll reveal the kicker to this lengthy saga. Like Groucho Marx, the clueless man glared at us with a bewildered gesture and blurted, "I cannot find a spleen of any size in this boy at all."

My brother left the room in disgust as the rest of my family all chimed in simultaneously, "HE DOESN'T HAVE ONE!" My initial reaction was a silent, "Duh, no kidding you moron." My first real dilemma since I had flown home from Seattle and this is my first impression of the things to come. It's a bit funny now as things often are retrospect as this pales in comparison unfortunately to events lying ahead that I experienced: "Absolutely stranger than fiction". This gentleman did not last but a day on my case and this was the same fate for several other male and female "specialists" if you will, on and off the job just as quickly as they started. Due to these same lame types of procedure formalities I hope.

I'll reiterate that all too many of these Mickey Mouse episodes occurred post-transplant. Not revealing the various hospitals or incriminating circumstances, I'll just state that it was more than a few. In fact, I can only recall two or three hospitals in which everything went smoothly without a red light of stupidity occurring at some point. That's two or three out of at least ten! So, as not to become too redundant, I'll recant just a few more of the believe it or not experiences. Perhaps a sequel can exclusively pertain to the blunders of butchery.

Returning to the theme once again after this brief bit of sideline details if you will, I find myself still in the hospital very ill with my usual quote of days going by and still no explanation of what was happening to me. The sticks, stool and urine samples, blood draws and overall atmosphere were all too familiar to me. I mentally regressed eons in terms of optimism and confidence. Relapse, death, depression, death, and fear times one thousand and again death ravaged my mindset. Did I mention death? I wish that I could somehow convey the emotional peaks and valleys of transplant patients that have serious complications on top of them.

Eventually my blood cultures and conducted tests revealed the E-coli bacteria. This news confirmed for me an instant reservation of at least another ten days for sure as a hospital resident. That was just a conservative estimate if every thing went very well and I responded to the impending courses of antibiotics. Every thing didn't go well, in fact, everything went wrong! I believe the super drug Vancomycin was implemented after a host of other drug combinations were initiated. Only then, after approximately twenty more days of hell at death's door did I once again respond. Not before, however, septic shock set in along with the collection of chills, sweats, ravaging fevers, diarrhea, vomiting, profanity, tears, thrown food and non-sociable mannerisms. Mix that in with alternating shifts of good nurse/bad nurse groups and it was almost enough to want to die for just from those experiences. I'm still really not clear as to how to describe E-coli manifestations in layman's terms. Just picture yourself as a solid food being placed into a blender—turn on the switch, pour out the contents and there you have it, my analogy of E-coli.

This duration had its share of medical blunders including my I.V. bag once again filling up with my blood like I mentioned earlier, except these episodes were clearly tagged with the markings of negligence all over them. My family once again standing guard was vital to saving my life. I talked earlier about their extreme role in my survival scheme of things both emotionally and spiritually.

Besides the single incident in Seattle where Carol noticed my back hemorrhaging, which was a very possible dilemma to be wary of at the time as I mentioned. But these "at home" hospital incidents should have never even come close to happening. If only I had been the type of person to file lawsuits. Boy, I could be wealthy today. We always joke that I have my own wing in this or that hospital due to my very lengthy tenures but, really, I shouldn't be jesting about all of the wings that I could own from court rulings. I would still like to think as a Christian that any incurred accident was just that and not intentional, then or ever for that matter. Who knows if I should have acted?

Now that this E-coli saga had unfolded and for the most part ended with a recovery, I still didn't know at that point what permanent damage, if any, I had incurred from it. My graft vs. host disease had roared and surged taking and giving like high and low tides. This clouded up the medical picture and made it tremendously hard for my 'real doctors' to sort anything out. With all of the immuno-suppressive drugs that I was taking, the irony of counter-productivity was present. I.E., suppress the immune system and try to control graft vs. host disease, while hoping that it would remain intact and strong enough to defeat germ enemies such as E-coli itself. Go figure! We are supposed to keep track of these intricate workings, imagine how patients' bodies must feel and, if those very same bodies could express themselves, what the heck would they be saying, "Other than expletives and profanities?"

Clearly, the crapshoot of risky decisions on the doctor's part had sucked us all dry of a bit more life. Essentially this was a no-win situation at the time due to the yin-yang balancing act that they dealt with, i.e., examples of GVHD and losing the graft vs. impending opportunistic infections. Fortunately for me, I suppose, that the lesser of the two evils that being the E-coli was slain. Imagine E-coli being a lesser of two evils, huh! That places one factor of GVHD in a better perspective for you of how terrible a condition it can present.

Yet again the doctors performing as if with light shows and mirrors seemingly rescued me from death's door again. I'd bet that God had just a bit to do with it as well, don't you think. Unfortunately this skirmish gave way to a serious GVHD setback though. Some minor kidney, heart and liver functions had clued us into this occurrence. Otherwise, at this point, no visible symptoms outwardly showed other than the fact that I was pretty irritable with the whole world by now.

Remaining in the hospital made monitoring of the GVHD somewhat safer. Severe diarrhea and occasional bleeding here or there episodes were quickly headed off and treated on 'good staff days'. Many prayers and just the ticks of the clock got me through the rough days. Having said that my prognosis as a home out-patient at this point would have led to my passing away I'm convinced. So, as with most things in life go, the bad comes along with the good. Day after day episodes played broken record repetitions of the same symptoms and existence in my mind. Feeling frozen in time problem-wise, if I have any personality quirks from all of this, my foundation for them was reinforced during this timely stretch. Besides all of the physical illness, my mind I'd say was past it normal coping peak. This could explain why I didn't have many visitors during this period. To be fair though, I'm not sure what the I.C.U. policies were on visitors or if anyone had even tried to see me during this stretch.

The somewhat strained relationship that seemed to be healed between my fiancé and I had taken some new flak with all of this local hospitalization going on. Those long distance phone calls that she had made from Seattle every night weren't needed any longer, she now could simply leave the hospital. My parents and family could also go home when they felt like it. So, in that respect it was positive for them. Some people's families don't even bother to visit their own kin so how could I be upset! I should have been happy for them but my reflection leads me to believe that I used even this against myself for torture.

I presume that some feeling sorry for myself stints ensued along with anger and jealousy following as well. Things like 'all right, be that way, just go off and leave me, that's right'; 'who needs you', 'screw this place', or "I don't need anybody anyway' etc. The truth was that I did need help and support. I desperately wanted out of this mess. Like a little kid who could count on his mommy and daddy to make it all better, I longed for a magical hug, a tuck in bed and a good night kiss, 'the bad dream analogy'. My body hurt so badly. So did my mind, my spirit and my heavy heart.

Well, February turned into March and about eighteen or nineteen days into that month earned me sixty or seventy more days straight on to my medical resume. March was a big birthday month for our family as four or five birthdays fell in it. They rolled in and by as well with me now fighting off bedsores instead of visiting and eating cake. Monotonous views of the overhead ceiling tiles clearly exemplified the depressions debilitating factors. With another cliché, of a coincidence-sounding episode on deck, the sheer oddity of the timing would have you think it was just that—a "b.s". line. It wasn't though as on my mom's birthday my condition seemed to vastly improve so it seemed, just two days before my own birthday in fact.

The perverted, cynical and fickle of a thorn GVHD decided to rest a bit. I thought this mostly due to the signs of my increasing vigor and energy levels comparatively. Say the ability to go the rest room just five feet away as opposed to kicking my family out of the room to use the bedpan. For me that was a phenomenal feat. Also with this came a burst of increased appetite and the leveling off of my organ functions.

What then ensued was either preplanned or scripted by my family, or pure luck with good fortune. It was arranged so that I could leave within the next day if I stayed stable. As always I was really so broken hearted and sad to get out of that personal cave of insanity. It would take a wheel chair cruise and a father-brother escort to the car and again into my house. The escort was them carrying me, of course.

A funny feeling that I still occasionally get is one of serenity and disillusionment combined, if that is possible. This personal phenomenon developed in this trip home from the hospital. After being hospitalized for so long and upon returning to my supposed 'normal' confines, this manifestation would begin. I may have touched upon such things as using your own bathroom or lying in your own bed and things of that nature. For whatever reason, these kinds of areas induce the feelings that I'm talking about. I'd say that it consists of a total relaxed state of relief first of all. A sensation kind of analogy would be if you were to stand on your head and allow the blood to rush to your head. As you continue this, there is that tickling in the limbs and feet from less circulation, along with a bit of pins and needles effect in with it. If you have ever felt anything similar to what I'm speaking about here, then that feeling I describe with my episodes of serenity and disillusionment equals that of your body upon standing upright once again: That being the blood rushing all at once sensation.

With this unique feeling going on, I sometimes have flashbacks of many traumatic experiences that I've incurred along the way. Instantaneously preceding this is a calm defense mechanism type of a voice telling me that I am safe and past the flashbacks. Heart misfires and most likely adrenaline rushes preside, and at the very least I am in my home surroundings or 'protected' if you will. It is often times in lying down and turning off the world, perhaps for an hour or two as if I go comatose for a spell.

I touch on this here because not only did it happen this night of my first return home from a hospital stay since I'd been in Seattle but did, in fact, occur thereafter enough times for me to make a statement on it as something of merit rather then that of mere coincidences. It's funny to me that I think about this misnomer of a diagnosed occurrence. I suspect that being cooped up for so long and swelling on possibilities has burnished these memories of sort pertaining to the traumatic episodes that I've experienced in my mind and in my life. However, I have no idea as to the complicated physical manifestations such as the mental voices of "positivity", the heart misfires and blood rushes, etc. I suppose only God knows the current rationale' but for whatever reason it continues to occur here and there. I wonder if other transplant patients have experienced anything similar to this.

My having attempted to explain that to a certain degree, my recollection picks up here with a better night's rest in my own bed. The very same bed I'd last slept in seeing castles and fields. No knights or dragons this evening, so from that perspective I was better. More irony had me being home for my birthday. Although I was in lousy shape physically, it was much improved over the last sixty days or so. I was determined to try and have a nice birthday and in getting a great gift by being released from the hospital, it got off to a roaring start! The next thing that I knew, late that afternoon I was convinced into taking a ride with my girlfriend to her aunt's home for some silly reason.

With my not having ever been to her aunt's new house, that proved to be the selling point and prevented me from being suspicious of any trickery. Gullible me, with my family and friends, I should have picked up on 'something' since it was my birthday and they all had successfully duped me on several occasions before with surprises. I must have been the perfect target for them because in all of the previous surprise parties, I honestly was fooled One hundred percent, and I might add that it's the greatest feeling to be conned like that! This was no exception because I lingered in the foyer and quaint sitting room for several minutes clueless. Upon turning the corner to the dining room, the gang ambushed me and caught me totally off guard. Of course, the funny thing is that I am usually very suspicious and wary of things due to the city life and all.

They pulled off another successful surprise party on me! Fifteen or twenty of my friends enjoyed the evening mostly playing the game of Pictionary and deciphering absurd attempts of renderings and stick men. All in all it was a fun evening except for my wavering energy level and the noticing of my girlfriend and my friend touring the empty upstairs hallways together. Harmless in the hallways, I suppose, if that's all that they toured. The party came to a close and my girlfriend drove me home where I again looked forward to the cozy bed that I slept in best—mine!

The morning and afternoon of the next day came and I felt even more rejuvenated then the day before with the party and all. Two straight nights of sleep at home replenished more than a total week of rest in any hospital bed for sure. My girlfriend and I spent the afternoon at her Brother Mike's house. As always, Colleen and Mike were helpful and compassionate in helping me out. I felt as comfortable there as I did at my house, my girlfriend's grandparents' house and Carol's house. That is saying a lot if you were me back then.

Colleen and Mike were refinishing a room in their house so I figured that I could lounge around and be a back seat spectator. I always enjoyed tinkering with carpentry also, so I thought that it would be fun. Again with my being pampered by Colleen and the family, I failed to pick up any signals on my friend and girlfriend leaving in his van to pick-up some paneling or something. Still innocent enough in its own right but the patterns were now clearly apparent in retrospect.

For the next couple of days, it seemed as if I held my own health-wise but I now was as bloated as ever. My mood swings were horrible and sporadic. Two more instances of frustration and helpless feelings being trapped inside my body involved my girlfriend and the same guy. The first involved us being invited to a function of some kind, perhaps a birthday or wedding dinner. It involved this guy somehow.

I hadn't worn a suit in at least a year and a half by this point and it never dawned on me to try it on beforehand. Naturally the time came to get ready with the usual shower and everything else. I proudly accomplished the shave, shower, socks, etc. and then the everything hit the fan. My thighs eased into the trousers and my shirt draped over me fine that is before I buttoned it. The sleeves were okay; I buttoned all the buttons except for the top one in which I always left last for the tie up. This was road block number one and I dismissed the problem simply thinking that I would tie my tie up over the collar and by tightening the knot "I could get away with it"—so I rationalized.

Next came the back breaker with my steroid fuse rage looming to ignite. The pants would not even come close to fastening. No belt trick or tape job could help me this day. I was so taken back by my misjudgment to calculate the overblown gut of fluid that I just lost it! Like a barbarian, I thrashed through my bedroom fueled by drugs and awakened adrenaline. Chucking and launching any object in my vicinity, I trashed my only private sanctum. When it came time to leave, I informed my girlfriend-fiancé that I wasn't going. She outwardly sulked a bit and called this guy that she'd been becoming close with to cancel, being more disappointed than I. It's funny to me now because these people were supposed to be my friends. Love really is blind.

Topping that episode was another instance of more serious proportions. I am very fortunate to have 'scraped' by this horrendous piece of bad judgment on my part. What happened was a typical drive with my fiancé having turned ugly. The scenic routes that we used to take on back roads became a stage of stupidity for me. In my defense I have to attribute this irrational behavior to the escalating side effects of all of the medicine combinations that I was taking. I'd say that I was a laid back state of mind kind of person for the most part in the early stages, post-transplant; Perhaps even being close to my old self at times, maybe not. As quick as the turn of my fiancé's car's steering wheel was on a windy road, something was said between us and my fuse was lit. I still cannot recollect the topic and exchange of words, but it was more than enough to push my fried and frail buttons to the extreme. With the car cruising along and us arguing in a volume level confined to two closed doors and six windows, I finally blew the veritable fuse so to speak.

With a flash of anxiety, frustration and even despair from no sense of closure to this nightmare of a life, I launched myself out of the moving vehicle onto the asphalt and concrete below. I say below because that's where I ended up all right.

The sensation of falling and everything in super slow motion, my mind assessed the foolish move and informed my body that this ship was going down. I recall being aware of my going to hit the deck and preparing myself for landing but now not really having any say in the matter.

The Rolodex in my brain pulled the file on a football tackling drill I'd experienced many times before. The concussion of the helmet to helmet contact or 'spear to spear' incidental collision that all players are familiar with, took the stage. My skull was my helmet, the highway was its own helmet and I don't know who had the harder head.

The 'cush' sound with the slapping of a belly noise ensued. One eye glanced and saw the silhouette of the upside down car door cruising away, as the other eye couldn't stand the thought of impact. The distant and constant whooshing I realized was coming from my ears and not from the highway traffic surrounding me. "Plainly stated I got my bell rung big time."

Coming out of orbit I examined the rest of the situation. My fiancé made the u-turn and started back toward me. I sighed with relief as no blood or pain surfaced that I could see at the time. I got up, dusted myself off and ignored my fiancé and her offer of a ride. Walking beside the flowing traffic, I journeyed on selfishly but not having a clue as to why I was acting this way. Ironically I ended up a few miles later at this then friend's house totally exhausted. How I didn't simply collapse on the road is beyond me. This guy was "generously" alerted that I was heading his way by her and he eventually drove me home, 'what a guy'.

A possibility to all of this rage and over-reacting may have been related to what was quietly brewing inside of me. I'm not certain, of course, but it makes some sense to me since these actions were way out of character compared with my old demeanor.

Not more than a week after my being released from the hospital, I was rushed into the doctor's office and from there I was immediately admitted once again to Two South. If the walls could talk they would have said, "Oh man, not him again!" As for the staff they could in fact talk and I'll bet many of them did just that. I had suddenly collapsed at home with a raging fever, which is what led me to this particular hospital stay. It was clear to the doctors that I had another serious infection. The all too familiar task of assessing my condition was initiated. Except for a new face here or there, we were all on a first name basis by now. I should have been on the payroll I tell you.

The first order of business of tests and sticks did not shed any light on the situation. It quickly became a matter of beat the clock because my enigmatic symptoms were worsening by the minute. I may have used this description earlier but I had several instances that apply to being near death. If I ever should have died this was the episode. My analogy of a blender that I tossed in previously in the book was accurate and hard to top, but this mess had me buried so deep in my bed that I felt like I was literally under or apart of it. In the sense of weight on top of me, being trapped under it, not mobile and quite frankly as lifeless as the bed was itself. The controls changing bed positions functioned better in fact than my body responded. There was no doubt about it that I was once again in danger of dying.

With the traumatic ordeal concerning my spleen back in Seattle, I really didn't think that I could envision any situation other than whatever the moment of death itself was being more heart wrenching. Probably never before did I feel so helpless and beaten. There just wasn't anything left to give and by the looks of things it was only a matter of time before I would expire. Even the doctors were handcuffed because nothing could be detected to fight. All of the immuno-suppressive drugs that I was taking did, in fact, mask any attempt to culture bacteria or get conclusive results from any procedure attempted.

Furious manifestations ensued in any format that you could think of. I've read about documented cases of the Ebola and Hunta viruses so they surpass what was going on in my body if for no other reason they are most definitely fatal. Survival is rare in those cases. I bring these up because my symptoms mocked very many of those viruses' characteristics. Short of bleeding to death out right, internally or through my pores, I experienced bloody eyes, nose gushes, mouth and rectum bleeding, and even blood in my urine. Throw in with that diarrhea, vomiting, chills, profuse sweats, burning skin, every possible joint pain that you could imagine, and finally lapses in and out of consciousness. So you can agree why I think this was most likely the worst obstacle to face yet to this point. It was very close.

Some evidence of E-coli did emerge and aggressive therapy was initiated to counter the infection. By the time that the antibiotics should have made some headway, it was apparent that things were not improving. In fact if I could have gotten worse without dying, I did. Around the clock shifts worked on me and from my mannerisms that was good because I wasn't capable of giving anybody any kind of flak. Silence was my new M.O. with an occasional 'charge' or groan of some sort. My blood pressure began falling dramatically so the risky decision was made to completely stop all of my immuno-suppressive drugs. These you recall are responsible for helping my new bone marrow graft as well as combat the graft vs. host disease from killing me—another catch 22 to have to deal with. Talk about your tough decisions to make!

With no other alternative, the drugs were in fact halted cold turkey. Since I had previously given the power of attorney over to my sister Carol, she agreed, as did my family to try something to help save me. I must have been real close to death for them to take such a drastic measure. I had total confidence in everyone working on me this time, not that I was aware of anything though. I was in 'la-la land' with a large twist of pain. Borrowing time from God's graces, I lived on fumes for another few days while more cultures were taken and analyzed. From what I was told, my sister said that the doctors scurried in upon discovering a missing piece to the mysterious saga. It eventually panned out as more bad news being a bit of somewhat good news. You can see what I mean.

In no way would this discovery have been made in time without the courageous and bold move of stopping the suppressive meds. The risky maneuver should have all but sealed my fate and it actually looked like this was the case initially. What ensued was perhaps another unprecedented medical occurrence involving me, I'd confidently wager. Not only did I have confirmation of another bad strain of E-coli but fortunately and unfortunately, I acquired something known as TTP. A hideous virus or disorder that rips and shreds the body's platelets as they are produced basically rendering them useless. In keeping with the truthful but melodramatic occurrences, this ailment was also deemed fatal. The platelets as you are probably aware of by now are responsible for survival. If the doctors had treated me for E-coli exclusively, it would have been all over for me. The TTP would have remained camouflaged and silently taken me out swiftly. God was amongst the physicians for sure when these decisions where made.

TTP in and of itself is usually fatal. I still don't understand all of its specifics and inner workings, but I wouldn't wish this one on anyone. The E-coli and TTP were targeted and protocols were formulated respectively. I was 'Heroshe-mad' and 'Nagasakied' out the wazzu with the GVHD, TTP, and E-coli over new bone marrow after leukemia and unsurpassed levels of total body radiation. So much in fact that Fred Hutchinsons magazine Quest printed an article stating that patients like me in 1986 were give the equivalent doses of radiation that was measured at ground zero of Heroshima. Ridiculous amounts of toxins, on and on, man! So much antibiotics in me in fact that I'd guess my body harbored drug store quantities. Vancomycin, which I've mentioned, something else 'sin', ansis, trates, ors, ing's, er's and an alphabet soup of letters of medicines. If you could pronounce it I probably carried it in stock, along with a Gieger counter!

A tiny improvement in consciousness had me recall my buddy Father Fahey make a rare cameo appearance away from his parish and administer Last Rites to me Yes, once again. Some small talk conversation and a few cool pops slushed in me gave some room once again for a little wiggle room for optimism. This whole mess lasted all of April and well into May, I believe, with my omission of many innuendoes and occurrences. Not to leave you hanging though, I do have some unbelievable doozies to share and enlighten you as to their 'flavor'.

With all of the immuno-suppresive meds being halted, the E-coli and TTP were ultimately defeated thank God and a few good doctors. The problem next was that the graft vs. host disease was given a free highway to exceed the speed limit and wreak havoc on my body ala solo pilot. By the TTP and E-coli being out of my system, I did feel much, much better. Even to the point of conversing, eating and attempting to use the regular bathroom again for the first time in several months. What I didn't feel right off the bat was from the progressive damage that had set in on me. My family too, in fact, was oblivious to the changes going on. How could you blame them with all of the other life threatening things going on to contend with; I'm sure that they were as happy as I was to get those infections taken care of. So, with that, different observations could be noticed now with those other distractions getting cleared up.

A particular morning found me halfway off the side of the bed deciding whether or not to attempt the tight rope walk to the restroom just about five feet to my left. I quietly maneuvered over so as not to wake the roommate on the other side, that being my fiancé, who was fast asleep on the pullout sofa. If I made it I could boast of the improvement and accomplishment, if not I would just wake up her up, that's all! Settling in to the restroom I closed the door gently and hit the light switch on while carefully escorting my entourage of companion pumps. The tiles on the floor vibrated like a horse and buggy on colonial cobblestones as I whipped the poles into position near the sink.

With a sigh of enthusiasm from that accomplishment, I raised my head to get a glimpse of my face for the first time in weeks. Although I was no Rip van Winkle with the beard, for me I initially resembled Cro-Magnon man upon further scrutiny. In the blink of an eye, I dismissed the scruff to a simple shave and immediately centered in on a terrible shock of a sight—my complexion. The bright fluorescent lamps revealed so much scarring and burn mark type blemishes that I gasped with frightening anxiety. These new souvenirs, all compliments of the leukemia, total body irradiation, chemotherapy, toxic drugs and, of course, the graft vs. host disease. These very same marks that would have a 'family member' scar me further and say things like I'll connect the dots on your face…Tasteful and compassionate, huh. That will bring me to touch upon other residual carry over transplant stories as we go along.

Now having my complexion shot, my observations learned that I'd suddenly also lost the ability to perspire, my pores were closed up due to the scarring or glands shutting down, my gums were so damaged that the only thing leading me to detection was the severe pain from the cuts in my cheeks. That again was caused by the mucousitis back in Seattle and now had intensified. Even more damage revealed a 'drop foot' diagnosis in which the foot literally loses the ability to function. No more toe moving, ankle wiggling or up and down gas pedal acceleration movement. All of this in about the span of a month I'd estimate. I don't know if it would have occurred later on down the line but I do know that everything that was now wrong wasn't before all of the drug's were halted. What can you do though? It had to be done; I paid yet another terrible price to continue living. Naturally, when this was brought to the doctors' attention, I was reinstated on the massive doses of drugs. "Just like the old days, only worse"

On top of all of this, my moods became green and hulk-like at times. This further reinforced my theory that once again those heavy drugs made me a mad man. I just didn't figure it all out at that time though. What came about was my being miserable company for anybody and anything.

My fiancé brought in wedding books and arrangements that we'd started working on beforehand. I got so fed up with all of it, that the last thing I wanted to discuss right then was our wedding. Of course in my right mind I would have gladly, but being the ogre that I was and not in my right mind, it wouldn't fly. I suppose my girlfriend didn't understand my situation and it didn't go over well with her. I wish that I could have been more accommodating then, I just was too sick.

The GVHD had induced so much pain that I was again on morphine and Demoral shots at times. I became addicted to Demoral and entangled in the vicious cycle of drugs. My days and nights existed revolving around the shots of meds and pain management. It was the only effective therapy for me until the immuno-suppressive drugs could try and make up for lost ground on the GVHD damage incurred, while I was no longer on them. My favorite nurse at the time was whoever was in charge of the Demoral.

Without realizing it I was slipping away again. This time it was my mental state. My fiancé continued to stay nights on the hide abed to watch over me. Actually she was as beat as I was and caught Zs as well as she could. Altered states, was my new persona and distant stares in and out of reality were evident. So many drugs, so much radiation, I'd love to have had a Gieger counter aimed at me back then. I'll bet I still buzz if not have nuclear submarine power capabilities.

One evening found me restless and miserable during the wee hours of most people's sleep. I was so sick of that milk bottle urinal that I made a break for a bathroom pit stop. Having no light on and being without night vision, I haphazardly reached out and felt the dark grabbing air. Being so familiar with the layout, I knew it was a matter of distance between me and the bathroom. My fogged up state of mind failed to calculate the wheels of the pumps and poles being a part of the equation. In less time that it took me to raise myself out of the bed, my newly acquired drop foot met the pole casters and down I went. California redwood down! I crashed hard face first this time and came out much scathed. After coming around, I yelled for my fiancé. She was already moving to me while simultaneously hitting the lights. Blood all over the place probably scared her silly as it practically gave me a stroke out of fear. What happened was that I pulled all of my I.V. lines out inadvertently, so the bloody mess wasn't as bad as it looked. I didn't know that right away because at the same moment, my mouth and jaw were giving me excruciating pain nerve shots.

I surmised that the blood was coming from my mouth due to me being covered in it but as it turned out that wasn't the case, thank goodness. Further examinations revealed a possible hairline fracture in my jawbone. "Make it a double shot of morphine, please." These occurrences were becoming so ridiculous that I'd wager interested readers may at this point; begin to think that this is all just a hoax or a fictional exaggeration. But it isn't and is all medically documented and kept by the hospitals and my physicians.

I'm sure that I must have felt sorry for myself or was plain and simply psychotic at this juncture. I absolutely remember still being very unsociable when opportunities presented themselves. Most of the time I just harbored in bed afloat infused with pain killers and the once again ever increasing amounts of steroids to counter the GVHD. I exploded again into Yoda, akin to the old comparison my friend had given me. Pale complexion, hair from prehistoric times and the ever stylish and distinctive slump, bloat, and eye socket circles persona that actually did resemble the little green guy in Star Wars. I was a freak...

My girlfriend clung to the wedding hopes I guess at this point even bringing back the wedding books to mull over and pass time. She even settled on a gown boasting about how lavishly breathtaking it was. Of the few comments I made on it, I do recall mentioning how beautiful she would look in a laminar bubble suit. From there the ship of love basically took a hit starboard side. The torpedo was that someone impersonating a friend. Foolish me, I should have seen the signs long beforehand. Like one time he sat in the car while I attended Mass later telling me that that he didn't believe in a God. He enjoyed soliciting my religious stories, though I now suppose for amusement behind my back. He wouldn't have done that to my face though.

The rituals of my girlfriend spending nights at the hospital weaned off by now. More and more of her time was spent away from my room and that which I could certainly understand. Some people can only tolerate so much before showing their 'true colors', pardon the pun. A particular time that is forever frozen in my life's memory was about as painful as all of the other transplant procedure battles I went through. The stiletto of news came delivered to me by a totally innocent hit man of sorts.

One evening I received a compassionate visit from my senior prom date, Caroline. She had sincere and genuine feelings for me and stopped in after seeing a relative staying in a nearby room. Upon her visit with me, one of the first things that she mentioned to me turned out to be just that stick of a knife. In what has to be close to if not the exact quote, Caroline asked me posing, "Aren't you still engaged?" Of course, I responded, not thinking anything other than she didn't know. She knew all right and rebutted that she was a waitress at a local restaurant and happened to wait on a particular table one evening. At this table sat my fiancé and this "friend". In other words one who was supposed to be a friend really turned out to be just the opposite. Their mutual response according to her was, "No, the wedding was off and we weren't involved any longer". News to me...

If there was any part of my body that had eluded radiation, GVHD and all of the other toxins along with it, they had been destroyed right then and there. A part of me died but I remained slumped at the edge of my bed. That roller coaster gravity drop sensation lump in your chest feeling kicked in and emptied any life inside that I had left. My pulse then rocketed to Richter scale proportions. The all too familiar football concussion sound of the whoosh in my ears deafened my consciousness.

Nothing else mattered. I died. All that I hoped for in struggling for so long kind of evaporated in an instant. It seemed as if I didn't' have sufficient evidence to render a verdict, but I could recollect the growing scenarios that I touched on as far back as the Seattle calls. From then until the present time I weighed all of that and Caroline's testimony against one doubtful possibility, which was that she made it up. The scale broke in Caroline's favor and my consciousness because she had class and wouldn't do that. She had no motive to lie. The deadly stab was that my then fiancé had been steadily drifting off and yet still wore the ring that I bought for her and never confronted me with any of this. Why?

As this all too surreal story of my life has been dictated here, a further humiliating factor virtually sealed my fate. Ironically my fiancé had been expected to visit me that evening and never showed up. In fact, with the city being as rough as it was, I had the hospital security staff searching for her in the parking lot and the Chester police cruising around the area grounds as well. I even called her mother looking for her. I was told by a questionable source later that the whole lousy ordeal was basically a wait it out scenario of sorts in thinking that I would eventually pass away. Physically that is…A good part of me was taken out in a callous and cold manner all right but my shell of a body tried to remain breathing. Adding some more insult to my injury, I was later informed by a former friend of my then fiancé that this had been going on without my knowing for quite some time. That was a slap in the face that stung a bit more if it was in fact the case. "I suppose when you love someone it's easy to disregard mounting scenario's and equally when you really don't have those same feelings for someone it's easy to disregard their feelings as well".

With the evening approaching ridiculous hours for somebody to show up visiting, my then fiancé did mosey in to my room. My Clint Eastwood clichés applied here all too well as I waited like an animal in my lair to confront her. Skinny legs make that non-existent legs, supported a fluid filled pot belly enhanced with road map scars across the chest that which was my garb. Not being bowlegged, the lack of mass on my limbs gave me just as much space of a view between them to impersonate the cowboy motif, no spurs though. The expression on her face was the same as it had been. But by realizing what had happened here to me I concluded that expression had been the same look consistent with the mischievous hunches that I began accumulating since way back when. Without a hello or where have you been, I simply stated for her to give me back the ring. Some bickering ensued and with a teary outburst she said that she didn't want to give it back, while at the same time though she unscrewed it off of her finger; a Freudian slip perhaps. The tears then made me wonder what to think. Recanting this little story still stings a bit many years later, all of this time and still that sting.

Once the can of worms was opened, decibel levels were challenged, as mostly it was I blowing up big time. Practically at an uncontrollable rate I'd say as I ranted and raved until I collapsed back on the bed. I believe it was early the next morning when we resumed the bout as her defense was that of denial to the whole accusation. Could it be that I overreacted?

I reflected briefly but intently. The denial on my part wanted it to be true and in what I'd have to conclude as some type of traumatic defense mechanism kicking in with me just shutting down. There is a stretch in time during this painfulness that I just cannot recollect. From this point of amnesia I came back to remembering her traveling to Arizona to visit her relatives. Evidently all of the infections had been worked through successfully and the GVHD once again stabilized to the point of my at least being released home.

That memory, unfortunately, didn't get erased because from here it was two weeks of agony and self-torment. I envisioned the evening before my official breakup of the engagement. Anyhow, recalling my giving her a kiss good night, I wheeled my pumps over to her hideaway sofa in the hospital room and before kissing her stating that I loved her and wanted to stop arguing. I apologized for everything and filed the thought of the kiss as being distant and empty. That giveaway sensation the passion has gone on one spouses' part. "I wish I could have seen the signs".

During those two weeks I stewed in a pool of anger and anxiety. Any type of teenager love sickness that I had ever experienced paled in comparison at the time. I'd go from extreme rage to self-rationalization of my overreacting to the situation to more exhaustion. On top of all the medications, dry heaves was a companion much of the time. A call that I placed to my fiance's mother at this point muddied up my perspective a bit more. I was consoled with a sincere opinion of her daughter's relationship with me so I thought.

This compacted with a gift that I received from my girlfriend upon her return home had me dumbfounded as well. I didn't know whether it was a sincere gift of love or a token gift of empathy on her part. I say that because in all of the two weeks gone by, I heard nothing whatsoever from her. I'll bet for sure though that the other party involved was kept abreast of her trip. For all that I know the joke could have been on me with him traveling with her, who knows? Whatever the case may have been, it's easy to reflect on this now but at the time I was distraught to no end about the whole situation. The gift was a fishing lure, which I still keep as a memory.

Very shortly after her return, we drove to a nearby mall to have dinner and discuss the relationship. It was her idea and once again I failed to see the smoking gun pointed right at me. My enthusiasm had me packing my own heat. But it was the engagement ring that I had pocketed to give back to her over the dinner once things were smoothed out. Things didn't get smoothed out unless she was a steamroller and I was the black top pavement being laid down. The proverbial line of 'let's be friends' didn't go over well with me and after going through so much together was, in my opinion, devastating and cavernous.

Years of sincere love I felt and sacrifices on both ends that at times, resembled the Romeo and Juliet stories and Maria and Tony episodes in West Side Story. All of what I thought was harbored became reduced to three hollow words on what I perceived that she got out of it. Several huge clichés come to mind here. The first was a brief conversation we had years later when I called her one evening and simply asked her if what we had was real. A casual yeah was the sum of her answer. She fudged that call up by inadvertently calling me the other guy's name. Another brief talk led me to state, "same old you that I used to know and love." Where upon she answered back; "no, she wasn't" seemingly boasting, as she recanted about her new life of success.

I'm now thinking that the person I fell in love with did fade off somewhere along the transplant journey as far as I was concerned. She was definitely a different person then the one I knew and loved. She moved on and got what she wanted I guess. I hope it was worth it for her life. You just can't make someone love you.

The last irony to this story is that the very restaurant we dined in was just where we had frequented shortly after my return home from Seattle. That was a day that I wore the mask in public and became involved in a messy altercation. I was confronted by a jerk of a loser who oddly enough dressed and walked like a 'professional'. Alas, the adage of 'Don't judge a book by its cover.' This guy pointed in my face and said, "Look at this freak." The steroids that I was living on had no trouble helping my Irish-Italian-American Indian temper rise to the surface.

While exploding to grab this punk, I awkwardly reached as transplant freaks can do I presume and closed in for a swinging bomb, targeting his jaw for a lights out KO. It all would have unfolded according to plan except a bystander intervened. My timing was off and as the last tidbit to my shadow boxing bout were low platelets. That coupled with my rage and a wind up telegraph from down under equated to a rupture in my nose. My manila colored mask became a crimson sopped mass that spilled over to my clothing and onto the floor. What was left of my Florence Nightingale fiancé at the time saved the day again for me with a quick burst of first aid. She was awesome; "back then".

This whole breakup as I mentioned was mentally and emotionally about as bad as the transplant itself. I'm guessing that the damage is to some degree permanent due to my cautious approach toward women and trust nowadays. The initial check out of mental reality had me irrationally contemplating foolish deals with myself of all sorts to plea with her to marry me. Before I came to my senses I would even entertain thoughts of accepting her to see this other guy. That's how out of touch it got for me on the medicine protocols.

Clearly, the drugs and depression combined to manifest delusion's in me big time. The first stage of despair visited and I posed suicide for an instant. Quickly countering that was a boost of anti-depressant helpers and prayer. I guess it prevented some major damage but initially those drugs on top of the others were just more hell. I never acclimated to any kind of combination and, ultimately, took myself off of them.

My father often hung out with me with as much compassion as a Marine could outwardly express. One day we hit the ice cream shop and with my changing of his radio station in his truck, as I always did, this day backfired. The start of cliché music began and no better of a numbing song then a Dave Mason tune, 'We Just Disagree'. I must have twenty songs that remind me of her as I do with other girlfriends and life experiences for that matter. Maybe that's just the musician in me.

I suppose God let me have another breather for a spell from hospitals. Who knows what would have happened had all of this unfolded as an in-patient, the hiatus wasn't long enough for me though. Just about long enough to reluctantly visit my brother's new vacation trailer at the time on the bay. Something in me went along existing as I traveled in body but not in spirit. I was just a blob—emotionless and outwardly distant. I often times like to sit alone and ponder things. This was different though; I stared and saw nothing. Thoughts were for the most part non-existent and every so often during the course of a day I would come back to reality. A chuckle here or response there made me regress in guilt for allowing myself to flash back on everything that had been taking place.

My brother, Tom, had a new boat as well so they swindled me into getting on for a ride and do a bit of fishing perhaps. I was the sack of potatoes in lifeless body weight so they teamed up together to board me. They did, of course, and we hoisted anchor. I laugh again at the irony of all of these perfectly timed clichés because no sooner than we reached our destination, a ravaging storm erupted. We were, I guess, three to ten miles out at sea and small craft advisories were issued. In a turtle's version of a b-line pace through the swells, we finally made it back. The ride that seemed to never end for me torched my equilibrium and hijacked my bones! I literally air walked on deck and would have made Michael Jordan or Julius Erving proud. The not-so-funny part of this was that not only did I chum for blues out of my mouth but my father literally had to grab me bodily to prevent my falling overboard. I really did think we would be overtaken by the swells back then. The drugs may have enhanced that notion but I do know that I flirted with water skiing without the skis.

With this trip ending my father informed me that my ex called and wanted to collect her belongings. Things such as stuffed animals, clothes, pictures, etc. This and that but ironically she left her dog to us. I made it a point not to be anywhere around for the collection run. It did rekindle though what I'd have to be careful in describing. I can say that many a connection of sources didn't approve of how this relationship ended and particularly by some of the actions by the other guy involved. It does take two but the guy can be thankful that I truly loved my ex and had self respect for myself. I extinguished some really serious threats toward this person that for sure would have been carried out. The kind in nature that cannot be canceled once the order is given so to speak.

My sense of gratitude did shamefully show through in having so many influential people approach me and, or my father with these 'family notions'. Simply put, some caring people misconstruing "the family" and especially "military" connections for love with vendetta's when, in fact, it wasn't right. Somebody out there is a lucky person to be alive, not even realizing how close they came to not being so. It's not at all a nice thing to say; it's simply a fact. If I'm going to profess to be a Christian, I've got to at least try to walk the walk and love thy enemies as well as thy neighbors etc. or in this instance people who I still cared about. If I did in fact love my former fiancé, why would I want to bring any kind of unhappiness to her? I'd want her to be happy; And him also for that matter.

I wish her everything great and blessed and hope she is very happily married. Not that I would want to run into her but I'm sure she could never be more satisfied with such a great life. My prayers seem to do alot for others. I still pray fro them both. As for the dirty deeds, I thank God that I was informed before hand because the last thing that I needed on top of leukemia and a broken engagement was to be framed or accused of a plot. Thanks to all concerned but that's why they have *Goodfellas* and the *Soprano's* on disc.

Getting back on track somewhat, if you have been noticing the crash and burn patterns, this is the time to have the scenarios recycle. I'm thinking that I had a small layover after this ordeal, mostly hanging around with my dad and trying to get into something to keep busy with. At this time we bought a band saw and began woodworking and cutting wooden figures for the house and lawn sales. Just a small operation out in our shed but it helped I suppose here and there. Making squirrels and ducks and wheelbarrows and chairs and Christmas decorations took time to finish, so otherwise empty spells stewing in grief was instead spent dodging sawdust and saw blades. Another serious infection came calling and no sooner had I entered the woodworking apprenticeship tenure, my true calling as a hospital patient took precedence

These pounding infections were amassing in totals that made me surrender to the front line head counts. This time it was a more mild form of a staph infection if there can be such a thing. That's what was explained to me but you couldn't tell my body that because I got slammed. Perhaps my psyche reverted back to the seemingly conditioned routine of bed stay as being a fixtured in-patient. The hospital ambiance didn't do anything positive for my disposition but what can you do?

During the course of this messy stay I developed a new twist of physical sensations. I wouldn't call it pain per se as far as my head and sinuses were concerned, because I'm generally a-symptomatic. With more antibiotics jockeying and vying for position against the graft vs. host immuno-suppressives, my sinus cavities swelled in pressure sensation to the point of "crying uncle". Not one to ever really experience a headache other than eating ice cream too fast, I was very fortunate in that respect so this experience was new to me.

As if someone was reaching in to pry my eyes out of their sockets, that feeling was not enough. Fireworks of chirping and creaking scoured my cranium down to the vice forcing wedge, out on to my healing fractured jaw bone. I take it that my jaw was healed by then but even today I still get nerve shots when it feels like it needs attention. The menagerie of sounds and symptoms up there in my head forced me to white flag for help. Get ready for another unfathomable occurrence of a witnessed story you won't believe happened in what was the twentieth century

Upon conveying these problems to my main attending physician, I was given the option to have a sinus tap and try to relieve the damned up pressure inside the cavities. In an uncharacteristic decision on my part, then, I hastily approved of the proposal without mowing over my alternatives. With the urgency I openly expressed to whoever would listen. My doctor quickly rustled up the first "sinus specialist" he could find. Evidently this gentleman he ran across was either on the floor at that time or in nearby proximity, so he got the job. I still have to believe that this was a sincere and compassionate gesture on this sinus doctor's part but it is very difficult to comprehend the motives of what he did.

Not one to intentionally judge anyone, I was taken back somewhat when this man entered my room. With my ears popping at this point from the extreme pressure akin to those airplane takeoff sensations, I don't believe that I heard his formal introduction. The unforgettable silhouette of his arriving dressed in a conservative suit was a different story.

Just as an appearance can be termed as being dressed loud, this man stood out in quite the opposite fashion. Very astute, in dark garb, the prominent features of the doctor were unique in oval shaded glasses, a bright bow tie, and brown suit and only seen on the Walton's or Little House on the Prairie days of old, the big black medical bag. This vault of a mailbag opened up at the top along two jawed hinges to access the instruments needed. The trusty stethehoscope "Ice cold I might add" and the ancient flashlight that I'd swear was illuminated ala candle power.

This was all very amusing to me in 1988 but again, "to each his own", and I harbored no ill feelings or apprehension towards his participation in helping me. "That is or was up until this point". Topping off the time warp session was a brass straw like tube and a miniature toy like hammer, which looked like something out of an Erector set or the likes.

With my family in the room and my attending physician Dr. Mike also present or in the area, the sinus tap fiasco began. In not having any reason to doubt the competence of this man and with my family present for relaxing reassurance, I braced for what I thought might feel like a punch in the nose or something like that. "No major deal I figured", considering what I'd been through this would be a piece of cake for me. Relief as well as having the drain opened with this sinus mess. I dug in mentally and prepared.

So the sideshow began. First, I had a bowl placed under my chin that reminded me of that oat bag hooked under horses' mouth's to feed with. The next step had the brass tube inserted up into my nostril until it couldn't move freely. Then with the miniature hammer, the tinking began. Tap,tap,tink,tink. Tap,tap,tink,tink. You could hear the notes aloud but inside nothing except foggy discomfort. This would be so easy I thought .Up until the doctor informed me that he wasn't making any progress. That meant what I felt wasn't painful only because nothing was happening.

After several minutes of this nonsense, even my drumming reflexes couldn't prepare me for what was coming next. In a split second and blink of an eye, simultaneously while reaching for the receiver end of the telephone, the doctor muttered something like "I'll try this". I can't say that it was intentional, out of frustration or what. This guy could have lost it in the heat of the moment or perhaps made an honest attempt to make headway. "Pardon the pun" but this actually happened. With the swing of the phone receiver, impersonating a bigger hammer, the doctor launched it right at my nose hoping to finally get that steel tube through into my sludged up cavities. All that I heard was a loud clack and suddenly major internal swirling ensued.

I couldn't see and blacked out for a period. Then, I was awakened by incredible major shots of pain traveling across my face, my ears, down my back and around again up to the ends of my jaw bones. The doctor had included my nose outside as a target whether inadvertent or not as I stated, so the phone receiver left a blazing mark on my nose and cheek! I believe everyone present was paralyzed in amazement and total shock, as was I.

Subconscious first aid maneuvers kicked in when the blood started flowing. This doctor had to realize what he had done because he left so swiftly. We didn't even get our bearings before he had vanished. I had my sinus tap alright and relief of all of that pressure. Unfortunately though, I had once again traded one terrible ordeal with another. This time it was a tap for a broken nose. Would you have sued?

I remember coming to somewhat while regaining my vision but still flying with the utter dizziness. I immediately began choking as I gasped for air. Then with the closing off of my throat to try breathing through my nose found that I couldn't do that either. My eyes squeezed shut and the mixing ringing of panic and pain set in. The huge bowl under my chin was now filling with a dark mass of infected matter. My throat was closed off due to the overflow of the same substance. But my nose on the other hand was not as fast to respond as the bowl filled up with more mucous. When it caught up the blood had no problem surpassing the already spewed volume in the pail.

As soon as my throat cleared I did manage to inhale this time by the closing off of my nose. Now that was a big time waterfall of blood, which easily surpassed my mall hemorrhage story. The now apparent and obvious reason was that my nose was now broken and the exterior revealed why.

Now with my nose pummeled and the list of crap wrong with or done to me was way past pathetic proportions. The packed and infected sinus's appeared to ease up a bit if not altogether, albeit tentatively. This I presume was aided by Immuno-globulin infusions or "I.g.G" as known in the medical field. Basically donor pooled spin offs of subclasses that assist in the body's performance in fighting and preventing infections.

At this point I have very vivid memories of still life experiences that I encountered, endured or created myself along the way. I have amassed plenty of incidences to touch on but I have to mention that this segment may not be in exact chronological order of their occurrence. I can say once again that they did in fact happen with many an eyewitness to attest to their validity. Just the fact that I recollect nearly every account must have a tie in with a shock factor or traumatic defense mechanisms that were embellished in my mind.

Upon reviewing my thumbnail outline, I've come across episodes that now today make me just shake my head a bit in disbelief, as well as send chills shrieking down the very spine that I'm going to reflect on.

If none of my early religious connotations and memorabilia episodes had any effect on your opinion of this story so far, I'd have to think that just these bazaar and horrible reflections alone has got to make you stop and think about God. Even though my spiritual participation was nothing more than mental contemplation and meditation during this time frame, this along with the prayers of many had to be instrumental in my survival as far as I'm concerned.

Hospital releases to home were few and far between for months at a time once again. I lost track of everything from time itself to what enjoyment was or used to be. I was so lost and out of it that my mind no longer seemed to work like the "old me", and didn't seem to want to for that matter. A doctor told my parents one time that he thought I could die whenever I wanted to and I suppose this feeling that I'm describing was a related issue to just that. It almost seemed as if every closing of my eyelids "to rest" and escape myself could in fact shut me down for good. I remember debating and rationalizing with my inner thoughts as to how deep of a let go sleep I'd decide upon. If the doctor was correct I guess that I never drifted to far away because I'm still here writing.

A lip biopsy was ordered here, which in Seattle was fairly common as well as necessary for GVHD monitoring. A hole punch sized incision was always performed with a circular scalpel type of instrument. In Seattle yes but I was in my hometown hospital in this case. You'd think that I would have hired guards by now but it was my guard that once again let me down. It is easy now to be critical of my actions upon reflection but back then things just didn't appear to be so black and white. There aren't any books out to give you guidelines on how to go about these hospital stays', so how was my family or anyone for that matter really to know, other than some type of trust!

The old adage of fool me once shame on you fool me twice shame on me was a theme that I should have adhered to right from the start. Even with our acquired savvy of asking many questions and writing down lengthy answers to pertinent issues, it just proved to be not enough. I still pray to hold out thinking that none of these "blunders" were intentional.

A "so called" prominent doctor was called in to see me, and with first impressions received of her, she seemed compassionate and trustworthy. I expected a bit of differences in the lip biopsy procedure techniques but not too varied. Lying down and weak, I just accepted the pre-med shot of Novocain in my lips and around my inner gum lines. The drug took effect pretty fast and my mouth soon drooled and dropped numb. Speech became garbled which had my paranoia frantically in panic mode from not being able to communicate properly. Though it didn't play a part here, it was a reality that not being able to convey my thoughts could be trouble.

With no other way to put it nicely, this "doctor" plain and simply "metamorphasized" into a meat butcher! Unbeknownst to me or anyone else in my family, the inner flesh of my mouth was being practically carved out and severed from the base of my gums where the teeth protrude out, to my utmost lip area just missing full exposure due to my closed mouth. This was a two to three inch gaping gash by conservative estimates. I can envision the skinning of a fish or the carving of a turkey because the scar line parallels those same cut lines.

Instantly, the slight drool became that all too familiar red river of plasma exiting my body. Now this time it was once again my mouths turn to participate in botched festivities. I hemorrhaged and was swiftly shrouded in blood from my slit open mouth to down along my solar plexus, finally puddling across the sheets that draped my abdomen. Of course the startling sight of this mess reflexed me to shoot up as best as I could off of the bed. That of course allowed the stream of red to increase as well as change routes. The bed, the floor, my groin, my legs, uh!, it was just a terrible mess!

I could feel myself becoming cold and numb crashing back to my version of earth, that being the gurney. A hangover spin took me all over the place with equilibrium malfunctions. With the lethargy and numbness winning out, the mad rush to attempt and get stitches in to stop the ridiculous flow only felt like taut tugs up and down my mouth. A feeling akin to that of when you were a kid and your mother hemmed your clothes while you stood like a mannequin impatiently. It was an annoying sensation, the jiggling and pulling here and there. You could certainly feel something going on but there really wasn't any pain per say unless she missed the numbed area; "With the blade of her knife that is".

I wonder if my mouth felt the same as a fish's mouth on a hook. I file the barb down today when I fish probably due to this crazy quirk. My mouth now resembles the space shuttle's orbit shot of earth with the rivers and canyons, inside lines and directions every which way. I don't know who wins the best mouth damage scar award, the biopsy scars or the mucousitis scars…

With another infection destructively taking a foothold on me and picked up from who knows where, I suspect the hospital; "A real Watson deduction huh". When you consider that I left for home and stayed there two or three days at a time tops during these stretches. Another doctor was on rounds at this particular time and of course totally new and unfamiliar with my case and history. Like the innovative spleenectomy story and collapsed lung incident back in Seattle, I speculate that these eager and gung ho doctors longed to be the next Jonas Salk or some pioneering doctor discovering a new ailment, disease, procedure or cure conveniently on me. To all of the patients out there, as we know many times we have to fall into the guinea pig category. But at what price do we pay or when do we draw the line, is the most difficult dilemma to answer.

Getting back to things, and keep in mind that this is now not too long after my mouth was massively stitched up to heal the biopsy gone wrong damage. My new and green "under doctor" brainstormed and collaborated with everyone except my family and I as to her newly concluded diagnosis. I guess that I may have shown some signs of spinal meningitis, but to jump to conclusions and pronounce that I have it without sufficient documentation is ludicrous! Well that's what she did, as if all excited to grab her Nobel Prize. I had some kind of infection for sure and I knew what the Graft vs. Host Disease could do as far as symptom manifestations, so instinctively I refused to buy this meningitis theory until I could speak with Dr. Mike personally. Yes, yet again my dwindling nine lives were forced to claw from out of the corner and do battle.

As nasty and defensive as I may have been, I feel that I was justifiably placed into that situation. I often say sarcastically that doctors can clock out and go golfing but I am still stuck with what I'm dealing with. It's a great analogy I feel of placing patient's feelings in perspective. So as it turned out, we argued and verbally battered each other until I conceded and hesitantly agreed to have a spinal tap done. I in no way wanted to have a tap done on me but I had some guilt's of "what if there is something wrong there and you don't get it checked, with your luck you'll screw up everything you've worked for" I just needed an evening to get ready for it.

That habit of mentally preparing for a time beforehand worked wonders for me here because only God knows if I could have endured what was to come next without it. Especially after the amount of energy that it took out of me in ranting and raving my side of the situation as a patient. I've discussed which procedures were the most traumatic but at this point I'll simply let the reader decide for themselves because I cannot pick one now after reflecting on these unthinkable episodes.

One of the drawbacks I now can pick up on from back then was that my initial physician team of oncologists was not in the mix so to speak with all of the decision making, as they should have been in my opinion. It wasn't for a while later until Dr. Mike and his associates took over once again full time with all of the medical decision making locally. This was of my request, and most definitely too late to have saved me from some of these medical fiascos. I simply got lumped in with "layman's or normal patients" as far as care was concerned, when in fact I think it was premature.

With everybody being as ready as they could be from my understanding, the wheels were set in motion for the spinal tap to begin. For anyone not familiar with this procedure, my experiences have always had me lay in the fetal position on the bed with my back facing the doctors. A vertebrate sight is decided upon and a long fairly thick needle is pierced through the skin and backbone to hopefully extract spinal fluid. This is a wealth of information for doctors to work with, so I've been told.

This scenario unfolded just as I have described except that the two "men" performing it were total strangers to me. Further more; none of my attending physicians were present to monitor this spinal tap either. Once again I should have sued and often wonder if in fact those guys were competent or students, since it was a teaching hospital. Perhaps they just wanted to rub me out I don't Know, jesting tongue in cheek metaphorically speaking. "Remember, I was the difficult patient to many".

With extreme intensity and shall I say reluctant focus, I attempted to settle in as best as I could and participate. After all It was my butt on the line here not theirs. Just one wrong move and I could be paralyzed, incur nerve damage or who knows what if this procedure goes wrong. It is highly stressed not to flinch or move at all and for my sensitive back, the pressure of the stabbing needle was unbearable. Today, from the damage you can literally touch me with a Q-Tip on the sight and I go flying! "A Q-Tip mind you". Thank God it isn't worse.

What happened you ask? I'll tell you what happened .My being dug in and holding the bed rail firmly with my brother and father near my head for support, had me conforming to position as directed. As I stated it was imperative on my part to be motionless so as not to cause damage. Perhaps the two guys doing this spinal tap were performing the procedure correctly but I will never know. As the thrusting gristled through my skin and bone, I squirmed mentally but remained as still as the night is dark in body. Just like that, with the pressure push I could feel a deep head to toe clinch sounding through me like the sound made and felt by banging your teeth sharply while keeping the lips closed. That very same sensation only magnified ten fold! When a chalk board is screeched rapidly and that sound could be translated into a painful nerve ending throb that would describe this shot. You just knew instinctively that things weren't right.

Generally instincts do not lie and they didn't here. The spinal tap needle had broken inside of my spine. Half of the shaft was embedded deep in my back bone and the other end was at half mast sticking out of my back! Immediately and urgently the two men yelled at me not to move what so ever at all. I don't know how much spinal fluid spewed out and to what dangerous degree but I can tell you that I held on for dear life! The term "a million thoughts rushing through my mind" does not do me justice whatsoever here.

I had plenty of time for a million thoughts easily because the buffoon's or falsely accomplished incompetents had me motionless for a half an hour. In fact one guy reinforced my legs down to the bed while the other guy ran for help. There were phone calls, confusion, bickering and chaos all around me, and all that I could do was eavesdrop in on what was going on. I picked a spot on the bed rail and focused on the section of steel as a parameter or landmark. The discipline not to move is far and above the call of duty here. A fetal position freeze with a cold rod protruding out of your back .The feeling of moisture trickling and tickling your skin with racing thoughts abound, as well as urges to move must be constantly suppressed and overridden. I doubt seriously though if I could have remained perfectly still if it hadn't been for my father and brother holding me down bodily. I absolutely blew another fuse and lost some more sanity with this one. God bless the people held captive and tortured. I think about them when I reflect on this debacle.

The stinking needle was finally wrenched and eased back out while my infuriated father was out for blood, "or spinal fluid". Just like the sinus doctor, the two interns or doctors or whatever they were vanished without a trace. After all of that crap, the tests revealed that I had no signs of spinal meningitis what so ever. I never saw that diagnosing fraud of a doctor again after this incident either. I'd like to think that they were enemies foiled in an assassination attempt. Just my sense of humor on these outrageous occurrence's, otherwise I wouldn't have been able to cope with it all. As bad of a doctor that she was for me, she was attractive though. "Beware of wolfs in sheep's clothing or lab coats"...

That sense of humor didn't keep me from becoming immune to the pressure altogether, because shortly afterward, I went into a major tailspin. Several incidents of my freaking out and verbal diarrhea of the mouth headlined the agendas. In this stretch of manic lows, I peaked with the finally of stunts. In my usual attire consisting of under shorts and tee shirt garb, with the legs of a broom stick and arms as frail as peanut brittle, I barricaded myself in my room holding me hostage. In retrospect I cannot make heads nor tails out of this incident. I simply recall the experience as if I was inside of my body looking out of an uncontrollable entity through the eyelids.

How the heck I moved those beds, chairs, tables, trash cans and anything else that could budge over against the door only God knows. Speaking of God in this time frame, I'd presume that the footsteps poem could again apply to my story, because I felt abandoned somewhat but must have been carried through this.

Prayers on my part were scarce during this duration with nothing much else uttered except informal conversation. One liner's such as "help me please" under my breath or thinking it consciously, that was the extent of it. Back in my cell, the nudging of my room door and outsiders pounding to ignite a response on my end were not successful. Some "F"-bombs or growls of anger directed their way at least let them know that I was still alive and kicking. I must say I did a nice job building that levy of furniture because it held up for hours. Any beaver would have been proud.

Just like in "Dog Day Afternoon" or a movie of that nature, the phone in my room rang. I answered gruffly only to end up in negotiations with my sister from her work office back in Delaware. She got through and had my doctor on her other line. Carol was my mediator some forty miles away, with the doctor some forty feet away down the hospital hall.

How hysterically comical this is to me now but back then I'm positively certain that it was unnerving and annoying to the staff. You'd think that they would have enticed me to come out with my hands up surrendering to a gourmet meal or something. It ended up being more like plaster paris mashed potato's something or other.

That abbreviated fiasco ended peacefully and coincidentally I recall a string of unrelated nightmare's ensuing. I can't remember how lengthy this particular hospital stay was, but however the tenure, it was way too long that's for sure! By this time in my life an hour was too long for comfort. It wasn't long after this hospitalization stay that I was blessed with a reprieve of sorts and able to go home for some "normal lengths of time"

I could make a case for saying that my life felt wasted and ruined at this point. Hospital stays were way too commonplace with many two and three day venues at a time going on. A good friend of mine at the time, Regina tried her best to cheer me up whenever she would get wind of my hospital pit stops. It wasn't uncommon for her to come and go dropping off food and things to help me pass the time as best as I could. It definitely helped, as did the reassurance of some other but now dwindling friends. I guess you can't blame them, this script was so old and worn out by now, "one day he's in' the next day he's out, he's going to die soon, he's a little better' now he's worse"! "I heard he died" and so on. It takes true compassion and concern to put up with that kind of a cycle, and I'm sure that I was no fun to be around.

These ups and downs in my personal life and first "year" of post transplant era floundering with skids and slides led up to the one year evaluation back in Seattle, Washington. This seemingly pre scripted journey of destiny, called off the dogs of illness long enough to make the lengthy trip. I recovered to the point of being released home for a bit to rest, but no sooner had we caught our breathes in our own confines, new arrangements were being made to fly west for a week. It was a big relief in one respect to be out of the local hospital finally and once again home but on the other side of the coin was the can of worms opened up in my mind that had been partially stashed in the mothball fleet of the temporal lobe.

Being preoccupied with broken needles, broken jaws, broken nose, broken heart and broken dreams, the looming torments of a leukemia relapse only had time to prick and jab my psyche part time. Now the spotlight was centered exclusively on just that, a leukemia relapse. Those mental psychotic sticks became commonplace with anxiety knocking at every pulse of my heartbeat to remind me there of. Perhaps my faith waned here because I became my worst enemy overwrought with fear and yet even more stress internally.

I believe that I hurt my father's feelings by emphasizing that I only wanted to make the trip with my sister Carol. My dad was visibly upset and at the time, I didn't see it in the fog of everything. Now I wish that I would have opted to take him with us. The proud man that he was and I deprived him of parading through the very same hospital he once did as a father of a son who used to have leukemia; Yet another of one of my many mistakes.

It was Halloween time so the brisk air and falling leaves as well as football all but carried my morale. I did feel up beat at times with less re occurring anxiety in our departure, flight and landing. Even with a nice volunteer picking us up at the airport, settling in once again at the Monticello and walking around I felt up beat; Then came time to get down to business. The one year checkups were rather grueling in their own right. One of the promising brighter moments was visiting many of the staff members who had a big hand in saving my life. The main reason for the trip was just the opposite in anxiety levels. The bottom line was the relapse factor. That called for the heavy artillery of gouges in my story. The "corkscrew" as I've come to call it. Also with that came what I envisioned earlier as the tequila worm of bone sliver that they dig out of you for the pathology information as well.

Such a feeling of absolute truthful irony was that my scheduled combination bone marrow aspiration "corkscrew cocktail" was to take place on Halloween itself. So what's the big deal you ask? Nothing as far as extracting the marrow and bone from me were concerned. The now humorous side of this and I emphasize now because I wasn't in any laughing mood at the time mind you, was on how they went about doing it.

All of the designated hip sights for marrow extractions were all but exhausted with scarring from the many previous taps. The rash of scars resembled constellations akin to the Big Dipper. The area was so sensitive to the gentlest of touch that it would have been very difficult for me to cooperate successfully for them. An un-harvested plethora of delight to those guys drilling was my sternum. Yep, right over the heart. Halloween stake through the heart analogy, you get it? Furthermore, all of the well enough little patients who could participate in dressing up were cruising in the hallways in any fashion or manner possible. Lot's of "little monsters", "not literally, although one may wonder about a few", slithered and trickled door to door very often accompanied by those infamous blue pumps and piggybacks "whistling Dixie about the joint". Yet another reminder to me as to why I freak out hearing bells and buzzers. Anyhow, costumes such as Godzilla and even a red lobster were the two most adorable little patient's get ups that stole the show for me. These costumes were as fantastic as the little guys were courageous.

But getting back to my initial point, even a few of the staff members were dressed up in costumes. And just as my luck would have it, one of the attending nurses sucking marrow from me was disguised as Dracula. "I hope she or it was just a nurse"? This un intentional or intentional match of a vampire on Halloween doing a marrow on my sternum for the first time is still uncanny and humorous to me today. Looking up at the ceiling doing my Lamaze, breathing and having that unbearable pressure clamp down on my chest as the apparatus grinded into me, tops the surreal episodes that I've hit on. Only in America can Dracula legally drill through your chest in a "compassionate" manner! On Halloween yet! Well perhaps in Transylvania. Are any bone marrow transplant hospitals open over there on October 31st?

Just as impressive as the costumes were was the sucking out of my wind cavities, to the point of me internally panicking due to the new and unknown sensation in my chest. I, again as many times before felt like this was it and I was going to die due to the lack of oxygen that I was getting in. Most likely I was in no danger whatsoever, but I was very concerned at the time. I fidgeted to try and get anyone's attention, squeaking out "I…can't…br…ea…th…! That all too familiar throbbing in my brain akin to being under water too long from lack of oxygen I presume went on here. Of course I had air pockets present or whatever it is that prevents bone marrow from being extracted, so I had to have the stake driven into my chest two or three more times before hitting pay dirt. "Or marrow"

I have used this analogy before but it fits that very sensation perfectly so you can envision what I felt on the table. Enough staff members were on hand and you'd like to think that I was a valued commodity having survived a year up to that point. That was a huge deal in 1988 with my CML, non related donor, accelerated phase and all. Seattle had no idea what the last year back home had been like for me at this point, but then again they probably didn't care because I was still alive. Not many if any could say that back then. That in and of itself, is a great humbling thought to ponder on when I boohoo with self pity now and then. Believe me these reflections snap me right back into a good perspective of things!

With that ironic story out of the way, the weeklong stay included many other memorable scenarios; an itinerary sheet listed all of the many appointments and various doctors for the week. As was the case when I initially had testing done before my transplant, the procedures were spaced out to allow for some breaks. As it turned out, I really needed the time to recover between bouts!

Pulmonary function tests with breathing tubes similar to a scuba divers oxygen mask were performed on me. Breathe in and hold, blow out, repeat, exhausting all of the air out, while every move would be delicately diagnosed by the computers, to the exact capacity of lung air primarily. One bit of bad news that I received from this was that my lung s had gotten smaller in a years time. The Graft vs. Host Disease battles had tightened my skin and actually pushed my rib cage into the lungs, thus the decline of air capacity. This manifestation is similar to Sclera derma patient's difficulties.

Next came the treadmill tests, dental exams, eye exams, reflexes and coordination tests. Nutritional analysis, psychological evaluations, more blood work and dermatology exams about rounded off the schedule. "I may have missed one or twenty other similar types of examinations but this gives you an overview of the fun". So as not to drag this visit out too long, the synopsis of it was that overall, most of the results were acceptable. Although I lost some ground in terms of mortality related issues, I seemed good enough this far out. The toughest thing was in not knowing whether I had relapsed or had the potential to do so at this time. The pathology report would take a few weeks to get back so I wouldn't know those results until I got back home.

A structured interview, slash, conference was conducted with the head GVHD doctor and Professor of Medicine at the University of Washington, Doctor Keith Sullivan and myself. With almost a checklist itinerary like pattern, he described my status on everything. No bones are minced here, as they are professional and straightforward. Once again humble is the word as I quietly gulped with every statement as a quiver here and there shot up and down my spine. The analysis of things overall was that my GVHD had gotten worse and that I had lost ground since last year other than the leukemia itself. All of this damage was due to what had been done to cure this damned leukemia, or at least attempt to. I still wouldn't know for a while as I mentioned but what I didn't state, was that the key factor in determining a possible relapse short of an actual relapse itself per say was the re emergence of the Philadelphia negative chromosome. In lay mans terms, a genetic marker indicative of a leukemia relapse possibility. Not always mind you but often more times than not. The name by the way comes due to its discovery in Philadelphia, Pa.

My GVH had failed the first two "waves" or treatments to fight the disease. Some discussions of new experimental protocols were started with me to mow over as possible options. The sum of those talks was that I could be left horribly worse off or much better off for it. The "half full half empty glass" analogy I suppose. Amidst these proposals, still on the same day of Halloween, I'd like to slide off to another tangent briefly in memory of my sister Carol. In all of the months that we spent together in Seattle, 99% of the stay consisted of heart wrenching life and death issues. These two stories showed her great personable side that housed an abundance of humor not often able to spring out in Seattle.

This week of Halloween that I've clearly alluded to, found us relaxing in the Monticello, trick or treat evening. It was that or possibly the city's determined door to door kid's candy traditional night. Whatever the case, we both enjoyed handing out a bit of candy to the lads besides the patients. Pretty good costumes all in all, but as the children's traffic trickled down to a halt we all but closed up shop on our candy giving away evening. The schedule had us getting up early the next day for appointments, so we both settled in to our beds next to each other and shot the breeze a bit waiting to fall asleep, or try to at least. The city sounds eased through our walls so even the faintest meows of a cat could make its way up to our ears. Just under our rooms window was an alleyway that produced some of those eerie echoes of titillation of wonderment. "What was that?, who was that?, what's going on out there?" and so on.

After all of the passing kids bickering over candy or divvying up the rations subsided, the usual silence save for the damp resonance of alley noise paved the way for the feature presentation. The approaching of pitter patter's along with skip's and giggle's reached our ears as some late solicitors. Clearly the ruckus turned into chattering of siblings going at it, brothers and sisters verbally rumbling below our windowsill. Crinkling of bags and candy wrappers drowned out by wrestles and grunts of dominance and determination became the main event. In one corner was Tyrone. The challenger was Pricilla I believe. Sporadic giggles ensued amongst the thrashing and slips with more bag crunching business going on, so right away we knew that it wasn't a mugging or a robbery etc. taking place. "At least not a crime of police proportions"

From the onset you could here Carol being entertained by these characters. Our pitch black room gave way to the window silhouette that peeked a shadow now and then of our personal live performance. The street light overhung the alleyway, so the adjacent brick building wall, damp and dewy as it may have been, served as our big movie screen backdrop for enlarged shadowy silhouettes. The enlarged images scuffled up to our sills; "Tyrone give me my bag"…"Tyrone I said give me my bag"……Silence, giggle, crash, thud, crinkle, whoosh, giggle, sigh. Explosively, in a deep monotoned directive Priscilla lashed out; "Tyrone I said gimme my f——in baag!!" Carol lost it and ripped aloud with her unique and contagious laugh. On and on she went as if it was just what the doctor had ordered for her. Whatever pushed her button had released much compressed energy that was pent up inside like Mt. St. Helens. That sure hit the spot for Carol!

As if to out do themselves unknowingly, the two actors down below in the alleyway paused bashing each other to converse between candy bars. Tyrone I presume laid Carol out on her knees with this encore short liner. Carol was about teary eyed when he say's "Maaan you shoulda seen it boyeeee.I was over at Maac Donalts en dare he was. A biig olt balt headett, yellow mutha f——a wit a mask…jus liket over daat hospital. Musta exxcaped ah sumpin. A whoole bunch of umm.

Carol may have peed her self in stitches, as those humorous lines to her were therapeutically intoxicating. I took much humor from the spontaneous occurrence myself seeing it take her out. Carol was innocently naïve in some respects and the shock of ten year olds firing "F" bombs and busting on transplant patients blew her minds I suppose. So much for innocence…

With that personal memory expressed in stride of things, we found ourselves next killing time before more scheduled appointments the next day. I'd like to blame my callus demeanor on stress but by now you would think that I had a better handle on it. For whatever the reason, my sister and I passed the time walking and casually came across a quaint five and dime store to stop in quickly when we were accosted by an apparent street man. He was pressuring us for money when I out of character lit into him to get a damn job while I gruffly stomped into the store. I barely passed the doormat when my conscience bombed me into submission. "You jerk" I ripped into myself mentally, a total hypocrite in professing to be a Christian. In the blink of an eye I dashed out as best as I could to fill the guys hand with the change I had in my pockets. A meal worth I suppose as long as it did go for food. With that, at least I cracked back into a bit of my old self in time to help the guy out, or get ripped off. Only God knows.

The conclusion of this trip included me getting around or "coming to terms" with myself rather to make the trek up to the very floor where all of the action took place. I had mixed emotions as to how I would feel back up there. I experienced some flashbacks and anxiety but subconsciously I suppose that I need to get it done. Up the elevator, around the halls, brief pauses and pretty much all business like in mannerism I eased out of there. What a tremendous surge of relief it was once I got off of the elevator and out of the building, knowing that I didn't have to go back in as a patient. "So I hoped". Again, my heart truly goes out for all of those transplant patients and their families. "Nobody knows…"

A pressing issue while in Seattle was to meet with the financial billing dept. This was an "antacid required" visit for sure. My bills had accumulated so much to the point that two big brown paper shopping bags were filled to the top with statements and the likes. This exhausted me further physically and mentally between big debts and recovery. Perhaps the steroids and bulk of medicines aided in my activities here. When it came time to leave and fly home, not only did I fit the profile of a meltdowned patient and drop off me suitcase to a homeless guys lair, I encored that stunt by dropping both bags of bills into a trashcan in a Detroit or Chicago airport! After reviving my sister back to life with that doozy, I basked in false serenity during the long flight back to Philly. Needlesss to say, paying the debts wasn't as easy as slam dunking the bills in a trashcan!

The closing out of this trip had the particular airline overbook our flight and attempted to negotiate a deal with Carlo and I to sleep over and take the next flight. "Yeah right" Do you think they persuaded me out of a seat? Fat chance, I wanted home sweet home and the sooner the better! What did they think, that these transplant people are softies; Soft in the heart perhaps but not in frequent flier mixups.

CHAPTER 6

▼

I paused a bit here before resuming my story to reflect on things and once again visualize the correlation of these events. Picking up where I left off was easy as I recall stewing in "marrow pangs", as to my possible leukemia relapse test results. As things would have it, Carol and I ended driving around frequently spending time together and assisting each other to the best of our abilities to try and cope with these piling situations. She wasn't exactly her self, and her marriage was being compromised in every which way. This was obviously because of my predicament but unbeknownst to me at the time, more so due to her spouse and her personal health.

With us being so close, Carol took this opportunity to confide in me some dirty laundry flying around rumor town about my broken engagement. I think that she wanted to cushion any blows to the head that I'd be receiving upon hearing these daggers thrown my way through the stinking gossip airways. Only the Lord would know the real scoop for sure. But so as not to give credence to the pitfall I felt, I'll simply state that they had to do with the engagement itself, and some people other than my family or friends. It was another one of those "keep it from Johnny" stories, about people waiting for me to pass on and "move on with plans in life etc".

I'm not stating that any of it was true or untrue. I'm stating it because I heard it enough damn times, and knowing what I now know gives me ample cumulative evidence to wonder about it. The Creator upstairs in the court of morals and ethics, let alone love knows the real story. I would think that my last name was Kennedy with all of this mischievous conniving going on by various people out there. Carol and I each had a good cry and I remember the exact location on the particular road that we drove on when we talked about it all. I still envision our conversation upon passing it even today.

A few weeks or perhaps more passed by along with my slipping into a stupor over this relapse thing and certain dates and numbers that I'd notice became more than coincidental to me so for a spell. I equated them with my death or relapse. My irrational panic attacks were so opposite of my suit of armor in faith outwardly, nevertheless they existed. This was about the time when less people courted my company.

The ended relationship severed ties to what was like a second family of sorts of about twenty to thirty I'd estimate. The predicament for "friends" I suppose was relating, understanding or just being their old selves with me. I don't know if it was the easy road or the hard road that they took in not socializing with me for them, only they knew that. The "pet dog mentality" in me did take some token bone visits of compassion or guilt, like a Christmas visit or a football game sit through. After those sporadic pit stops, it pretty much reverted back to the same rut of plagued anxiety. That lousy ringing of the quote in my head "you'll be trading one terminal disease for another haunted me all the more...

The pathology reports eventually came in and revealed still no relapse of leukemia detected to the best of their abilities. In and of it self, that was very great news! I'd been informed that due to the severity of my GVHD, my relapse chances were a good deal lessened. I take that as being the new marrow's strong ability to suppress any new "old cells" production in me was the key factor in their reasoning. In any event the additional news was again that the GVHD was not responding to therapy.

By now the cycle of meltdowns were apart of me and the time was right to have one. The depression became so very bad that I can sum up many, and I'll stress many episodes denoting my behavior unfolding with stories like this.

An evening of unrest in my bedroom of stagnation prompted me to carry out and attempt to escape my own self. Without rhyme or reason I would randomly bolt out of the house and meander about to God only knows where. The few teardrops that could be mustered up ran down my cheeks for all of the ones that couldn't escape. Just like me, those tears were prisoners in a body that we could no longer recognize. The neighborhood was not familiar to me after about two blocks due to the move from the city as I mentioned earlier.

From frequent walks on the shoulders of I-95 in the past, I did head towards my old city's direction. Due to my horrible walking ability, capacity and speed, what would have taken a healthy me ten minutes to reach, covered at least ninety minutes now. My parents were so conditioned to my outbursts that they simply expected me to return or didn't see me leave. As I reached the ramp on to the highway itself, my incoherent mannerism kicked into overdrive. Thoughts of "I'll show em" I'd say were appropriate in describing my mindset, but show who what? God, my family, my friends, me, I don't know. I just wanted to escape this pressure and flea from it all.

The longest of ramps was also the darkest of nights. My eyes I believe were still fairly normal but my waddling across the gravel embankments and mini potholes made more fuel for my fire of emotions. As I reached the bottom of the ramp leading to a tunnel of sorts streaming under the interstate itself up to the highway, my fears overwhelmed me. The city street smarts that I acquired in Chester made me fully aware of the dangers that loomed in this all but too real setting of uncertainty ahead. Tingling senses told me not to go through this darkest of pits. I was out of my mind for sure, even to the point of seeing the passing torch of lit cigarette silhouettes about the black air. My irrational mannerisms pushed on with self thoughts of "big deal, so you get jumped or killed, you'll take somebody with you. Your dying anyhow so who really gives a shit!"

My real self was fearful and the rosary that I carried with me was company enough to sludge through meditating on the 23rd psalms excerpt "though I walk through the valley of death I shall fear no evil". I still cannot believe that I remember this or why the heck I even continued on. As it turned out, I was approached by the group, but oddly enough I wasn't bothered under there. I guess they figured that I was as crazy as they were to be in the tunnel, so all was left well enough alone. Not that I could have defended myself from a gang at that time, from the "Little Rascals" perhaps.

Anyhow, the insanity continued as I lumbered up the hill directly on to the highway traveling north on the south lane. There were moments when I actually walked right at on coming cars just oblivious to reality, so I think. I must have been crying out for someone or something but no one was aware to hear or see it. Even my being the one involved didn't understand the purpose of the stunt, and I still don't today. Like a zombie I was and I cannot fathom how some of those cars could have avoided me!

I just ended this exhausting journey with a collect call to my dad from a pay phone several miles away to come and get me. That whole bazaar but true story was only good for a solid nights sleep, or recovery? "I guess, that's what trauma can do to you".

Ensuing experiments with antidepressants blew up in my face as I never at that time found one that didn't make matters worse. After several attempts with different drugs culminated into negotiations with my mom and Dr. Mike on the phone to fine tune my dosages, we ultimately decided to call off the meds with so many others mixing on board inside of me. For whatever the reason, they simply couldn't alleviate any of my mood problems. I'd presume that all of the chemicals I'd been ingesting in those forms of medicines as well as the chemotherapy and radiation itself, had to have alot to do with it. Nevertheless, the whole situation was terrible and it all stunk.

Walking and collapsing turned into a "normal" routine during this period. I actually wonder if it helped to keep me alive in a funny sort of way. Despite the danger and apparent stupidity in the rationale of it all, it was physical activity of sorts. In attempting to cover all that I recall as pertinent insight, I'd say that I could write chapters on each little tidbit of information. But to keep things rolling, I'll move on having simply given you a window of where I was mentally, physically and spiritually.

This reminded me also of another ordeal to put far behind me. The Cyclosporin that I was taking, affected me in ways which I'm sure many patients taking it unfortunately encountered. Although they varied like a chameleons various color changes, this tenure had me walking a lot, but more importantly exploding with metamorphic negative residuals as my reward. I swelled to even bigger proportions when I didn't believe that it could be possible! Like a change of seasons my hair turned fiery shades of orange, to black, to curly brown, to baby thin, to a punk rockers front man look. Then when some of my fingernails split and cracked wide open with raging pain, others grew disproportionately. One toenail in particular embraced a mind of its own. It just enlarged and descended to the point at which I could no longer place weight on it. This was a flat tire of sorts because I couldn't journey out on my sporadic rendezvous any longer. To as I've mentioned, attempt to "escape my self". So yes another appointment and more rigmarole to see another specialist, this time a podiatrist.

A very nice man, when upon being informed of my condition, spiraled into the "china glass syndrome doctor". That's what I'd come to call the doctors who treated me as if I was a fragile piece of breakable goods. It was true but another blow to my ego, which took personal offense to those notions. My toenail had embedded itself as if overnight speed wise, into my skin, which encased my inner nail next to the smaller toe. This was so uncomfortable I tried Epsom salts, elevation and bed rest but they did nothing to ease the pain. What strikes me here in reflection was the extreme lengths which were taken to fix my ingrown toenail. After being bombarded and nuked with the radiation and everything that you have been reading about, I jested at this fuss over a simple toenail.

My attitude turned a nice and polite doctor rabid with disgust and anger toward my scoffing. He fired a phrase something like, "You know, Mr. Amatuzio, this isn't a laughing matter. Do you realize that you could die from this?" My smile and humor toward the toenail weaned a bit, although I didn't take him seriously at first, until I gazed at the stark, stern look in his eyes.

Again I had to saddle up for another operating room procedure; the cold stainless steel, the gowns, all the fun stuff "right, fellow patients." This all consisted of a lengthy lie down and fully conscious session on the gurney with only my leg being localized. I felt sensations of a lot of pressure and motion like a dentist working in the mouth analogy once again. When all was said and done, one-half of my toenail had been removed and bandaged up. "Big deal", I still thought, "give me a break". To this day I have half a toenail and it probably would look better all the way off.

I eventually learned of the many concerns being related to sources of major infections for me. It turned out that the bloodline from the toe to the blood stream was damaged and exposed to potential infection. I took the horse-sized antibiotics for a two-week course and still got lit up with one. Thank goodness it was a mild compared to what I was used to getting, you know all of the staphs, E-colis, gram negatives and everything else. My lesson learned is that an ingrown toenail is no laughing matter! "For me anyhow, not even if its a monstrous-sized Cyclosporin toenail." Taking care of the 'big toe' came and passed by with another bomb painted on the side of my battered fuselage. I notched another successful bombing raid on a cropped up complication but I was still leaking oil.

This all compounded my depression to the highest altitudes yet. I didn't cope with it well at all and went so far as to take off again to who knows where. The recollection of that wasn't so strange in the boundaries of my previous erratic behavior at the time. What was perhaps extreme was that I ventured a highway via automobile this time. I actually persuaded my mom somehow to let me borrow her car and I headed solo to Wildwood New Jersey. I had about a hundred dollars and a gym bag, not having a clue as to what I was accomplishing. Perhaps subconscious childhood memories tuned me into longing for a better time in my life. The earliest of which took flight at a very humble and modest beach hotel. This was a palace to a guy like me at the time, with my upbringing and annual family vacation destination.

A creaky somewhat damp abode filled with such charm that I just melted away in mental drifts of the season and moment upon every stay. While not elaborating too extensively on this place, it simply was plain, old, homey and in the center of everything taking place on the island. Nestled fifty feet or so from the boardwalk and beach while directly across the street sat a twenty-four hour bus station to add to the ambiance. Dracula's Castle sat a football field's length away and overlooked our porch usually on the third floor of four I believe, and notoriously echoed the mysterious and enchanting pipe organ theme that we all know. "Den nen nen den nen nen, doodle oo, doo doo, do", you know the rest. I hear you humming it right now.

A distant ocean surf layered over the organ as did the "click, click, click, click" of the roller coaster climbing to the top peak, surging down with the chorus screams of its captives. Even more titillating for the conscious listener were faded sounds of mocking birds babbling at the shooting gallery in from the not far off casinos. "Eh, eh, eh, eh, eh, eh, eh, eh", they sneered taking the quarters at will from those sharp shooters oblivious to the rest of the world surrounding them; the complete opposite of me.

Every sound "Watch the tram car, please. Watch the tram car, please", and "There's a winner every time" Buses rolling in and out with echoing announcer's dispatching departures, the routes and destinations. Motorcycles, police cars, cruising hot rods, all of those giggling gals, cooing babies and crying babies who did not get their way on the boardwalk. I'll bet that I could write a book on the Wildwood sounds alone. It was so great for me and all of this without having mentioned the visual aspects. Whew, where would I start? Water slide girls, life sized stuffed animals, concerts, bike rentals, humungous beaches and abundant ocean surf, party boats, seagulls, salt water taffy and fresh fudge aromas flowing abound; On and on and on and on.

I'll add some ingredients of salty misty air coating your skin and clothing ever so gently. That is unless you encounter hurricanes and they become a whole other story. Rocking in the chair on the porch overlooking everything from kid's trying to sneak into nearby motels and landlords' chasing them to clear moon lit nights setting over the ocean's reflected glow. "Stuka" dive bombing seagulls closing in on unsuspecting board walkers' and oblivious sunbathers' leftovers; some voluntarily giving up their food and some no so voluntarily.

It seemed like just so much to go and escape to. Yes, perhaps this is what I fled to or attempted to flee so I thought in hindsight. Whatever the case may have been and by briefly giving you a slight flavor and feeling of what my destination and motives were, I set sail.

Just stone cold and depressed to the max, I reflected on irony and trips from Wildwood back to home before the transplant. "Good old Box of Frogs tape" my buddy Larry gave me really helped back then but there weren't any songs to ease things for me now. I managed to get a room at the same old childhood palace, the Dubois Hotel. In fact, one of which that I'd stayed in as a boy. This was the very same connecting bathroom to share with who knows who and everything. It was a ghost town this time around and I actually had my own floor so to speak. The childhood palace as an adult now had the same flavor and ambiance as before but really was never a palace of luxury at any time. I mean this in a physical appearance but sentimentally it was the Taj Mahal in its lucidity.

Upon checking in and making my way up the stairs, I still can remember now my thoughts as I climbed up one by one, further and further. My legs had a bit of strength in them like pre-transplant days. Perhaps not the explosive bounce I had but at least a solid feeling of a foundation upon my push off and landing. This struck me because my limbs were clearly taking the brunt of the graft vs. host disease attack. I stopped and pondered overlooking all of the sights and sounds of Wildwood that I just mentioned, except for the bus station. Over the years it had moved across the island but even still without those unique sounds of travelers coming and going, it was all virtually still the same. I briefly rested in one of the old and most definitely the exact same rocking chairs that I had as a child. The weathered wicker seat swallowed my tiniest cheeks of a tush after which my eyes just hovered over the balcony banister. I drank in the refreshing flavor of the encompassing area and for an instant I thought that I'd been on to something as far as fighting the depression was concerned.

After a bit, I moseyed down to my room again and crashed on the bed as I was way past tired by then. Staring up to the ceiling light (bulb) I stretched my hands out and locked them behind my head. The breeze through the ancient screen allowed the sporadic sea mist as well as the surrounding sounds in also. I remember feeling my heart beat through my shirt and noticing the ever so tired ear ringing that I used to get when I became fatigued. With the hopes of just drifting away from my problems, as I mentioned, it turned out that I couldn't even drift anywhere.

My efforts to sleep were in vain and all for naught. I tossed and turned and come to mention it, I did end up drifting somewhere, right into a moodier, grumpier insomniatic state of depressed depths. I was alone. I drove ninety-six miles to escape myself and failed. My panic needles pricked my psyche and his friend, fear, stopped by also. If I could try to express this time frame of emotions, I'd fall short. The whooshing of waterfall thoughts from "What am I going to do?" and "Am I going to die?" to "I don't want to die." to "Why was I ever born?" and the infamous, "Why me?" comes to mind. Such an extreme sense of loneliness, and it seemed like I'd sadly adopted this tenant as a mainstay on my game wheel of life.

My stay lasted two days of which I reminisced and, unknowingly, fueled the fire of self-torture. I actually stopped at a few places where I had enjoyed wonderful memories of younger romances. I sat as a spectator gazing at the healthy water sliders zipping along the chlorinated caverns. I labored through crowds feeling like the freak show attraction, thinking that I was being stared at even if I wasn't. The filed emotional scars added up it seemed now upon reflection.

Ironically, the last evening of my "trip" featured a lunar eclipse. My mom used to say to me when I was a boy, "Look up at the moon and I'll be able to see you". I watched the eclipse with a stranger on a bench on the boardwalk and gave my parents a call from a nearby pay phone just to hear them. My whole mission didn't work out very well and I finally journeyed back to the "good old home sweet home", still lonely, still scared, still with GVHD and still depressed.

Other attempts to shake this grip of pessimism got shot down as well. I'd visit the guys and try to hang out but things were different. Some type of tension in awkwardness existed for whatever the reason. One day I brought my mail with me to go through at my friend, Larry's house. I discarded the junk mail and came across the usual batch of medical letterhead envelopes. I'd grown accustomed to this ritual of hospital "fan mail" and the majority of them were either statements or explanations of the financial goings on.

After opening one of the last envelopes for the day, my friend, Larry, could tell something was going on by the look on my face. As I recall, just combine the expressions of shock, laughter, surprise, fear, panic, disbelief and you must be kidding kind of looks. This was all spurred on by the accounts payable due by me in the some of fifty thousand dollars! "Misprint? I'm afraid not. Insurance mix-up? Nope. Mistaken identity? Obviously wrong again." I was responsible and what lousy timing to get this news and relight the smoldering embers of frustration and depression. The song "Dirty Laundry", said it best "Kick 'em when they're up, kick 'em when they're down".

In future appointments, I'd learn that the hospital would later agree to write-off much of it given the fact that I had consented to the governmental experimental protocol program. They expressed to me if, in the event that I could ever pay it off personally, they would accept it. As I mentioned though, the hospital worked it out for the most part. "That's mere chump change, right fellow patients." Well, comparatively in the overall expense of everything it certainly is. I just wish that I'd have been informed of all of this in a less stressful manner.

As more time trickled by, recollection of further graft vs. host disease complications and initiating more combinations of immuno-suppressive drugs to combat it were implemented. I just kept getting slammed with this or that symptom-wise. My humanity showed their "true colors" because I adamantly bartered with God for my kind of answers but to no avail in my eyes. To just see your own body deteriorating away right before you is so very frightening and demoralizing to say the least.

Off to the races I'd sputter, out of my house, down the street in the all too familiar direction. "Man, this was getting so old", I recall pondering. Anger accompanied me big time and in a story that my mom enjoys telling stems from my being so out of touch so bad that I actually thought that I was able to run. In fact, it got to the point where my father could spot me a head start in escape and within a few jogs of a pace he'd have me tossed over his shoulders. My mom laughs today explaining how my legs would still be kicking slowly over my dad's back as if I thought I was still making world beaters time. "Just like in the cartoons"

As I mentioned earlier, some days I'd have a bit of juice in me where I could walk to exhaustion and call for a ride home and other days, twenty-five feet would be the extent of my journey before collapsing. Everything felt so far gone that I was lost in this state of mind. I believe that the massive medicines brought me to this senseless mess of irrationality. I also believe that God made a pit stop by to sober me up j-u-s-t enough to "Houdini" me out of this binding predicament.

I exhausted all of my mental tricks to try and buy time to simply will myself better or whatever. In an abbreviated epilog to yet another long story, I was in possession of a large quantity of the drug Thalidamide. This was the sleeping pill that had been blamed for many birth defects in the fifty's or sixties. The banned and illegal drug now in the eighties had been rightfully acquired for an experimental study in Seattle. As a GVHD patient, I was one of the first, if not the first, bone marrow transplant patient to be a human guinea pig (again) to be included in the closed study. Evidently, in animals, Thalidamide showed great promise in battling graft vs. host disease.

Having filled you in a bit there gives you a clearer picture as to where I was at this particular junction. I was so desperate for relief that I would have consented to most anything that the medical community had to offer me. With a tall glass of water at my side, the bedroom door closed, my bed butted up to the knob and straddling the jamb, and I myself on top of that bed itself, made for more resistance to open it from the other side. I wonder if it was a cry to God for help, or a crying wolf if you will. I still think and wonder looking back on it.

Everything was in place to throw all of that work away. The course of Thalidamide all in all really did not change my GVHD if, in fact, I gave it enough time to work. I can't say for sure and it has since helped other GVHD patients improve their quality of life. I do know that one pill would make me so groggy that it would knock me right on my butt. So without question, twenty or thirty ingested would have turned the lights out on my recovery attempt for sure.

I still prefer to think of it as God's intervention because I did go through all the motions. I even went so far as to plead with my badgering brother at the door. "Tell me, what am I going to do, Tom?" True to form, my Mt. Rushmore-faced brother is a man of many words…the famous reply to me was and I quote, "I don't know what to tell ya." Perhaps, that lousiest of a cheesy response in my mind gave me enough insight to want to stick around and tick him off. Way to go Tom, you reverse psychologist you…

Whatever the case, my not doing anything foolish still left me back in the real world as a bone marrow transplant survivor with chronic graft vs. host disease in terrible condition both physically and mentally. I'd echo those words from the doctor in Seattle many times. "John, frankly we're going to go as far as we can to try and kill you without killing you." Mission accomplished.

Picture, if you will a spider web. Imagine any insect getting caught in the weavy threads. Once entangled, there is no escaping. This scenario is likely to be the analogy that doctors used to dub the infamous stricture that occurs in many bone marrow transplant patients' throats, affectionately known as "the web". Whether this manifestation is a result of the chemotherapy, total body irradiation or transplant wear and tear, I don't know, but too many BMT patients seem to involuntarily acquire them. This web consists of a ledge of scar tissue and muscle contraction control around the esophagus as being the main culprit. As you have been reading this so far, you can see the trend of 'if you could get it, I got it.' So naturally, the web takes center stage for now.

In attempting to do battle against a possible leukemia relapse and also fighting the graft vs. host disease, as most surviving patients do, we engage in a plethora of pill cocktails. A menu of twenty to thirty to forty or more pills a day is not unheard of. I'm sure, in some instances. From BB size to Tic-Tac sizes, to my range, which were Good 'n Plenty sized, aptly nicknamed the Herman Munster pill.

The latter of this group can get tricky for even the healthiest of a person's swallowing tube. As the web goes, even a ridiculously small size of a cake jimmy sprinkle can get lodged in the gulp process. Water and, for the most part, air can still eek its way through while at the same time leaving the object still lodged in your throat, i.e., the bigger the piece of food or, more worrisome, the bigger the pill becomes that much more of a serious problem to the patient. It took one or two close-call traumatic calamities for me to seek out help.

A Percoset, or pill of that aspirin-sized family got lodged in my throat one afternoon to the point of no air going in or out whatsoever. I sat along side of my bed taking a ton of pills and boom, my luck finally ran out. "Eh, uh, eh, uh, eh, uh", I chirped out. Before I knew it my head was searching for air. It pounded with dizziness creeping up swiftly and simultaneously. I recall thinking to myself, "Son of a bitch. All of this damn work to try and live and now I'm going to choke to death on a "F" ing pill." I also stood up in my oversized underwear, which once fit me. My skinny legs and arms began banging on the walls with lethal force for dear life!

My family, now tattered by and accustomed to these antics, luckily took an immediate interest knowing that something was wrong. I managed to come out into the hall where my father was just turning the landing corner to meet me. Of course, it's funny to me how he reacted, but at the time, absolutely no jokes were on my mind! "Mr. Cool, Sergeant Semper Fi, Charles Bronson or Clint Eastwood-like" in mannerism, he nonchalantly stepped up, analyzed the situation and with one non-telegraphic swoop, clocked me in the mid-back region with an open hand (catcher's mitt sized). He not only dislodged this stinking curse of a pill but he launched it airborne into the bathroom some eight feet away. His hand might as well have twirled as he re-holstered it and casually rolled back down into the living room sunset, I could hear the western music, "Ahh ah ah ah ah wawa wa". Of course, it was not really like that but it's how I like to remember that scene today. He was smooth and calm with his generic Heimlich maneuver though.

The time had come and arrangements were made for me to go into Philadelphia for a procedure known as a dilation. This from my recollection was an attempt to re-stretch or open up the closing of my airway due to the scar tissue build up or 'web' that I mentioned earlier. I recall this being one of the comparatively 'easy' procedures that I went through. Save for the severe sore throat and mouth afterwards, I zipped through with relatively no complications. The staff members at Jefferson Hospital were cordial and compassionate throughout the ordeal.

This pit stop lasted for about seven hours and back home I went. What a change from what I'd been accustomed to! Every action has a reaction though so mine was having more pain than the expected amount for usual tolerance levels. Thus, more doses of Demoral, Morphine or MS-Contin alleviated that without a problem but conversely that branched into a reaction of withdraw from becoming addicted to those drugs. Finally the drug Methodone, which is used to try and get "clean" from addictions, enabled me to cut loose and recover so to speak after tapering from that course.

With this now taken care of and my throat considerably improved, nothing changed though in terms of my mental outlook. I probably didn't feel as if I fit in anywhere at this point, in retrospect. I hadn't seen any of my friends for a good while and missed doing the things that we used to do. My mind longed for the good old days and in fact, even day, I go through that phase and wonder what if? On one of my next attempted visits with a good friend, the trip stood out as an example of a few other similarly eerie moments with society's lack of compassion and abundance of ignorance.

One of the most enjoyable things that my friends and I used to do was to go out for pizza. We had one or two favorite hangouts and one in particular was in a nearby mall. A close friend of mine Horace or 'Gus' as known in the business took me out for the first decent attempt at getting back to 'normal'. The moment is still clear enough to me years later but basically, in short, we just cruised out to the mall for pizza as I stated. We settled in and enjoyed the food as we always had many times before. Afterwards we took a stroll or shuffle in my case around to shop. I think we had hit the several record stores within the mall and found ourselves on the lower level needing to go back upstairs to exit. The nearest elevator was further than I wanted to waddle so I believe I decided to try the nearby staircase instead.

At this point my balance was not great and my feet hampered me considerably, as did my whole body for that matter. The steps numbered about ten to fifteen and then came a landing. A turn and another ten to fifteen steps, a last landing with more steps up and you were there on the upper level. Well, I began my ascension clinging to the railing somewhat slumped over, lifting one leg up to the next step and bringing the other leg up behind it. My hips were going so I imagine that I compensated for this subconsciously by only using one leg while favoring the other.

I had made it up to the first landing to make the wrap around turn using only the guardrail for balance when suddenly I could feel and hear a fierce rumbling coming from behind me. As I chugged up the staircase, I know that I made every effort so as not to look as though I was struggling to the public's eye, as well as my friend Gus. I also know that an Academy Award winning effort couldn't have fooled anyone about my frailty. No one perhaps except my self denial and what was left of any pride back then.

My friend Gus was next to me sort of incognito, not exactly holding me but close enough just in case I bottomed out or something. In his doing so we more than likely took up some extra space. Having said that we surely were cognizant of passers right to go by and would accommodate whomever needed to blow by my friend and yours truly 'Touche Turtle'. The problem arose though when that rumble I mentioned came and crashed into us faster than it could take most any-one to elude. Luckily I was already clutching the rails so all we heard and got besides the collision was a bunch of lousy mouthing off of expletives. Those being "get the 'f' out of the way mother f'er" and so on. Gus launched some 'f' bombs back while I got my bearings and when we finally made it up to the top level a spell later, our paths were blocked off by the same punks who rumbled by us. I'd say that about seven or eight of these losers confronted us about our comeback remarks back at them. Give me a break!

We shouldn't go up their "mother f'ing" stairs so blankety, blanking slow they said as we wedged through the barricade of posers. In the tough guy fashion, they were in our faces when the one guy reaches in his pocket and brandishes a piece (gun). Real or not I didn't know. "That a good way to get shot, boyeee. He boasted." My buddy Gus was still in their faces going off when I, like an fool in retrospect, fired back a brilliant release of penned up anger "Go ahead, shoot me man!" "You're a real-tough guy shootin a leukemia patient transplant dude". Go ahead shoot me, man! Come on, do it! I hope that I said that out of frustration and anxiety because my health was not up for defending me, or anyone for that matter. And why should I have to, I'm in a damn mall, not somewhere in the Middle East!

To show you how lame these guys were, the one with the gun says to me, "Maaan, we don't got no problem wit you. It's your friend noww." By this time Gus and my hearts were pumping with gallons of adrenaline and, as a crowd of growing spectators grew, we just jawed back and forth while trying to get meshed into the minglers and slip them. With my blazing speed, all that we could do was go duck into a nearby Roy Rogers for an hour or so. We outlasted them in a wait-ing game of attrition over a couple of burgers. The funniest part of it all was that both of our rush let downs came in the booth of the restaurant. He and I melted as the adrenaline dissipated and the residual shakes of nerves kicked in. I pray they were just bluffing because all of my families, friends and my hard work in this cure thing would have been wasted away in an instant due to my stubborn-ness.

After successfully eluding the jerks and having a nervous and phony smile on our faces (well, mine was fake), Gus sighed between catching his breath, and easing out, "I wasn't scared". More like I wasn't, pause, scared, pause, chuckle. I don't know how we ended up eating those hamburgers after the pizza though.

One of the straining effects from what the transplant had done to me that is evident from the previous story was my physical de-conditioning and frailness so to speak. I had earlier in my recovery attempt tried to rejoin a health club. I thought that I could pick up where I left off before leaving for Seattle. That's what I thought anyway but it turned out to be one more mental setback and huge let down. I really was a freak as I mentioned before, I suppose, compared to all of the club members. I'd been so mangled that I would have looked more at home cloaked in a tuxedo at some opera than to be exposed in say a pool or on a leg lift in sweats. This old club to which I belonged to at the time was more of a social arena than a workout center.

No one really interacted with me despite my outgoing efforts. I went in to work hard and get better, so that's just what I ended up doing. I worked hard all right but saw no improvements. A friend from the old school days, Joe Hart, was one person at that time that I can say treated me in the same manner that he always had. We were not extremely close friends but that fact that he tried to make me feel okay with spotting my lifts or watching the ladies aerobics from the pool or whatever was a real nice memory.

After a few months of spinning my wheels and getting nowhere at that particular 'club' I became very disgruntled. The back breaker was seeing an old girlfriend named Karen, not even acknowledging or recognizing who I was. That was tough. I talked with my dad some and one day while driving around, we passed by a rehab facility near our home that we had never noticed before. Upon stopping in to inquire as to the services that they had to offer, two things were so uncanny! The first was that this was a Philadelphia Flyers trainer's staff center, which were active in the fight against leukemia. Secondly, the manager turned out to be the friend and previous manager of the health club that I just mentioned!

Before by BMT I was feeling strong and said to this manager, "Doug if you don't see me back in six months, I probably won't be back at all"—what a crazy world sometimes—crazy with irony. We talked for a long while and everything seemed great when he said that his staff could accommodate me to rehab and it was only several miles away from my home yet! During my transplant he had resigned at the first club and joined staff with the Flyers and '76ers staff here.

Well rather than elaborating on this part of my story, I'll simply say that things seemed to be going fantastically until one day I was abruptly terminated. My friend Doug had suddenly left to work at another facility in Central Pennsylvania and the replacement manager motioned me to his office and precariously stated, "You can't come here anymore, your bill stands at five thousand dollars" There's a slapshot for you—right in the face

." The "great" organization that I'm still I guess a fan of for some reason, could no longer accommodate my presence (could it have been the money?). My insurance, after a squirmish, paid the five thousand dollars and stated that they could no longer cover me. I did receive a letter from the new owner of the '76ers at the time, informing me that he received their insurance payment so I didn't have to worry any longer about the bill. When I first opened up the envelope, I had hoped to see some kind of arrangement that I could resume my rehab but instead got the reassurance that their money was safe and sound; "what a guy". "Score one for the Flyers affiliate, zero for the leukemia patient". Whether it was irony or not shortly after the boot, I was hospitalized with another 'good, old infection'.

This leg of my encumbering journey spawned a slide and venture into further depths of depression. Another selection from the prescription menu had the doctors dish me a new type of antidepressant and some rounds of counseling as well. I actually sought professional help and was referred to the one I settled on. That blew up on me as well being nothing more than an absolute joke of a service. More like a disservice and mockery of the psychology and psychiatry field in my opinion. Sessions eased into my noticing this 'doctor' glancing at her watch at seeming regular intervals, while building no foundation or direction for help. In place of progress she built up her bank account with the insurance payments and lack of governing guidelines. I finally trashed the whole idea when I was informed that my sessions would have to be frozen while she took a summer cruise and would not be returning for two months, a victory for cynicism here; me cynical?

Perhaps the medications were not to blame for my irrational behavior that precipitated after all of this. I feel it was personal but I cannot say for sure. My brother had tried to settle back into some sort of normal route in his life again and had mentioned several times the possibility of us starting a business together. A time and situation presented itself to go ahead with his idea and he opened up a music store selling records, tapes, etc. This story itself could go on for chapters with its undertaking and my health, let alone attempting to look as if I could actually fit in and contribute, which I couldn't really.

One thing that I will add to give a feel of my ridiculous mindset was to recall my actually going in to work in bare feet and a cardboard tie that I made in the back room one day. I'm so baffled looking back as to why, and where I was mentally. I may as well have been an empty shell or a zombie at that time to do those types of things. It wasn't me. My brother didn't like it and who would? After all, I wasn't in Maui selling surfboards at the beach! I'll never forget a manager of the pet shop next door who told me that I looked like walking death one day. When she threw that at me I felt so empty I just stopped working there for good. It stuck with me so much and hurt so bad that I really didn't function and withdrew back to square one in my cave of a room at home.

All that time I never mentioned what that stinking girl said about me to anybody. What would it have accomplished anyway? I was lost again and nobody could help. I thought about whoever really cared anyway when it came right down to it. I thought about God a lot.

More infections came calling and short procedure unit stays took over as a norm with immuno globulin infusions. They as I've mentioned, try to combat the infections or boost my immune system that was being so severely suppressed. Think of it as taking pills to weaken your immune system to fight the graft vs. host disease and at the same time taking something else to boost it as well. Obviously, it's more intricate than that but in its simplest form you can look at it in that respect. My sinuses were blown out and barely functioning. I used to envision my sinus cavities as the Grand Canyon and then filling it totally up with mucous. Pretty disgusting I'd say but the non-stop cycle of chronic sinus infections was a smaller version for sure. That in and of itself could make you go insane just choking on and spitting this crap out twenty-four hours a day, seven days a week! The constant hacking had some friend's joke to me that I sounded like a "coke head".

Infusion after infusion of autoclaved donor pooled and spun off globulin to fight infections. Stick after stick after stick after stick after shunt; "Missed veins after missed veins, and scar tissue on top of scar tissue". How many mental fuses did I blow trying to be polite and cheerful while my lines backed up or my arm massively swelled due to a missed vein infusion? (That means the bag of stuff didn't go into my vein but into my arm tissue itself.) How many mental fuses blew while student nurses gouged my battered guinea pig arms? Compassion was a word very much lacking in their vocabulary along with personality more times than not. How much damage is done mentally due to those fine incompetents?

Thank goodness my doctors' staff was very good; otherwise I could really have stories to tell. They stuck me more often than anywhere else except at Fred Hutch in Seattle, and I will say as with all of my hospital stays and experiences, some of the people were God sends just to keep me hanging on in there. Not nearly as many that genuinely cared about me personally or my welfare added up to those who couldn't care less. I actually wonder how the numbers of those people got hired or had an interest in the medical field. For the ones who did care, my words could not do them enough justice. They know who they are and I'd like to think that God handpicked them.

Even more I.g.G. infusions came and went along with all of the other desperate measures to keep me ticking. The efforts paid dividends enough to keep most of the recent infections under control. Well, at least well enough to take a moral victory out of the procedures and continue convincing myself that I could survive the problems regardless of the setbacks brought on. Only the Lord knows if I did the right things or not with many of these hospital stays and decision making.

Moving along, the calendar flipped a bit and my hair began falling out and changing colors yet again. The strands left growing were brown originally and then turned to dark black curly locks, and then to orange waves of baby fine hair. Perhaps some white and every shade in between. I again hid my anguish behind a fake sense of humor during the orange period. I brought attention to the stigmas as if it didn't faze me, with jokes and wise remarks, often volunteering them in order to beat any possible incoming flak. In reality I just emptied out all of my emotions silently. I often felt the chest pains or heart races overlapping and just concealing it all.

I worked with this cover up until the appearance couldn't be worked with any longer. I didn't want to be in public looking that way so I pursued the good old hairpiece, wig, hair hat, carpet, whatever you like. Instead of getting into each story, I believe that the course took me through three or four different companies, so much money—which I never had to begin with—and cold-hearted thieving stinking mongers that prey on vulnerable people such as me; (A cancer or former cancer, limbo kind of a patient.)

I did find a decent enough place of business that helped to a certain extent but, all in all, we are all just numbers with money that they want. I now wonder if God sees that as vanity or gluttony since I was ripped off with stinking, lousy crap. Some people may be fortunate to get a decent establishment with good service from which to purchase these products. But how many patients like me got sucked in, desperate to fit back in to society as much as possible with everybody else. It's a shame that this world is so sick and biased that you can't fit in just as you are without being a target for violence or torment.

Well, I finally had my orange hair dyed and covered to the extent where I could go out 'comfortably' and try to socialize. I began attending Mass once again. A story to remember was my attempt to drive some ten miles away to my favorite old church and visit my buddy Father Fahey at St. Rose of Lima's. My plans went array that morning and I should have stayed in bed! It's all a bit humorous to me now but back then I just raged with fury and anguish!

To begin with I woke up sick. I was so goofy-minded that I had thoughts about God not giving me blessings if I didn't make it, as well as other irrational notions. My pride had me again driving a big truck with huge tires and why, I'll never know. Perhaps another attempt to force doing the things I used to be able to freely do. I love trucks but I had no strength in my hips or legs, though I still insisted on being 'normal' and live my life. The thing is that I had to use a milk crate tied to the driver's seat bottom with a cord to get in and out of the truck. I'd open the door, reach in the back and toss out the crate. Even with that setup it still took what seemed like forever to finagle myself up and into the cab.

The truck had a seven inch lift I believe but wasn't super huge by big 4' x 4' standards. My first truck was higher but this one was still a nice rider. In any event I managed to get in, being so ill I don't know what I was accomplishing. Perhaps God would acknowledge my great and gallant effort and poof me down a miracle or five! I was feverish and weak but managed the drive over.

Upon making it into the parking lot maybe one or two minutes late, just as the last of the parishioners were making their way into church, I pulled in and parked, opened the door still coughing and everything. I dropped anchor (the milk crate) and prepared to dock reaching my leg down to the top of it, as that was my step to land. Just as soon as I made foot to crate contact and put my weight on my leg, my whole body gave way and went limp. I crashed to the pavement and scuffed my hands up pretty good. Luckily, I only hit my head slightly on the door going down, but by the time I realized what was happening I was totally laid out on the ground.

With Mass going on there wasn't a soul around. I was hoping for a late arrival to flag down for assistance but none came. I used every bit of my energy to attempt to get up with but it was to no avail. It felt just as if my lower extremities were paralyzed and I couldn't move them. I couldn't use the big monster tires, I couldn't use the bottom of the truck door and I couldn't even get up on the frickin' milk crate. I believe that I panicked a bit and became infuriated with rage. Not the good kind of rage where you turn green with the strength of the Hulk and all, but the "poutey", feeling sorry for yourself frustrating anger that gets you nowhere kind.

The parking lot poles just in front of the truck looked like a way to shimmy back on my feet if I could just crawl to them; which, is exactly what I attempted to do after several long minutes of rolling and scuffling around. This was all going on outside the church and nobody had a clue that I was out there. Unbelievable! Mass was usually about forty five minutes to an hour and the time that it took me to crawl to the pole, get the energy, work my way to sitting up, catching my breath and finally get back into the truck was about that length of time too! I was so "p-o'd." My view from the rear view mirror could catch glimpses of everyone leaving Mass. I went home to bed, watched bruises pop up all over me, and then recovered from the flu.

The total irony of it all was that about a month or so later upon going back and visiting with Father Fahey again. He asked me why I didn't stop in to visit him the last time I was over. He said that the other priest, Father McMullin, was angry with me because I had been rolling around in the grass during Mass with my old girlfriend. He was in the rectory watching me the whole time from the kitchen window and those ninety year old eyes of his, saw a crate and me as my girlfriend and I frolicking. This was the very same priest who gave me back a Christmas gift that I bought for him and stopped Mass, because of a girl smiling as I spoke of earlier in the book. Believe it or not, he really wasn't too bad of a guy! But milk crates passing as ladies?

Shortly after this stretch, I was able to get some stability if I can use that term. A promised fishing trip with my friend Larry and my father had been slated if I could get to the point of fitting it in healthwise. Once again I miscalculated my stamina because, when we finally made it out to the lake where we had always enjoyed fishing in Amish country many times before, I didn't last very long at all. I'd say that it probably took longer to get there than the time we spent fishing.

We pretty much set up and cast a few times until I was wiped out. I did feel bad but also had a very good time while it lasted. The surroundings and the lake itself can pick you up tremendously, so it was a victory of sorts. Every little experience that I enjoy goes into that column. I just couldn't improve on stamina at that particular junction, so it would have to do for now as a 'closest to normal function'. As readers can see, stamina, energy, fatigue, lethargy and mental exhaustion play a monumental role in the interpersonal interactions between patient/former patient and simple tasks of daily living.

With probably a few back porch barbecues or TV sports events watched from the couch, I amassed a little bit of real life recreation to boast about; enough so to distance me from another problem, which I had been dealing with shortly thereafter. I'd been experiencing a throbbing in the back of my eye socket that would wrap itself clear around my neck so to speak. With that also were intense nerve shorts that beat in tandem with my chaotic heart pulses. Sometimes, again the likeness of having eaten ice cream too fast would ensue as well.

You may think how could you not recognize this as being serious, or how could you be so foolish as to ignore it? But I'd have to state that in with these transplant side effects and complications, so many sensations would travel here and there that if you questioned every single occurrence you would absolutely go insane. I believe I mentioned that earlier when initially that was just the case. I would become paranoid of every creak and sensation that I'd notice. I suppose that I may have conditioned myself to de-condition myself to those occurrences.

With several months passing I was examined by an eye specialist who immediately zeroed in on the problem. This particular diagnosis was that of a torn retina. This is as you may know a type of a ligament shall we say that connects a muscle to the back of the eye itself. Speculations were that I might have had it for a long time. As far back perhaps as teener league, when I was once hit by a baseball in that same eye playing first base. Other thoughts were that it could have occurred in the hospital when I fell and fractured my jaw. Nevertheless it was very dangerous from the doctor's point of view in that they emphasized that I could lose my eyesight.

There were procedures that could attempt to repair this damage, but as the way things seemed to go with me, no one really wanted to touch it. In fact, the doctor who initially diagnosed this torn retina said that he wouldn't touch me with a ten foot pole and doubted if anyone out there would. He wished me good luck in finding somebody. This all had to do with my medical history, and the "china glass syndrome I'm sure.

We called around and eventually were referred to the Scheie Eye Institute in Philadelphia. Upon a consult with several of the doctors I believe, we finally found a team that had agreed to try and help me after corresponding with my home doctors as well as the Fred Hutch staff in Seattle. Of course, I had to sign everything you could think of away in order to protect their rights and I kind of respected that. I can see why but I also felt like an alien.

Once all of the legalities were settled, an appointment was set-up and I went in for surgery. After the good old waiting period of glancing through magazines, looking out the window and things like that, I was escorted to a tiny room (although huge compared to laminar room standards). After some formal procedures, I believe that I recall placing my face into a catcher's mask type of stationary apparatus, a bit similar to that which we all use at the eye doctors. Then a pipe-like instrument was placed in my eye so that the eyelid itself could not function and impede the procedure.

I was told to focus and concentrate, then once we began, what felt like many rubber bands being constantly snapped at my eye was the result of a laser beam attempting to reattach and repair my torn retina. I would surmise this was to be accomplished by burning it and letting the scarring retake a hold. Perhaps like the melting of candle wax and allowing it to cool and reform itself in a weld like fashion. Although it stung a good degree, I'd say that it was more annoying than anything else, especially when concentrating on not being able to close your eye with this pipe like apparatus inside of it. But, all in all, the whole procedure went pretty well. I touched on this briefly, as the chances of my retina being related to the actual transplant itself are not exactly known. Getting it worked on was another story.

For no apparent rhyme or reason though, shortly thereafter this eye procedure, I began another particularly fast mood swing downhill. Just as if invasive procedures set off internal bodily triggers. This was to such an extent that I again began taking my nomad walks here and there, only to be rescued by a pay phone call. I suppose that I reverted back to the pattern, which I mentioned earlier concerning my walks and now typecast behaviors. I still wonder today why I would simply take off and roam, besides the attempted escapism's and possible therapeutic aspects of it.

Anyhow this is probably both the funniest and worst, of the "take off and walk" stories for me as I think back on it now in retrospect. As I journeyed one day in a huff I made it several miles or so perhaps from my house, which was significant for me at that time being the turtle that I was, I found myself out engulfed in a very, very hot sun. This particular day was a scorcher and the fact that I was now not perspiring greatly added to my physical problems. I'd even begun to carry a squirt bottle to travel with me when I'd walk away from the problems that I couldn't walk away from. In any event I overexerted myself in a big way.

In an unplanned episode that found me not having the ability to muster enough energy to continue to the nearest pay phone, I basically collapsed suddenly on a stranger's front lawn. Once these nice people noticed me on their grass and seeing the condition that I was in, I asked them to please call an ambulance. I did have some chest pains and a flying heart rate. I'd been all too familiar to these symptoms in the past but this spell seemed a bit more intense. I looked really bad, my body was a beat strawberry red all over by the time the ambulance arrived.

I had the ambulance crew take me to my local hospital for fear that I may have been worse off than I could estimate. I was definitely dehydrated and running a fever probably about one hundred and two or so, but that could have been due to the sun and not perspiring. Regardless, with me it could have been any damn thing, so I had to take every precaution. For me to have called an ambulance was out of character but in any event I did.

Once I entered the hospital through the emergency room, I immediately found myself taking a number because the whole ward was filled to the rafters. Once again I made a stupid mistake by expecting some professionalism out of this emergency room. I guess once they saw me breathing and appearing to be able to sit in a chair okay my stock dropped dramatically. Of course they couldn't see my insides or know how I was feeling but that's the way it goes with me sometimes, in this emergency room anyway.

Several fellow patients waiting their turn had made some noise to the window about my condition. To humor them I suppose, I was then escorted to a nearby curtained room that we all know. But only this time it was a female gynecological exam room used for female purposes. So I essentially was placed on the table that housed angled stirrups for the legs and feet. Of course mine weren't secured but you might have thought they were. The joke in the unit was my being in that room as local transient cops with their donuts and coffee in hand would peek in along with other staff members and gesture smart remarks—real professionals that they were.

I had to undress down to my underwear and, upon waiting for evaluation, getting steamed and stirred while listening to patient after patient being taken care of before me. The back breaker for me finally was when a nurse outside the curtain mumbled to a fellow nurse something like, "What's this guy in here for?" There was more laughing and mumbling, then stating that they needed a room burst in through the curtain while directing me, "Sir, your gonna have to leave, we need this room."

That's all that it took for me to get up, grab my shirt, slip on my shoes and walk through the emergency room hallway in underwear and sneakers with pants in hand, while at the same time giving everybody the finger and 'f' bombing the whole world. I walked out and took about a mile journey up to the corner Hardee's hamburger joint! How on earth I never got arrested I'll never know. I managed to get dressed eventually but, in the meantime, I must have blended in fine because one of the hospital's mental wards was adjacent to this restaurant and they often frequented the store on breaks to get coffee and loiter you might say.

I mean I fit right in there, as I awkwardly got dressed. Using the pay phone outside I'd call good old Carol to come and rescue me. I think I waved to a couple of on-looking cashier's. This was something right out of a Seinfeld episode for sure…I'll tell you the stories that I could touch on from being in this local hospital alone were simply unbelievable! Keep in mind that I'm just trying to give you a flavor of some of the events that were going on at the time because I am leaving out bits and pieces to keep things flowing along.

Obviously, I didn't die from that episode; I was severely dehydrated and actually taken better care of at home by my sister and my mom then I would have been in a hospital. I paid a bad price that day for taking off and walking and being stubborn about it. There was a time that I more or less refused to confide in my family when various ailments would arise, such as the episode I just mentioned. Perhaps out of anger or thinking that I didn't feel loved or feeling guilty for putting them through all of this, I don't know.

You'd think that I would have learned, and I guess that I did. At least I didn't call any ambulances after walks in different directions at night. The last "trek" that I can recall I believe had me landing at a place called The Purple Cow. This was an ice cream store that was closed. It had a pay phone outside so I called my sister Carol and her friend at the time Harry to come and get me. But I think by now that the walking phase was coming to an end. I wonder if any other fellow transplant patient ever did seemingly absurd things like that, or is it just a blown fused quirk of mine.

My temperament seemed to level off I'm presuming as I came back down to earth and socialized a bit. And as I talked to you before about the hairpieces and the scarring of my scalp from the radiation and or GVHD, hair hat number four came into play I think. I don't even remember counting actually but it seems like a good number for the amount of times that I went looking.

I desperately wanted to still try and fit in and I had my sister and Harry take me on a long journey out of state, after seeing some TV commercial that made you look like a million bucks. Actually some of the actors were portraying people needing hair looked a lot worse than me, so I thought again that may be this was something that could help my self-esteem or paranoia. Of course they were all too happy to oblige and humor me. I remember scraping more money that I didn't have only to get my new synthetic bouffant hairdo. I should have just bought one of those plastic 'Devo' wigs looking back. I guess it made me feel a little better for the time being.

Thinking about it now I don't know if people would have looked at the scarring more or could they even tell that it was a fake? And if they did, would someone tell me the truth? My mom and I kind of enjoy picking out hair hats on people now, and I debate sometimes whether to tell them or not that you can spot them out. I don't know if that would be more demoralizing than to not tell them at all. I guess that it's "to each his own' there, everybody views things differently. I wouldn't want to ever hurt anyone's feelings especially cancer patients.

All through this same stretch, I'd continue taking rides with my sister here and there and sometimes a long drive to go out for ice dream with her and the kids. One particular day we took a drive and Carol informed me that she was getting a divorce. This was really upsetting to me because I immediately thought that I was the reason. I even felt worse for awhile, when her husband actually in his case through the lawyer claimed my sister to be an unfit mother due to the fact that she was helping me with my transplant. Can you imagine! I can only hope this was due to some asinine legal advice. Thank goodness this didn't go over well with the courts and she won her divorce due to the concrete circumstances stacked against him. .

Carol was clearly upset and the whole proceeding took a lot out of her as if she had anything left to give. But all in all I suppose life is what it is and these things take place all of the time. She was concerned enough to inform me in the way that she did, and it made it a lot easier for the most part, if that was possible. Now in a sense I lost another side of family members when I lost my brother-in-law and his relatives.

I started to get close with some other girls attempting to move on in the relationship category and actually had some fairly nice connections, including one girl, Christina. I think some things may have worked out wonderfully if I would have had a little more time to get back on my feet. I'm not sure if she understood the magnitude of what I was going through at the time and what it would take to recover. She was a little farther along than I was at the time and was ready to settle down and ultimately didn't want to wait a while before talking marriage; she's happily married now and we are still good friends. I still stay in contact with Christina, as well as her sisters Julie, Maria, Vera, Franny, brother Mike and their whole family. They have all supported me in my recovery attempt in one way or another.

Just when I seemed to get somewhat of a breather, not so much energy-wise but health-wise, I had to be scheduled for yet another skin biopsy to check on my GVHD low and behold, I went to a local dermatologist—why I'll never know but I did. I basically was hole-punched, butchered big time in my arm and the huge scars that remain were unnecessary and preventable. Aside from the scars, the biggest reminder that I have of this guy was his explanation of graft vs. host disease to his nurse. His description was as elaborate as it was full of bull.

I didn't even bother to correct them. The "Doctor" and nurse would have only scoffed at my statements anyway. After all I was just the patient, what would

I know about GVHD? There are a lot of fantastic doctors out there; I'm simply stating that I had more than my fair share of lousy ones. Boy did I pay for it! Thank goodness I'm still alive to speak about it today, and can perhaps inform a future patient or two of the awareness it may take to prevent these medical blunders from occurring to them.

This was the very same visit had me actually fall in the hallway lobby and have not one but two people, walk right by me. I wouldn't be surprised if they had to step over my legs instead of giving me a hand up. I don't know if this was just because it was in a rough city or this kind of treatment happens across the board of society. I can remember being on the ground and watching these people leave me, as I gazed at them in amazement.

As for the fall, it was one of those cases where you clearly know that you're going down and it seems to take like forever; you can actually think to yourself "I'm going down, I'm falling" as you hear the timber sound in the background until the thud of your body hits the ground. You assess the damage and kind of laugh. Then you have to figure out how to get up. Luckily my sister-in-law Denise took me and then found me lying there, or rustling around trying to get myself back up. With her assistance, I was quickly back on my feet and on my way out of that joint.

Back home at the house one evening, we received a phone call from Seattle informing my family that one of the patients, Chris, had passed away. He had grown close to my family while I was going through my ordeal. Chris was a younger boy who had grown accustomed to calling my father Uncle Ralph. As I mentioned, I really didn't know Chris very well because I was in the bubble dealing with my situation. Upon hearing my family crying in the house reflected just how patients and their families can get so personally involved with each others' cases. As for the little girl, Paige, I have not heard anything about her for awhile. I actually was not aware of the magnitude to which my family was involved with the cases of the other patients. I could feel myself getting sick to my stomach when I heard any news along those patients lines. Even though I didn't know Chris personally, I was mentally placed right back up on the floor of Fred Hutch's transplant ward.

Since this roller coaster of a pattern at this junction in my story seemed to be on a downslide, this series of events kept it going even further in that direction. Shortly afterwards my brother informed me that my father was sick. We were driving in his truck somewhere on the highway when he broke the news .All of this just kept coming in waves, it really did. My brother, Tom let me know that my father had lung cancer. At this point they didn't know to what extent, but from what I remember, he told me that they had given him a short time to live unless they could start treatments. Obviously he did just that and initially the prognosis was optimistic.

While this was taking place, I had myself in another bind because prior to my knowledge of my father getting sick, my curiosity on graft vs. host disease treatments had led me to a hospital in Pittsburgh, Pa. There they were initiating some new clinical research protocols of using drugs to possibly reverse the effects of GVHD, so by contacting and pestering the heck out of them, I was eventually accommodated into their research program. I was scheduled to fly out to Pittsburgh as a patient in yet another hospital for another lengthy tenure with more battles to come. Now in finding out about my father's condition, I wanted to cancel everything, but my dad would have none of it. He was adamant about me going out there and taking care of my situation.

My father had to go into the hospital for his radiation treatments on the East side of Pennsylvania. While at the same time, I was trying out this new procedure called photo pheresis in a hospital on the western side of Pennsylvania. Actually, the title was U.V. photopheresis (ultra violet). In a nutshell I was to be given a drug called Psoralin that would somehow activate my t-cells to be susceptible to being destroyed you could say, after being exposed to the ultra violet light. This was made possible by two separate catheter lines being placed inside of me. One in which my blood would exit and spin-off through a machine and the other would enter back in to me along with the flow of blood to my body. The ultra violet light itself was encased inside of this machine, so as the blood flowed out from me and into the machine exposed to the light and back into me, the t-cells theoretically in numbers would be diminished.

The Pittsburgh stays for the most part weren't exactly great nor were they horrible. They kind of just were. So in skipping much of the details, I would simply like to touch a little bit on the procedures that I just explained. One of which was the initial horrible reaction that I had to a pre-med which name I cannot remember. This episode still sticks fresh to me after all those years. It is very vivid in that the medicine had me crawling out of my skin in a very panicked state of mind. I had a very difficult time conveying this to the staff because they must not have seen this in any of the other patients. Quite possibly they didn't believe me. Even my brother who had accompanied me on several of my trips, I would venture to say, tended to think that I was over-exaggerating it a bit but that wasn't the case I can assure you. God knows

The sessions as they were set up would have me flying from Philadelphia to Pittsburgh for one-week stays rotating every other week. This was to go on for several months, so in the time frames that I had to spend in Pittsburgh, I communicated with my dad quite frequently. Upon several weeks into these P.U.V.A. sessions, my father had experienced some complications and was probably a lot worse than I was led to believe. We called each other from hospital room to hospital room across the state and one day his voice had basically left him. All that he could muster up was a scratchy whisper. I'll never forget a phrase that he used to use, I'd always ask him how he was feeling and he'd simply reply "pretty good". This time the pretty good was barely audible. I really knew then that something was worse than I had been informed of and it didn't help me in any sense or form. I was devastated.

One of the P.U.V.A. side effects itself was a very dark tan as if I was from the tropics or something. This drug has that effect of a reaction on a patient, and when you are exposed to the sun, you can develop an extremely dark complexion. Aside from this, I was very fatigued and had severe stomach problems especially holding down food. I knew that this was a pre-explained price to pay for a possible GVHD improvement, so I tried to go with the flow.

Back and forth to Pittsburgh we'd go, and upon coming home I found my father sitting on the couch in the down in the rec room; a sort of promotion to a home hospice program, which I knew nothing about at the time. This is all very clear to me now but back then, I really was oblivious as to what was going on. I just assumed that my father was going to be better and that was that. It wasn't the case, however, as he clearly struggled with this disease of lung cancer more so than I, at the time, could think.

One of the requests that he asked me to get him was a microphone and an amplifier from some of the old band equipment. My brother managed to pick him up something to use from a local electronics store, I think. This was one of my dad's hopes that he could communicate easier by increasing the volume of his scratchy whispers. It really didn't work out very well and I feel a lot worse now about it than I did at the time. It just didn't occur to me how my father's losing control of his voice made him feel trapped and isolated communication-wise. This is another segment of my life that stays with me as I wish that I'd have done, or could have done so much more.

I believe that I put one or two more weeks of photo pheresis treatments off in Pittsburgh because my dad was clearly struggling. In fact it was so bad that he didn't leave the couch in the rec room anymore. He remained confined to the downstairs except for one or two scary ambulance trips to the hospital. I have to reiterate one more time that I was just so out of tune mentally to what was going on. I'd like to term it as shock because I simply wasn't prepared to have my father pass away ever, especially at this point in my life when I wasn't clear headed or any sense of "the old me".

With the fact that home oncology nurses were coming in and out while taking care of my father, I really didn't equate that with him being in such bad shape in my mind! I'm very resentful to my family members for sheltering me so much because I didn't really have any say in the matter. Not that I should have had but I felt I could have been informed as to what was going on to a much further degree than they did. I don't know what I could have done, I just know that it 's a salted wound when ever I look back on it.

I guess you could say that a good amount of time went along until there came a period that my whole family settled in to stay at my house. It just became a ritual that everyone stayed there with my dad around the clock. One night for whatever reason, I found everyone out except my mom and me. My father and mother were downstairs and I was upstairs in bed. I could hear him choking and struggling to breathe while my mom attempted to comfort him. I painfully recall yelling downstairs, "I'm coming, I'm coming." My struggling limp of a walk scurried down the steps as fast as possible to try and get to him and see what I could do. In all reality I was helpless. There wasn't anything that I could do other than rub the back of his neck and shoulders and hold him trying to comfort him.

I hope that my dad realized I was there for him as best I could be, but eventually it came to be where he would just lay there and stare. He recalled a lot of his WW II battles and had quite a few nightmares as well. My dad would often wake up out of his sleep as if he was back on Okinawa or Pelilu or any of the other wartime Pacific islands he fought on. The one ironic and, I'd say religious story came to play in an again surreal moment.

One particular night had me settling downstairs to just try and spend some time with my dad knowing that he was sleeping for the most part. I came down and sat beside him and, just for the heck of it, had started talking to him in a religious context. I was saying something to the effect of, "Dad you're going to be ok, you're going to be with Padre Pio and all of the saints soon, and especially you're going to be with God." Just then, my father came out of a deep sleep immediately after I mentioned that to him. He promptly mustered up enough strength to give us a nice big grin while opening his eyes very wide. I can't say for sure how he felt exactly, but I do know that he made the effort to open his eyes out of a sound sleep and smile. With that he laid back and went off to sleep.

The rest of the night was pretty quiet. I went to bed and tried to get some type of sleep and I believe I did; I was exhausted and dozed off very well. Early the next morning my brother came up and gave me the news. He informed me that my dad had passed away. His words were "Dad's gone" This was all too over-whelming for me and I had no reaction outwardly whatsoever that I recall. I was just there on the side of my bed so lost and in a deep daze. I didn't cry I didn't have a reaction; I was just gone mentally and emotionally like he was physically.

The funeral was a disaster for me. Somebody dressed me up. I guess my sister Carol, in a suit that didn't fit me because I was now a walking skeleton. Just the opposite of where I had been. I guess I looked as okay as I could have. It reminded me of a show that I saw on a St. Jude's Hospital Telethon for Children's Leukemia Fund-raising one year. This proud little boy was all dressed up so handsomely in his suit. It really left an impression on me because he looked like a small version of me that day. His family had dressed him up and under-neath those nice pressed clothes was a skeleton of a body. But the cancer that seems to be killing us all in this story wasn't going to be enough to stop us; that little boy in his shining moment on the TV show, or me from going to pay respect to my father. My Dad…My Dad!

I think that it was my Godfather who assisted me out of the car and into the Veterans' Cemetery for a full-color military funeral. Fellow marines were there and soldiers fired a twenty one-gun salute while *Taps* ranged out across the open air. I remember just sitting. It was a nice sunny, clear day and I just stared for miles into the distance. Every time that I hear *Taps* now I think of my dad.

I didn't pay much attention to my family that day or anybody for that matter. I had a couple of altercations that I tried to not let get out of hand with some people who visited my brother's house afterwards; Names of which I won't men-tion but they still sting now. Here I am just losing my hero and great friend and these people are just stuffing their faces with anything they could mooch from on the table; Sitting down next to me explaining about their promotions or this and that. Can you imagine that, or is it just me?—A part of which wishes that I would have gotten up and punched him in the mouth but it was what it was and I just thought I'd mention it.

The time going on from this point really hurt. I was even more alone and it's funny how I've come to feel different levels of loneliness. I had no religious signs that I could take comfort in or brag about, I really didn't have any friends that were visiting me on any regular basis, and I really didn't have good health to speak about. We all had an empty household, especially inside our bodies. That empty feeling just wouldn't leave.

I remember one day I managed to get out to the mall to get a piece of pizza by myself, and I went to a pizza parlor on the first floor this time. Damned if I didn't sit near the window looking out into the mall and have a bunch of guys come up to my space walking by. They all gave me the look and one of them gave me the finger—just for no damn reason. He had that "stupid ass poser look" that in a healthier version of me, I'd like to think that I would have got up in his face real fast, right or wrong. This is one time that still gets to me to no end because I didn't get up and confront this guy or do something. I ultimately let some time go by before getting in my car and go looking for them in the parking lot. As if I could have done anything about it, but if for no other reason than to question this jerk. What the hell is his problem?

It's funny how that moment tops off a culmination or serves as an example of what I was feeling inside. Maybe part of me wanted to take out some of my vengeance on this punk whereas another part of me didn't know why I would even think about doing something like that. This is a good way of explaining how I was. Man, all of my emotions, my whole sense of being was just a mess, awash in a tirade of dissention.

This was supposed to be such a great recovery story and it wasn't materializing out to be. I was still alive, which don't get me wrong, for that I am very deeply appreciative. It's just by now after having you read all of this, you can easily see the many perverted scenarios that maybe I am now becoming aware of as an adult, that this is just what life is. Maybe I was so sheltered that I had no clue. "Instead of me thinking that I'm the only one who could be going through this or try and understand that other people can go through this, I'm trying to understand how anybody has to go through this…!"

One of my dad's last wishes that I believe he told my brother was to make sure that I would be taken care of along with my mom and sister. He also stressed that he wanted me to keep going to Pittsburgh to try and get better. He said a lot of things to my mother that I don't know and doubt I'll ever hear about. I get little bits and pieces here and there but that's the way it is with husbands and wives and children. I was probably behaving like a real jerk during this stretch, getting in a couple fights and skirmishes with different people for whatever reason. I'm sure this was mainly a result of the way that I looked and or felt.

A good stretch of time passed with me being 'out to lunch' as to what was going on in life. I tuned back in a little bit for a spell and recollect another drive with Carol venturing out for a gown as she was preparing to get married. With the horrible and bitter divorce long since past she attempted to start a new life and eventually kindled a relationship with a long-time friend. She and her friend Harry, who assisted us in some of the transplant preparations, seemed to be a 'perfect match'! Pardon the pun.

He was always a terrific friend for Carol and it seemed fitting after what she had to go through with everything, and I stress everything, to have much deserved happiness and a good husband for her and the girls. It just was what it was for me. I went with her to shop for a gown and can remember being so short of breath in one particular store that I had to stop and sit almost hyperventilating. I can't remember what she looked at or anything else except my having a hard time breathing for some GVHD reason. One more example of how unexpected complications from the transplant can crop up out of nowhere and vanish just the same, never knowing the origin or reason for the occurrence.

The time came for Carol and Harry's wedding. It was a very nice afternoon and all in all I'd say that I remember struggling pretty hard physically through the day. I was extremely weak, again in a suit that really didn't fit me and seemed to be experiencing a major stiffening of my back and lower extremities. Other problems now that I was facing were more on the lines of fatigue as well as increased joint pain and flexibility (range of motion).

My lower back had become extremely stiff and it was so difficult to even try and act somewhat normal to simply walk across the floor or go from table to table. I guess at the time I thought that I might have been doing an adequate job but I know now that there's no way. I probably looked as though it was just what I was doing, struggling to try and look okay. Nobody said anything, everyone treated me fine but they were also all well aware of my condition and "my de-conditioning for that matter".

I stopped the ultra violet photo pheresis treatments, (PUVA) because I just wasn't getting the type of response that I hoped for. That plus the fact that I would have needed to continue this procedure for an ongoing lengthy period of time. I don't believe that I was prepared to handle flying back and forth to Pittsburgh every other week and endure the kind of treatments I was getting. It was too much on my body mentally and physically. Even spiritually I'd add here. I would have either had to stay in Pittsburgh indefinitely or find a center nearby that offered the same procedure.

Unfortunately at the time the Pittsburgh Hospital was the only facility doing clinical research protocols with Psoralin and leukemia survivors with chronic graft vs. host disease phase two, in this manner. One of the ironic things to happen was talking with some nurses and staff members in this particular Pittsburgh hospital about goings on at another in-town hospital. This time my interest was for physical rehabilitation purposes. This was a so-called, renowned center for physical therapy and so forth.

I eventually contacted that facility and somehow got entered into the program. I became friends with a girl named Karen who was my occupational therapist. Actually I corresponded with her for a long while after leaving the program. I believe her father was diagnosed with CML some time later. I've not heard the outcome of his case or from Karen in a long time. She was a very nice girl. Having said that, there was a time when I would commute from one hospital to the other hospital across town, and then fly home and check into a third hospital nearby. This was a terrible juggling act for me. My health, my family and people involved trying to accommodate me travel-wise.

The Rehabilitation Institute of Pittsburgh offered some great techniques for, if not improvement, at least more relief in the sense of pain. The most of which was hot water therapy that is basically self-explanatory. I would get into a heated pool of about ninety-eight to one hundred and one degrees or so with three or four physical therapists working on my joints and range of motion. This included Karen who was easy on the eyes and I enjoyed her company the most.

The problem with this protocol was that I would stagnate in a hospital room doing nothing all but for an hour or so a day. This was not at all conducive to my mental stability. God bless the 'resident' women patients down the hall who asked me to have community lunch and to play bridge with them but I just wasn't that kind of guy. "Sorry ladies."

The juggling of these hospital trips took an even further toll on me, and my moods. One particular Doctor or Corpsman handled herself just like a linebacker. We never hit it off and didn't get along very well from the start. In fact, in one episode she had me sit on a chair in the middle of a circle of other chairs. From there she sat among students and colleagues while they all each took shots interrogating me on my condition, state of mind, and things of that nature. I did not take a liking to this format whatsoever and once again felt no type of respect being somewhat degraded by their demeanor.

This woman without much knowledge of my case history interjected her opinion and pseudo pop psychology diagnosis/remedy rather abruptly (and absurdly I might add). She proposed placing my lower extremities in a total body cast for several months. I want to recall saying six months, which I believe was her quote but to stay safe with her call I'll remain at several. This must be documented somewhere, but at this point I really had to reconsider my motives for even being in this facility. I'm sure it is a terrific center for many types of ailments but as I was becoming accustomed to finding out, my problems were not fitting in with any categories that anybody had seen.

The body cast recommendation freaked me out to say the least. I had the drop foot that I was aware of and they fitted me with these plastic splints "velcroed" around my legs. I may sound a bit pushy myself, but I hated them just the same. I later found out that I was documented as a difficult and cynical patient by this Navy nurse, or what ever she was. It's probably a good thing that she was shipped to the Middle East and Operation Desert Storm for both our sakes. I don't know what would have happened if not for that but the irony in the situation was my contemplating escaping this place and vowing never to return. I became somewhat paranoid of the whole environment and the treatment I was receiving. I'm sure I had a part to play in it but when I began looking at the bars on the windows and the older ladies down the hall and the differences in the types of patients, I just got a creepy feeling that I didn't belong there and no longer wanted to be there!

A great day came when my friend Kev and his wife Mary visited me totally by surprise. They were in Pittsburgh visiting family and got directions to where I was staying. They brought me some fast food and snacks and visited for a few hours. I most definitely contemplated having Kev stick me in his trunk and get me the heck out of there because they were driving back home across the state. With Kev's driving I could have been home in about six hours.

What I did do was coordinate a tactic that I got a kick out of. I conveyed to this center that I needed to transfer over to the hospital across town for my resumption of ultra violet photo pheresis, which in fact was true. As I mentioned earlier I juggled both treatment centers as much as I could. This all took place just before I was being slated to stay as an in-patient for several months at this very center I was planning to go AWOL from. This was the straw that broke the camel's back. There's no way that I wanted to stay in this joint for three more months, after going through what I had been through and with my brain having conjure up the crazy inklings that it was doing!

I remember with my little duffel bag getting out of the wheelchair outside to a cab thinking, "I'm never stepping foot in this freakin place again". I got in the taxi that indeed took me to the pheresis procedure hospital, which oddly enough was a refuge sign of relief. That's funny to me because going to any hospital isn't fun at all. It gives you an idea of how fearful I now was of being misdiagnosed or 'committed'. I felt I had successfully escaped and to the present day I haven't been back. Even an employee who corresponded with me agreed about my treatment being erratic at best. I was forewarned of certain employee's reputations for zany behaviors and they came to pass.

This attempt to improve my graft vs. host disease didn't fare too well. The hot water therapy felt terrific and I'm still looking into nearby facilities for that aside from this one procedure that was about it. I think a real important area to mention here is that my mind still seemed to remain sharp—sharp enough to be sarcastic with a smidgen of cynicism but I was still feisty, somewhat bitter and always on guard that something could do me harm. Perhaps a bit of paranoia yet a healthy kind if that's possible. I've explained this many times before that you always have to be alert and cognizant of what's going on and question things. The more informed you are, the better your chances are I feel and definitely subscribed to this school of thinking. I just hope other patients don't have to learn the hard way as I have by perhaps being to trusting or lax in certain areas.

While I was still trying to keep tabs on new GVHD procedures around the country, being in Pittsburgh enabled me to get bits and pieces here and there of what might be coming up on the horizon. This and touching base with Fred Hutch, in Seattle, along with any other center getting news. Loyola of Chicago, U.C.L.A., Sloan Kettering, Johns Hopkins, you name the facility and I had my nose, if not my foot, in the door at all of these places somehow.

I was very gung-ho and perhaps a bit too gung-ho to present myself as a candidate for clinical research protocols in looking for possible cures for chronic graft vs. host disease. I did this mainly because the disease itself was totally ripping me up, and my quality of life was suffering immensely. As advertised, I was trading one horrible disease for another and I didn't want that nor will I stand for it today if I can do anything about it. I do not want to become a self-fulfilling prophecy of what one of my doctor's said to me many years ago.

On CNN one day there was a short segment about an experimental drug called FK-506 developed by a Dr. Starzal and his colleagues. This was yet again being researched and developed in Pittsburgh primarily as an anti rejection drug/immuno-suppressive for liver transplant patients. Here I am lying in a bed looking up at a doctor roaming the halls on T.V. somewhere in this very hospital.

This place harbored a new so-called anti-rejection drug that was helping significantly with patients who couldn't tolerate Cyclosporin or other immunosuppressive drugs. So immediately the light bulb in my head went off. I calculated mentally that if this FK-506 could help some of these new liver transplant patients, perhaps it could possibly take the place of everything that I was on or could work in conjunction with them to do so for me! As to how I was going to go about weaseling in and getting it was another matter.

My mind was once again racing and rejuvenated with the notion of theoretical help. "Pretty sharp" I think, considering how fried my up and down body and overall condition was. It had dwindled away to the point which I have a difficult time expressing. They did take medical photographs that would give an accurate assessment of my status but I haven't been able to track many down.

I began making some noise by tracking down social workers that gave me leads or dumped me to somebody else who could after becoming annoyed with my persistence. These cold calls and dead ends were pursued while actually still being in the hospital for photo phereses itself as a patient or from back at home across the state via the telephone. I eventually spoke to a nice woman who led me to a Dr. Fung, who is one of the world's leading liver and organ transplant specialist. He was a colleague of Dr. Starzal. Dr. Fung was a very cool, personable, respectful and down to earth man. I think he respected my intelligence but mostly me as a patient, as well as understanding my motives for wanting to try and improve. The problem was getting him cornered long enough to elaborate on my thoughts and motives.

Some of the nice nurses in Pittsburgh along with several doctors were helpful such as Jean Bakey, Dr. Bloom and Dr. Titchner. They took a liking to me I guess; enough to smuggle in Dr. Fung himself in order for me to meet him for a pow-wow during a photo pheresis session. This was perhaps a five or ten-minute consult covering my intentions and how I could go about getting myself on this FK-506 protocol. This is the extent to which you may or may not have to go to in the desperate attempts to acquire information and or assistance. "You've simply got to make noise and be heard". I mentioned earlier Father Fahey telling me to storm Heaven through prayer for attention, and getting your point across. To make noise you have to "storm hallways, offices, medical centers, insurance companies, newspapers, television stations and a tool that I never had at my disposal in 1984, the internet for sure". Do whatever it takes…

So by having Dr. Fung hear my case and seeing my side of things, he ultimately helped out a great deal. Having him as an ally was like having all of the Cardinals with you to try and influence the Pope—"well, almost". I think that it took another couple of weeks or so to iron out the paperwork but I managed to squeeze my way in on the protocol as the only bone marrow transplant patient to be given the "FK". It was exclusively being administered to liver transplant patients with the possible exception of a kidney patient or two. This was the drug that went on to help Pennsylvania Gov. Casey so much, as reported on CNN. I found myself now being up in another wing of the hospital, I then was transferred to the third different hospital in as many days. "I thought how many hospitals are there in Pittsburgh?" They needed to do more skin biopsies and do everything that I've talked about hating all over again.

I bit the bullet and tried despite having another sarcastic jerk in the form of a nurse tell me, "You couldn't pay me any amount of money to touch your skin with a needle". And, "I wouldn't touch you with a ten-foot pole" the way that my skin was. Real nice, comments like that, well, lady, in retrospect nobody could pay me to touch your sorry butt either, you were no raving beauty yourself. I had leukemia, what was your excuse.

Ambulances and private services would escort me all over town it seemed, between hospitals, although it was only blocks, in reality. I met a real nice room-mate who had undergone a liver, kidney and stomach transplant, I believe, from Saudi Arabia. Although his family didn't care for me because I was a Christian and they were Moslem, when they would leave Masude came over to talk or watch TV. We got along real well and that just shows you the kinds of ridiculous stereotypes that people adhere to with religious beliefs and so on.

Masude and I communicated as best we could, he spoke broken English and I spoke no Arabic. He got a kick out of watching TV wrestling while I grit my teeth grinning and bearing it while he intriguingly reeled himself in as a gullible spectator. He also told me that he really enjoyed listening to Michael Jackson but that it was difficult for him to get his music in Saudi Arabia. I told him I'd try to send some tapes when he went home but I'm sorry to say that I lost contact with Masude. We both had difficult long hauls to overcome but I pray that he is alive and well.

Student doctors (to be), continued to flock in and analyze me in droves as they always seemed to do whenever I was being worked on. One particular day early one morning, when I was still awaiting news on being given the FK506 administration instructions, a surgical team blazed in and surrounded my bed. This group of carnivores insistently persisted to take a "sliver of my liver". This was of course a biopsy but I was not slated to have it. I had to promptly don my Joe Frazier boxing gloves again and corner myself in the room preparing to do battle, because there was no way in hell that they were going to cut me open for a liver biopsy.

I wasn't giving anything that I didn't need to be giving. Big, loud arguments and problems ensued because I was the labeled "difficult patient". Finally one of them stormed right up to me with all of this paperwork to sign. Evidently this was to indicate that I was not consenting to the procedure. Pretty soon they would see that it was not me in fact but "they" who made a big deal out of my "difficult patient status".

CHAPTER 7

▼

The biggest problem here is again, I felt as if none of these "students" or co-workers, whatever they were, gave me any respect of politeness whatsoever. I simply told them that Dr. Fung was personally taking care of me at which point they simply scoffed at the notion. Sarcastic rebuttals such as "Oh, Dr. Fung is taking care of you is he, Oh, yeah, where is he?" I got a lot of those cat calls and finally said, "Look, he's coming whether you want to believe it or not."

I said a lot more things worse than that I'm sure and I regret using the tone of voice that I can sometimes have but again I felt extremely cornered. That's a really lousy predicament to be placed in, it makes you almost have to be the kind of person that you do not want to be.

Just out of another cliché from a western movie, the abrupt silence brewed echoes as right then in walked Dr. Fung himself. The parting of the waves took place as all of the students seemed to bow and squirm backwards, opening up a clear pathway up to my bed. Dr. Fung casually then came further in, tapped me on the shoulders, shook my hand and shouted, "Hey, John, how's it going?" I'd say that perhaps one or two of the cronies acknowledged that I wasn't "b.s.ing" them, as their heads stared down or away from my eye contact. I was of my right mind and probably in some cases as smart a person as some of these prospective scholarly doctors. Their bedside manner 101 course got an F if I was giving the grade.

Dr. Fung kind of snickered a bit as I explained to him how they wanted a slice of my liver so desperately and how I wasn't going to give it. He gave them explicit instructions to listen to what I had to say and explained to the students that I was in fact a bone barrow transplant patient treated for leukemia. He stated that I was on the FK506 protocol and not at any time a liver transplant patient, even though I was on the ward and not hallucinating or making any of this stuff up! I mean how hard it would have been for these people to check my story out! Needless to say, I spared my liver from going under the knife, though I lost some sanity and more seconds off of my life with all of the stress probably.

I still had to wait, as this FK506 was made in-house and at the time was treated like gold. It came in very tiny, minute powdered amounts that you wouldn't believe could be so potent or lethal. Dr. Fung came back to visit me and joked a bit several more times with small talk. One evening he came in eating M&Ms peanuts, all decked out in scrubs chewing away and with a dry sense of humor said to me, "You want the stuff, you really want this stuff. I'll give you the stuff" laughingly. Out he walked and I was basically ready for the next morning's initial dosage to begin.

Masude and I watched TV until my protocol preps began. After my weight, height, skin, muscles and so forth were all charted, it was worked out that I would initially get started for several days on the medicine in this hospital and, if all went well, I could fly back home to continue therapy. The FK506 drug would be shipped to me a couple times a week due to the close dosage monitoring. I would, of course, have to go to my local hospital weekly for more blood work doing all of the too familiar sticks in the arm rituals.

I sound a bit catty with my descriptions of this particular GVHD recovery attempt. I'll definitely say that I was still regressing pretty badly in my being extremely weak and to the point of now needing a wheelchair. I could walk from my bedside to the restroom if I needed to, or perhaps forty or fifty feet if I had to. But all in all it was now commonplace for my brother to cruise me around in a wheelchair, lift me into a car, into the house and so forth. The problem was now my brother had business to tend to at home, so I was there by myself as I have mentioned, extremely weak and worn down and needless to say stressed out.

The FK-506 initially didn't give me any noticeable side effects other than maybe a heart eurhythmy here and there which I had previously, or a hot flash, so I couldn't count that for sure. Possibly, some more hot flashes or further loss of appetite, but nothing that I would have been unaccustomed to or unprepared for knowing that I had been given an immunosuppressive for this GVHD.

The instructions given to the particular airlines that I would be flying home on must have been phoned in from the hospital or an unknown source to me at least. I never felt so strange on a plane, ever. Whereby after being dropped off by a volunteer driver at the airport, an airline escort dropped me into a wheelchair and scooted me on down to the early pre-board preparation area. The flight attendants were extremely nice and assisted me in to the very first seat on the plane. This was terrific and I thought everything was going great. I was excited to once again be getting back to my house.

The flight was comfortable and not untimely. We landed in Philadelphia and everything seemed fine, other than my being in the condition that I was in. Good old Philadelphia airport I thought, that is until the plane itself taxied out onto the runway eventually slowing down to a complete stop. Only to have the pilot to announce to us that for some particular reason the terminal gates that we were scheduled to arrive in were closed and off limits, so we would be required to have what you would think of as one of those emergency-type of exits.

We had to taxi over to a remote part of the airport's runway where they would bring the steep manual wheeled staircase, that we're all familiar with when you see the President or some ambassador or the Pope exit their planes. They actually wheel these steps over to the plane's front door and everyone leaves via that route. Well, this was just the case for my flight, which definitely caught me off guard. Since I was in a considerably frail condition at this point, this presented a problem for the airline staff. Everyone on the plane de-boarded except for me. I was instructed to wait until the plane was cleared and they would assist me in getting off. The plane steps themselves were steep and ramp like, to extremely steep in my estimation. It's not like this was any type of a bump or an easy grade of an angle to descend down on.

What the staff came up with for me was a wooden stretcher. They somehow convinced me to lie back on this thing and then proceeded to strap and secure me in from the neck to toe, to the point that I could not move. I was reassured that this was simply a standard procedure in emergencies for patients in my condition and that this was not a problem. That was easy for them to say because I don't know how many times they've de-boarded a gurney down those cliff-like steps. Usually I would just cruise right off in a wheelchair through the tunnel and into the airport itself. Not the case this time, for down below was one of those gas powered or electric cars you often see flying around the airports waiting for me as it's cargo.

As I now lay securely strapped in or 'on' to this stretcher, a gentleman clutched the handgrips to the front of me and another gentleman grabbed hold of the handles at my feet. I was lifted up and all that I could now see was the ceiling of the plane and a little bump I noticed moving up towards the cockpit. That and in making the left turn towards the exit itself was bright daylight. That was all fine and easy enough to take as they made their way out to the exposed stair platform itself and began the descent. No sooner than the sky and clouds started to slant from my eyes' stiff perspective, the way that things have gone for me previously, dictated the next shocking performance. My head suddenly slid radically and tipped about along the steel railing, where my vision could clearly notice that I was turned sideways. Just as if you were on a sliding board out over the edge with your head protruding off the corner as you descended!

What had happened was that the gentleman behind me plain and simply lost his grips. Lost the grip I tell you! I cannot see how I wouldn't have just slid and gone off the side all the way if it wasn't for the man at my feet. But for a good two to three seconds, I mean that seemed like forever with the proverbial 'your life flashes in front of you statement'. I could see and feel myself slipping and sliding down with no ability to control myself having been strapped in. So I don't actually know how high it is from the top of the cockpit of an airplane to the bottom of the runway 'and I really didn't want to feel it either'.

Those cold shivers you get, the whooshing in your ears, the chest pains, the fireworks, everything that you would think would happen in that situation did in fact happen in my mind. All while I took a bit of a slide, just a casual stinking slide down the rails of steps on a runway at Philadelphia airport! I guess my Guardian Angel kept me from slipping over all the way. That's just par for the course right, all bone marrow transplant patients have their head stuck out over a stairway of about a fifty foot descent on a sunny day. That's just standard procedure, in the protocol right…

For the most part I got through that 'unique' experience and added it to the file of my 'How to transplant resume book'. My sister picked me up at the airport not having seen the entire fiasco and took me home to rest in bed. For the next several days it was just normal routine stuff going on. Hanging around the house, mood swings here and there and ingesting my slew of pills, while waiting it out. More trips going for my counts at the hospital, probably catching some TV and trying to eat, whatever the case, whatever 'normal was back then'.

I'd put a lot of stock into this FK-506 miraculously healing me. I was still relatively feisty and hungry for a reverse or cure of GVHD I was still somewhat green in the knowledge of how and if it could be reversed. It probably stemmed from a lot of my confidence and cockiness in the ability to pull off the transplant coup initially, given all of those odds and obstacles that we had overcome to this point. I really convinced myself with reasoning that it would just be a matter of time before the Graft vs. Host disease symptoms would be reversed due to the strength and power of this new wonder drug as compared to Cyclosporin, Imuran, Prednisone, Thalidamide, ATG, Interferon, and all of the many other drugs that I'd been given previously.

The problem that was coming around the corner like a Mack truck for me was that this FK-506 was too strong. I had mentioned to Dr. Bloom and Dr. Fung I believe that I had experienced problems in the past with sensitivity and dosages of medications. That is to say I personally believe that sometimes I do not require nearly as much as the prescribed doses offered to most patients. I know that is the case with the Medrol and Prednisone like corticoid steroids that I take because the amounts I now take, most doctors would likely scoff at due to their minute amounts.

Initially, of course my dosages were ridiculously astronomical and about as high comparatively to other patients as they now are low in this area. If I don't take them, I am in for big trouble and will very much aggravate my symptom status. Again a little bit goes a long way with me it appears, and the initial FK-506 doses that were worked out in the lab took its time to 'attack' or react to my body, or at least feel anything.

One evening, just lying in bed actually feeling somewhat relaxed and comfortable, I suddenly experienced extreme and intense unrelenting pains, which exploded across my chest and in my heart. Shortness of breath and the branching out of unbearable pressure all over my upper torso erupted as well. It felt like the tightest vises of pain I had ever known in my life until then. As if concrete slabs were sandwiched around me and no matter what I tried doing it wouldn't go away.

The only good thing about these impacting symptoms was that I knew they were severe enough not to ignore or try and remedy them at home. I quickly called for an ambulance and remember speaking to the dispatcher explaining my symptoms. Maybe it took five or six minutes for the ambulance to arrive, but yet once again, I found myself flying down I-95 in an ambulance looking up at the ceiling and arriving at the emergency ward. This time I didn't give anybody the finger because there wasn't any time to.

I was wheeled right up on to the heart patients' floor and one of my attending doctors met me. Dr. Jim was on that night and after my reasoning with him for a few minutes and answering some questions to his satisfaction, he administered some moderate doses of morphine, which took the edge off of the pain somewhat. But as I stated earlier he is a cautious and methodical doctor so we had to wait and see how that conservative dose panned out. That was one time when I wished that I would have responded to the low dose. We tried discussing a couple of options though eventually I convinced him to increase the amount for me, and at least make things bearable for the time being.

Doctor Mike followed up with me once I was placed in my own room. When we were done mulling over what had happened, we both concluded with my pushing the issue a bit that the FK-506 was the probable source of the mess. It took a lot of pain-killers and a few days for all of the chest pains to subside but I remained as an inpatient a while longer for observation. The initial EKG read-outs were erratic and clearly showed a heart problem was evident. The severity of which was uncertain though. That could only be determined by a heart catheterization.

We took a wait and see approach and ultimately heeded the advice of Dr. Mike who stated that I really didn't need to go through any more procedures if I could avoid it. I was feeling much better so decided against it for the time being. In all probability I had some degree of a heart attack but it would only be more procedures and more uncomfortable poking and prodding on me to confirm this for certain. His personal opinion thought that it wasn't necessary so that was good enough for me. Needless to say, I took the wait and see approach.

I believe that I was placed on 'my' old floor—2 South—for easier observation by all of those wonderful nurses that 'just loved me'…I graciously ignored the 'Oh, no not him again looks and smiled as my gurney cruised by the nurse's station. I blew kisses to everyone, I was such a model patient…that's just the kind of guy I am. All that I had to do was just hold out and hope that no more chest pains would crop up and I could be sprung out of there pretty fast.

I had a visit from my sister and mother where upon they informed me that a friend of mine, Laura, was hospitalized also just a couple of rooms down the hall. Laura had recently come home from a Pittsburgh hospital where she underwent a bone marrow transplant as well. I didn't mention that earlier but, after my BMT, I tried to help several families with their transplant struggles. Whatever I was able to do whether it be answering questions, referrals, phone numbers and so forth. I'm sorry to say that in the long run none of the patients or families that sought out my help did very well in their procedures, but Laura did become a special friend of mine.

Ironically Laura was connected somehow to a coworker of my father's and that's how they tracked me down to talk. Laura was doing very well until an infection that she picked up evidently set her back. She was much more active and outgoing post-transplant than I was. Shopping, raising her family, the beach and so on. It seemed like she was doing so well but the infection could not be shaken off. Laura was a very pretty woman and something about her made you enjoy her presence. I often think of her and it reminds me that I must still be here for some reason. Many times I wonder why when I think of people like Laura.

I was able to send her messages from room to room through my sister and mother. Actually Laura's husband and sister visited me once. I don't think her family even understood what it took to get through this type of procedure we had done to us, or what it could do to a patient. I wish them all the best and this all brings to mind, another friend that I had, Bob, who lived in New York. Through the Padre Pio Center he would call and write to me as he was battling AIDS. Bob would call me for prayers or just someone to talk with. He struggled a great deal and stopped communicating with me once his t-cells went under thirty I believe.

He was a bit angry at the world and everything and I could understand why. Bob and I talked about God and why things happen. He went through phases of questioning, to buying religious medals, to reading every book that he could to changing his favorite saint. This was a real apparent cycle of desperation for somebody to reach out and help him. I'm sure that God took good took good care of him and as I, in this position of just almost having serious complications from this drug, now getting to see two friends pass away, seemed to reaffirm that my still being here was for a reason. I just couldn't understand why.

Facing these situations of death over and over really makes you question and think about things especially when you find that you get no measurable answer. With human nature the way that it is, us not understanding things, animals killing animals, people having to suffer the way that they do, tragedies and so forth, it just doesn't make any sense. So some times it's difficult to fit God into understanding why these events do occur. Nevertheless, I cling to my faith and try to hope that I can make something make some sense to me.

Another thing that I had done along the way and especially during this period was to spend a good amount of time and money searching for different kinds of equipment that may be able to help my deteriorating body and waning proportions. I was wasting away but I figured if I could just work hard enough, find the right leg machine or chest machine or abs machine, anything that would have to equate to progress, I'd find a way to recover.

I had to find a way to not give up. I even went so far as to put my trust in a company in Philly to build me some custom equipment for my hips and legs. Of course as always, using money that I didn't have and ended up getting ripped off by a couple of jerks to put it politely. After a good run on these machines and several thousand dollars later, I ended up giving them to my nephew to give to his friends. (Another mistake that I can only attribute to the drugs and irrationality)

One day Carol bought me a treadmill and simply showed up with it. Of course, charged on her credit card. I mentioned something about wondering if a treadmill would help in passing, so she picked it up to see without my knowing.

Those were the kinds of things that Carol did. The treadmill worked well on my stamina but my ankles, hips and knee joints couldn't withstand the impact back then. My niece Danielle ended up getting that nifty machine.

I was so desperate for some kind of magical cure. I was also willing to put out the effort but couldn't find the whereabouts to do it. With a good amount of time on my hands other than expending energy to try and rehab, I investigated the area's local dermatology centers inquiring if any of them were familiar with U.V.A. treatments. Those being Photophoresis or 'P.U.V.A' treatments, Psoralin ultra-violet augmentation I believe. Even though it was tough to get through I figured, if I could come up with a center closer to home instead of resuming my treatments in Pittsburgh. I might be better able to endure all the number of treatments they had said it would take to initiate some signs of GVHD recovery, if any would occur at all. As it turned out I was able to work out a program with a nearby dermatologist who had ultra-violet light facilities. They were setup in the format many of us see today in the sun tanning salons. Basically the same type of beds or standing shower stalls, which have the light tubes surrounding you. These machines could be used and they had them there.

We set up with the different doctors a way for me to come in two to three times a week. Then I would have to take the Psoralin drug at home and my mother would drive me over. She'd wait in the car while I would get 'crisped and fried'. I had to wear those very dark huge "terminator-esque" sunglasses to protect my eyes and cover my body head to toe so as not to be exposed to any sunlight. "Just like a vampire." This ritual continued throughout my treatments. Naturally that meant that all of the time after these procedures was to be spent in the house virtually in the dark. They were even so adamant as to instruct me not to use bright lights in the house for fear of possible cell damage. By the way, curtains were to remain drawn a la Dracula.

.It wasn't long before I had the darkest of tropical tans. A disturbing occurrence that I noticed was that I could actually smell the distinct presence of my burned flesh. I could always walk around and be able to smell my own burnt skin. That sounds a bit disgusting I know but my sense of smell seemed to be enhanced bionically, somewhere along the line during this transplant. I was always very self-conscious about people being able to pick-up what I was noticing. I wore cologne, of course, with antiperspirant but no matter how nice I may have smelled, I could still pick up on the underlining burned skin smell from the P.U.V.A. damage.

I think I could say that some things felt a little bit better during these treatments but unbeknownst to all of us, I was still sliding backward due to the fact that I wasn't eating nearly as much and my muscles were severely atrophied. With my practically being a shut-in and covered up in bed, other than being naked inside of the tanning cylinder, nobody really had the chance to compare my progression or regression. Things such as skin checks and a periodic once over by the doctors just to look for out of the ordinary symptoms were done, but nothing relative to my overall physical or muscle condition I'm sorry to say.

Fairly deep into these treatments I went in to see Dr. Mike whereupon he did give me this once over that I needed earlier. By the look on his face you could see that he was concerned. This man was not always one to easily give away his thoughts by facial expressions but he noticed how horrible my legs had become. It seemed to happen overnight because as in times past, my family and all parties concerned failed to pick up on the changes, myself included. We all were oblivious to it just happening as I mentioned. So basically, my lower extremities were now skeletons covered with a saran wrap of skin.

That's how bad they were and I was still using them to try and stand on without realizing this, believe it or not. I'm harping on this fact but it boggles my mind how such a metamorphic change can occur without a single soul including me be aware of its happening. Between wheelchairs and canes and being carried it was just a terrible mess. We all seemed to be caught up in a coma-like state because nobody reacted. I keep reiterating that but I don't know where the time went between having muscles in my legs and some meat on my bones, to then having them both disappear. By the time we realized this, it seemed to be too late.

This was a horrible time for me as I weighed in at only eighty nine pounds. This was the lowest I'd ever been (as a patient, of course). Evidently it is my guess that the Psoralin combined with the tanning lamps (the activator), all of the stress and anxiety along with the physical toll it took on me physically simply shut down my ability to eat. Two bites of this, a bite of that, a gulp of this and that was it, I was totally filled. Perhaps if I had remained in the hospital as an inpatient this would have been noticed much earlier but you just can't live as an inpatient your whole life. I know I couldn't, what's the sense.

With my family at a loss, I don't know who the exact decision-makers were but one day I was informed by my sister and mother that they were going to bring in a staff of home care nurses to take care of me. I freaked out initially because I had harbored some ill will toward the nurses that came and took care of my father. I'm very cynical about some of these situations, especially they way that they took care of my dad. I don't know all of the details but I just had a bad feeling pertaining to the whole way that his situation unfolded.

I was really prepared to probably be a difficult patient when I first found this out but it was pretty hard to do that because they all were very good looking and cordial. Every nurse that came to work on me was attractive in some way or another. Perhaps that was one of their diffusing types of tactics. Isn't it funny that as deathly sick as I was and falling apart, my libido still had time to work?

This home care nursing probably helped me more than I would have liked to have thought back then in retrospect. It was a bit of communication to the outside world. It was a little bit of companionship and I'd like to think at least some of it was sincere and not simply acting on their part in playing the roles of the compassionate Florence Nightingale. In any event I'll choose to think they were sincere for the most part. Needless to say they would do all the duties necessary such as blood work, heart rate and overall monitoring. They even worked with my doctor heeding to his instructions during this duration.

Eighty-nine pounds was obviously not cutting it so not long after the staff began taking care of me one particular nurse that I formed a decent rapport with asked me how I felt about getting a peg tube placed in me. As frail and wiped out as I now was I didn't put up much resistance to this idea. So skipping along a bit further, I was lifted into a wheelchair and scooted on over to the local hospital to have this feeding line put in. I think this procedure was done downstairs in the emergency room in one of the makeshift short procedure areas. This mind you is the very same hospital that I've had the pleasure of giving you all of these other 'unique' stories from, so I made sure that both my sister Carol and my sister-in-law Dee were there to accompany me for this one. I gave strict orders not be left alone...

I lucked out because it turned out to be a first class surgeon working on me, Dr. Haith, I believe. We got along very well and I can remember this being a relatively simple procedure. With a pre-med I.V. to put me under and from what I remember of Dr. Haith's explanation, they were simply going to turn out the room's lights and place an illuminated scope down my throat. From there they would slide it down into my stomach and turn it up brighter like a flashlight. Thereby having the light be able to shine through my skin that was used to pick a target to make the incision into my stomach. Finally, the tube would be forced down my throat and pulled out of the hole, which was just cut. "That's kind of interesting, going inside of me to mark a spot outside of me to cut to pull a tube from inside to outside." I'd be stitched up a bit and let the healing take place around the tube. So when all was said and done I had a long tube hanging out of my stomach. Dr. Haith performed other surgeries on me, one of which was a Foley catheter in my groin so I had full confidence in his abilities.

This new tube was going to be used to give me hyperalimentation or 'hyper al' as commonly known, basically liquid food. There's no doubt that we could have more fun joking about what types of food that I was ingesting through this straw-like apparatus in my gut. "Surf and turf, filet mignon", liquid goo is all that it looked like to me, especially if you got some on your hands and allowed it to dry (or harden). You could peel it like a rubbery and gummy cement substance from your fingers. I wondered what the heck it did in my stomach. I remember having sarcastic thoughts of those cans of fix a flat that you spray in your tires when you get a flat.

I can have no idea of the amount of cases upon cases of this nutrient that I shot into me! Two-Cal, Ensure, Ensure Plus, Insta-Cal and who the heck knows how many others as well, which incidentally, spawned more bill collectors with insurance and account discrepancies. The stress that these callous people induce is unbearable especially when you let them get to you. I had legitimate receipts for bills and coverage for all of this and yet a certain care company still tried to squeeze me for double payments. Only after I had to threaten to get my own law-yer, and send copies of statements along with a doctor's letter did they cease and call off their dogs. Dogs are just about what they were to.

I'm sure that the nutrition helped me but all that I can remember is having a bloated potbelly and still no legs to speak of whatsoever. None of the nutrition appeared as if it had made its way into my muscles and I remained extremely de-conditioned. This was most definitely yet again a threatening period for me physically but especially mentally as well. I mechanically acted out oblivious to the seriousness of my condition but the heart still beat. That motto which I keep inside of me but I was more of a possibly lethargic, serene state of being now, lying in bed waiting for the nurses to arrive and check on me during the day. I 'rested' virtually sedentary and wasted away indefinitely trapped in this web of cancer's residuals.

From the group of home care nurses that tended to me began another home physical therapist named Sue. She attempted to see what she could do to offer her services for me. We would stretch the color bands and do this and that motion-wise but pretty much were not able to make any headway due to my con-dition. I really liked her a lot and our personalities clashed a bit in a healthy sort of way. We were both feisty and headstrong. Eventually we both concluded that the sessions weren't working so she stopped coming over. When that attempt failed I next looked into a local rehab center, which again had high acclaims back-ing it up.

This center was located in the city so a transit service provided me with the transportation. That's a whole other can of worms dealing with those difficulties, but I'd have my mom help me out to the curb where I would be picked up. She and the driver would assist me into the bus and I'd be strapped in and whisked away to this facility. What was to come, as the normal look I would receive from therapists was that of having just seen a ghost. My first consult at this center was with an older man having the mannerisms of an experienced, seasoned therapist.

Looking stooped and dumbfounded as to how to go about initiating some type of rehab for me, his stare was that of bewilderment. I recall being laid out on a table and having weights placed all across my joints to try and physically push them down. During all of this atrophy my joints started to buckle and "freeze up". In other words my knees would not lay flat; they would arch up in a tent-like state. Likewise with my elbows and shoulders, the same pattern arose. The drop foot was for the most part out of the question at this point in time in terms of addressing. Some hot wax was tried but I immediately had to warn the gentleman not to proceed too hastily with this method.

I may not have mentioned this but in Pittsburgh during hot water therapy; my wrists were split open by the pressure that the therapist placed on them during a release technique. Needless to say, I didn't want to go through that again, so I was adamant about explaining this to my latest therapist. Whether or not that made him more apprehensive, I don't know, but we ceased the use of hot wax.

Over the course of one or two more visits I'd say, I was shuffled around to some ignorant seemingly high school students talking about their spring break and how much drugs they did. With no respect or professionalism whatsoever, I'd find myself simply sitting around and waiting for some type of assistance.

I'd finally be shuffled along down the line and eventually being placed on a gurney and wheeled to a whirlpool of sorts. I was then finagled into a sling and hoisted up over what looked like a vat of boiling water. This was terrific though, the transition went smoothly and I remained to stew in there for a good hour or so. It made me think of a Bugs Bunny cartoon where the sliced up vegetables were dumped into the smoldering vat. I just soaked and repeated the instructor's movements that I was given.

The problems began when I was prepared to be lifted back out. Once again the crane-like apparatus swung over me, and the slinged harness was lowered around me in place. I slid into it fine while still in the hot water and prepared to be hoisted up. I was picked up and lifted over the stainless steel tub walls edge, preparing to come down on solid ground again. Something went wrong that was not of my doing since I was held in motionless unable to be released from the harness.

Whatever it was launched me and the harness backward on a decline, allowing me to slide right off and tear my back open on the tubs wall before hitting the floor head first. The middle-aged to elderly lady pleaded with me not to report this or her for fear of her losing her job. The 'great guy' that I am didn't say anything about the matter and was ultimately treated for a staph infection back in the hospital. All of this ridiculous crap just to try to get better and, as I mentioned earlier, you go out of your way to try and be polite. You try to force a smile and be pleasant even when you don't want to be or don't feel good and then things like this happen. I know accidents occur but after a while, I mean, come on.

A big temper tantrum out of frustration had me freaking out and throwing things everywhere. Whatever I could lift (which wasn't too much at that time) but another stupid thing that I also did was to go ahead and rip the peg tube right out of my stomach. I would bet that I came close to having, if not have had, at least one nervous breakdown during all of these turmoil and stress related incidents.

Just a silent stare is all that I can reflect upon from my reflection of symptomatic tendencies during those particular weeks. I did learn something funny though from having an exposed hole through my stomach. It sounds a lot worse than it actually was really. I simply held a cloth over the marble sized opening, nothing gory like you might imagine with massive bleeding or discharges flowing out from the substantial sized cavity. Carol and Dee drove me into the emergency ward and a doctor basically reinserted another line right through the existing hole. Amazingly enough, that's about all that it took with me, as I experienced only a bit of air forcing in with some sensations and about a minute of pressure pushing down on my abdomen. Just like that I was plugged in again and luckily for me, for whatever the reason this time I suppose, since the hole was already there, no scarring took place so that enabled the doctor to do it in that manner.

This was at a time when I found myself back at home and once again bed-ridden for the most part. So just like in times past, the homecare nurses still visited routinely to monitor me. Without having a way to gauge everything that I'd been through for lets say "accurate severity", it very well could have been the worst of times. I just know that it was to the point where perhaps everybody was simply tired of me, and frankly I was tired of myself, especially trapped in this body.

My mother inadvertently sprung on me that there was talk of placing me in a home from the nursing staff, which absolutely freaked me out all the more. After what I had seen and gone through in all of these hospitals, there's no way that I would be taken alive so to speak and go to one of those places. I have nothing against any of these centers per say it's just not something for me, not at that time in my life anyway.

With nothing really to lose I thought that I'd investigate some more into some other types of physical therapy or recovery miracles. I'd come this far and done virtually everything that my mind could conjure up, "You might as well go out trying", I figured. I believe that I contacted the boss of an old gym, Doug, from long ago who helped me at the two previous centers. After explaining the intentions that I had, he referred me to a gentleman that he knew who was still in my area.

I called the number and, upon initially speaking to the answering machine, it didn't take but a second to realize that I had gone to high school and played football with this gentleman. Yet one more full circle link of irony to that quote "It's a small world". This trainer referred by Doug was my friend Greg. We were always friends, although growing up we didn't hang out together but were better than acquaintances. So, after hearing my story, he enthusiastically but reluctantly agreed to come down and see what he could do. I say reluctantly because I don't think Greg knew if there was a lot that he could offer for me. According to my mom, after he first visited me to evaluate the situation, when he was leaving they had a private chat. She pleaded with Greg to please help me but he had a worried look as if he had seen a ghost or something. My mom placed all of this stock in Greg to solve my problems, which only added to his list of pressures to come up with in this life saving comeback of a game plan…

We rekindled some of our funny childhood stories growing up in Chester and discussed to a certain degree what I had been through and what I was going through. He proceeded to tell me what he could attempt to do and what type of goals we could try to set. But clearly from his face you could still distinguish that 'just seen a ghost' of a look which was all too familiar. I'd been used to having all of these pretty ladies working on me, so for Greg to start it wasn't nearly as appealing to the eye. "No offense, Greg", but I did recant to him some of the things that the previous therapist Sue had told my mom. One of which was how de-conditioned I was and the other of which was that she felt that I needed some type of a heart procedure. She was very skeptical as to my recovery prognosis, as was Greg I'd bet, but he didn't let on as candidly.

I recall here briefly taking comfort in the fact that I could go to the bathroom without pain or bleeding despite being so terribly weak. But the next order of business was to yell down for my mother help me off of the seat because believe it or not I was simply not able to get up. That is where I was at this juncture and now preparing to try and improve. Try to imagine yourself being so weak that no matter how hard you tried, you could not get up from the bathroom seat. What was I thinking? What was anybody thinking?

The first area to attempt working on was to try and initiate some type of stretching on the floor. Keep in mind I was almost totally reliant on a wheelchair or being carried at this point. One doctor went so far as to state that I'd probably not walk again. Greg wanted to get me to the point where I could attempt to come out of the house again. On a good day, I could leave my bed and lumber to the bathroom about twenty feet I'd guess.

So with a lot of very hard and tedious effort, we worked in increments of getting to the hallway, then to the front room, then to the front door. From that point right outside, next to the curb, and finally what was at the time a big turning point was literally a walk-up the street and back. This tallied about a hundred and fifty feet or so. Every one of these advances equated to a week or two of work and time from each progression to the next.

After a couple of months of more work, I reached the point where I would have a cane in one hand and Greg assisting me on the other side holding me up. Just like with the flashbacks to the laminar room in Seattle, with those laps and my struggling around the hallways, the peaks and valleys were unbelievable! So, I guess on a positive note, which I could insert here to patients and readers is that no matter how well you recover or how far you fall, it seems as though you can find yourself in the same position over and over again. This, I suppose, could be looked at as a good or a bad thing, but most definitely I would say that if you're that far gone and down so to speak, you'll always know that you have capabilities to get back up once again with that line of thinking. The trick is in staying up there without getting the setbacks obviously.

Greg and I used some equipment that I had and some that he brought as well. We worked extremely hard, I'd say, although I'm one of those people who thinks, that I always could have done better. After several more months and quite possibly closer to a year by now, we transferred our workouts to a nearby Gold's gym. I had worked out a deal with the manager and now friend Jim, who allowed us to work out in there at our own pace. Usually personal trainers are not permitted due to company policy but they waived it for me. The progression to the gym itself brought its own obstacles from a few idiot bodybuilders giving me some flak about being in there but it only occurred a couple of times. For the most part, everyone was cordial and pretty helpful. I made some good friends and got to see a lot of pretty women, which further helped inspire me to keep moving more so than it did to just give up and throw in the towel.

A gluttony of monotonous plateaus was for the most part frustrating and much more mentally than physically. I would work as hard as I could and find myself losing some more weight and strength. The peg tube infusions put ten to twelve pounds back on me but I only tipped the scales at about a hundred and four pounds or so. I think that was potbelly fluids as well, if you ask me; so, obviously I couldn't afford to lose anything at this point. After which, for me, our sessions became so strenuous that I would feel beat up everyday after leaving and just go home to bed. This was normal activity for healthy people's routines so I would simply pray to God that my body would respond and recover like it should have.

The peg tube infusions continued and I maintained the hundred pound scale line so, in that respect, it was something to be pleased about. If I only could have gained sixty more pounds or fifty or forty! I think Greg was a great sport, a true helper and friend. All in all I may have gotten under his skin one time through everything. He was instrumental in getting me back on the right track. Honestly, everybody that I have mentioned played their part in which I don't know if I could have done anything without their help.

Even though I was making some improvements by no means was this any kind of astronomical break through; I don't know how much out of danger you are being a hundred and five pounds as opposed to eighty-nine pounds, but I was walking, albeit not a lot, and I was driving just a tiny bit. I guess that I could also state, although that's stretching it a little, that my quality of life did improve. A little is way better than none at all.

Anything is better than simply living in your bed. So I don't want to come off as sounding ungrateful for those improvements to anyone reading this who may be in the same predicament. I guess human nature gets greedy and every time that you see an improvement you're not satisfied. You want more and more. My goals were to run once again and play ball, etc. Delusions of grandeur, for a total recovery back to what I used to be. In reality, however, that's probably not the case. I'm just now beginning to realize that. That's how hard of a head I have and how irrational my lofty goals have been.

I think that one of the keys could be early realization of how you have got to adapt to what trauma your body has been through and make adjustments accordingly. For me though, unfortunately, it's easier said than done. I would frustrate myself by trying to go out on my own and attempt riding a bike and just fall over, or throwing a ball, or shooting a jump shot or a foul shot for that matter. It all blew up in my face so badly because I was once someone who could dunk a marble or hang on a rim on occasion depending upon the courts and how I felt, to now not even be able to arch a basketball over my head and launch it.

The ego in me was just destroyed. I found myself attempting to do the things that interested me before and as they, one by one, seemed to backfire, I was losing interest for everything in life. The vicious cycle of depression that I keep touching on doesn't just get up and leave when its best friend is frustration. How I admired the people when in their right mind of just being laid-back and easygoing. I remembered a time which I likened myself to them. Friends from high school used to tell me how laid-back I was. What a far cry from where I used to be, to where I now was in this transplant recovery scheme of things.

One of those attempts I made was to have my brother take me up to a Penn State football game. I believe it was Penn State vs. Miami. I found a travel agent that booked us for a 'party train' supposedly. It turned out to be a long 'plain Jane' ride with practically no one on board, only to find us rooming with the Miami Hurricane football team themselves some thirty miles outside of State College. Talk about nightmares! The entire lobby was covered in orange and green, the last lousy thing that I wanted to see! Upon our arrival, I fell off of a transport bus—head first. Thank goodness that my brother grabbed my coattail and the hotel escort caught me or I would have been in big trouble. My legs were giving out and, although the weather was fantastically breathtaking, our game seats had me basking and baking in the sunlight of Beaver Stadium's corner end zone. I was determined to tough it out whether it killed me or not. It just about did, although I escaped any serious complications and enjoyed the trip to a large extent although not as much as I would have liked. It seems that you can never match what your mind's expectations are with reality and physical limitations at times.

We all went up for another game later that year, I believe, with virtually the same thing happening, the weather simply wore me out. This time I had to be carried and then escorted by an emergency vehicle all the way back to our truck, which was eons away in the far end of the mountains fields. Why I placed myself in these predicaments I do not know; I just had a stubborn will to be the old me who wouldn't take no for an answer sometimes. Especially when I was told I couldn't do something—health-wise.

Back home at the local hospital I was scheduled for some type of an endoscopy procedure again. I can quickly give you one of those truly 'great stories'. I was placed in a room when lo and behold the attending nurse was a friend from high school who I used to skate with. Her name was Shelly and she and I talked for a little while. It was just small talk as I got the impression that she was feeling awkward seeing me in my present condition.

As we passed the time away small talking, before I knew it the gurney along with a couple of goons arrived to wheel me down to the operating room. From there I was placed on the cart and trollied down. The biggest problem was that the girl who I was speaking with or someone else there was supposed to give me my pre-med and failed to do so. This was to relax and sedate me but I didn't know anything about it. So here I am lying down in this procedure room when the staff promptly turned the lights off beginning the endoscopy. I was asked how I felt; so, not knowing how to feel I said okay, of course.

With my being restrained a good deal to the table, the doctor started to slide or 'jam' the tube like apparatus into my throat as I recall it. My supposed to have already been prepped and pre-medicated for this was news to me, and my gag reflexes, so of course I immediately began to gag and retch. With the way that things often went for me at this hospital in the past, nobody gave me any type of respect or acknowledged my attempts to stop the procedure whatsoever. It must have registered to them as the difficult patient but it finally took me to free my left hand (luckily), grab the stinking scope and jerk it away from the doctor's thrusts.

My arms grasping force practically slung the scope right back at him once I yanked it out of my mouth. You'd think that the idiot, in seeing and hearing me gagging trying to mumble out some kind of communication to him, would have ceased at once! Or at least cordially incurred as to what I was urgently trying to convey, but no not with me. Only after I escaped so to speak and blurted out that I could feel all kinds of pain, somebody finally came forth and said, "He didn't get his pre-med"...Can you believe this? Stephen King's fiction would be proud coming up with some of these bizarre stories, I tell you. The only problem is that unfortunately these accumulating blunders were real life stories!

With not even so much as an apology or anything, the jerk simply walked out mumbling to somebody to reschedule me again; "Fat chance in hell, moron." That wonderful trip had me leaving with nothing completed on me, or any conclusive results from the initial directive to have it done in the first place. Finally, the old friend nurse that I mentioned said to me, "You have to speak up next time", muttering embarrassingly.

These Mickey Mouse operation blunders go on all of the time I'm sure and just to be fair once again I'll say that there are a lot of good doctors out there too! I just had a knack for encountering some horrible ones sprinkled in between the good ones more times than not.

This was all lousy timing for me as I entered into another horrible phase of my life. It all had to do with my family trying to shield me from bad news. My newly married sister had been sick and complaining of problems here and there that no one would let me in on. "Just keep it from Johnny." Carol's sickness was much worse than I would have ever imagined. It all began with mere small talk of how she wasn't feeling well to her being hospitalized.

When I was finally able to get some feedback as to what was going on, they told me that she either had Non-Hodgkin's lymphoma or some type of cancerous tumor that could possibly be removed. Everybody downplayed it so much, even the doctors, from my point of view and it annoyed the heck out of me. I think now that she should have been in a better hospital that was more qualified to deal with her specific problems but what do I know.

Carol and I talked here and there about it and she was pretty scared. She would make small utterances to me like, "Do you think I'm gonna die?" and the like but, of course, I thought that was absurd and it angered me. I'm thinking, no, don't say stupid things like that. Maybe then she knew more than I did…Carol was in and out of the hospital probably more times than I know but one day we were at her house sitting on the back porch and decided to take a walk. Actually Carol wanted to take the walk. My sister-in-law Dee and I escorted her around the block and I could tell right then that she was clearly not taking this walk well at all from her breathing. She was back in the hospital not long after that in yet another room and I would go daily to visit her still struggling myself to become more mobile and walk better. Actually, the walks through the hospital to Carol's room were more than I had done in the gym at physical therapy with the elevators, the hallways and so forth.

Just like at her wedding, I had to really work hard to stand up straight and get in there and act like I was feeling okay when in fact I wasn't. As compared to my sister, she was in the hospital bed this time around and I wasn't, so who was I to say anything! I just tried to sit with Carol and comfort her as best as I could. Only later did I realize what it was like for her seeing me in the bed having her watching over me. I was the one now overlooking her wondering what I could do to help. It's the worst helpless feeling. Any member of the family that gets hospitalized affects the whole family no matter who's in as a patient or who's next to the bed. Simply stated both situations stink!

A couple of more weeks passed by and then there was talk that Carol would be okay, "just like they said about my dad". Some news had leaked out though along those lines and at the time I felt that it was hearsay. I overheard my mother saying that the doctors opened up my sister for exploratory surgery hoping to get the cancer out but simply closed her back up immediately. Someone said that the cancer had rapidly spread and was too far-gone to successfully accomplish. This doesn't sit well with me at all to this day. I think its all politically correct b.s. and I could then feel the stress just ripping right through me, sucking dry all of the progress I had made and going back to square one. I was mad, I was annoyed, I was frustrated, I was scared, I was exhausted, I was devastated, I was probably antisocial and withdrawn. I was just so angry at the whole world! "F the world", probably was "I".

I got caught so off guard and destroyed one night when I went in to see Carol. Everybody was huddled around and I pulled up a chair to sit right in front of her, when at about that moment she began gagging and choking. No sooner had I gotten there then this all began to occur and no one else appeared as if they were aware of her choking. I'm sure that wasn't the case but no one took this episode as anything different than that which was going on "normally". I could detect a real effort just to breathe coming from the cadence of Carol's mouth.

Evidently she might have been going through this for a longer period of time than I was aware, because as I mentioned the nurses were oblivious to it. I began yelling and screaming at my family and at any body else who was in the way. As hard and as fast as my taut body could try, I trekked to the nurses' station and began cursing everybody out to get any doctor that they could before it was too late. I wanted something done immediately for my sister. I was teary eyed, burnt out and now hoarse from my screaming feeling so helpless. Layers of your inner being die off in not being able to do anything for a loved one.

I had been trying to get arrangements made for Carol to be flown to Sloan Kettering Hospital but with my being who I was "just John", the little baby brother who doesn't know anything, nobody seemed to pay me much mind. At least that's I felt about the issue. I can remember crying, with my radiated body's version of mustered up tears trickling down and sitting in a corner waiting room by myself—feeling just so empty. That feeling of emptiness is difficult to express verbally, but I simply couldn't handle it.

Most everyone was expected to leave within the next hour, so I had somebody drive me home sooner than later. Since I couldn't get anyone to listen to me, there wasn't anything else physically that I could do. I'm sure that I at that time put in some furious personal prayer barrages to storm Heaven. No sooner than I got home and lay down in bed, I just felt that something horrible had happened.

About an hour or so later my mom came in and informed me that my sister had died. I felt robbed. Robbed of dignity and I became disgustingly infuriated! The resentments that I had harbored I guess were focused on my family members, my doctors and God, not really knowing where they were supposed to be directed. Perhaps to myself which, is the perverted and vicious cycle of self-guilt. My thoughts of inflecting all of this on my sister for what she went through in helping me with my fight against leukemia. It does haunt me some with painful anguish in that I possibly took life out of her in assisting me, which she may have used to help herself. I have to really work hard to not let that line of thinking get the best of me.

What was left of the family tried to get through these funeral services with some type of dignity. There really wasn't anything left to give from what we'd been through. I didn't even want to pay respects to my sister. I didn't want to go; I didn't want to see anybody. I refused to believe that this was true. I recall just sitting in the funeral home chair mechanically shaking hands, "Hi, how are you? Thanks for coming" in a somber tone and then thinking, "Next", as people came in to give respects to Carol.

I made my way out into a corner room and then outside I believe. I acted as if I was okay when asked when in actuality; I could have cared less if the whole roof fell in on me. I kept thinking, well, God is keeping me alive or should I say existing, and everyone else is going and I have no understanding as to why. My not understanding all of this is one of my biggest crosses to bear because of how I can let it get to me.

Believe it or not Christmas was only about one week away. It was the worst Christmas ever. It was just empty, or hollow would be a better way to phrase it. There were no feelings, my niece Nicole described it best when she said that it felt like we were all living in a morgue. This thing called life can really pound and pummel you...For a time after Carol was gone; there was a period in which I cannot recollect much of anything. I suppose that it was just another one of those blackout spells in my life memory-wise.

The next orderly recollection had me the following spring somewhere or perhaps into the summer having to go to a dentist for more chronic problems. I had been politely kicked out of my previous dentist's business due to the fact that I wasn't a doctor or lawyer or corporate executive. In other words, I wasn't enough of a high profile type of client, which is what they upgraded to in my stating that politely. I was recommended to a clinic in which I reluctantly agreed to try having my sister-in-law drive me. This visit in itself was an unpleasant experience for sure as I had a significant reaction from the sedative or extra epinephrine or something. Possibly they reacted with all of the other medication I was already taking but, in any event, I became extremely disoriented with a distinct burning in my esophagus among the other symptoms.

I became ridiculously hot internally, perhaps not so much with fever but just wanting to be cooled off. I eventually got so lightheaded that I had my sister-in-law Dee help me into the house and up to bed, whereupon I got a little smart with her enough so to place some friction on our historically up and down but for the most part good relationship. This wasn't what I needed to have happen with the family dwindling down like it was. I think that with over time and our history of family setbacks made things right and perhaps even closer for it. That dental ordeal was overcome with the simple passing of time and the drug reaction leaving my system after a spell. This was as best as could be hoped for at the time I presume, but just the fact that these things kept hitting me without much of a chance to regroup was exhaustingly strenuous to say the least.

I had another one of those engulfing and rejuvenating desires shortly thereafter to try once again to fit in or improve my appearance, mannerisms or wanting to be accepted. This stemmed probably in part thanks to some peoples apparent understanding. Of that handful fraternity, Tom and Dee came to see me one day in the hospital as I had a 'quick' but serious infection to do battle with. I took comfort for some reason in that particular visit. Anyhow I even looked into getting some new clothes and so forth, never realizing how bad I looked at the time.

Nothing that I could ever wear could make me look any different than I was yet this never sunk into my cavernous mind. It's like you can't paint up a dented, beat up old Volkswagen and make it look like a brand new shiny Ferrari. Bear in mind that I never realized this back then, it's just now in hindsight of what a fool I must have made myself look like. When I say fool I should say more like a patient. If a person is chronically ill, the outward appearance more times than not will come off as looking like a chronically ill patient no matter what he or she is wearing.

I 'd spoken with my doctors about possibly trying anabolic steroids, growth hormones or anything to try and get my legs back into some sense of usability. So after researching all of these areas, we started out a trial run by giving me small doses of testosterone cypionate. The levels were then boosted up gradually but still very conservative amounts by any body builder standards. I wasn't trying to be Mr. America just Mr. Claymont as my doctor used to joke. I had met another gentleman named John at the gym after Greg had changed professions. This guy ironically went to the same high school that we did as well. He agreed to help me for awhile in which time we gave it a good run effort-wise, although nothing significant came out of it progression-wise.

All that the steroids ultimately did for me was to increase my libido and irrational behaviors to the point of flirting with practically every lady I would encounter. Thank God I was conscious of this and kept my doctors posted, so as quickly as we initiated the steroids we also fazed them out. One more busted attempt to get my legs back on track. While on the doses of steroids that I was on, I may have gained eight or nine pounds perhaps, getting closer to the one hundred and twenty pound area. As soon as I stopped the use of them though, I deflated back down to maybe one hundred and fourteen pounds.

The feeding tube was gone by now also so all in all, the only thing that I can say is that I made the effort to try these ideas. I quenched the notion of what if I didn't try and this or that would have worked? Now I have an idea and for any other patients in my position, the steroids didn't do too much in the amounts that I was taking. I'd say that you would have to use significant dosages and stay on them indefinitely, risking other residual health problems. Possibly someday I may give them another chance if I cannot induce any significant growth in my limbs by other means and if my legs keep failing. As for the peg tube, speaking for myself I do not believe anything significant was gained in my case. If it did serve a purpose it must have been underlining and subtle. As with my other experiences and observations every patient responds differently.

With my inquisitive theories for improvement I was also ridden with guilt about my irrational behavior fluctuations. My overall demeanor, the mood swings, feeling sorry for myself, being bitter, and being disrespectful to my mother and family etc. One day my brother made the remark that if I ever get better, he wanted to kick my ass, which we both joke about today. "You wish, Tom…ha ha".

I'd go to confession and church searching to get juiced up spiritually to try and keep going on. For awhile it would work. It became a vicious cycle of being content, to getting frustrated, to going back to confession over and over and over for most likely trivial reasons upon reflection. This of course because it was happening to me and I had to insert what I had been through, as the culprit or at least a big part of the reason why; "that good Old Catholic guilt".

I would touch base with some of the people that I mentioned earlier at the Padre Pio center or my friend Paul or other close confidants, to see how they would cope with their own problems relative to them in life. I guess the naïve me learned the hard way that there are no easy answers a lot of the times. Everybody's got problems and that was a bit comforting for me in one sense because it's so easy for you to think that you are the only one going through troubling times, or why me. But in reality everyone's got things to deal with. I'm learning for myself in a stark vivid fashion from what I've been going through that life isn't easy or fair. It just seemed so much more tolerable being healthy in coping with many of these problems.

My future presented many thoughts and questions for me as to where I could go or what I could do in my precarious condition. I was now staying with my mom, not as yet having any way to make a living and most of all not knowing how my health would continue to affect me. Before I became sick with leukemia, I had a lot of delusions of grandeur and real possibilities with my artistic ability and imagination. It didn't really materialize as of yet but I know this was due to the result of my health having a big impact. This wasn't simply a matter of my going out and getting a job as a carpenter, or roofer, or using my physical abilities. Nothing would work if I couldn't use my mind or strength properly. Now having that taken away I had to come up with some other type of way to set some goals of something of which I could attain. I just didn't know what.

I had a lengthy period of a lull you might say, with no problems to speak of health-wise other than simply the plateau of staying in the same condition. So as not to get out of character with this book, it wasn't long before my eyesight started to get cloudy and dark. Everything in my vision eventually began to become muddied, hazy and blurry. I got caught up in a web of complacency once again because it still to me didn't seem to have occurred all at once, and yet I didn't properly recognize or do anything at all about it.

I found that my ability to read and focused things of that nature became more difficult. The color of the sky, the birds, the grass, everything was just eerily fading. So finally, off to the eye doctor's I journeyed again. Initially the diagnosis was cataracts. This was a residual present that I was going to receive from the massive doses of radiation I had to have as well as the chemotherapy. The doctors previously had warned me that possibly as many as sixty percent of bone marrow transplant patients with Chronic Myelogenous Leukemia non-related patients, who survived long term could contract these cataracts. If they were to arise, a routine and relatively normal procedure for most people could repair and restore better sight to the patient, requiring glasses afterward. Of course, I'm not a normal patient let alone a person, so appropriately fitting was the doctor informing me that my condition was a lot more serious than first thought. Why? Because of all of the complications that I dealt with previously and namely the partially detached retina I incurred. The doctor mentioned to me that with those two combinations and the physical condition I was in, he didn't think there was a doctor anywhere who would be willing to touch my eyes and perform the procedure.

Just like the time before when I had the retina problem, we had to go searching for a doctor that would consent to do this cataract procedure on me. It all ended up coming back full circle as the initial diagnosing physician came in to play again. I was able to twist his arm and convince him to do the operation at the nearby hospital. Of course, this wasn't without a lot of major arguing and debating because he was emphatic and adamant about the real possibility of me losing my sight. I had to sell him on the notion that I didn't have anything else to lose with my current vision as bad as it was and my floundering quality of life. That plus the fact that I had to give him legal protection so to speak in the event that anything went wrong he wouldn't be liable.

With those details taken care of we were now going into the hospital for what seemed like the millionth different procedure performed on this body of mine. I'm beginning to wonder if there is an area left that hasn't been targeted on me. It was just a comparatively simple operation with only a few incisions into my eyes themselves, though for safety sake we chose to do one at a time. I prepared as I always did to get up mentally for it and try to do the best that I could and hope for the best. Praying to God although wondering if he was still listening at this point (I'm sure he was).

A bizarre story happened one night when I was laying in bed and for a brief spell could swear that my eyes were healed. I was praying to all of the different Saints to plead to God with me for a miracle and just praying in general, when my eyes seemed to clear up. I jumped up out of bed and hopped on the phone calling the Padre Pio center. The Calandra family, as I mentioned, are friends of mine who run this center. Anyhow, I called excitedly informing them what was going on. I could see fine so I thought. I could see! I could see! I must have been hallucinating or had some freak nerve pressure change or something, because I couldn't see just like that. Talk about an up and down moment! The next morning my sight was a s cloudy as ever. I had everyone's hopes up for this great miracle from God including mine and then evidently, I don't know how to explain what it was, perhaps it was just my emotions getting to me and wanting something great like that to happen. In any event, I know what I saw and then couldn't see, so I still had to go in for the operation.

With the cataract procedures after you get them cut out and removed, you have to keep the eye patch on and clean it several times a day wearing those Frankenstein like goggles. The coolest thing that I remember about the cataracts was that once I was able to take a patch off and look outside the explosiveness of the colors and vivid brilliant light was simply overwhelming. It all jumped back at me instilling a renewed vigor. Although that sensation eventually weaned off, I wished that I could have kept it because it was just such a high. I'm assuming that my eyes acclimated themselves to the light and the seemingly bionic colors became what we all know as being normal.

Although I wasn't totally blind, I would say that I was legally blind. To go from losing your perception and basic vision to regaining it back again was an incredible experience, "and a miracle." I then had my glasses fine tune all of this brilliance and it really made everything almost get back to normal, vision-wise. Other than the fact that I had an astigmatism that prevented contact lenses, the only minor adjustment initially was getting used to wearing glasses for the first time. I now have an expression that I use called 'coming out of my frames'! This is where my eyes move around looking above the outer frames or around them so to speak and the glass lenses themselves not following along. Most anyone surely would accept this hindrance for having eyesight! This transition took awhile to get used to and affects the bridge of my nose in a brush burn manner as far as irritating the skin itself. For whatever the reason this graft verses host condition has made areas of my skin paper-thin. Of course, the bridge of my nose is one of those areas with my luck.

As I am not attempting to reflect upon all of the things as they occurred along the course of my 'recovery', this point of my life in the story has me dangerously frail. I've used that term a few times earlier in my story but it is the best phrase to convey my overall condition to this point. I did seem to hit a plateau or rock bottom with my muscle atrophy combined with roaring mood swings now going way off the Richter scale.

This particular time in my story finds me not improving or really regressing any further in a noticeable manner. I'll never know for sure what damages I incurred consenting to all of those experimental research programs in attempting to alleviate the graft vs. host disease. That's another annoying problem in itself because I torture myself with inner thoughts as to whether I would have been better or worse off not doing them at all. My reverse psychology tactics just reassure my conscience that I wouldn't have been here to debate the issue were it not for my persistence in these endeavors.

With notions such as bad timing coming into play for most people at some point, that phrase had no room in my vocabulary or life. This "thing" which it was didn't need a label because now my last seven or eight years of my life to this point became a virtual existence of nonstop bad timing, always an assault of some kind from one side or another. Now it was targeting my dog and buddy Yuke.

Yukon went promptly from a tenacious half tamed wolf of a dog to a docile and fragment shell of his old self in what again seemed like the blink of an eye.

He clearly didn't seem as if he felt well but it seemed like the type of thing pets can do if they eat the wrong food or have a stomachache and so forth. His K-9 shepherd like ears no longer reached for the sky standing at attention, they now simply bowed out to the sides of his mane. Listless and void of his characteristic personality traits we were fondly accustomed to, it was time to run him into the vets. I should have sensed that there was more to the situation then I did when he couldn't carry his own weight and needed to be bodily placed into the car. I myself had been carried out in about the same fashion only to return home at some point, so I dismissed his harbored body language. I was shook up all right but I didn't think that it was anything that couldn't be remedied.

Eerily similar to the countless times before that I'd been rushed into the hospital only to be experimented on by a student, poor Yuke drew the same straw. Why the hell I didn't see it I'll never know but I placed trust in very questionable hands in my opinion. As the examination began, a drawn conclusion assessed that Yukon was simply dehydrated and needed some I.V. fluids. As any owner would be, I was elated with this news and gladly consented to getting fluids infused in Yukon. Perhaps I'm hostile or resentful and extremely defensive now but this was a supposed prominent animal hospital, not some backyard "R.n. Ellie May Clampett Raccoon Ctr". I'd like to think as a college graduate that I'm not so ignorant as to choose bad care for my pet. Having said that I presume that I did what all good pet owners would do and seek what you hope is the best care for your pet.

Well as I stated, perhaps I'm being too critical but no sooner than this man inserted the needle in Yukons back, the blood just poured forth in a relentless manner. I believe another site was immediately probed for as if a blunder had occurred. The second indiscriminate attempted stick went in but the bleeding was incessant and a giveaway. Such deja vu for me, I just snapped inside and suppressed my anguish. More than a few layers of gauze pads were taped on the geyser to subdue and I'm guessing attempt to clot up the bleeding, while the I.V fluids drained into Yukon at the other site. As that was that, we were told to go home and await improvement.

The problem was and my mother is partially responsible for this, as she stated that she didn't want to upset me, the profuse bleeding ensued later that evening and she never told me. Instead she used a towel to sop up it up. I have to think she was in denial from all of the previous shell shock. The next morning upon my becoming aware of Yukes lack of progress, I rushed him back to the vet where this time he was admitted and tended to. The fact of having to leave him flashed visions of my other dogs Sam and Kong who I mentioned earlier as having lay on the damp cement floors with them.

The day went by and the next afternoon had me being informed that Yuke appeared better by their estimations, so I made plans to come visit him that evening. I had started an art project at my Godmothers daughters house painting Winnie the Pooh characters on her new baby's room, so I went to work. When the night hours arrived I eagerly went over and spent the evenings lying down with Yuke in his cubicle as best as I could. He looked so sad and distant from the old guy who bit me in the chest rough housing what was now some ages ago. I was really choked up and "sinusy", feeling helpless in comforting him. I don't know what they saw in him but he wasn't the same at all. I smuggled him in one or two M&Ms to boost his morale and as best as he could he lapped them out of my hand while still remaining on his side. A couple of "rare tears" emerged on my face when Yukon licked my cheek with some mustered up love he still had to give back.

The time went by and I was asked to leave as I usually remained long after visiting hours. The staff was cordial and seemed very optimistic of his improvement. They stuck to their guns of Yukes being simply dehydrated and now a bit anemic. I recall being emphatic about sparing no expenses to help him, Even transfusions if need be. I just hope I pleaded my case with the right people. The next morning I prepared to go and continue my art project and had my mom phone in and check on Yuke. The reply and news said that he seemed a little better and could come home later on that night. I was so high with joy and relief! It was a happiness I'd not had visit me in many years. What a great sense of weight falling off of me I felt.

I shot down to my artwork site and painted with the fervor that Michael Angelo would have admired. Painting a Tigger never felt so good. The afternoon whisked away as I all but finished the mural save for a few details. I cleaned up and packed my brushes and paints up and was ready to roll. In fact I had the urge just to go straight over to the animal hospital and break Yuke out as early as I could. I believe I asked my Godmother to call my mom to make the arrangements. In the meantime I'd talk to my Godfather about this and that.

Perhaps five minutes or so went by and my Aunt Joann entered the doorway as I smiled over at her appearance. With a somber, quiet and subtle voice, she got out the sentence that "your mom called the vet and they said that they were sorry but Yukon died" WHAT? If you've ever seen the movie The Outsiders scene when Johnny dies and Dally's gonna blow, that's a bit how I reacted to this one. I callously passed by, said good by abruptly and got into my car. The fuse of irrationality just blown was directed right at God.

A grown "man", I broke down and spewed out "verbal vindictives" to my God. I'm sure that it was a continued carryover straw of sorts that broke the camels back but what the "F" I thought. "You punk, you louse of a friend, who needs enemies and so on" The Padre Pio leaflet I had on my dashboard I ripped into shreds. Oblivious to my Godfather seeing this, it devastated him as he was a very faithful and reverent Catholic. I tore up a holy card of a man of God, to him, a blasphemous ritual only something a mob member would do in a make ceremony.

I peeled out of the driveway and tore off my Blessed Mother statue from the dashboard and launched it out the window. I felt so disillusioned and consumed with rage. I would have liked to "not be" then. If I killed myself in my right mind, I'd go to Hell? If I went to Heaven, did I want to see God? If I drove home did I want to see anybody? "I just didn't want to be right then!!"

"All over my dog…? Probably not". This was simply the culmination of all of the events, which kept adding weight to my load of which I wasn't capable of handling or rationally coping with any longer. I imagine that I blew the biggest fuse of my life alright and spiritually it's been a difficult and long road back to stabilizing my belief in "blessed are they who believe and do not see". As well as a few hundred other lines of ambitious scripture for the believer to fuel up on.

I bounced back somewhat after a long, long way coming to acceptance of God not giving you more than you can handle. I envy and admire trying to be like Job. He willingly accepted his cross. I honestly still grumble while accepting mine, which is a far cry between the two scenarios. The breakdown I experienced here humbled me after deep mourning and attempting to heal and move forward someway. I believe that God forgave me if in fact it was sinful in the first place. That doesn't relieve my sadness for my actions but all of the stress, the tons of medicines and canyons of mood swings can go along way in swaying emotions.

I didn't want to come off as sounding ungrateful for my blessings. I know many people are going through worse times than these. I simply wanted to be candid in my behavior and give some insight to those who may not know what trauma and catastrophic experiences can do to a person or patient. A seemingly unrelated issue to a "spectator" can have major implications in the course of life of a traumatized individual.

As time seemed to be flying by in one sense and not moving at all in another, one of the burdening issues was still what I could do with my future. If in fact there was to be a future. At this time I was probably coming close to nine or ten years of a 'recovery', which I had self-deemed as a trademark of an answer when people asked how I was doing. When, in reality, I don't know if you can term yourself as recovering when you're approaching ten years post-transplant. That test of time reassured me just a little bit as to the staying power the bone marrow of 'Jim's' had in me. But at the same time seeing yourself wasting away has you calculating the amount that you have deteriorated in that same time span. Trying to figure out how much longer you could continue going on at that same pace of a slide which becomes a formula of survival versus one of attrition if you will.

I pounded myself consciously about wasting time on futile future plans and would reaffirm my thoughts of simply existing rather than living. The inner voice of 'as long as the heart still beats' could be placed in either category. But hopefully coupled with a sound mind I could rally all of this together into a continued positive outlook. Another attempted mindset to fight and strive to make something out of this topsy-turvy ride through Hell, into some sort of an acceptable life.

I attempted to contact Penn State University and the Art Institute of Philadelphia, both of which I had been a student of prior to my transplant to see what I could do to re-enroll and get my college degree. For starters I didn't know where I could fit in or be accommodated in the job field but I had to do something. Going through the motions to be re-admitted as a student, I was enrolled in the home study program or 'independent learning' as they termed it. I spoke with some counselors and social workers for disability and disabled job networking.

To spare more negative details on these experiences, I'll say that after being shuffled around like a number and re-introduced into different programs, one vocational rehab facility attempted to place me in a position filing papers in an office with other handicapped and physically disabled coworkers. How it is legal, to me I don't know but this program paid three dollars per hour. I recall someone mentioning to me that this was an initiation of sorts to graduate you into the job force. But still I don't know anybody in the U.S.A. that can live off of three dollars an hour. Needless to say, that job lasted about two hours and then I withdrew myself from the program. I decided to take it upon myself and go about this career thing with an independent approach. Perhaps those government programs do work but from my vantage point and what I encountered, I saw failure and red tape loopholes written all over them. Call me cynical but I know what I went through.

During the course of those inquiries, I contacted the local chapter of the leukemia society and for the most part they didn't have any services that were helpful to me. They're big priority is fund-raising but I did agree to attend some of their functions and public fund raising services. I'm sorry to say that I didn't have many good feelings with the particular chapter I dealt with. One of the good experiences I had was in meeting several 'partners' that I was paired up with in their Team in Training campaign. All of who were nice people but in particular was a partner that I had named Jackie. She was a very energetic and bubbly person who would go out of her way to try and make you feel better. I don't think Jackie understood though the magnitude of what I'd been through. I know the local chapters' staff had and has no clue but Jackie at least attempted. She tried to get a feel of what I was going through as well!

During our fund-raising efforts, Jackie and I had some spells of miscommunication with each other, you might say, but all in all I really keep those efforts that she made trying very close to me. I'd say that the biggest memory I have of the Leukemia society DE. Chapter and Jackie back then was a big national function to be held in Disney World. Jackie pulled strings and did what she had to do and then asked me to travel with the staff, her and her son.

Jackie was a great cross-country runner and was scheduled to race in the team in training marathon. This event is held yearly all over the country at different sights and from what I've seen it seems to be very successful. Evidently I was slated to speak at this convention in Disney World itself but it never worked out. I literally boarded the plane from Philadelphia, flew to Florida and was in Disney World perhaps four hours before I became very ill; "The good old frailty of a transplant patient and his or her lifestyle"…"You just never knew when something will flair up or arise."

This alone can stand as my point and example of how difficult it can be to find a position in the work place without being perceived as irresponsible when illness comes calling. What company do you know who's going to say, "Okay, take two days off or a week or even an hour for that matter". Many people have a hard time getting more than a fifteen minute break without being docked!

Anyway, I was able to eat a nice meal inside the park with Jackie and her son along with a couple of team in training runners. We got to walk around just a bit before I had to sit down and collect enough energy to walk back to the hotel room. That also included one ride on the monorail around Disney World's complex but that was the extent of my seeing Mickey Mouse.

Emergency calls were made back home to the hospital and instructions were given to a local pharmacy to get me started on antibiotics. My condition warranted an emergency flight home so Jackie and the coordinator made the arrangements for me. I was wheel-chaired, escorted, taxied and gurneyed onto the plane and flown home where I immediately was taken to the hospital. This time it was for yet another blistering infection. If nothing else came out of that trip, I hope that everyone involved got to see first hand what transplants can do to patients even long after having one. I believe that I volunteered to help out with one or two more fund-raising campaigns but for personal reasons I just withdrew from their program.

After recovering from the latest infection, which was now becoming the norm and mounting up almost weekly, I still couldn't shake a residual bug that lingered with me. At the same time I continued to burn with a desire to rid myself of this graft vs. host disease. I searched for developments in clinical research and especially anything that could possibly improve the muscles in my legs that were just dying off. I also kept in contact with some of my previous trainers and in this particular instance I tracked down Sue again. I wanted her to try a muscle stim unit on them to and hopefully induce some muscle growth. The doctor was all for it but initially we introduced a tens unit to gauge the pain tolerance levels and reflex responses.

Sue stopped over one day and lit me up with some electricity. The feisty "PT" was back and I liked her so much as a person but we just always clashed professionally in the patient/therapist setting. I think she ignited me three or four times in the legs before I freaked out and booted her. I simply couldn't win. Instead of feeling electricity through my legs as I had envisioned, it was more like placing a loaded hornets' nest on them. I think not having the correct calibrations was the culprit but my legs were so frail and thin who would have known what the heck calibrations to set them on anyway! I later found out after buying my own muscle stim unit and spending money that they didn't work on me. At least for my conscience sake I can say I tried it out. "Yet one more bold and desperate attempt without a positive outcome". As far as my legs were concerned, I didn't make any improvement wha:soever.

As I just mentioned the infections were coming in relentless waves by now. There was continued speculation that I harbored a lingering bug that was resisting treatments but that couldn't be proven. I myself, meanwhile, was left with furious and constant sinus problems in a big way. It got to the point where I would start off symptom-wise with a persistent tickle in my throat. That would signal to me the early warning system that infectious bombardment was imminent.

The symptoms would range from my throat tickling to becoming clear, to an all out brutally sore and raw intensity. One side of my nose would clog up and the other side remained open for clear sailing with air pouring in freely almost with a teeth grinding sort of bite. The chirping and whooshing in my ears would build as the fluid was mounting its masses on the front lines. "Just like the old days." In whichever direction I laid my head towards on the pillow I could be rest assured that the sinus fluid build-up would follow suit and pack full throttle to that side.

So as not to gross you out too badly, the discharges were just horrible in color and not pleasing in aroma. It was so persistent and overwhelming that I simply stopped grabbing tissues and used 2-liter bottles to fill instead. How many times I blasphemed using the Lord's name in vain I don't know. I hope that it wasn't as many as I speculate in that frenzied state of mind. I'd rather hope that it was taken as prayer to just help me with this demoralizing pounding that may have broken my spirit again. As we discussed earlier about the Lord not giving you more than you can handle, so I believe that He understood my heart those times. I reasoned that it must have been better to rid myself of the mucous instead of keeping it in but then again I don't know if it would have even mattered. My body kept producing and producing this mess. I simply couldn't find a medicine to work or way to shut it off! I would collapse in exhaustion from the physical demand these onslaughts would place on my body.

I was a bit concerned in hindsight that none of my doctors ever established any kind of testing or inquiries as to why this was going on in the first place. I'd simply be given an antibiotic prescription and that was that. Some physicians in fact wouldn't even go that far except for Dr. Mike and perhaps one or two others.

The infection would run its course so we thought, but it got to the point where I'd get a ten-day cycle of twenty pills, five hundred mgs. of this or that. I'll beat a dead horse, in hindsight it's easy to see how this pattern could go on like this but when, in fact, it was continuing over and over and over for months and months I never put those factors together, just always trusting or accepting. Here I am telling everyone to be alert, ask questions and don't always trust everything you're told and I myself was at fault here, "at least partially anyhow", for these very same reasons.

I'm almost afraid to say what I'd like to coin as the 'drive thru' McDonald's mindset of doctors. "Just so busy and impersonal, not taking or having the time for that matter to give genuinely concerned care." I've got to live with this stuff and they can punch the time clock and go golfing, leaving works problems, which are my real problems, etc. I could very well be off with this feeling but as you will soon see, I do have a good selected case mounting for my basis of aggravation.

I'm going to move along here because basically what ensued during this time frame in my life was just that, constant sinus infections of the horrible magnitude mentioned. So much to the point that one day, while doodling in my notebook,

I had a whim to call the drug store and see about acquiring a computer print-out of my prescription history. Once I found out that this was possible I had them pull up the last three years. After highlighting all of the prescribed antibiotics and attempting to formulate some type of pattern, I realized that there was only one pattern—constant illness!

There wasn't a particular day of the week that stuck out as an indicator of when I would call in for the antibiotics. If there would have been I'd then planned on going back and see if my habitual patterns were indicative with picking up a bug. That wasn't the case as every day had its share of prescription pick-ups. It was simply month after month after month of these constant infections. Cipro, Augmenton, Ampicillin, Amoxicillin, etc. etc.

As embarrassed as I am to mention this, I'm equally embarrassed that this is all true. There were almost thirty infections in thirty-six months on the printout chart. That's in three years, so it doesn't take a rocket scientist to do the math. I may as well have been eating antibiotics like candy. How the heck can nobody be aware of something like this going on? It's not simply a doctor or a group of doctors; I was seeing many, many doctors. Did they simply dismiss this as a graft vs. host disease commodity? I'd really hate to think that it was because they didn't care.

After all, most of the mortality rates among graft verses host disease, bone marrow transplant patient survivors are attributed to infections. But did anybody besides me ever take a good look at the patterns of my charts? And why was I out to lunch on this for so long while enduring such beatings from these disgusting infections? Was it because I became too complacent or was I just a disparaged soul confused to the point of being consumed in a fog?

I'd been having some dental problems most definitely as a result of the radiation weakening tissues in my mouth. I had already become too familiar with the cut scars in my cheeks from the mucousitis I had incurred back in Seattle. But now with these 'minor' dental problems posing potential infection areas, this couldn't be ruled out as a possible candidate as to why I was getting sick all of the time. Due to the nature of my sinus problems however, and its disgusting nature I might add, I had to believe that's where the source of the problem stemmed from.

In looking for an answer to my problem which quite frankly having been accustomed to living this way, I picked up some ridiculously quirky habits of compulsively moving furniture in my rooms. The weekly family dinners on Sunday would always include a joke or two of where my furniture was this week. I'll admit that I was climbing walls and still do from time to time and I probably enjoy a change of scenery so to speak now and then, but I had never been this erratic before my bone marrow transplant. The artist in me has always done eccentric things here and there but I'm talking about moves weekly to daily at this point. It got so bad that my brother-in-law Harry would joke to me and say I was ahead of my time and that the future interior decorators and designers will build houses and furniture with wheels to accommodate those types of frequent moves.

Moves and moods, my swings were all over the place again—full circle back to the crazy "psycho man'. Once again in a rut looking on all of the things that I wished I could have changed. Thinking about what this insidious disease Graft verses Host was doing to me, and how it now monstrously overshadowed Leukemia by leaps and bounds, when you broke it all down to how I actually felt physically, spiritually and mentally.

All of the stinking drugs, Cyclosporin, Cellcept, Methatrexate, ATG, Interferon, Imuran, Myleran, Hydrea, Vancomyicin, Amphetericin, Cypro, Amoxicillin, Ampicillin, Prednisone, Medrol, Demoral, Benydryl, Busulfate, Bactrum, Zoloft, Prozac, Ativan, Paxil, Elavil, FK-506(prograf), Thalidaminde, Psoralin, Morphine, Oxycontin, M-s contin, Testosterone Cypinate, Heprin, Dilantin, Versed, Buspar, Megace and on and on and on and on!. I'm positive that just as many drugs, which I have mentioned here, there are that many more that I have skipped! Plus all of the massive chemotherapy and lethal doses of total body irradiation, how can that not have severe adverse reactions on your body, on your psyche, your mood swings, endocrine functions, spirituality and so forth? It's just as if I'd become a toxic waste site, with legs…

All of the stories, all of the people I hurt—the feuds with my father, the disregard, the self-worthlessness, the ups and downs, the hate and disgust, the sorrow, the anxiety, the compassion, contrition, and the confusion! Complacency although rare, all blended in, was to be known as the stare I'd give frequently when people would just perceive me in the wrong manner.

I really dislike the sayings, "If you'd walk half a mile in my shoes", or "You don't understand", or "It's all relative". With a degree in psychology I still haven't found the words or a way to express what I'd like to convey. Though that's the case God still keeps me going and I've said to my mother, sometimes I do wonder why the good Lord didn't take me back in Seattle. I say that because I felt so close to Him then, a closeness that has been unparalleled in my life to this point. Now that I am still alive and existing, sometimes I feel as though my sins accumulate like the national debt sign that keeps rolling over. It's one of my biggest challenges to still hold on to my strong faith and after seeing what I have been through and how I have survived all of this, why should I have the audacity to even question things.

The expended blown wind that was just these few previous paragraphs are thoughts in my mind which come and visit me at least a couple of times a week. I don't know that you can address them per say, you simply deal with them when they arise, reflect upon them and attempt to move forward somehow.

Getting back on track, one day had me call another hospital with a bone marrow transplant unit that I had not dealt with in the past. Upon discussing matters with a bone marrow transplant coordinator, I was given the name of an ear, nose and throat specialist by the name of Dr. Teixido. In order to see him for a consult It would take several months due to the extreme popularity of his services. Upon finally getting in and being evaluated by Dr. Teixido, early words coming out of his mouth sounded like optimistic music to my ears. He immediately could tell that there was severe damage in my sinus cavities, while I answered his questions if I've ever had work done to them previously. I discretely tried to slip the sinus tap debacle with the phone receiver story to him and, once I did, you could see the light bulb go on over his head as to how I got so messed up in there in the first place. His rebuttal I recall was something like, "That's why it looks as if you've had a diabolical procedure performed on you".

He informed me that he could operate on the internal cavities in my sinuses that would have in his opinion a great impact on the decreased rate of my recurring infections. From the time that the "Mr. Magoo" doctor destroyed my nose with that Flintstone's type of sinus tap "procedure", the scar tissue, which reformed literally blocked up the natural draining process that we're all supposed to have occur. The sinus cavities simply had nowhere to drain whatsoever! The fluid would just mass and build up to the point of exploding while leaving me as the victim.

The deviated septum as many of you probably called it is the procedure that comes closest to describing this repair job here. I eventually was admitted to Christiana Hospital whereupon I had my deviated septum "un-deviated". This was absolutely no fun either. If you have ever had your nose severely broken or re-broken you know all too well that besides the pain comes the blood and long term major clotting. The shunts up the chute, the Waterpik attachment to blow salt water through each nostril for two minutes a side five times a day and the repetitive healing residue to put it nicely, etc. This ritual continued for about three months post-op also, so my cavernous cavity of reconstructed roadways became, hopefully for me, the highway for clean air and little to no infections.

This recovery period was more aggravating than painful. I simply had to wait it out and allow my body to heal itself to see the results. All of the follow-up visits showed that the doctor was pleased with the work, which was done on me. Now it was up to me to go live and see how I'd make out with regard to infections. I sarcastically joke with my friends sometimes that God above and His associates must keep a Rolodex with my name in it. I may have mentioned that earlier in the book but it seems as though whenever things begin to go well my name gets pulled out by some one above reminding them to 'give me a zap in the tush to bring me back down'.

CHAPTER 8

▼

I literally went almost a whole year after my sinus cavities were operated on without getting sick. I couldn't believe what I had lost and missed in living! A good portion of the burden with my being perceived as miserable and moody could now be placed squarely on the shoulders of those horrible sinus infections. It's a true miracle in itself that the infections alone didn't kill me. I can honestly say that I was never 'healthy' ever at any point in time after initially incurring that sinus damage. I was living sick thinking that I was feeling the best that I could feel after a transplant when, in fact, this was not the case at all. I just became accustomed to what "feeling well" was, when in fact I didn't know that I could be feeling so much healthier. My version of what well was simply a lesser degree of being sick. That is until Dr. Teixido fixed my sinuses.

I could feel such a noticeable improvement that it went to my head. 'No pun intended.' This is funny because it just happened fairly recently but I would go bragging to everybody how I hadn't been sick since February 28, 1996. I knew the exact date since the last time that I had been sick up until that point. It was a year at least! Although initially after the operation I would hold my breath feeling like 'here it comes, I'm going to get sick, I'm going to get sick', but it didn't happen. I probably came close to feeling like all of the healthy people who are reading this because if you don't get sick with those types of infections that often, you cannot know how it would impede and collapse your lifestyle.

Unfortunately I had to find out sooner or later but as Aerosmith sings in *"Dream On"*, 'You've got to lose to know how to win'. I can certainly apply this analogy to my infections. If I didn't know what it felt like to be so helplessly pinned down by perverted sickness, I couldn't appreciate feeling well on a normal day as being anything other than what it was—not nearly as much. Everyone needs something to compare things to sometimes.

Occasionally I would reach for the Waterpik nasal hookup to shoot up my nose due to some psychosomatic skeletons. Although my boasting of not getting sick wasn't all in seriousness but also in jest, I did however confidently let anyone asking how I was doing know about it though. That's when the Rolodex cue card came in.

A quiet calm before the storm that I didn't even suspect was creeping in silently to slam me though. One late evening in what started out as a very subtle ear throb exploded into a vicious pounding and culminated into a bloody ruptured eardrum. I was paralyzed by the pain, strewn out down on the floor as a grown man in the fetal position and groaning for my 'mommy'. Not even my old standby M-S-Contin, which is a morphine derivative, could fend off this piercing onslaught of barbaric proportions. The crescendo of pain leading up to the bursting pop was the fiercest I'd know in years most certainly. Just when I'd given you my charted analysis on all of the types of pain that I'd been through, then this new front runner of an entry comes along...

Perhaps my pain threshold isn't what it once was, I don't know, but this pain was brutal. Then when I saw the blood trickling out of my ear all over my pillows I definitely blew a fuse and panicked crashing to the floor. First of all, I couldn't hear anything out of my ear. I rushed in to see my doctor and waited for what seemed like hours in the waiting room, holding cotton up to my ear, which had coagulated to a crusty barrier by then. So, really once I got in he examined the scabbed up area and simply smiled. "You've just ruptured your ear drum", chuckle, chuckle. I muttered something serious to him like this isn't "F"ing funny—what are you laughing about. But his laugh was not one of a humorous nature; it's just that he had experienced one himself and seen a hundred others before and knew the likely outcome of what it would be for me.

He directed me back to the doctor who had done my nose work since he was an ear specialist as well. Upon visiting him he lanced the eardrum again which totally rotted but was needed in order to relieve the additional building pressure. The only theory we came up with after retracing my patterns was that possibly the 'Waterpiking' produced a residual water backup that made its way from the sinus cavity to the ear canal—thus the ear blowout. I was given antibiotics, so forth and so on. That itself took a couple of weeks to resolve itself pain and hearing loss wise. I would say that my hearing now is about ninety to ninety-five percent of what it used to be but to tell you the truth I'm ecstatic with that. I actually wasn't aware that hearing can come back at all after a ruptured eardrum. Maybe

that's why Dr. Mike snickered. He knew that more than likely it wasn't as traumatic as it appeared to me. I never really had an earache in my life, so that stands
to reason why I became so paranoid in this particular instance.

I'd grown somewhat accustomed to being vulnerable to many things. Just
being in the company of a baby or child, sitting and dining in restaurants, people
coughing in public, people smoking in public, etc. I won't even begin to speak
about second hand smoke as that would be a another whole book to write but
you get the idea of how patients come to see things as being a possible danger to
them! I mean you have to live. You have to go out and try to make something out
of your life. When you have these inner voices of previous experiences conveying
how susceptible and prone you can be to injury, infection, and public scrutiny,
I'll toss that in there as well, after undergoing a transplant, especially when fighting graft versus host disease to boot.

With my lifestyle having taken shape to represent the chaotic ups, downs and
in betweens of which you've grown accustomed to reading thus far, this story still
has a bit more windy roads to travel. During my Walt Disney World trip, which
I previously mentioned that ended suddenly due to a raging virus, one notable
coincidence did occur. On my flight home, to pass the time as best I could, I
browsed through the familiar airline magazine strategically located in the kanga-
roo pouched seat directly in front of me. As sick as I felt and not really paying
much attention to the pages, a quick glance at an ad for a correspondence university was duly noted. California Coast University offered an opportunity for me to
transfer my Penn State and Art Institute of Philadelphia credits and initiate
enrollment in the B.S. of Psychology degree program, of which I did. After a brief
gathering of my transcripts, letters of recommendation etc., I was accepted and
began my courses.

With my health being as fragile as it was this was the perfect alternative and
solution to finishing school and getting my degree. I wasn't able to physically
attend classes on a regular basis, so this long distance program enabled me to do
all of my core work in the confines of my home and if need be attend the local
PSU campus for a proctored exam. Once I became acclimated to the workload
I'd say that it took me a little under two years to graduate and "receive" my
degree in psychology. This was in itself a big personal victory of sorts, if for no
other reason than a completion of my schooling up to that point. I felt that all of
my previous education left in limbo due to the leukemia was now not in vane. If
I never use the psychology as a career at least it is a useful tool in my life of daily
interactions with others. Like I mentioned it's a nice feeling to have completed
what I started now many moons ago especially under the awful circumstances of

which to do them. For the record nobody in my family ever really congratulated me for my neat little accomplishment. I was bummed, but hey it's all good...

My health remained a time bomb of nitroglycerine ticking and set to blow at the slightest wake of disturbance. My flare-ups and or infections would play peek-a-boo and hide and seek on a daily basis. I went in to the doctors probably at this point about once a month unless trouble was brewing. I could drive, I could walk and "interact" so to speak socially and I could pull off a pretty mean smoke and mirrors act to "fit in" socially. I'm sure that I didn't look the part of Carrie Grant but in this stretch of time, I was okay enough with myself I guess to attempt the first real stab at getting back into the "mainstream of life". This by no means meant that I felt great I just think that the sense of urgency and panic set in to a greater extent.

My brother called me one day and asked me if I thought I was up for the challenge of trying a job that had been brought to his attention. His friend Ralph Nagle held a flexible position at a prominent super market food chain in the area. Ralph asked my brother if I might be interested in a unique kind of position available in the company so he asked me. As an independent contractor I would be responsible for going to competitor's stores and comparing prices. I would be a "spy" of sorts and gather virtually every price of every item that you could think of. From woman's products to ice cream you name it. Some of the other competitors had their own infiltrators working covert operations in the company for which I worked as well but not many.

Once I met Ralph and became pretty good friends with him actually, he and I prayed for my continued healing and things of that nature. His son was dealing with some health related issues as well. When I became familiar with the methods of operations my job entailed I set off for my initial outings. The distances varied from ten to thirty miles from home each way and consisted of me having a big logbook, filled with the top levels needed information. I would have a week or two to complete my inventory tasks and could come and go as I pleased as long as I acquired the price comparisons. Some of the irony to my travels was the various people that I knew in the competitor's stores, other words employees who knew me. My cover was blown and it wasn't soon after that, until I would be confronted by the "enemies'" bigwigs". Many of these people had worked for my brother in his previously owned supermarkets.

When the dust settled I was able to do my work in some of the stores but always had the feeling that "big brother" was watching my every move. The job itself enabled me to work around my feeble health. Some days would have me work a half an hour before getting into my car and making it home to bed. Other days I found myself being able to stay on my feet for several hours at a time. This job didn't really pay much and only lasted I'd guess six to eight months in retrospect but I did enjoy the overall experience it provided me.

Ultimately this position was phased out due to the competitors not allowing me in to spy on the prices. The reason being the company I worked for wouldn't let anybody in to do them, that which what I was doing to the competitors. I couldn't blame those food chains for banning me if they didn't have access to the same information. A real cut throat business those food chain wars. This brief attempt to get back into the workforce turned out to be a good experience for me overall. As frail as my health was I did get to socialize and "wet my feet" so to speak and see what it took to get the job done. In other words I knew where I stood physically in the scheme of things. My conclusion was that I still lacked much of the stamina and mental longevity needed to participate on a consistent basis.

The fact that my position was being eliminated probably became a blessing in disguise. Perhaps a week or so later I was struck down once again by a severe flair up. This time my symptoms were not so much of the "physically ill type" but more so related to the extremely weak kind in nature. Basically it came down to being bed ridden for virtually the entire day, for days at a time. The Epstein Barr Virus was suspected but never conclusively diagnosed. The thing about my transplant related complications were that they manifested themselves in so many different forms, that it became almost impossible at times to diagnose me properly. I have mentioned this earlier but I could be showing the symptoms of several concrete black and white conditions and yet not have the apparent perceived condition. This is something that I believe set me back time and time again.

With the bedridden weight bearing on my psyche and atrophying muscles, I again lost any of the ground that I may have acquired during the brief work tenure. One day while lying dormant in the body but being restless in the mind, I furiously rampaged mentally to come up with something else that could rescue me from this awful predicament. I could always take more doses of Medrol, which would inevitably boost me up physically to methamphetamine levels. "Fake energy" you might say. Some would argue that energy is energy and if you can get an advantage go for it. I was somewhat fortunate in that I could count on a physical hop up off of my Medrol anti rejection medicine doses. In fact I only took four mgs. daily to "control" the GVHD

Of course every action has the reaction and the Medrol has nasty and devastating side effects right along with its usage. Over the course of about thirteen years now and counting at this point of my story, the long term side effects evoked on me from the Medrol were severe muscle atrophy or "muscle waste" as known in the medical field. Secondly was the cataract damage to my eyes, which I mentioned. Unfortunately the side effects from long-term use of these catabolic steroids went further than these prominent two that I spoke about.

I could speak at length about the pros and cons of Medrol and Prednisone use. I won't do that but I wanted to try and briefly explain scenarios of why I couldn't just pop the Medrols. In fact in retrospect I overstepped my bounds with that drugs use and caused my body much more harm than good. At least that's how I feel about it. You could make a case for the half full, half empty glass analogy that if I hadn't of taken the amounts that I did, perhaps I may not be alive writing this story today. In any event my main point that I wanted to emphasize here is that with the graft verses host disease and the symptoms, which it can manifest, the situation becomes a terrible catch twenty-two. If I were to increase my doses of Medrol in this particular situation, I would increase my energy level most assuredly but at the same time be damaging my body in the long run as well creating more of the extreme fatigue and lethargy conditions which I sought the medicines use for in the first place!

I liken this vicious cycle to a living entity that in a science fiction movie may bring a quick reward for the drug use. Giving a boost of remarkable energy initially, and after a moderate to lengthy high, the side effects bloom into the very symptoms of weakness, which you are attempting to fight. It's like a self contained virus that cultivates its own existence.

Having attempted to give you some idea of the Medrols' web of addictive vice, my thoughts from bed had me scan the remaining hospitals that I had not been to for any treatments. I thought to myself if any centers were doing anything or similar to for that matter to Fred Hutch in Seattle. In hindsight I should have simply relocated to Seattle where I felt most secure in the quality of care I received. Well I didn't do that.

This was about the time when my friend Kevin or my brother Tom gave me a modest second hand computer to use after they had upgraded. I believe one of them helped me go online and do a search for leukemia, bone marrow transplants, graft verses host disease, treatments etc. I eventually made a lay mans version of an outline from what I could gather as being pertinent to my situation. I obtained addresses of several prominent centers this side of the Mississippi and began to formulate a game plan of who to call, what to ask and what protocols were being offered if any. I ended up narrowing my inquiry options down to two or three centers after a lengthy thought process.

After deciding on the center I had in mind to contact, I prepared my thoughts and simply broke down what was a lengthy spiel into a simple sentenced inquiry. Something on the lines of, can you tell me if your facility is currently doing any active ongoing research on graft verses host disease and related complications? One particular center piqued my interest as I found out that they in fact were doing ongoing research on bone marrow transplant patients, long term survivors and graft verses host disease etc. The only problem was that the usual waiting period to get in for a consultation was about several months. Whether or not I happened to lucky with whom I was speaking to on the phone, after I explained my situation and that I had my transplant now some fourteen years ago at Fred Hutch, I was told that they would get back to me. Actually I received a phone call later that day asking me if I could be there in a week. I was very surprised at the immediate attention I received. I made the tentative arrangements and agreed to go stay at the hospital for about a week's stay of consisting of consults, workups, evaluations and so forth.

These entire sudden fast moving scenario's unfolding after what seemed like "a forever of nothingness" without any progress was once again a strange pace of a change to get used to. My initial trip down to Baltimore was in itself a surreal event. I traveled alone and had most of the time consuming my thoughts with everything I had already been through as a person and a patient. I think I had my brother drop me off at the train station and I window seated my trip reflecting on everything while staring out of the tinted glass. What seemed like the millionth trek to wherever for whatever had gotten so old by now that it was a part of who I was, whoever I was. I still had a lot more of the apprehension and fear factors than the optimistic and at ease sensations I'd much rather have been harboring inside. My past track records really didn't give me much with what to work with either for that matter, but it was about all that I had to go with for a shot at a recovery and better quality of life.

My train ride lasted only about forty-five minutes to an hour at most as I recall and with it being my first day into the city itself, I took a cab ride right to my assigned outpatient hotel. I believe the name of my hotel was the Hackerman House, a very modest and quaint patient home away from home respite. I found the people there to be compassionate, friendly and as understanding as they could be under the circumstances. My room consisted of nothing much more than a bed and a dresser with a rest room in the front. I brought an alarm clock and a radio luckily. In order to watch television the tenant had to go downstairs into the community living room. One of my funny memories was watching Mother Angelica on EWTN late one night and thinking of the irony with my being

Catholic and watching a Catholic show in a Jewish run outpatient facility. It actually was quite peaceful that evening, the calm before the storm so to speak.

All of my impressions of the employees at Johns Hopkins Hospital and the people I encountered in Baltimore were virtually all very positive. I'd say that about nine out of every ten interactions with people were great and I was impressed with those odds. I even ate a Roy Rogers dinner with a homeless man one night while walking around trying to get myself a decent meal. We only small talked a bit but I was humbled by his politeness and appreciativeness. He was nicer than a majority of "well to doers' you or I typically encounter in our everyday lives.

Once I had registered and "settled in" so to speak, my itinerary called for a serious of mini consults from which we could formulate a game plan to work with. The initial meeting consisted of two doctors and a mediating head nurse. We compiled a general history of my leukemia and everything that was seen as relevant to my case. In retrospect I wish that I could have a giant wall chart to show me exactly just where I was with protocols and progress etc. but as it stood, I think it boiled down to something like a seven step outline for my particular case. It is easy now to reflect and be opinionated but back then or when a patient is in the trenches it couldn't be further from the truth. Opinions and decisions get lost in the shuffle, which again is a critical need for a patient to have help in those timeframes. Regardless of how well intentioned some medical staff members may be, the tendency to get overburdened and overwhelmed with patient to doctor—nurse ratio can't be ignored. Initially I didn't see this as a problem and consented for the most part to all of the ideas they had for me.

One of the biggest pressing issues was to determine if in fact I still had GVHD or not. This was a critical initial problem for me that I feel I dropped the ball with, because in my case there was no concrete way to conclusively tell whether or not I had active GVHD. Yes, lip, skin and in some instances muscle biopsies could be performed but it is an inexact science in the big scheme of things. What I mean by that is a biopsy result could show residual scarring, active GVHD at the site or no present activity at that particular site. You could have made a case back then by simply looking at me and visually diagnosing me as having GVHD, perhaps even today as well. It's simply not that easy though as I have mentioned.

There was such a heated debate right off the bat between the staff members as to whether or not I had GVHD at all. In fact I recall going back and forth with several doctors and their theories of why or why not. Writing this now upon reflection is unsettling to me but some five or six years ago it went right by me. I could look at myself and feel physically that I was a long way from being okay, so

I simply attributed it all to GVHD. I guess this was a school of thinking that was embedded in me somewhere along the transplant lines. If blood work could show that I was "normal" in all mechanics of function and now cancer free, it could seem logical to attribute everything else symptom wise to a graft verses host effect. How I wish that I would have challenged that line of thinking back then.

Anyhow, things had gotten off to a very good start for me and I had a genuine sense that this staff was taking a sincere interest in my case. Again the biggest problem for me was the decision making. Some theories were being given to me as to why they thought this or why they thought that and so forth. For the short term I didn't need to make any hasty decisions so I continued with some further breakdowns of my protocols. One area that could be investigated concretely was my endocrine levels. What I feel now as being perhaps the single largest factor in contributing to most if not all of my physical problems. Again, at the time this was not registering as a significant area for me to pursue and I probably am to blame if anyone can be. I simply focused so much energy in areas that I thought were of concern when in fact I missed my mark. Not with effort but with the target.

I believe that I've mentioned I'd been taking synthetic Prednisone or Medrol as known in medicine for some thirteen years straight up to this point. If I could go back and change one thing medically or "medicinally", omitting this drug would be the one. I believe that I elaborated on some of my Medrol setbacks earlier with the cataracts etc. To my knowledge, no bone marrow transplant patient is ever kept on a constant protocol of Medrol. In no way am I being critical of my home physicians, it's just so painfully hard to now see all of the major damage this drug did to me. With my symptoms being so bad and the Medrol seemingly bringing me back to life on false energy, anyone could see this as a logical alternative. As I alluded to previously, the Medrol use gave me false energy and masked the real damage it was causing me internally.

Well I may have beaten a dead horse by now with this extended use of catabolic steroids but the fact of the matter remains that it was and is a critical hurdle for my body and mind to overcome. In the course of the protocol evaluation breakdown, getting an appointment set up with an endocrinologist was one of the most important issues. As a matter of fact it was my second exam. I was scheduled and got to see Dr. Adrian Dobbs, a well renowned and highly regarded endocrinologist in the area. Upon our consultation, she set up a battery of related thyroid tests among one of which was called an ACTH stim test. This turned out to be a critical targeted area to pursue. The test could determine how much if any cortisone and adrenaline, etc. my body was producing on its own.

When the first results came back in they revealed that my body was not producing any of these chemicals at all. The glands or mechanics in the body that go about producing these hormones and chemicals had been shut down from all of the years of drug use. My body was now relying on the drugs exclusively to function. The task at hand was now to try and ween me off of the Medrol in such a way as to not cause my body any more undue harm. This would entail a lengthy timeframe of some months of testing and tapering.

One of the things that irked me and seemed to fit right in with what I'd grown accustomed to was the fact that no facilities in my area could or would do these simple blood tests. I couldn't believe it! I mean nobody when I say it. All of this meant that I had to commute to Baltimore once a week for a simple blood draw and result. I know that's not such a big deal but it sure added to the complexities of everything because as I said earlier, this was only one facet of the "recovery protocol game plan".

Without elaborating on the timeframe it took to get me off of the Medrol after all those years, I'll condense those experiences and say that ultimately I was able to do so. My body once again began producing cortisone, adrenaline, etc. I have a personal theory that with transplant patients, simply because a blood test result can show a "normal" count number, to me does not mean that those cells are in fact functioning properly. I bounced my thoughts off of my home oncologist Dr. Mike and he agreed that my theory could be possible.

Trying to articulate this segment of my story is a bit challenging. Attempting to keep the reader abreast of all of the intricacies that the doctors had going on with me is difficult for me to keep exactly in chronological order; that as well as my ups and downs at the particular time. For example this brief explanation of my endocrine situation was one complicated and serious matter to address but it was only one cog in the sprocket so to speak. As one defined targeted area was being worked on the other "levels of things to try and fix" were going on simultaneously.

A perfect segue for this would be my very first official doctor appointment once the listings had been formulated. I was to see Dr. Dermott Moore O'Feral, at the time Professor of Medicine at Hopkins. Most likely after the spinal tap gone horribly wrong incident I discussed earlier in my story, that's when my legs stopped working properly. So it was determined that Dr. O'Feral may be of some help to me in a diagnosis and or treatment. Right from the beginning this visit had mess written all over it. Upon my arriving to the particular hospital examining room and going through the undressing, gowning up and sitting on the steel table with the paper towel ritual, I immediately began to freeze. It had now easily passed my appointment time and my patience was wearing thin. My itinerary had me scheduled to be across the hospital for my next appointment within the hour now and still no word from anybody as to where the doctor was.

I iced over this table for yet another hour which would end up being literally a three hour wait until Dr. O'Feral arrived. My appointments for the day were shot. I can understand emergencies and contingencies but with me I feel so much rides on respect. Here I am trying to muster up some positive waves and look for hope in a recovery somehow and not one single person could even check in on me or fill me in as to an update of what was going on.

In any event, what I would now place into the staff being overloaded or spread to thin category, things finally materialized into the much anticipated consult. With everything having previously gone so well my first impressions left on this doctor and his protégé were miscalculated. After having been left out on the gurney to freeze for so long I was in no mood to be bubbly and cordial at this point. I felt that it was disrespectful to leave me in a room with no directions at all and I was going to let them know it.

I don't recall being given a reason as to their tardiness but the recollection I do have was my profound statement that put me behind the eight ball for time, sanity and what else first impressions. After a lukewarm introduction I made the simplistic and sincere statement that "this was my last attempt by a doctor to get well". With that the kiss of death was placed upon me and I was banished into the difficult patient category for what seemed like the rest of my tenure to some degree.

Things resumed with this particular consult such as motor skills walks, hand eye coordination, background information, range of motions, etc. Everything seemed cordial and respectful after the smoke had cleared. It wasn't until this appointment was over that I was informed that I'd have to see one of the staffs social workers and psychologist because of what I had said earlier. What I said earlier, what did I say earlier I thought? My whole brief sentence about this being the last attempt to get well through a doctor was I feel taken totally out of context and how I'll never figure. Doesn't anybody factor God into the mix anymore I fumed inside? Doesn't anybody factor in the fact that I'd been doing this now for some fourteen years of my life. Why does this simply get shuffled into a line of thinking that I was irrational in my statement as best as I could figure.

I was placed in a slot I presume that I was suicidal and in imminent danger to myself, when in fact I was just expressing the truth which was fueled by a very late and freezing appointment that's all! There's a huge difference from someone willingly attempting to improve and someone who just shuts down. My feelings were genuine in my mind when a time comes where you explore all of your options and decide what the best strategy is for your particular predicament. That may or may not include going home and placing your faith in God to see things through. To me it's not rocket science. I could possibly see being stereotyped or misread if I was just out of the gate with many options to pursue but as I said in my case I'd been to virtually every center in some capacity, tried every protocol and experimental drug available and expended years of my life to try and get well.

With that, if I intended to continue any kind of medical care at this center I had to consent and go through with these psychological evaluations. I was quickly set up to see a young lady by the name of Holly. In a funny way of looking at it this woman was in charge of my either continuing on with treatments or being sent home due to my diagnosed mental state of mind. When we first began to go through my psychological and medical background, I felt pretty relaxed for the most part. Even though I continued to be put out with the whole situation I at least had some sense that this girl was sincere with her approach to me. I believed that she respected me enough so that my truthful answers would vindicate and justify my reasons for being on edge yet still a sane man.

Holly treated me fairly and after about four or five more days of interactions with her she finally gave me a hug and said something to the effect of "John, I can say that you're fine and as stable mentally as could be expected under the circumstances and I believe that you're not going to harm yourself". I had to laugh inside when I heard her remarks to me. Not at her of course but at the asinine irony of the whole predicament I'd somehow placed I in by being honest from the get go. I knew that I was "fine" and it took a week of sidetrack interviews to a psychologist/social worker to solidify my already known state of mind. It doesn't seem so terrible reading this now after the fact but in retrospect back then it was a serious matter. If I sound like I'm making too much of the situation I'd respect that opinion. It's just that when this all unfolded I was caught off guard and it seemed to set the tone for my outlook of the whole situation.

Well after elaborating some on this mini setback, once the staff was informed that I was "cleared for continuation" the appointments commenced. I picked up about where I left off with Dr. O Feral. He and I got along very well I felt and I respected his insights. Among some of his recommendations he suggested that I have some nerve conduction studies done on my lower extremities. Most doctors felt that I had permanent damage to my legs and feet due to the broken needle in my spine during the botched spinal tap. This left me with a diagnosed "drop foot", i.e. the inability to move your feet or ankles. If I could get some test results and have a conclusive diagnosis, I'd know where I stood. This would also entail some specific blood tests as well. As luck would have it this was messed up also.

The doctor decided that it would be easier for me to have these tests done back at home instead of here at Hopkins. I was okay with that but everything got all messed up when the proper doctor's appointments to be made at home were initiated. This is another example of why and how I became so irritable, disheartened and discouraged. How is it that competent doctors cannot make the proper arrangements for patients? Each of the doctors were good guys and meant well I hope but in all of the time gone by this is one category that has never been accurately addressed.

How this came about was through an initial doctor who was contacted at my local hospital from a recommendation by my home oncologist, Dr. Mike. This doctor took care of the nerve conduction studies, which consists of placing wires along your legs and feet and delivering electric shocks to the sight while progressively increasing the current. The objective is to induce a response from the targeted area. This would be a muscle twitch, a painful shock or burn like sensation or nothing at all. The latter would not be good news and most likely indicate that there was in fact nerve damage. There are other responses and involvements, which I am not knowledgeable on. I had the nerve tests taken care of and as I recall the doctor was only as polite as he needed to be. During the course of the testing, there were times when he hurt me pretty good with the electric currents and there were times when I felt nothing at all. When I tried to obtain the results he was very funny about telling me anything whatsoever relevant to my case. He told me that I would have to talk with the doctor back at Hopkins for any information.

This kind of condensed the nerve conduction study testing experience but it didn't address the blood test that I needed to have. I didn't think much of that as being a big issue since I'd become the king of blood and sticks. What did turn out to be a problem that still isn't solved even today was the particular test that I needed. From Dr. O Ferall telling me about the blood test I needed, he never gave me a name for the particular test itself. I recall him telling me that the nerve conduction study doctor would know the name of it. When I confronted him about it he didn't seem to have any idea what I was talking about. It was the same with my oncologist, he didn't know about it either. How can this be I'm thinking as I write this down now.

I'm hoping to solve this dilemma in the future, but when I attempted to coordinate the doctors to help me get this now mysterious blood test name tracked down I had zero success. I'm guessing that's because of the short handedness and communication breakdowns on their part, plus the fact that I had a seven step plan implemented on me; and furthermore, about as many different areas to monitor while being the patient at the same time. It's difficult to figure out why and how I couldn't get this area once and for all diagnosed. It may not have been a priority to the doctor's staff in the scheme of things but in my mind it was and still is a critical area to address for my quality of life and closure for that matter.

With the protocol rolling along in all of the other areas at full steam, my pursuit for the legwork to get done must have been placed on the backburner. Dr. O Feral returned a call of mine one day and told me to contact him if I needed any more assistance. Since we never resolved the first issue to begin with I may take him up on his offer some day. That is if I can come up with a new medical insurance breakthrough coup to cover the costs, which will be another story down the line.

Meanwhile back at the roundhouse my endocrinologist continued to tinker around with the ACTH stim tests and start me on Synthroid, a drug hormone replacement therapy. Of course I had to stay true to form and have difficulties in obtaining the correct levels. If I didn't discuss this area already I'd say that yet another horribly discouraging mountain to climb was the inability for me to get any regularity with the drug levels and dosages. Whether it was me or not exclusively I cannot say but I found that with so many of my drug dosages and varieties, they never seemed to get regulated properly. Either I was oversensitive to the dose or unreceptive to the dose or didn't get any anticipated response whatsoever. With the experimental medicines I could see having some ups and downs but as I said I just always seemed to have difficulties with drug doses and desired results.

With this dilemma I had in regulating medicines and dosages, I know that it gave the doctors problems as well. Mentally sometimes it wore me out because I felt perceived as being a difficult patient. I may have developed a bit of a complex through the years due to so many of these situations arising. I know in my heart that I went into these situations with as much enthusiasm as a patient could have and wanted them to work. I can't imagine any patient not wanting the meds to work. Nobody, I don't think would want to just take a bunch of potentially dangerous drugs for kicks would they. By the same token if you don't take the meds and therapeutic levels I might add, what's the sense of trying to get better anyhow? Most of the time I figured that the medical staff concurred with that line of thinking and would take whatever I told them at face value but I didn't always get that feeling from all of them. Those were the ones who cast doubts in my mind about believing me or not. What does a patient have if he or she is not believed?

Having touched on this problem I had, I don't believe it was a case of believing or not I just never got the physical results that were desired with the Synthroid. One nurse after I believe seeing my thyroid T3 and T4 results told me "you're not going to believe how good you're going to feel in a couple of days to weeks". I was naturally excited to hear that profound and unsolicited statement and prepared for the coming expected results. Time passed and nothing. No difference that I could see or feel anyway. I was disheartened to say the least but I'm positive that it was and still is today a case of getting the dosages right for me. This has been the search for the Holy Grail so to speak for me, getting it right; a seemingly unreachable star for some reason or reasons. I hope to soon try yet once again to attempt and find the right dose of thyroid replacement therapy.

In backtracking a bit if I hadn't mentioned it the reason for the thyroid replacement therapy was that all of the radiation I had in Seattle destroyed my thyroid glands ability to function. The amounts of T.B.I. I had been given were so toxic that it shut down many of my bodily functions, i.e. being virtually sterile, not perspiring, tear production etc. If I could only solve the mystery of how much and what it is that I need I feel that the quality of my life could be so much more. Again the overload that the doctors have with patient to doctor ratio I feel contributes to this problem immensely. The Synthroid works it's a proven fact, I just need to be regulated and monitored and monitored and monitored until a breakthrough arises. I'm sure many patients out there are in the same predicament as I am in this area. There is help and a solvable solution but how the heck you get to it by yourself is beyond me. I've often wondered if it would matter if I were the President of the United States, would anything differ in my quality of care or should I say quantity and intenseness of care. I feel, "you bet your tail it would". I'm just not going to be the President anytime soon so this is my story to tell.

I guess this was about the second ingredient in the grand plan to fix me up. With heated debates still going on as to whether or not I continued to have GVHD or not, a particular pow-wow one afternoon with me took me to a big decision making roadblock. It was proposed to me to try the drug known as Prograf alias Tachrolimis and formerly known as the numbered drug FK 506. If you recall I had the pleasure of being probably the first BMT patient to try this drug some years ago in Pittsburgh. I thought then and commented to everyone that I felt it was a wonderful drug. I just felt it was too toxic or powerful for me in the then prescribed dosage.

The doctors at Hopkins had teetered on the conclusion that I still probably had some form of GVHD and wanted to implement this protocol as well as possibly a few other drugs eventually. I had confided and conversed with the staff by now so much so that I felt a good sense of security in who they were, what they believed in and my ability to trust their opinions, especially one doctor in particular. His name was Dr. Jeff Margolis and from the beginning we seemed to have a very good rapport. I trusted and respected his insights. He would later let me down in a big way but for this timeframe he was about just what you would want in a doctor.

With this decision looming on the horizon I needed to be assured that I would have a strong support unit around me with contingency plans and the whole works ready for if and when something was to go wrong. I had previous experience with this medicine and came away with mixed reviews so I knew that I needed to be prepared. Well in mapping out our tentative game plan Dr. Margolis assured me that he would be there every step of the way. He went so far as to give me a phone number where he could be reached during rounds etc. I felt pretty good with this and his explanations probably tipped the scales in favor of trying the Prograf one more time.

Now Dr. Margolis wasn't the only physician on my case, he was the main attending physician I guess you could say for me. The go to guy who was supposed to pool all of the incoming information from the various other doctors, specialists and sources. I had several other doctors and nurses who assisted Dr. Jeff initially. For a long time I felt pretty comfortable with everyone involved in my case at Johns Hopkins.

After going home and thinking it over briefly I decided to go ahead and try the Prograf. I'd be able to have my blood levels checked at my local hospital so that wouldn't be a problem. I still had a handful of other doctors and specialists to see at Hopkins so I had to continue the commutes accordingly. One of which was a physical therapy evaluation. The appointment and visit itself didn't turn out anything monumental per say but the telling moment from that trip was meeting a family from New York. They had a son about tenor eleven I'd guess who had been through a bone marrow transplant similar to mine. He had GVHD and a handful of other complications to deal with as I recall. The strange scenario that unfolded for me was having the mother of this boy come up to me and began talking with me. Obviously she saw similarities in her son and me. As we talked and became familiar with each other's situation, she mentioned to me how I wouldn't believe how much better I was going to get within a year or so. She sounded so excited for me and went on about how bad a shape her son was in when he first got there about a year ago previously.

Evidently I fell into the being oblivious of my appearance category because I didn't think that I could be spotted out and diagnosed by someone who didn't even know me. I know that you can look at me and tell that I've been through a lot but not to the extent that you could pinpoint it down as she did. Perhaps because she was a mother and had a son with similar things wrong with him to deal with that gave her an insight others wouldn't ordinarily have. In any event she went on to elaborate on how he looked just like me when he came in and she must have envisioned the same improvement for me. The boy's father was even a Jet fan so I took the good omen and went with it for some much needed "positivity".

I'll spare the mundane details of most of the other appointments and prognosis that I received along this initial stretch. They mostly consisted of some gastrointestinal exams, liver prodding festivities, oodles of blood sticks and a partridge in a pear tree. All of this was still relatively condensed into a month or so getting the show on the road with this assembled plan of attack.

A funny thing to me was the order in which I was accommodated, or not in my travels through this monstrous hospital to get to my scheduled appointments. By this time I really didn't have anyone in my family who was able to escort me as in the "good old days". Thank God I was able to commute via train or car if I was up to the drive. Getting there was one thing, getting around in there was another!

Obviously with my being as frail as I was, even appointments in close proximities to each other would pose a brisk challenge to anyone in my shoes. The now humorous point of it all was that these exams and consults seemed to almost be scheduled as far apart from each other as they could be. Allan Funt for all I knew could have been the brainchild for the distances in appointments for excerpts on his Candid Camera show. Initially I winged it and walked at my usual Touch'e Turtle's pace but I quickly realized that it wouldn't cut it. One report from a therapist or specialist of some sort complained about my being late and not being able to complete the consult. I had to improve my commuting times so I Inquired as to if I could borrow a staff member, volunteer and wheelchair.

I don't recall them as having a setup for outpatients scooting around so much but a solution was found. I somehow got onto the "Loop" of inpatient escorts. These people, some of them anyhow turned out to be prison inmates on work release or a program, which allowed them to provide this service. I'm assuming that they got paid and should have asked. I had plenty of time to because depending on my destination it could be a wheelchair cruise up a few floors, across a bridge and down a corridor or an all out assault on hospital track records to make it on time. More than a few times my driver would buckle me in and head to the basement tunnel virtually used by hospital employees and independent contractors, vendors etc. From there we would put on the afterburners, which would be whatever brand sneaker he preferred and his feet. We had time to strike up small talk conversations and I must say that the guys were some of the nicest people you'd ever want to meet.

As it stood, this method worked out pretty well for scooting around to my various appointments. I continued another group of consults and the battery of tests that went with them to the point of leveling off and just about having everything I needed squared away. That is, I had the group of drugs and directions the doctors wanted me to be taking settled on. The drugs I started out with initially were Prograf, Bactrum, Synthroid and Cellcept I believe. Basically they consisted of two very strong immuno-suppressives, an antibiotic and a thyroid replacement drug.

I had pretty good communication lines open with the group of doctors and nurses I was working with so I felt comfortable enough then to get started with everything. Dr. Vogelsang, Dr. Margolis, and nurses Viki and Phyllis were my primary caregivers so it was all basically a go. It all came down to taking five or six pills a day after all of the fanfare. Very simple in pill numbers especially from what I'd been accustomed to in years past. I could go home, take my pills, get my blood levels drawn there, resume some kind of routine and wait for any improvements. This was the hope anyhow. I also had to be aware of the toxicity factors with side effects as well.

So this was the culmination of all of our work and to take one more shot at attacking my host of lingering problems, which continued to plague me. I began treatments from home and waited for anything. From a psychosomatic twitch to realistic itch my mind was on guard. Initially I seemed to feel alright, I guess. Other than the usual initial phase of drug adjustments, i.e. restlessness, stomachache, fever, chills, etc. whatever the case may have been I'd say that I got off to a good start.

We had to make some adjustments to my Synthroid due to a tachycardia problem, which may or may not have been related to it. The Prograf I feel gave me a handful of minor side effects and the Cellcept just made me feel "yucky". My initial symptoms could have been the combination of all of them in conjunction with each other I don't know. It's difficult to link side effects and symptoms to a particular medicine sometimes so my views here are just that, my views based on how I felt taking this or that particular drug.

I continued this ritual at home for an indefinite period of time and rolled with the punches. Some things seemed to respond and improve while other areas may have regressed somewhat. It was as always extremely difficult to distinguish exactly where I was with the medicines or what was going on with things. This may be difficult for any reader to fathom who hasn't been in a situation of dealing with many medicines, their combinations and reactions. I can understand that but believe me when I tell you how complicated this mess can get. Things can seem all neat and organized wrapped up nicely to the observer's eye but it's simply not always the case on the insides.

I got used to feeling the way that I did with what I'll describe as always having a queasy and slow sensation inside of me. I don't know how else to phrase it, I could use a hundred different adjectives but that's not the point. The point is that I could definitely tell that things were going on with my body. My ability to get around in spurts was about the same except if it was a hot or humid day. When the next time came around to go to Baltimore for a checkup I was well enough to drive myself so I did.

The mental marker for this trek south was my blown tollbooth episode. The Delaware to Maryland pay lanes can bottle neck you in before you know it and I forgot to know it. My cruising speed had me trapped in the EZ pass lane with no way out. So as the sign says to keep moving I did. Actually I pulled over once through to try and get out to pay but the traffic would have had me hopping about like the Frogger game. I went on my merry way to Hopkins wondering if I would be pulled over by Maryland's finest later on down I-95. Since I never did I then wondered if I'd be tracked down sometime for my two dollars, which I was. The mailman delivered me my notice complete with the mug shot of my vehicle leaving the scene of a tollbooth. Once dragnetted I sent the cash and explained my situation with everything being fine, something which they probably see everyday.

With this same trip I also recall more of the same moods to music trend, which I had grown accustomed to seeing in myself. It worked as a kind of therapeutic preparation for when and what I'd be gearing up for at the hospital. My hour and a half drive could be stressful in itself sometimes with the lot of raging maniacs blowing by me left and right despite my being just on the arrow side of sixty-five. For the times when traffic wasn't hell to play I did sometimes enjoy the scenery and music combination to sooth my mind as best as could be. For the readers who have used the car and music in tandem for mental escapism you can fully appreciate this real life tidbit of mine.

Visits during this time frame in my story focused on that seven-step progression I mentioned earlier. Targeted areas were broken down to I believe something like my thyroid being the endocrine area. Second was the Prograf and Cellcept teamed together which was hoped to lower my T cell count among other things and directly attack the problem of suspected graft verses host disease. Third was the antibiotic's, used as an extra protection layer for my considerably compromised immune system. Another area to target was my weight issue.

If I haven't mentioned this yet it's a very common occurrence for bone marrow transplant patients to have weight issues. If you throw in dealing with GVHD your chances are much more likely. Some survivors don't have any problems but as I said most do. One of the theories about this manifestation of weight and muscle loss is something called a necrosis factor. I never made it to this step, as it was the last to target I recall but the staff only briefed me on this necrosis factor theory. I presume that it has something to do with the body's metabolism and endocrine inter workings possibly but I'm not sure.

The next breakdown area to address I think was physical therapy. I visited with several nice therapists and a couple of not so nice therapists to be evaluated. This was a road I'd been down many times before and for the most part during my consults I just grinned and bared it. One constructive aspect of these visits was range of motion measurements that were taken. This was a way to access tangible numbers to show regression or improvement. Other than that it came down to money, facilities, and quality of sincere help.

Another area was nutrition. This consult was about the worst in terms of quality, relevant concern for my wellness and being on a par with the standards of the other areas I mentioned. It may have been that I happened to have a novice nutritionist or intern on the day of my consult I don't know. I'd been to a handful of other nutritionists and dietitians before so I feel I had some good sources to compare to. I think this area is extremely important to be involved with it's just in this instance nothing positive really materialized.

The psychosocial category for me was and is about the most important area to keep healthy. I could go on and on about my experiences and rapport with various doctors here and at other facilities as well. Collectively if you polled all of the many Physicians who've ever worked on me psychologists and psychiatrists alike, I'd say that positive opinions of me would far outweigh the negatives. As my luck would have it though, at Johns Hopkins I got the feeling that most of my grouped staff core members always seemed to have it in for me. What I mean by that is the overbearing redundancy of constantly bringing up my mental health state during my time as a patient there. Save for a handful of doctors and nurses of whom I always felt like I could be myself and be respected for, that simply wasn't the case across the board. I'll elaborate on this as I progress through my story but as I mentioned, this was and always is going to be a part of any major protocol.

I guess that about rounded up the plan of attack, which had been coordinated for me by the staff. Depending on who would be present during a particular consult usually dictated how the visits went. From what I remember the first group of say four or five commutes to Baltimore went pretty well. My medicines for the most part were figured out and I seemed to be tolerating them okay. One of the things I requested early on was to receive a copy of everything paperwork wise that would be sent to my various doctors and hospitals. This way I could keep a good track of what was going on myself as well as have a personal copy of just what my doctors were doing and saying regarding my status.

During the course of my visits to the hospital, my description of myself here as feeling okay simply meant that I wasn't ill to the point of being admitted or bedridden. I still had many ups and downs to finagle with and one of them was the commutes back and forth to Hopkins. I wasn't always up for the drive and as I mentioned my family wasn't in the position to take me either. So for a good amount of my trips, as I mentioned earlier I chose to take the train. My brother would pick me up at home and drop me off at the Wilmington station. From there I was on my own to be punctual. What a challenge this turned out to be with the train schedules and my health I'll tell you.

One of the funny stories for example was a particular hospital appointment that I had which was scheduled for an early morning/mid morning time frame. I myself have never been an early morning person mood and function wise. I love mornings it's just that my body never really went along with the program so to speak. I can remember as a teenager struggling to get out of bed at three or four in the morning to go fishing with the guy's and simply dying inside. I forced myself big time to "fit in" and it would usually be hours before I even came close to feeling my normal self. Even then I felt that old hangover sensation in my head, eyes, brain and just about everywhere else that mattered.

Anyway getting back to my train ride adventure, this particular trip came at about the time when I began to have some minor to moderate side effect symptoms arise. One of which was shortness of breath upon exertion. Basically the out of shape feeling or a de-conditioned state is how it felt. Upon my arrival into the terminal I went through the motions to hunt down the designated track for my trip to Baltimore. Everyone who has used a train before is all too familiar with the overhead muffled voice of the dispatcher. As if distinguishing his or her crumpled inflections isn't enough to steer you off the beaten path, getting to the announced track and then having them change it on you at the spur of the moment is.

The frail and de-conditioned state of which I was in placed me in the predicament of walking very slow and gingerly. After arriving an hour before my scheduled departure I realized that did me no good because they didn't list the relevant track numbers until about five or six minutes beforehand. Once I did hear the muddied message broadcast about, I reaffirmed what I thought it was that they were saying by bouncing it off of other prospective passengers. I kind of followed the crowd and looked for signs pointing me to the correct area.

Having felt like I accomplished my mission and could sit to re-catch my breath for a minute that wasn't the case. With about two minutes or so until the train was supposed to pull in for boarding, another one of those distant but loud and inaudible sounds beckoned. This by the looks of the crowd was another last minute track switch. With everyone around me scurrying up the stairs I was literally left in the dust by the group. As I said I'm not at my best in the morning to begin with but this scenario spawned a heaping helping of stress and anxiety right on my poor body

With no one really around to give me a hand I felt overwrought with anxiety and shortness of breath on top of that. I muscled my way up the steps one foot at a time while holding onto the banister. I tried to keep myself in check by mentally counting time and rationalize that I'd somehow still make the train before it took off. Once I finally made it up the staircase in what seemed like an hour's journey I took a shot at the closest terminal and descended back down towards this trains doors. By the time I reached the landing I was visibly shaken and worn out.

With my backpack slung over my side and leaning slumped at an angle, moving at a snails pace through the causeway I attempted to board a car. My being now in visible range caught the attention of a conductor who jogged over and helped me board. The only question I had to find out now was whether or not my gamble to catch this particular train was the right one. Once I caught my breath and explained to the conductor my dilemma he rolled his eyes with an "oh brother" look. He stated that I was on the right train but in first class not expecting me to have a first class ticket. He was like "you probably got it wrong" as I handed him my ticket but the funny ace in the hole was that I did in fact happen to have one on this particular ride. It didn't matter by then anyhow because the train was moving and I was going wherever it was taking me…

All of this little tidbit story about a train ride to Baltimore may have sounded trivial and winded to some but I thought it would be another real life episode of my journey in which the reader could relate to. We've all had life experiences to deal with similar to catching a train, whether it be actually catching a train or not.

I wanted to convey how the "simplest" of what are looked upon as routine tasks in everyday life can become a monumental challenge for patients and people in general who are compromised in any way. Needless to say I made my scheduled appointment on time although totally spent of energy, focus and charm.

Episodes like that took place occasionally and added up in the big scheme of things. They do take a toll on you cumulatively. In what probably contributed to the struggles I'd been experiencing when traveling I began to really fatigue at times much more so than the norm. I'm hesitant to use the word disoriented here but I could sense not feeling right, in what I'll call "foggy". There didn't seem to be any pattern or rhyme or reason to these spells other than the fact that I could attribute them to the medicines I was on and their inter workings in me. I couldn't recall the same side effects beforehand so I just left it at that. I'd inform my physicians of these occurrences and stay the course.

As I continued with the protocol, this timeframe placed me in the early stages of spring there or about. The doctors seemed very optimistic with some of my blood test results and expressed positive notions with me. A very nice gesture on Johns Hopkins part was the fact that they had successfully created a huge fund-raiser called "Plunge for Patients" and they offered me a free trip to attend it for a week. Normally, when something like that would be offered to me I usually take my time in deciding but when they told me that it was held in Wildwood N.J. I couldn't refuse. How ironic I thought after having so much to say about Wildwood previously in my story to the reader.

The Plunge for Patients fundraiser is a weeklong event, which includes many volunteers and athletes from around the globe. It consists of several big swim meets in the ocean where a swimmer will race as a sponsor for a patient. The athletes solicit contributions all year I believe, as obviously the idea is to raise funds for the cancer research program. Patients are welcome to race if they're able. Anyone in fact who is fit and cleared by the staff can participate. They may have a big run and a walkathon in addition to the swims as well.

For the patients who are fortunate enough to be able to attend it's a week of the beach, rides, ocean and fun. That's not to mention all of the sights and boardwalk activities I talked at length about earlier in my story. It is definitely a noble and charitable event worth looking into. In addition to the patients and athletes involved, many companies are signed on as sponsors who contribute greatly as well. Getting news of this vacation of sorts in the upcoming months was a definite shot in the arm to my morale. I would use this new found circled date on the calendar as a positive boost to the days leading up to it. At that point in time my goal was to evaluate where I was with everything and where I thought I should be with things all around.

In the meantime I was still engaged in the ritual of taking the medicines and attempting to go about my daily routines as best as possible. I always seemed to have some type of side effect hovering around visiting me. One of the doctors in a sent out directive alluded to the fact that I was experiencing these symptoms from psychosomatic manifestations. I was burned up to read this and resented his view. It kind of said to me in so many words that my explanations or complaints were not respected. Patients know how they are feeling better than anyone else, besides when your shins start to turn beet red and burn I'd say that was not psychosomatic. I'd be a rich man if I could induce visible symptoms at will.

Anyhow I discussed my displeasure with the statement and things went on as usual from there. I once again had the same thing happen with respect to the Prograf and Synthroid meds. I experienced some episodes of rapid heartbeats or slight tachycardia, which didn't seem to be taken seriously in my opinion. It wasn't until I went round and round with this particular physician that my doses were adjusted and the symptoms dissipated. In retrospect these incidents of what I perceived as negative rapport, "land mines had been buried" and from that point on I always carried that wary feeling inside with me. I think it's crucial to have confidence in the doctor-patient relationship and feeling as though they have your best interest at heart. At this point in time I still felt pretty confident with the staff as a whole but some erosion had taken place.

Perhaps I had been a patient on this protocol for several months now and it placed me right into the summer season just in time for the Plunge for Patient Wildwood trip. To assess my progress at this point in time would be way too premature but I was self conscious to embrace any inkling of improvement. This was of course the timeframe in which I designated in my mind to unofficially check in and compare "then to now significance". Right off the bat I could say that a bit of the burn marks or blotches on my complexion had improved and not regressed. I possibly had some improvement in my range of motion as well; nothing dramatic mind you but at least a start in the right direction. This was all that I really had to go by as far as tangible evidence to go by visually.

I still had bouts with extreme fatigue, strength and mobility restrictions as main areas of concern. Most threatening and worrisome of all was the vulnerability to infection. I couldn't gauge this area very accurately at this time more than likely due to the strong immuno-suppresives, which I was taking. Actually I may have been even more at risk to catch something during this stretch because I was so suppressed. As I mentioned before any crowded area, children, confined buildings etc. are potential danger zones for transplant patient's even years out post transplant. To catch a cold could easily escalate into a whole big ordeal. The biggest fear for any immuno-compromised patient would be to have a simple head cold or sinus infection case of the sniffles turn into a life and death crisis of pneumonia. I'd been pretty fortunate up to this point since beginning my protocol of not getting to sick. The trip to the shore would be fun for sure, if I could get through it unscathed that is.

The moment of truth had arrived. My buddy Paul and I had our bags packed and the car gassed up to navigate the drive to Wildwood. Of course I didn't forget to bring my cache of drugs along for the ride. Actually I was getting car sick routinely by now which I attributed to the meds, so any thought or mention of them fueled the queasiness even more. I never really got carsick before or after taking that particular protocol so it makes some sense to link the two. Nevertheless we were on the runway and cleared for takeoff so that's just what we did.

I recall this drive being fun and relaxed, which was a feeling that had eluded me for quite some time now. The drive through South Jersey from the Pa. side for me has always been enjoyable. Time goes by rather quickly through what is still many miles of farmland, produce stands, ponds and lakes to catch the travelers eye. In fact some days you can see flea markets and yard sales briskly doing business with prospective customers or simple browsers akin to something out of a Norman Rockwell painting.

As I said the drive stood out in my mind because I seemed to be in a good mood for the trip. I believe that it carried over to the arrival at our motel where we stayed. It was a good hike to the boardwalk from our unit but at least I was there. Settling in for me was about as entailed as tossing my suitcase on the bed and attempting to make it up to the boardwalk. I traveled light and didn't anticipate doing anything extravagant anyhow.

Once there I relapsed into the induced state of serenity of which the beach and ocean bring to me. The amount of energy I expended to get to the boardwalk from my nice little motel room was well worth the effort. Most of the ambience, which I spoke at length about earlier in my story was out and abound with zest, vigor and fury; basically, therapy in a bottle, or should I say island.

I got to meet and mingle briefly with some of the other patients and their families while we were up on the boardwalk and back at our motel. It was clear that the range of problems and severity of issues varied greatly from patient to patient. For the most part I believe that the patients here were made up of leukemia, a-plastic anemia, brain and head related cancers, and related branches of those groups. I may have missed a few other areas but this gives you a general idea of what patients participated and benefited from it.

We all had a calendar of events and some mandatory functions to attend. The rest of the time was ours to enjoy as we saw fit. For me I wasn't able to do much of what I'd love to have been doing, i.e. riding waves, partyboat fishing, getting on some aggressive rides and baking in the hot sun laying on the beach. I was at least there and could watch others doing these things, which sometimes felt good and other times blew up in my face because I could no longer do them.

Nevertheless I did have things that I could do and enjoy. The tramcar for starters was the taxi of sorts for the boardwalk. Its pricey fare hit you a little in the wallet but for a guy like me it became a great way to relax while traveling the length of the boards. I could also get out on the beach but only for a very brief time by order of the doctors. One of the drawbacks with the meds was that they made you prone to skin damage and other health problems through prolonged exposure to the sun. In addition to these activities I had all of the shops and nook and cranny stores to browse through. I had plenty of things to do, most of all like I said it was just great to be there.

I made the most of my trip and overextended my bounds with all of the exertion. This was a problem that eventually would catch up with me in a nasty way though. The worst of which came one night during one of the patient mandatory gatherings. This was at a dinner and slide show where homage is paid to former patients who have passed away. Basically what got me was the heat. During the course of my earlier activities combined with goofing around down on the beach at the events tent, I expended way too much energy and I don't really perspire.

As I touched upon earlier in this story my perspiration glands were damaged so as my body's temperature rose so did my core temperature, with no real way to cool itself down. I've mentioned that I use a squirt bottle to try and regulate the heat but in this instance the misting simply didn't cut it. I hadn't been in the water at all due to the weakness in my legs so there was no relief there either. The worst part of it all was and is still today is the fact that my body doesn't have an early warning system to let me know that I'm overheating. Of course I can tell when I'm getting "normal" hot but there is no distinguishing from the gray area and feeling a little warm. Like I said my body simply doesn't kick in any longer with the automatic cooling system, so obviously this combination or lack there of, was the formula for heatstroke.

When I sat down on the makeshift picnic table under the nylon circus like tent temporarily set up for the venue, the world around me began to swirl. The distant lights, which emanated up through the nighttime skyline from all of the amusements and activities seemed to rush in on me like the ocean's surf. My skin forced a wicked shiver spasm on me with its' clammy cold exterior but under the layers harbored a feeling of massive heat sensations building up. The rapid heartbeat and not quite but close to the shortness of breath accompaniment told me from past experiences that I was about to be dropped once again by big time overheating.

I slumped over the table progressively and rapidly getting worse until I called attention to myself to a nearby nurse. My friend Paul hung around to assist me as best as possible but there wasn't too much he or anyone could do at that point. The immediate consult amongst the medical staff present called for a volunteer to drive his car down to the shoreline about where the tents were located on the sand. From there I was assisted, or basically carried into the backseat for transport back to my hotel room. From there the nurse could work on me and further assess whether or not I needed to be hospitalized or not. Thank goodness I didn't need to be but with most of the symptoms of heatstroke present on my plate to contend with such as nauseous spells, sunburn like skin sensations, dehydration, feeling disoriented and extreme fatigue, I was just happy to be on the bed packed with ice and in an air conditioned room.

Unfortunately this had become par for the course in my journeys so I had no choice but to grin and bare it until I recovered. I'd say that this heatstroke episode was certainly serious in its own right but in the scheme of things with respect to my physical condition and current medicine compromising protocol I was on, this pot hole of sorts only ranked as a moderate setback.

My main therapy "in house treatment" at the motel called for lots of rest, plenty of fluids, cold compresses and air conditioning along with the nurse's visits to monitor me. I basically had to hang around the motel room until I clearly saw an improvement, which is exactly what I did. Besides lying around in the room I felt comfortable enough to sit right outside in one of the motels lounge chairs. The combination of the misty ocean air fueled in by the swirling breeze gave me the sensation of a complete body sprinter atomizing me all over. My lethargy remained although steadily improving gradually over time as long as I didn't exert myself.

The one pitfall, which really stung was the fact that the motel landlord's children were mental terrorists for the self-conscious patients. They launched stinging salvos, some of which having malicious intent and others which, simply came from upbringing and ignorance, rivaled each other for their painful content. Almost from day one, this group of two or three sisters seemed to lurk the pool grounds for any potential patient prey they could heckle. Why their mother or father didn't put a clampdown on this behavior I couldn't say but I know their actions bothered me and most probably the other patients in the motel even more.

The notable comment I recall towards me was directed at my being so thin from all that I'd been through. Of course they had no idea what I'd been through but as kids often do they speak freely from the heart I suppose. In this case it was a series of phrases something like "look at that guy, look how skinny he is" repeated several times over. Other audible outbursts included such as "uh, that man is so skinny" and "can you believe how skinny that boy is". As if those innocent enough sounding statements to the reader didn't way on me, the coupling of them with giddy laughter and finger pointing afterwards sure put salt on the wounds. Maybe for me it was akin to how someone may feel after being told they were fat or a whale etc. By now the drugs had made me a bit oversensitive perhaps but you just know what you know when somebody is making fun of you.

I myself had much more important issues on my mind to deal with so I could file it and move on. I'm not so sure about some of the other patients I met during the trip. A couple of patients in particular I think were really affected by the snide remarks. You could just see the expression of a couple of patients change drastically while in the pool after hearing themselves being made fun of, while just simply trying to get away from all of the pain and anguish being felt on a daily basis. It really stunk.

I think I made a comment loud enough so that the mother could hear me one time and I was passively humored by her, with an almost sarcastic reprimand. I can't blame the kids as much as the parents in this instance. We all know how cold life and people can be sometimes but what can you say. I just hope that the other patients who were harassed about their wheelchairs or scars or no hair etc. were able to move beyond those negative life experiences. Sometimes you can and sometimes the words become "a part of you", like the person who told me that I looked like walking death one time and the other person who told me that she would connect the dots on my face. You just can't take back words once they've been put out there. For me there are a handful of painful remarks etched in my mind, which I cannot shake. Like the children's remarks, many are shakable but as I've stated some cut like the knife and never heal.

With that said of course life goes on and so it did. I still found myself here in Wildwood for the rest of the "plunge" and came out of the heatstroke enough so to participate in some of the evening activities. I mainly recall a dinner social and a remembrance ceremony to honor all of the deceased patients who went to Johns Hopkins Hospital. I ended up having a difficult time with this part of the trip as it opened up all of my feelings for my father and sister as well as the broken engagement and all of the other upsetting waves, which previously occurred. I didn't externally show any visible signs of anxiety or emotion that I was aware of but it definitely was affecting me big-time. The events themselves were nicely organized and for the most part everyone seemed to have a great time. Besides my having the reaction to the slide show memorial, I was pretty comfortable physically and as I alluded to, I filed the anguish and socialized with the fellow patients and attendees. It wasn't until I got back to the room that I melted down about everything

The week's trip carried on and culminated with a somewhat relaxing day just doing nothing. A couple of fellow patients along with my friend Paul decided to go across the street to a comedy club but I just wanted to hangout by myself for awhile and simply "be". I watched people doing their thing and listened to the sounds around me etc. I found this to be very therapeutic and relaxing, "a nice change for a change". So with that for the book's relevance my first Plunge experience was duly noted and one for the record as they say. After a nice drive back home I settled in and for the most part got back into the swing of things with respect to my protocol being the main focus pretty much of my life. It was now approaching late summer or they're about and I hoped to look forward to a positive and happy fall/winter season. So far I'd made it through what were now several months or so of intense medical mayhem, "medicinally speaking".

Well if I thought that I could avoid any of the gray area symptoms or problems, which could be included in this token medical mayhem label I was gravely mistaken. In what seemed like no sooner than I had settled into some sense of a rhythm, somebody somewhere up there pulled my name out of the rolodex once again for a crisis session visit. With little more details to give other than the fact that I got "lit up big time" with raging pain and discomfort it was a cut and dry situation. Simply put one night out of the clear blue sky my lower limbs exploded in a feverish frenzy.

It started out as a tight, warm sensation and escalated from there on out. The next thing I knew my entire lower limbs from the kneecaps down was super hot and quickly turning a strawberry red. I initially envisioned this as some sort of bizarre infection, which was contained only by the thin layers of skin draped over top of them. Perhaps even thinking of boiling a hot dog and visibly watching as the expansion of the meat from within pushes the outer limits of the hot dogs shelled skin. That's just about how it was for me with this enigma of complications to deal with and try to combat.

I gasped and sighed simultaneously to summons my mom through the shoddy plug in intercom system I bought. This made for easier floor to floor communication with her for just such an instance. By now I could feel the intense fever in my legs increasing as well as spreading now to my whole body. The dense red patches, which covered my shins and calves spread continuously until stopping at my knee's border. Now my entire lower leg below the knee was ablaze with this mysterious intruder of discomfort. My breathing remained difficult not because of any obstruction or lack of oxygen to inhale but only as a direct result of the pain. I may have looked like a mother in labor since I've watched the learning channel many times and seen the pummeling many moms take while giving birth.

As soon as my mom entered the room and gained a visible sight of my condition you could clearly see by her face that she was terrified. Whatever this was that infiltrated my body and or immune system or what have you was definitely cause for big alarm. Instinctively my mom soaked a couple of towels and molded them to my shins to try and bring the heat off of me. The thermometer revealed that I was cooking at one hundred and two degrees. Of the areas left on me that still "eked out" any resemblance of perspiration, worked overtime to trickle out what they could. As I mentioned earlier virtually all of my sweat glands were "fried" from the amount of radiation I underwent so needless to say it wasn't much.

My mom did the Tylenol, fluids, icepacks and everything else she could think of to help. Of course the calls were made out to the doctors but as many patients are acutely aware of, late evenings and or weekends can be treacherous to the patient in a crisis situation during this timeframe. If I haven't mentioned it earlier in my story, I have this theory from my own personal experience that things only get done in the hospitals from Tuesday to Thursday. Of course the other days some things do get accomplished but I'm talking about those primarily serious in nature. I'm not suggesting that anyone here has to agree with that notion but for me it's been a trend I simply couldn't ignore.

Nonetheless, I still stewed in this inferno now from head to toe and couldn't see or feel any relief in sight. My fever throttled me at one hundred and three. I felt hallucinatory yet again. My mom was a mental mess with the stress and she now pleaded with me to call an ambulance and get me to the hospital. Maybe for the first time in my long struggle with this leukemia and transplant recovery, I just felt like I'd had enough. However many years at this point it was I don't know fourteen, fifteen or whatever the case I just didn't want this kind of life any longer. This lifestyle of being a patient as a profession had become in fact my lifestyle. I guess everybody has they're breaking point wherever that parameter lies and I felt like this might have been mine.

My bed was now completely soaked down to the mattress from the wet towels, icepacks and what little perspiration my body could muster up. I had refused to have an ambulance come to my rescue because really, deep down inside I'd been down this road several times before and didn't think they or anyone was going to be able to rescue me, save for God perhaps. One time Father Fahey and I were chit chatting about pilgrimages and the likes and he made a really cool analogy of sorts, in that God is everywhere and I didn't necessarily have to make a trip to Lords or Fatima to be heard. A pilgrimage would be fantastic don't get me wrong but in those instances where it's probably not feasible, that doesn't mean it's the end of the line. So conversely the thought of being "sirened" in to the hospital via ambulance and basically in my opinion, stagnating in a room wouldn't do me any more good than just remaining home and riding out the storm in this instance.

My mom's next idea was to entice me by having my brother escort me into the hospital in his truck. She in fact had put the call in already and he was on the runway awaiting further instructions from her. I recall striking a deal with them that if my fever rose any higher I'd oblige. This in retrospect was absurd because I doubt if there was any significance at all between one hundred and three and one hundred and four degrees respectively. Anyhow, I actually feel that my family simply grudgingly went along with me not because they felt it was the right thing to do but because they were themselves wiped out and also wanted to honor my decision somewhat. Yeah that's what I guess I feel about that.

As the night drug on into the early morning hours nothing seemed to subside and I pondered as to whether or not I had made a big mistake by deciding to stay home. The chills, which now ran ramped through my body, seemed to use every nerve ending as a highway. Between the pain and the shakes and the fever, the combined sensations brought a new light to my track record. I've spoken about death during the course of my story but this is one vivid moment at home where I felt I might pass away. My mother and I even talked about it as gently as we could.

I remember having the driest mouth even after drinking and nibbling on crushed ice and thinking, "what the hell is that all about". How can you drink and not have the liquid stick to your mouth? I attempted to sit up on the side of my bed and plunging backwards only to land on my soggy mattress. My mom attempted to change them in a makeshift manner and she partially succeeded despite my failing body floundering in her way. Once again like the old days I had to master the bedpan, which wasn't really a bedpan this time around. Who knows what it was but I presume that it served it's purpose.

As I spoke of having a deep faith in God as a Christian, I've also touched upon having the peaks and valleys during my life as well. This night was one of fear and anxiety that of which it is difficult to articulate. Simply stated, a rush of emotions, fears, thoughts, self-reassurances, doubts, exhaustion and uncertainty would be some of the main ingredients here. How you can be so deathly ill with painful distracting symptoms and still function mentally is beyond me. I'd like to think that I was coherent enough to make some sense during this sickness but as I mentioned, I know I was in and out of being in rational states of consciousness.

The faith that I like to think I have played a role and once again boosted my spirits here and the timing couldn't have come at a better moment. In the heat of the battle to break the hold of whatever this enigma of unexplained origins was on my legs, I internally pleaded with God for relief. The incessant fever and burning nerve endings along with a perverted and tormenting tickle was taking all of the life out of me. In a quirky sense I could explain it to the reader in some respects as we all can recall from childhood memories. Those times when friends, family members or neighborhood thugs may have held you down helpless, while at the same time, tickled you to the point of hyperventilation. Not that any of this is funny mind you, just the similar sensation of being helpless to escape on top of the relentless torments.

This symptom of my lower leg brutality was the lesser of the two evils. The raging pain won the honors hands down for sure but I guess I wanted to make the point that the tickling torments reeked havoc on my psyche as well as my endurance. When I was probably at my weakest hour with respect to this particular crisis I'm touching on, that's when I personally found that God lent a much needed helping hand. So much so in fact that I later recall in retrospect, jesting in anger that I virtually had to be at death's door just to get God's attention to step in and intervene. Obviously that's not the case but I could probably also joke with God that some of my stories cumulatively could come close to showing otherwise.

More than a few times in my long battle with this leukemia/transplant/recovery history found that things had to become so grim and hopeless, only to have a miraculous turnaround. With this situation concerning my limbs now coming to a head, it was the cue up to Heaven from my bat signal of internal conversational prayer to God, which seemed to finally induce a welcomed response. In the span of perhaps an hour or so, my one hundred and three fever simmered down to a balmy ninety-seven point five. Along with the fever went all of the swelling and irritation that came with it. I welcomed this relief with open arms figuratively speaking and my mother, bless her heart, conked out on her couch from both exhaustion and relief. I feel that God did once again intervene here. So be it if this is looked upon as a mere coincidence, just as the entire boat load of others at this point in my recovery. That's okay with me but it sure is something, to constantly be going from one extreme to the other in these climactic fashions.

Why it is that I've had to be repeatedly subjected to just about all of the things, which could go wrong to a person post transplant I cannot say. We joke about it, my family and I but what can you do. You try to make the best with the cards that are dealt to you I suppose. I harped on this particular incident because it was a prime example of the so called trivial complications that can arise out of nowhere, do their dirty work and leave without rhyme, reason or origin. The patient is left dumbfounded along with the physicians many of the times. Kind of like someone who claims to have been abducted by a UFO. and has no way of convincing anyone except eyewitnesses or fellow abductees who may have actually experienced what they're trying to convey. I can't say of course if UFO's or their abductees exist but I can empathize with them in trying to convey something to others, which they haven't experienced; So much for that analogy and long winded attempt, to get you seeing where I'm coming from.

With that I'll come back to earth and place you as a co-pilot in my car, somewhat recovered from my "crop circle leg scorching episode" driving down I-95 to John's Hopkins for a check up. Just as I've touched on during my story, these drives can be cathartic and introspective in their own right. I never had any company with me but if I did they would know what I mean about its' therapeutic value, as well as the loneliness a patient can often feel even amongst others.

The rigors of the continued visits through hospital hallways and basement caverns ventured on in my protocol travels of layered steps. I completed the necessary recommendations up to this point but like I mentioned before several times, my wariness to this toxicity and turmoil was wearing thin. I received an interesting visit one day at home involving a Delaware State Trooper and myself. I'm lying down in bed pretty wiped out and all of a sudden I could hear the distinct sounds of a police radio dispatcher just outside of my window. With my curiosity getting the best of me, I made my way slowly over to the window and much to my dismay was in fact a State Police car parked in my driveway. "What now" I gasped! I'm thinking "what did I do now" and "what kind of trouble am I in" and thoughts like that. The next thing I heard was a loud banging on the front door.

Since no one was at home besides me, I had to go down and become the recipient of the news. As I opened the front door slowly in peered the brow of this trooper's hat bill. This hat was attached to a "got ya" grin as it was my friend Sean who I met from the hospital. He also had a bone marrow transplant for a-plastic Anemia and we became friends at the first Plunge for patients I attended. We visited for a good while exchanging thoughts and basically shooting the bull about "normal stuff". This was a nice change of pace to be hanging out with a regular guy who happened to be familiar with some of the things, which I had to deal with. Even though there were vast differences in our protocols, just bouncing off some thoughts off of each other was helpful to some extent.

At the time my friend was doing much better than I was as he was functioning as a police officer so obviously he had to be physically able. I myself was in no position to do much of anything during this time period. The encompassing task at hand here for me was to try and simply persevere through these difficult medicines side effects and the symptoms for which they were being theoretically administered for in the first place. I felt like I was progressively getting worse but I couldn't put a finger on why or what it was specifically. I just kept sucking it up and stuck to the prescribed regiments, so as not to rock the boat any. I had an upcoming hospital visit pending anyhow so I braced for that trip and tried to find focus.

My scheduled appointment was with Dr. Margolis and the pertinent staff members to update all of my goings on and determine if I was on track with things or not. One of my steadfast factors of assurance at Hopkins was my friendship with a nurse named Phyllis. She assisted me from day one and always seemed to show up for me when things weren't going well to lend a helping hand. On this particular visit I felt that any kind of momentum I had built up took a significant hit when my friend slash nurse Phyliss informed me that Dr. Margolis was leaving the hospital. No sooner had I got there then she gave me close to a quote of "can you believe Jeff is leaving?" I was like what! Phyllis went on to break it down for me on how the chain of command was going to change for me, and what I could expect in the future.

If you recall this was the same doctor who assured me that he would be there for me every step of the way and oversee the whole operation. I internally blew a fuse of rage and more importantly one of fear. I placed a lot of stock in the fact that this gentleman would stay the course for me. As a matter of fact I consented to some of the medications due to the fact of my confidence in his oversight. With now over sixteen years of hospital and doctor interaction experience under my belt, this curve ball was not anything that I couldn't handle. What infuriated me was a feeling of being disrespected. Things happen and opportunities present themselves for doctors and people in general but some courtesy should be in order. It would have been nice to here the news face to face from the doctor himself but it wasn't the case. Being the kind of person that I am for better or worse I went on a mission of sorts to track him down, which I did later in the day.

Upon my finding the good doctor I confronted him as to the reasons why he didn't intend on personally informing me of his move. Though his tone of voice wouldn't have given away his persona of being uncomfortable, the strawberry red complexion on his face gave a glaring notice that he was embarrassed about the situation. He went on to elaborate on the opportunity to open up a private practice in Michigan I believe. That was all well and good and God bless the man but on a personal note, it left me high and dry and once again feeling disgusted with the whole stinking system. We small talked briefly and eventually went our own ways through the corridors in opposite directions. A fitting testimony to where we were both going in life at this point. He, off to a new and promising career and I, still left struggling with my deteriorating condition. I ultimately finished up my visit seeing staff members that I was familiar with to a point and on the surface it would appear that everything was still kosher enough I suppose.

This derailment of sorts threw my game plan off somewhat in terms of how I was approaching my protocol and potential setbacks. I'd always been accustomed to tapping into a particular Doctor or Doctors rapport and building what I'd like to think was a mutual respect kind of relationship for the long haul. With this now not being quite the case, I had to yet again reassess my line of thinking. The up coming holiday season couldn't have come at a better time to figure out how I was going to proceed with my treatments. I would use Christmas and the lengthy time to calm down internally and mentally for starters. "Regrouping and recharging my batteries" so to speak was and is a tool every transplant patient probably adopts to survive. I had to remain steady to my commitment with all of this and stay the course despite of and regardless of who was now overseeing my treatments. How to go about it though was another story…

This holiday season for me was mostly peaceful and about as relaxing as it could have been under the circumstances. I continued to struggle with physical problems and mounting side effects from the meds. At least that's how I saw it as a patient being in tune with myself. During this period of about a month or so I'd say, I figured that I would try to continue my exact dosages of the drugs I was being given and be meticulous in my charting of everything going on. I'd set the relatively short-term goal of continuing everything until at least the summer season and again re-evaluate my situation at that time.

Surprisingly to me the months of January through April were non eventful as toxic protocols can go. It was no picnic of course but by that I mean that no significant setbacks or extraordinary occurrences took place other than the regular routine "slop". I'd become so accustomed to living with a continual stomachache and the overall queasy feeling which accompanied the pallet of pills to be ingested like clockwork. You could just tell that the drugs were hard at work reeking havoc on my immune systems functions. Cells were being hijacked and taken out by the thousands upon thousands and in an indiscriminant manner at that. Any thing in sight was fair game if you were a T cell especially or an accompanied red or white cell in the region. That region being limited to my whole body…

I made it through the springtime months in about the same manner as the preceding winter months, constantly queasy, lethargic and a bit nomadic. At least mentally I wandered and wondered about anything and everything. My thoughts did focus on my second Plunge for Patients summer fundraiser and any positive things that I could pull out of the upcoming outing. As far as my life was going I'd say that it was still extremely difficult to deal with my physical problems and interacting with people in general. By that I mean most everyone that you see in public is for the most part functioning normally. They aren't struggling with the simplest forms of things that we all usually take for granted; such things as perspiring and the fluid movement in your ankles, wrists, joints, etc; the blinking of your eyelids without difficulties and the loss of strength and energy to boot. Just coordinating your self to attempt to "fit in" in the first place are among the top of the list of difficulties in simply interacting. And it goes without saying that when you're not feeling well for any particular reason on top of that, it's all the much more challenging to interact and be your real self. I'd been doing this act of a routine for so long now up to this point that it would have been fruitless to stop now. My show was continuing and my next public appearance was going to be once again in Wildwood for the fundraiser/vacation.

CHAPTER 9

▼

My thoughts of modest excitement arose somewhat over my trip at just the idea that I was going to be able to spend some good time down at the shore. Of course by now you have heard me talk about the beach a hundred times so you get the idea. For this second year as a patient at this particular hospital and participant in the fundraiser, my beach hotel room was much closer to the boardwalk and center of activities than last years was. I once again asked my friend Paul to come down for some vacation time and relaxation. I was real happy with the accommodations and the decks view overlooked many interesting sights to see so to speak. Sometimes there isn't a better medicine than to go where your heart pulls you too! At least that's my feeling.

My week wasn't that filled with commitments so I was pretty much free to go and do whatever I so chose to do. A lot of that would be hanging out up on the boardwalk and attempting to stay in the shade "if there was any to be found" as best as I could. The ocean breeze quenched my warm and rising body temperature so I was able at times to do many "normal" activities. Of course the evenings were even better so I again stretched my activity limits to the max as best as I could. The weighty fill of the medicines would nag and follow me wherever I traveled so no matter how much of a surrounding ambience I enjoyed, the bulk of that toxic slop inside prevented me from totally escaping.

On one of the first or second day there, I encountered a bit of a sticky wicket for lack of a better term and stepped inadvertently on a dog biscuit. As it turned out the motel that we were staying at was one of the few places to allow pets. Somehow the maid must have missed these chunks or fragments and my foot didn't. In taking my shoes off to flop down on the bed I somehow must have stirred up these pieces from just out of sight under the beds blanket. Before I knew it or could say aoough, the chunky landmine tore up the underside of my heel. Of course it was painful and bothered me to place much pressure on it but I didn't feel like it was a medical emergency. Of course I was wrong once again. With the simple task of asking for a bandage and some peroxide summoned the nurses and peanut gallery of onlookers and newsy bodies.

My foot swelled a bit but not as much as the gossip, which ensued. You might as well have thought that it was an assassination attempt by the way that people talked. It was a stinking dog biscuit people get a life! Anyway the nurses were very nice and helpful fixing me up and of course I had to add some more antibiotics called in stat for me to feast on along with all of the other pills; "Woopee".

Of the nice nurses who assisted me were Phyliss and her sister Phyliss. I kid you not. Two of the nicest ladies you would want to help you. We actually hung out by the pool and ended up going on the boardwalk together and stuff like that. "Phyliss squared thank you".

Throughout the week activities went on and on some to watch and some not to watch. I particularly had some difficulties with a slide show ceremony for patients who had passed away. This opened up many painful memories for me to cope with and I had a change of gears so to speak with the way that my moods went the rest of my trip. What was also hard on me was the fact that it was brought to my attention that two little boys who I had been introduced to the previous year and got a kick out of had also passed away. I personally felt no uplifting moments from this experience. I absolutely see the act of respect given to those brave souls in a tribute I just didn't handle it very well that's all.

The week came to a close and all in all it was a worthwhile experience. Possibly I was physically better, compared to a year previous I couldn't definitively say. My spirits were at least the same I suppose but without anything concrete to hang my hat on it was just about a crapshoot still. I'd stay the course and continue the protocol indefinitely I told my inner self. I can remember looking out at the ocean by myself on the boardwalk singing "Knockin on Heavens Door" by Bob Dylan and feeling the irony of self lies. You know how you can tell yourself something internally to try and believe it, to really want to believe in yourself and will everything to be alright but somehow deep down there is a sinking bellowing feeling which haunts you. Yet another battle to fight in fending off those inner feelings of human emotions, mainly fear in this instance.

Everything ended on a good note I'd say. A logbook or patient journal of sorts was passed around for all to write down a brief phrase for reflection and would be forwarded I believe at the next years function. I entered a conundrum of "don't kill bugs" and with that left my calling card for those who chose to solve the underlying metaphor. Who knows how it was construed but I didn't have the time or the energy to worry about it either. My "Spidey Senses were tingling" as my body gave hint that things weren't going as smoothly as they may have felt if even for just a week at the beach. Plain and simply my protocol was taking its' toll.

Once I got back home things for me continued to go on about the same as they had been for the most part. I could function with basic interactions and "slug" my way through the days feeling weighed down by the intensifying toxicity. I took a ride to see my old friend Pete at his new home and to just hang out and catch up on things. One of the great breaks to this visit was that Pete's home had a beautiful in ground swimming pool, which he graciously allowed me to "float around" in. My versions of floating were more akin to cinderblock water skiing than anything else at this point. Nevertheless it was water and extremely refreshing to simply lope around in and escape my real problems if only for a spell.

Pete and I shot the bull for a few hours and had a good time philosophizing as we often did. Eventually I had to depart and make my way back home up into the confines of my bedroom and "scenic ceilings". This was my routine resting and recharging abode for the most part. At least through many of the impending sickness spells I incurred, a given was that my bed, covers and the ambience of my room (as cluttered as it could get at times) were always a comforting refuge.

At or around this time period I believe was when my Grandmother on my father's side became seriously ill and soon after passed away. Now in retrospect I can clearly see how mentally in a fog I was with some things. I wasn't extremely close with my grand mom but enough so that I had some great memories as a boy visiting her on her farm. She was also very instrumental in finding my donor Jim due to her having that rare 244x chromosome show up in her blood work like myself. The problem I have with it now is that I don't recall reacting in any particular manner. I'd now attribute it to a numbing effect or a continuation of the post-traumatic stress disorder issues. In any event it didn't seem to really register in my mind at the time as real for lack of a better term. Perhaps it could be for various reasons but I'm mentioning this here because I feel that some of the medicines side effects or toxicities played a key role in the reasons why.

Before I knew it I had another scheduled appointment to see the staff for a periodic checkup. This was probably the first or second visit since the previous Doctor had left for greener pastures. Some of the topics discussed at this session were my weight loss and the tightness in my extremities. The drug Megace was administered to me as a possible vehicle to enhance my appetite. Megace is a chemotherapy drug, which has a known side effect of producing an increased appetite in most patients treated with it. I reluctantly agreed to give it a shot mostly to stay compliant, as I personally didn't want to add any more drugs on top of what I was already taking. The other drug Etretinate I believe was to try and loosen up my tight ligaments and fascia areas. I put that treatment off for the time being as the staff also concurred that I should wait on it until I could see more evident progress with the other meds.

The last related topic discussed was the theory of a necrosis factor. This in my travels has turned out to be a search for the Holy Grail of sorts because I was treated with some tidbits of information here and there as to what it was thought to be but never really getting close to its substance. By that I mean I heard that the necrosis factor was thought to be the key as to why some bone marrow transplant patients who used the protocol that I did had significant problems gaining weight post transplant for what ever reason. I know I've mentioned this stinking necrosis factor more than a few times but I mean if it is thought to be the key to the whole mysterious problem, why bring it up repeatedly and yet be so vague about it. To this day I still don't know what the heck a necrosis factor is or actually does.

My doctor visit concluded with some contentment on my part with respect to the change up in staff members. I still felt pretty good about things and the people taking care of me in Baltimore. The mundane ritual of going home, taking the medicines, dealing with the side effects and waiting for some results continued. For those of you who know the old adage of waiting is the hardest part you may be right in some instances. At least partly in this area for me I can say because getting up day after day trying to squeeze any possible improvement out of the treatments can be mentally exhausting.

At this point things seemed to be going okay for me besides that tugging inner feeling of the self, telling me that something was wrong. Outwardly and physically I was surely no glistening picture of health but at least I fell into the profile realm of a patient on the drugs that I was on. Not long after I recall feeling "okay" as I mentioned the levy broke so to speak in terms of my health. I recall a particular evening going to sleep feeling relatively relaxed and actually looking forward to a round of sound "Z's". I'd say that it was about two in the morning when the disaster side of things came calling to jack me up big time.

I woke up from the internal fire in my shins, which scorched the rest of my body with raging heat. This wasn't the first, second, or third degree burns that I incurred back in Seattle now some fourteen or fifteen years ago. This was the recurrent fever in my legs, which seemingly had no traceable origin. I screamed from a pain that I hadn't felt in a long, long time. Calling upon my mother to come up and help me was a ritual that we had grown accustomed to over these years of "recovery". I had no time to worry about what this was until I could be relieved of the pain. My mom instinctively soaked towels in cold water to reduce the fever. Crushed up Tylenol didn't even make a dent in the lower limbed throbbing. From years of previous experience, no phone calls out to any doctor or hospital short of the emergency ward would do anything until early morning. We've all been to the emergency room before so we know what that's like right...

The night ended up being long and exhausting for both my mom and I. Her applying the constant soaks ended up breaking the beast of leg lashings as even a sprinkling of Holy Water was just as much a vital role in my mind to induce the perverted fever's remission. Even today you can visibly see the roadmap of battle scars that these hideous bouts of "leg pummeling" episodes have left as a reminder to their existence. These hotspots have continued to haunt me for years especially if I exert myself physically for any length of time. It must have to do with elevated body temperatures or something related.

Now with me just having explained to you how difficult these leg flairs were to deal with, my next segue to discuss relates to this topic and you as the reader will probably think that I'm crazy for what I attempted here. The scenario will unfold and appear to take some different turns. As to what side of opinion's scale your thoughts fall on I can't say, I just know how I feel about it.

Not too long after this bout with the lower limbs took place, I'd say that it was about a month or two to be more exact, my desire to improve pushed the limits in some people's minds but I didn't see it that way. I had purchased an electric muscle stim unit a long time ago and never really spent time using it on a regular basis, so the drive to get well provided the impetus to give it a try now. The process consisted of wetting these circular pads about the size of mini pancakes. This was to provide the conduction of electric current through the pad, to my skin and into my targeted muscle area. A simple and for most people safe procedure I suppose.

The unit had a control device to regulate the amount of current going into you at pulses as fine as say a massage. The higher the setting the more intense the pulse would get. The happy medium was to be able to tolerate the highest "sting" if you will of the zaps. My threshold here was about that equal to a thick rubber band being "slingshotted" at the skin. But make that many bands pulsing all at once for a period of say, thirty-second intervals. Then a break, of between five and fifteen seconds before you got lit up again. Since I hadn't had any serious symptoms in my legs for a good while, I decided to get started with my "treat-ments". I just had to try something to induce growth in my legs!

I guess things went okay doing this muscle stim process in the beginning for the most part. The idea was to fatigue the muscle in tricking it to believe that physical exertion was taking place through constant contractions. Thus in theory the muscle would have to regenerate bigger after each session, much like normal weight lifting does. In my situation my legs were so atrophied that I couldn't at that time use many of the conventional machines, which were out there. Well it turned out to be a situation of being damned if I did and damned if I didn't, as you will see.

In retrospect I probably shouldn't have initiated the muscle stim unit at a time when so many medicines were in my system and I was experiencing so many post transplant complications and physical symptoms too boot. I can't emphasize enough to readers who haven't been through cancer of some kind of how desper-ate and obsessed a patient can get to become better. Well as I've mentioned I began using the unit without too much of a hitch and briefly fed off of the initial high of self-empowerment. I jolted my system with determined expectations to will these legs well. I actually thought that my brainstorm was working when I sensed some gains occurring but it pretty much turned out to be a mirage.

What followed was the beginning of the end for me as a patient at Johns Hop-kins at least for the time being. The culmination of everything going on mixed together in a vat of confusion unfolded with the very same legs, which I've been boasting about. The increased girth in my legs may have in fact been the building up of fluid for all I knew. With the blink of an eye the explosion of pain along with the very same incessant fever exploited my body and soul. Without a doubt this was the most significant setback I'd faced since first coming down to Hop-kins. Not only did the pain reign supreme but my level of consciousness was in serious jeopardy as well.

Once again my mother was right by my side to try and do what she could in this all too familiar predicament we were in. Even the most experienced veteran of chronic illness can meet their match and for me I about thought that this was it. To be consumed burning up with fevers that seem more lethal than the ther-mometer indicates and be craving to have the helpless feeling lifted from your midst, is all that mattered in life at that moment.

I thought I truly was going to die within the evenings end and succumbed to the life threatening moment. You kind of let go and relax somewhat at least from my few serious scrapes at death's door. A strange serenity of sorts where you hope to pull out of the nosedive but realize that you're pretty much helpless and have done your best to handle the situation. I talked to God a little bit and blanked out from there. My mom placed a call into Hopkins but it would take at least another day to get there because of transportation arrangements and staff scheduling quarks. A call to my nephew Tom Jr. was put in for his possible assistance to get me to the hospital and he graciously obliged. I'd like to think that my family is always there for each other and we stop and make time for whoever is in need whenever there is a need.

Without any sleep and being accosted by the fever and spreading nerve shots, my nephew arrived early to get me to the hospital for treatment. I had to be bodily placed in his Mustang and blanketed over even as I was burning up inside. Some of you may have experienced a bad fever and at the same time be freezing out of your mind. Well this is what I was going through if you know that feeling. Without sounding melodramatic I informed my nephew that I felt like I might not make the trip and how much I cared about him. We made our way down to Baltimore in a usual time frame I'd guess. Once in town and after the usual traffic holdups we arrived on the hospital grounds only to find that the doctors I needed to see had moved to a new facility elsewhere on the property.

My doctor's new offices were extremely nice and in better condition, I may have appreciated the comparative lavishness from the old basement area I used to see them at. My nephew single handedly got me to the place I needed to go piloting my wheelchair through caverns and carpeted hallways. I was in no real better shape when I arrived then from when I left home so at least the staff would get to see the real symptoms as they manifested themselves.

Once I finally got into my designated exam room the walls spun about as I braced for a possible fall from low blood pressure. It was all that I could do to get my sweatpants and garments off of me by my self. A nurse came in and drew blood and then I waited to see whoever was going to look me over. The wait was about as long as it felt as this routine of sitting on steel tables and counting ceiling tiles had finally reached a crescendo. The overseeing nurse Viki entered my exam room and politely informed me that things would be very hectic with my visit. As sick as I was, in the room next door was a patient closer to death than me; that plus the fact that the new move caused some natural setbacks with red tape and everything.

My nephew waited down the hall as my makeshift exam continued. It was clear that this was a case of bad timing all around. I suppose Viki did the best that she could do for me but the staff was clearly overloaded with patients to clear-cut care ratio in my opinion. Viki's status enabled her to do many of the same duties that doctors could do. Perhaps like a physicians attendant would. My head to toe once over concluded that I was roughed up for sure. As to why I was like this brought about the beginning of the end to my confidence in the program. I'll just state here that my opinion of the staff and hospital are still very high. I would recommend them to other patients for the most part. Some of the nicest people I've encountered through my years of being a patient worked at Johns Hopkins.

If you could envision your legs from the knees down as being nothing more than skin tightly wrapped around the silhouette of your bones but with a "fluidy substanse" to them, that's what was going on. For all of the explaining I've done here to let you see where I was coming from this all to anticlimactic scenario came down to the choices I had to make and reasons why. After over the period of about an hour and a half of in and out of the room tending to several patients at once, Viki assessed my condition. She felt that the protocol medicines of Prograf (FK506), Cellcept and the host of other meds were not working. She attributed all of my problems to Graft verses Host disease and immediately wanted to prescribe a massive bolster round of Prednisone to counter this furious onslaught. I'm probably talking about doses higher than anything I'd ever taken at once in such a short time frame.

The idea was to shock my immune system back into acceptable ranges and if successful then take it from there. I expressed theories about my simply irritating my legs to the point of flaring the peripheral neuropathy but I felt they were dismissed or taken lightly. Viki informed me that now I'd be stopping all of the previous medicines which I had been taking all of this time and be starting a new drug called Rampamune. I'd finish of course the Prednisone course of a week or so and begin this new drug at that time.

As sick as I was I had nothing in my mental gas tank to argue, debate or otherwise with. All that I wanted to do was get back home into my bed and be rid of this horrible pain throughout my body. I had one last pit stop appointment in the same room I believe so that saved me much inconvenience to deal with. This penciled in exam was with the hospitals pain and management team member named Candice Morrison. She was so understanding and seemed to react to my descriptions and analogies to symptoms as if she knew just how to zero in on my problems and alleviate some of them.

Candice prescribed the pain meds Neurotin, Desiprimine and Oxiconten in amounts that I could regulate as needed per pain flairs. What a Godsend it is, when you can solve a problem or at least manage and reduce the symptoms of pain. That blessing gave back much more over time but at this particular moment as I mentioned I just wanted to go home. I could have elected to be admitted to the hospital itself but honestly I'd had my fill of floor time residency for sure.

I left the hospital disoriented and still in about the same condition as when I arrived. Perhaps the kicking in of adrenalin and stressed out nerves camouflaged some of the pain I don't know. I do know that simply by getting into my nephews car in the parking lot felt so good just to be on my way home. To be sitting in traffic or cruising on ninety-five at that moment was such a cathartic escape. I've had to many moments where I get so beat down from it all that I just didn't care what happened any longer. I'll stress not a giving up sense of not caring but an at a loss for what else can I do kind of feeling. I've mentioned the experience we all have had of looking out the car window and gazing out at everything and having your mind escape and wander. This was one of those times.

From too much past experience with Prednisone, I was disappointed to have to use it again after such a tough ordeal it was to get off of it. The up side to it was that I was pretty confident that it would beat my body up back to "normal pre leg pain days". As I mentioned though, the massive doses terrified me, so I called my longtime oncologist Dr. Mike at my local hospital. Once I caught him up with everything he agreed with me that it was an extremely high dose of Prednisone for me to be taking in his opinion. Every hospital has their own standards based on standard norms but tweaked somewhat. I told him that I would begin the directive as prescribed and take it from there keeping him informed.

It didn't take but a day or two before my exhaustive leg saga cleared itself up. The pain was gone for sure although my mind was clearly being fogged up from the Prednisone. Once the high doses hijacked my immune system I was in for a lengthy ride of mood swings, sleepless nights and an overall funk like you wouldn't believe. I didn't like this at all so I picked up the Bat phone and called Dr. Mike. I probably should have called down to Baltimore but by now my heart told me to go with who knew me the best. I made a call to Fred Hutchinsons Cancer Research Center and spoke with a couple of friends I had on staff for their input on my situation. When all was said and done I had to make my own decisions on the matter and chose to take a significantly less dose than what was initially prescribed. A dose more in line with what had kept me in check all of the previous years. I felt that it was a case of less is more in this instance.

Whatever the case may have been it worked for me and now I had to focus on a critical choice for my future and possibly my life. I probably was a bit vague in my explanation of my muscle stim scenario and Graft verses Host Disease dispute. The fact of the matter is that we went round and round on this issue and I feel that none of my opinions were ever really duly noted or respected. It came across to me as more of a humoring and skimming over of what I had to say for input. "After all it was only my life being tinkered with or guinea pigged on". This was clinical research and experimental across the board so I felt that I had a right to give some concrete input to the situation.

My feelings were that the muscle stim unit had induced this horrible leg flair by irritating and enflaming the nerves and that it was not necessarily GVHD If you recall earlier in my story it was heatedly disputed in fact if I even had Graft verses Host disease at all anymore. So I didn't think it was a stretch to speculate that I had caused my leg flair and that it was not a case of the previous medicines failing to work on me. I wasn't altogether sold on the idea of bailing out of the bulk of meds I had been taking for just about the last previous two years. I can't say that monumental recoveries took place while on them but at the same time, if I had invested all of that time staying the course with the protocol I wanted to make sure I gave them the best chance to work despite the side effects. Not only did my gut have a terrible feeling about this next wave of drug taking but my heart, soul, brain and everything else connected to me was screaming out against it. Beings that I was home taking the instructed course of Prednisone (albeit shaved amounts) I had some time to decide my next move. If that doesn't sound like difficult decisions to make to you please excuse me while I wonder how much Valium you're taking...

This is such a tough predicament to convey when you're in a position such as I was here. The pressure was building and I could feel it coming from everywhere to get it right. My panic spells lingered deep in my head underlining and undermining any attempts to focus normally. In a mad rush to find constructive feedback I tried to call my acquaintance friend Sean who was also a patient, who I've talked about earlier but to no avail. I made repeated attempts to contact him and even tracked down my good neighbor Larry who is a State Trooper himself and asked him to relay the message. For whatever the reason I never heard from the guy again. Basically I didn't have anyone to bounce my concerns off of who was a patient. My family, friends and Dr. Mike were about all that I had to gain strength and input from as best as they could give it.

My biggest fears were the extreme toxic feelings that I had talked about earlier going on inside my body. I felt like my body was telling me to stop or I would be killed from the piles of poisons in me. Perhaps I was or am mentally ill with these notions but personally I am a firm believer of instincts and inaudible voices inside guiding you or at least making you think on things. I couldn't help but think that if the staff wanted me to try this new medicine Rampamune it would have to be stronger and more toxic to me than the previous protocols were. Maybe that wasn't the case but it seemed logical to me as aggressive therapies go. Usually you start out with the "less severe" of the meds and gradually increase the levels or intensities accordingly. In any event I just know that for me my body had had enough and was telling me so.

For the sake of argument I went to my drug store and had an extensive contraindications sheet printed out on this new drug and compared it to the much shorter list I'd been given from the hospital staff. I'm not suggesting that side effects were deliberately hidden from me it's simply the case that my bigger printout revealed many more as far as I'm concerned. I fully knew that these protocols were dangerous to be on and that it was an individual decision to make to decide if in fact the risks outweighed the benefits. It was about at this time when I pooled in all of my resources and collectively made my decision to stop these powerful drugs.

This was a process that took I'd say about a week to finalize my thoughts on. I convened with Dr. Mike as to the possible ramifications, which could or would follow my decision. I valued his opinion highly and when he more or less gave me the green light to do what I felt was in my best interest I did so. At least I had in my mind a clear-cut reason for my halting this protocol. This new drug was and is probably a wonder drug for some patients, particularly kidney transplant patients. As I've harped on I just reached a point after years and years of taking some form of chemotherapy or another that I wondered if this was the right way.

The drug store information sheet of dangers and statistics was a vehicle I needed to re-enforce my inner self's voices of enough is enough! Having read the drugs contraindication sheet and breaking down the possible scenario's which could happen to me such as recurrent leukemia, stroke, blindness, organ failure, paralysis, heart attack, kidney failure, liver failure and death among other relevant problems was what further sealed the deal for me. Many protocols that I took part in previously had their share of possible dangerous side effects for sure. It's just that in this instance some of the possibilities screamed out right at me. For instance I'd already been through kidney failure and liver failure so I figured logically thinking I would be placing myself in more jeopardy straining those organs any further. With that said I decided to make my decision. I was going to stop everything and place it all in God's hands. The biggest fear was whether or not it was a wise decision or another stupid move, which was going to kill me. At this point time could only tell.

The time came and I believe that I informed Viki at Johns Hopkins by phone that I was taking a break from the treatments and was hoping to leave an open door so to speak if I ever needed their assistance again. I wouldn't say that I was treated badly at any time ever but I surely do not feel that my opinion was ever really valued either. I could attempt a high road low road approach and sugarcoat the experience falsely or express just the opposite side venting with negative fury in the same manner but I'll choose to do neither. It was what it was and I'll leave it at that. I will say that the copies of my files, which I requested for my own piece of mind "thank goodness", painted a much different side of things than how I saw them. Like I said "it is what it is"...

I can remember when the time actually arrived to stop the medicines having my mind blast off with every type of fear and possibility of what could go wrong with me now that "I've up and done it". Like when you're a kid and something happens and a friend, neighborhood local, brother or sister or whoever say's "oooooo you did it nowww, your in biiiig trouble". You know the feeling, except I was an adult and it was I who was conjuring up the torment. No matter what decision I would have come up with my mind would have still attempted to betray me or frazzle me out somehow. Now with the verdict rendered having stopped all of the medications I had to hold my breath and see what was going to happen next.

EPILOGUE

▼

The first evening of not having taking one pill in some sixteen years came about and even though I'm guessing that my body couldn't tell the difference at this point one iota, my mind was sure aware of it. For a while it seemed like every breath that I took was the precursor for the beginning of something to go wrong. It took a whole lot of getting used to and some time had to pass before my mind gave any kind of slack in worrying. I really did have anxiety over whether or not I made a wise decision in choosing to stop all of the medicines. My mainstay for buoyancy was thinking about all of those horrible contraindications, which they brought with them and how my inner voice posed the warning signs to me. I had to believe in myself, and my ability to make these decisions.

I can't say that I felt any less "toxic" anytime soon after withdrawing from these courses of medicines but it did lead me to the self theory of much time would have to go by before I "de-toxed" so to speak. I mean I had this concept, envisioning beat up cells inside of me, and spaces filled up like inflated balloons throughout my body. Realistically I knew different but the notion made for a good analogy of how I saw things back then.

As time went by I felt slightly but progressively improved. My feelings about this were that even if I was as bad off as I was off of the meds it still would be worth it and a victory in its own right. So long as I didn't regress any further at the very least this would be a success to me. Anything else at this point would be gravy. Some people in high places speculated that I would experience significant complications and ultimately die due to infection or GVHD. I bit my tongue on that issue and followed my heart and the inner voice that I'd like to think had tie

302   Does the Sun Shine in Heaven

ins' to God. After all I did place myself on Autopilot in Gods hands many times before.

Not too long after this duration of my attempted escape from the bondage of med's and experimental drug incarceration some more of the medically related update letters were delivered to my door. The double-edged sword of having requested copies of your medical transcripts be forwarded to you is in the reading of what is stated. You expect to be rattled sometimes from the medical aspects pertaining to your physical condition and progress or lack there-of. What really stings is when you read personal comments about yourself from people who you've placed trust in who portray you in a negative light. Especially when you absolutely do not agree with what is written.

The medical dictations, which followed played me out to be a suicidal, introverted and non-social, uncooperative person. I was tabbed for resisting repeated directives for therapy treatments and compliance in general. Among a list of what I feel were very unfair and inaccurate statements was the spin placed on my being so difficult. Further suggestions of my not having any friends or outlets put salt in the wounds all the more. You might have thought that these people had first hand knowledge of my life, what I went through on a daily basis and were in the position to make these kinds of calls. It couldn't have been further from the truth let me tell you.

I was just so infuriated to read these comments about myself knowing full well how way off the spin was on me as a patient and more importantly as a person. I can say that I'm glad to have the reports on hand to refute any of the statements made about me if need be. But by the same token how many people can read or have read a file on me that I have absolutely no control over of how they perceive me. They go strictly speaking on the "technical sterile side of medical jar gin" without having much of a clue about the person behind the stated directive. This is something that can happen to all of us and it reminds me of an episode out of "Seinfeld", where Elaine is labeled as the "difficult patient". It was funny in that confine of comedy but in real life it isn't for sure.

Dealing with the comments in the files was draining but after discussing this over with some respected doctors and medical staff members, I was placed at ease somewhat as to the nature of the business. I had more pressing issues to deal with and so I continued on with this new recovery strategy. The combination of fear and hope mixed together like oil and water for this out of the chute duration so to speak. I experienced a "painful lull" of sorts through this time frame in terms of complications or even worrying for that matter. Of course I had an element of fear as I mentioned but at this particular time I couldn't say that I was consumed with or experienced any bouts of worrying per say. It actually was a nice and welcomed place to be mentally now that I think about it in reflection. Perhaps akin to the cramp or lactic acid burn you sometimes feel after an intense workout.

As I look back everything here was taking place around the late fall of 2000. The timing for me to "quit" the protocol or reevaluate my options, as I'd like to think of it couldn't have come at a better time for me. As I've stated how I love the Fall with the East Coast change of seasons and colors, brisk air, holidays, other goodies including football of course. I once again used all of these enjoyments to my advantage and coaxed my body into a healing mode. I still believe that the mind is the vital tool to tap into for the body to do its' best work. Not that I've cornered the market on any unknown secret, it's just that I don't hear many people or patients out there advocating that angle too much. Well anyway this part of the year had worked well for me to make progress in times past so it was a natural fit to give it another go.

The fact that I wasn't taking one pill or one I.V. line or one sip of liquidly goop or one shot of slopped up **** (fill in your own expletive here) was a victory in itself. For this time being I was going to enjoy being "normal" as far as not ingesting anything toxic or poisonous other than the assortment of football feasting snacks from the local supermarket. I continued to see my regular doctor Dr. Mike and figured that I'd buy myself some time thinking on what my next move would be if any. From this time on was the beginning of a change in all of the aspects of my quality of life period. I could sit here and try to break down all of the whys' or what's as to solving the mystery to this enigma of occurrences but I'd like to leave this to each and every reader's discretion.

As time passed on and the fact that I wasn't experiencing any significant complications continued, I saw no reason to change my newly found game plan. "If it isn't broke don't fix it"...As a matter of fact I'd say that I did improve a tiny bit all across the board. The most telling sign was the fact that I didn't get sick from this time reference on for two years! I'd gone from having chronic sinus and chest colds bi-weekly on a consistent basis to nothing for two full years! When I did get another sinus cold I actually felt almost normal. Everybody gets sick now and then but not on a weekly to monthly basis.

This turnabout was so dramatic for me that I internally attributed it all to God and some finally answered prayers in the form of what I was asking for. Externally I vocalized God alright but the fact that I stopped all of the medicines had to make you wonder what they were doing to me previously as well. Given the fact that I had those internal voices telling me to stop kind of bundles the two together nicely for me. All that I can say is that the turnaround was dramatic for me compared to where I'd been prior to this point. I don't know that you could have looked at me and noticed anything different but the best way to describe it to you as a reader is that "we stopped the bleeding".

My newly found lease on life had me cruising quietly through the holiday season and snowy landscapes. I enjoyed fine-tuning my perspectives' on life with about my hundredth different outlook in as many months. I was as keen as ever with determination to rebuild my legs. I took my most comfortable pair of Nikes, two skateboards I purchased cheap and a steel meat defroster from Ron co or some infomercial company like that and went to work. Out to the shed I trekked to build my latest miracle leg rejuvenator. I cut and bended and drilled and bolted until my brainstorm was ready to unveil. I probably looked like Wile-e Coyote minus the jet pack with all of my padding, equipment, goggles and make-shift ski poles I threw together.

This "invention was simply a pair of roller skates that I made to conform to my bad ankles and limbs. I used the steel defrosting plate cut in half for a perfect mounting deck for the shoes and skates. The wheels and truck mounts came straight off of the skateboard itself and I drilled holes through the soles of the sneakers, then the steel and bolted everything up together for the perfect pair of roller skates. Once they were finished and my having found a sense of optimism being off of the drug therapy, I envisioned cruising my way to getting the old legs back again. I wish that I could say my super idea paid huge dividends but unfortunately it didn't.

After all of that work I was able to stand upright and comfortably walk around on the skates but that was about it. Upon my attempts to get rolling once suited up in my combination motocross, lacrosse, football pads and any other device I thought would work, it was about the end of the line for the time being. My ankles evidently were so damaged that I couldn't lean forward enough to start momentum or thrust off with any kind of consistency. I made four or five major attempts over the course of about three weeks before deciding to pack it in conceding temporary defeat. I still believe it can work someday or at least I have hope that it will eventually but for this time frame in my story my roller skate idea was not to be.

I was really bummed out that the skating idea didn't work out but after a short spell of sulking and thinking I figured that I could still walk "okay enough" so that's what I'd start out doing again. The bodies in motion stay in motion theory. Before I knew it I was walking out at a local track and setting new goals to reach in terms of stamina and balance. A big worry for me was and still is the sun. My being prone to getting skin cancer has risen dramatically since having all of the total body radiation and procedures, which I've had. Not perspiring very much if at all lights me up big time with the over heating possibilities and dangers which that presents. I have to carry a squirt bottle with me most everywhere I go. It's been a great lifesaver and something that I thought of trying after hanging down at the beach and feeling refreshed often times by the oceans misty breeze. The waterslides atmosphere of atomizing sprays from churned up pumps and chlorinated pathways also cooled me down even when just sitting around nearby.

My walks continued regularly for several months with some slight improvements from where I'd initially been physically speaking. I didn't experience anything monumental in terms of a huge recovery but what was important to me was that I seemed to be on the right track, no pun intended…I was able to do some things now such as get back into my woodworking and artwork, which I hadn't been able to do for some time. In fact I began building my mom a scaled down version of a Santa sleigh for her two feet high Chris Cringle figurine. The real Santa Clause would be proud.

I managed to finish a few of the kid's room artwork jobs that I lined up as they were presented to me, which in itself was fulfilling to accomplish. I did some daycare centers and a Gold's gym nursery mural pretty much rounded out the menu. I also was commissioned to do an oil painting and a pen and ink lithograph along the way. These were normal things that I hadn't been able to do for years so that's why I mentioned them here to give you an idea of what was taking place not all that long after my decision to stop med's.

I continued to have many periods of lethargy and times when my body would let me know that I needed to simply lie down for sure. In fact more times than not in some instances I'd be bed ridden more than being up and about but it still was a better overall place to be at. My symptoms were more of a tiredness that was not fun by any stretch of the imagination but not a sickly pain infested stagnation kind of a thing. The oxycontin and neurontin kept any pain in check for the most part during a flare but I think around this time frame a pattern was being formed where I needed less and less if any at all. As a matter of fact I was eventually able to go for months at a time without a pain pill. I'd call that progress.

My health still prevented me from really entering the workforce on a full time basis due to what I call "power outages" of complete fatigue and lethargy but I had hope that this would also pass. I attempted to remain patient and try to be thankful for everything that I had and keep pressing on taking what foothold I could gain with each passing day. Similar to the rope in tug of war, I wanted to keep a grasp of every inch of rope of improvement I maintained without losing any gained ground acquired. To do that like I said I had to focus on patience, hope and calmness. The three things I've been challenging myself to master since this epiphany of sorts.

A cool boost to my morale came one day when I got a call from the Queen Latifah television show about possibly coming on to tell my story and perhaps meet my donor finally after all this time. I was asked to FedEx a package up to their office with some information and so forth and await a return call. They were very nice and actually scheduled me for a program with everything looking good up until the very night before traveling. I received a phone call that the topics were being changed and I'd possibly be rebooked sometime down the road. I even think I was to be on the program the same day "Lil Kim" was performing. I just tell my friends I got bumped for "Lil Kim" and they get a kick out of that. What can you do?

My routine doctor's appointments with Dr. Mike continued and went well actually. I'd not progressed any but surely hadn't regressed any either' so for me that was and always is a victory and good news as the scale goes. I'd become accustomed to the slower version of me so to speak. The Touche Turtle M.O. was I so for the time being or immediate future I adjusted accordingly. Some of my short trip excursions were to visit my Godchildren and nieces and nephews as best I could. I built my Goddaughter Elisabeth a dollhouse, which turned out to weigh more than a ton. The only thing good about that was it could withstand my Godson Seth's mighty wrath of boyhood mischief. I'd play with my great nephew Anthony and great niece Hannah during the regular Sunday dinners as well. That progressively got better also as time went by. Nothing monumental mind you but again anything in the positive direction was well, positive...

Fred Hutch center sent me my annual questioner and for the first time that I could remember I could answer in a somewhat positive manner. I always made it a point to elaborate on my symptoms or relevant information so they could possibly benefit from it for research purposes. This time was no different and I followed through with what I hope was a thorough reply. At about the same time I attempted to contact my donor Jim again and I'm sorry to say that I didn't have much success on that front. I'm sure that I'll track him down and perhaps even hand him a copy of my story of which he is a Star character.

My friend Paul took me fishing one day at a place in Pennsylvania called Muddy Run Recreation Park. It felt so good to just sit out on the lakes shoreline and cast a line in. I gazed out over the lakeside only to spot a group of White tailed Deer grazing while checking me out at the same time. Birds squawking and an Amish family talking completed the scenic moment for me. This was one of those flash frames that I've filed as a reminder of how all of the horrible hell I've been through was worth the suffering to get through. I believe that someone in my position needs to constantly refocus on positive moments and memories if they are to have any chance of beating the odds. I'm thankful that God gave me a pretty vivid memory to reflect back on for just such an instance. This way I can focus and hopefully look forward to many more "flash frames" of life's wonderful timeframes.

As I mentioned earlier I didn't improve physically much more than the "de-tox" kind of cleansing I felt that I experienced. My stamina improved from what it was and I hadn't been nearly as sick as I used to be. I reached a plateau so it seemed and ventured to improve continually in any way that I could. With my faith being the glue for this whole predicament to stay together I chipped away at trying to attend Mass more regularly as in times past. I'd say that I didn't do all that great of a job of getting to church regularly during this stretch. The Masses I did attend however were powerful in their own right though. The big problem's for me lye in the scheduled Mass times and my bodies internal clock of energy coinciding. It simply wasn't a case of going into church whenever you felt like it, the era of open doors are gone in this day and age. Nevertheless I did what I could and figured that God knew the scoop.

I would say that my mental sharpness or awareness has improved since the medicines were discontinued. Not that I would have considered myself mentally "un-sharp" before this time, it's just that there was enough of a change for me in my opinion to where I had to mention it. Perhaps this was and is today simply a case of realizing that I have to focus more on "real world problems and decisions and maybe not quite as much on the physical health side of things. In other words when your whole life is consumed with dealing with saving it first and foremost nothing else really matters comparatively. There isn't time to think about a career or family or buying a house or anything along those lines. In fact all of those regular things we do as adults get pushed way back out of the picture. When you expend all of your resources to getting better, if and when you get to the point of recovery this sets the stage for a restarting period back into the game of life. That in itself brings on a whole new batch of potential problems.

Don't get me wrong it would be a welcomed set of problems to deal with compared to the bone marrow transplant and plethora of complications. But to give you a minor taste of those roadblocks, let's take trying to obtain a mortgage for a home. What W-2 forms would be worth any clout? Life insurance, forget about it; "Savings, what savings?" Trade skills, career experience? The last time I checked there weren't too many openings for Laminar airflow unit life experience credits. Nevertheless I threw those tidbits in there for readers to ponder. I can send you my resume...

I'm not sure if I mentioned that my medical insurance at this point had been whittled down to Medicare and Medicaid only. My Blue Cross and Blue Shield provider who had been instrumental for me at one point now found a way to cut their losses in me. Actually it was a couple of ways. Some very bogus loophole enabled them to drop my policy due to the state I lived in and a plastic handed gesture to transfer me over into a new policy never materialized. I was sent some new application forms to "apply" with after now some twenty years or so of being a paid subscriber. The new forms came nicely packaged with astronomical premiums as well. Costs being so high and unaffordable to most, that it makes one wonder if it was purposefully calculated. I know that I wonder. Perhaps I dropped the ball here by not seeking out legal council but you know sometimes you just get so fried and beat down that your responses aren't always as quick as you'd hope them to be. I heard a quote one time where are gentleman stated that "he wasn't a quitter but knew when he was beaten". Again I'm wondering if they don't just have a staff unit who calculates these scenarios and wagers on the odds attempting to cut losses here and there. After all they are out to make money no matter what their nicely packaged television commercials tell you.

Nevertheless, I moved on with the show and my attempt to get back into the swing of life. I think I may have used the analogy of trying to hop onto a moving train car as it whizzes by you at a hundred miles an hour. The moving train being life and the workforce and myself of course being me and trying to figure out how to go about getting on this thing now in my predicament. To be honest with you as of this writing I still haven't figured it out. I'm attempting to look into whatever I can and keep moving forward whatever forward is. With that being said I did make a pretty good transition from a person being practically a professional patient to becoming a semi patient/somewhat "normal guy" again, God willing.

I started dating regularly again and even have played drums professionally again on a small scale. My artwork is going well, slow but well. I'm able to consistently exercise and do little things that I couldn't do for a long time. There aren't any major breakthroughs it's more of what I mentioned earlier that being I've not really regressed, so that's the victory for the short term. I hope to continue to improve and with any good fortune have something come along which would allow me to make a respectable living, purchase my own home and even get married who knows.

I've recently been back in contact with some old friends and girlfriends. Some full circle feelings have been reconnected with special people and relationships, which I highly value. One in particular being between a special woman Jennifer and I re-connecting after all of the hardships is one great example. Two other distant but close longtime friendships rekindled in Sherry A. and Lisa G.'s. I don't know if we would have been able to do so if not for my transplant and situation. I wouldn't have met my friends like Paul, Mike or Bill if not for my ordeal. The same goes for all of the Calandra Family, the Walsh's as well as all of the wonderful nurses and doctors who've taken care of me over the years.

A good amount of my old friends have come in and out of my life for nice flashback reminiscing and well wishes as well. I'd always hoped to rent a huge billboard or some type of highly visible sign to let everyone know how much I cared and appreciated their friendship and kindness. I could never make a perfect list of all of the names of those people accurate enough without missing someone along the way so I hope that if they (and you know who you are) ever get a chance to read this story, you will feel my sincere appreciation and value for you having been in my life.

As of now I can't say where my life is going to take me or what will happen to me either. But then again all of us could probably make that same statement which could lump me in with everyone here as a "normal" thing...I do struggle with depression and anxiety flares with kindling's of "where do I fit in or finding my niche" so to speak. There have been some people taking cheap shots at me, accusing me of fabricating stories and statements. I heard a quote one time from Dr. Phil stating that "you probably wouldn't care about what some people may think of you if you realized how seldom they did" You can't control what people say. I know this story is accurate and so does God. That's good enough for me.

My physical ailments dictate most of what I'm able to accomplish so often times I feel like a spectator in life. Needless to say I'm misunderstood more times than not and struggle with this on a continual basis. My faith is holding it's own I'd say although it has taken some heavy barrages through the years. Perhaps it is evolving or growing which would be nice though I cannot say for sure.

It's funny how human nature works. With all of the spiritual happenings and unbelievable occurrences unfolding for me in my story, the mind can still grow wary even after living through such wonderful healings. Sometimes I think of when Jesus spoke to the apostles saying "ye of little faith" even after they witnessed miracle after miracle right before their eyes. I'd probably be guilty of some of the same scenarios since I still find myself feeling weak in stretches even after experiencing miraculous blessings.

I still hope to gain a more positive outlook on life although the fact that you run into so many negative people with no real clue of what problems or tragedies really are. That's not to say that all problems are not relevant either. Tough times are tough times regardless of the package their wrapped up in but I've seemed to run into buzz saw's of people with nothing to complain about at all. Instead of counting their blessings and being so very thankful for the littlest of things it's more a case of more, more, more. I like to joke and say that unless they were and Egyptian King, with a pyramid to stash their goodies they can't take them with them! Nun the less it is what it is in our struggle with hardships. Life goes on and we can only do our best with what has been handed to us. The will to live is a powerful weapon against all odds and obstacles. In struggles against cancer and seemingly insurmountable odds be it most any predicament I still feel that the personal power of one's self, coupled with a great faith in God can overcome tremendous obstacles.

I'm not only speaking of my particular situation but for everyone placed in times of terrible hardships. I guess that what I've had to deal with could have happened to anyone reading this story. I can only speak for myself but I also believe in what I've talked about throughout my whole story. That being don't ever give up, trust in yourself, more importantly trust in God however hard times may get, trust in the doctors to a large extent but remember especially in times of pessimistic or terminal news that they aren't God. I believe that doctors can be the hands of God many times but God is in charge. For those who believe no explanation is necessary and for those who do not believe, no explanation will suffice. I'd say to those who choose not to believe, if I'm wrong it won't matter much anyhow and when our time is up it won't make a difference but if I'm right and have chosen to follow faith in God, the eternal gift of life is there for us.

Perhaps tragedies like mine were placed here for stories to be told to convey messages to those in very difficult situations. Messages of perseverance and finding hope in hopeless situations. My hope would be that each and every person reading this book could draw the strength's and ingredients that they would ever need in a time of crisis. Throughout my duration of writing this story I never really had a focused reason to finish it other than some type of personal closure but the more and more I pushed on to complete this story (as incomplete as it really still is) I gained a larger perspective.

There are no blueprints or golden books to read for enduring traumatic life experiences. I can only try to give readers my reflection on hope and success in whatever the predicament one is placed in. Regardless how insurmountable the obstacles may be, the fuel of hope can do marvelous things. Never give up. Never give in. Never say never and in borrowing a line I used several times before in my story "you know that you will always have hope as long as the heart still beats"

Again I would like to express my sincere appreciation to every single person who ever played a role in one shape or form in assisting me. My words can never fill the void in attempting to thank everyone fully enough. From the people who have been by me throughout my struggles with leukemia and complications, which followed to all of the kind hearted people that have been sprinkled in at just the right time so it seems. Thanks to Dr.Mike Soojian and the entire staff at Crozer Hospital's Vivaqua Cancer Center. To Dr. Lebetta, Dr. Keough, Dr.Vivaqua and all of the many Doctors who have assisted me there. To the nurses and staff members who have been nothing but fabulous to me always. Angie, Redee, Therese, Sue and Debbie have been there for me the entire time. Along with Gail, Sharon, Carol and all of the other ladies on staff, they are the nicest people you could want for help. That speaks volumes considering the many places and people I've dealt with over the last 20 years.

I'd like to thank Marion McCarty and the entire staff at Fred Hutchinson's Cancer Research Center in Seattle Washington. Marion is so instrumental in my story that it would take a book just to write about her. There are literally a hundred people at Hutch at the minimum who stand out as tremendous caretakers for me. It's probably more like several hundred if I knew each and every staff member that worked on my case behind the scenes. Wonderful Doctors and P.A.'s such as Rick Naon, Dr. Lee, Dr. Hickman, Dr. Buckner and of course last but not least Dr. Donnell Thomas himself. He, being the pioneering doctor who was awarded the Nobel Prize for his bone marrow transplant concept. Nurses Linda, Laney and Ann, Doyla, the Puget Sound Blood bank and Dr. Fred Applebaum, the list just goes on and on and on.

Thanks to Dr.Fung, Dr. Bloom and all of the staff at the University o Pittsburgh Hospital. The staff at Johns Hopkins Hospital and again like I've mentioned it's very difficult to recant everyone who deserves my gratitude for their help.

Thank you to the staff at U1.net in Boothyn, Pa. Thank you to Mary Lamplugh. Very special thanks to my close friend Kevin Van Horn who has been like a brother to me and has been instrumental in getting this story finished. Thanks to Maryrose, my family and a select handful of special friends who know who they are. Of course the story couldn't have been told without my donor Jim Murphy. What an incredible man, who as of this writing I have not yet met in person. I've mentioned this throughout my story and in the future perhaps I will be able to do so.

Once again I can see the pattern of how difficult it is to list each and every person who has helped me in one way or another. A part of me thinks I have simply stated a generic thank you to suffice all. That seems incomplete, as does this approach so I'll close with this format about how it is I suppose. The main gist of this "thank you stuff" is "Thank you everyone"!

Most importantly I'd Like to thank God for the blessings that I have been given. We cannot understand so many things in life, diseases, traumas and tragedies being among the vast amount of baffling mysteries. I only hope God allows my struggles to result in some kind of good for myself, loved ones and everyone that, I may encounter in my life for the better. I hope that people could see God in the things I've tried to do, have succeeded to do and failed to do right, which unfortunately is many things. Thank you for reading my story and I hope that you can take something good away from reading it all; May God Bless You.

978-0-595-31219-1
0-595-31219-5

CPSIA information can be obtained at www.ICGtesting.com
Printed in the USA
LVOW08s2310291013

359203LV00002B/149/P

9 780595 312191